Acknowledgments

The publisher and authors would like to thank the following people for reviewing the manuscript and/or participating in focus groups as the book was being developed:

Ana Maria Aguilera, Lubie Alatriste, Ann Albarelli, Margaret Albers, Sherry Allen, Fiona Armstrong, Ted Auerbach, Steve Austen, Jean Barlow, Sally Bates, Sharon Batson, Myra Baum, Mary Beauparlant, Gretchen Bitterlin, Margrajean Bonilla, Mike Bostwick, Shirley Brod, Lihn Brown, Trish Brys-Overeem, Lynn Bundy, Chris Bunn, Carol Carvel, Leslie Crucil, Robert Denheim, Joshua Denk, Kay Devonshire, Thomas Dougherty, Gudrun Draper, Sara Eisen, Lynda Elkins, Ed Ende, Michele Epstein, Beth Fatemi, Andra R. Fawcett, Alice Fiedler, Harriet Fisher, James Fitzgerald, Mary Fitzsimmons, Scott Ford, Barbara Gaines, Elizabeth Garcia Grenados, Maria T. Gerdes, Penny Giacalone, Elliott Glazer, Jill Gluck de la Llata, Javier Gomez, Pura Gonzales, Carole Goodman, Joyce Grabowski, Maggie Grennan, Joanie Griffin, Sally Hansen, Fotini Haritos, Alice Hartley, Fernando Herrera, Ann Hillborn, Mary Hopkins, Lori Howard, Leann Howard, Pamela Howard, Rebecca Hubner, Jan Jarrell, Vicki Johnson, Michele Kagan, Nanette Kafka, Gena Katsaros, Evelyn Kay, Greg Keech, Cliff Ker, Gwen Kerner-Mayer, Marilou Kessler, Patty King, Linda Kiperman, Joyce Klapp, Susan Knutson, Sandy Kobrine, Marinna Kolaitis, Donna Korol, Lorraine Krampe, Karen Kuser, Andrea Lang, Nancy Lebow, Tay Lesley, Gale Lichter, Sandie Linn, Rosario Lorenzano, Louise Louie, Cheryl Lucas, Ronna Magy, Juanita Maltese, Mary Marquardsen, Carmen Marques Rivera, Susan McDowell, Alma McGee, Jerry McLeroy, Kevin McLure, Joan Meier, Patsy Mills, Judy Montague, Vicki Moore, Eneida Morales, Glenn Nadelbach, Elizabeth Neblett, Kathleen Newton, Yvonne Nishio, Afra Nobay, Rosa Elena Ochoa, Jean Owensby, Jim Park, John Perkins, Jane Pers, Laura Peskin, Maria Pick, Percy Pleasant, Selma Porter, Kathy Quinones, Susan Ritter, Martha Robledo, Maureen Rooney, Jean Rose, David Ross, Julietta Ruppert, Lorraine Ruston, Susan Ryan, Frederico Salas, Leslie Salmon, Jim Sandifer, Linda Sasser, Lisa Schreiber, Mary Segovia, Abe Shames, Debra Shaw, Stephanie Shipp, Pat Singh, Mary Sklavos, Donna Stark, Claire Cocoran Stehling, Lynn Sweeden, Joy Tesh, Sue Thompson, Christine Tierney, Laura Topete, Carmen Villanueva, Laura Webber, Renée Weiss, Beth Winningham, Cindy Wislofsky, Judy Wood, Paula Yerman.

A special thanks to Marna Shulberg and the students of the Saticoy Branch of Van Nuys Community Adult School.

We would also like to thank the following individuals and organizations who provided their expertise:

Carl Abato, Alan Goldman, Dr. Larry Falk, Caroll Gray, Henry Haskell, Susan Haskell, Los Angeles Fire Department, Malcolm Loeb, Barbara Lozano, Lorne Dubin, United Farm Workers.

Authors' Acknowledgments

Throughout our careers as English language teachers, we have found inspiration in many places—in the classroom with our remarkable students, at schools, conferences, and workshops with our fellow teachers, and with our colleagues at the ESL Teacher Institute. We are grateful to be part of this international community.

We would like to sincerely thank and acknowledge Eliza Jensen, the project's Senior Editor. Without Eliza, this book would not have been possible. Her indomitable spirit, commitment to clarity, and unwavering advocacy allowed us to realize the book we envisioned.

Creating this dictionary was a collaborative effort and it.has been our privilege to work with an exceptionally talented group of individuals who, along with Eliza Jensen, make up the Oxford Picture Dictionary team. We deeply appreciate the contributions of the following people:

Lynn Luchetti, Art Director, whose aesthetic sense and sensibility guided the art direction of this book,

Susan Brorein, Senior Designer, who carefully considered the design of each and every page,

Klaus Jekeli, Production Editor, who pored over both manuscript and art to ensure consistency and accuracy, and

Tracy Hammond, Art Buyer, who skillfully managed thousands of pieces of art and reference material.

We also want to thank Susan Mazer, the talented artist who was by our side for the initial problem-solving and Mary Chandler who also lent her expertise to the project.

We have learned much working with Marjorie Fuchs, Lori Howard, and Renée Weiss, authors of the dictionary's ancillary materials. We thank them for their on-going contributions to the dictionary program.

We must make special mention of Susan Lanzano, Editorial Manager, whose invaluable advice, insights, and queries were an integral part of the writing process.

This book is dedicated to my husband, Neil Reichline, who has encouraged me to take the road less traveled, and to my sons, Eli and Alex, who have allowed me to sit at their baseball games with my yellow notepad. —NS

This book is lovingly dedicated to my husband, Gary and my daughter, Emily Rose, both of whom hugged me tight and let me work into the night. —JAG

A Letter to the Teacher

Welcome to The Oxford Picture Dictionary.

This comprehensive vocabulary resource provides you and your students with over 3,700 words, each defined by engaging art and presented in a meaningful context. *The Oxford Picture Dictionary* enables your students to learn and use English in all aspects of their daily lives. The 140 key topics cover home and family, the workplace, the community, health care, and academic studies. The topics are organized into 12 thematic units that are based on the curriculum of beginning and low-intermediate level English language coursework. The word lists of the dictionary include both single word entries and verb phrases. Many of the prepositions and adjectives are presented in phrases as well, demonstrating the natural use of words in conjunction with one another.

The Oxford Picture Dictionary uses a variety of visual formats, each suited to the topic being represented. Where appropriate, word lists are categorized and pages are divided into sections, allowing you to focus your students' attention on one aspect of a topic at a time.

Within the word lists:

- nouns, adjectives, prepositions, and adverbs are numbered,

- verbs are bolded and identified by letters, and

- targeted prepositions and adjectives within phrases are bolded.

The dictionary includes a variety of exercises and self-access tools that will guide your students toward accurate and fluent use of the new words.

- Exercises at the bottom of the pages provide vocabulary development through pattern practice, application of the new language to other topics, and personalization questions.

- An alphabetical index assists students in locating all words and topics in the dictionary.

- A phonetic listing for each word in the index and a pronunciation guide give students the key to accurate pronunciation.

- A verb index of all the verbs presented in the dictionary provides students with information on the present, past, and past participle forms of the verbs.

The Oxford Picture Dictionary is the core of *The Oxford Picture Dictionary Program* which includes a *Dictionary Cassette,* a *Teacher's Book* and its companion *Focused Listening Cassette, Beginning* and *Intermediate Workbooks, Classic Classroom Activities* (a photocopiable activity book), *Overhead Transparencies,* and *Read All About It 1* and *2.* Bilingual editions of *The Oxford Picture Dictionary* are available in Spanish, Chinese, Vietnamese, and many other languages.

TEACHING THE VOCABULARY

Your students' needs and your own teaching philosophy will dictate how you use *The Oxford Picture Dictionary* with your students. The following general guidelines, however, may help you adapt the dictionary's pages to your particular course and students. (For topic-specific, step-by-step guidelines and activities for presenting and practicing the vocabulary on each dictionary page see the *Oxford Picture Dictionary Teacher's Book.*)

Preview the topic

A good way to begin any lesson is to talk with students to determine what they already know about the topic. Some different ways to do this are:

- Ask general questions related to the topic;

- Have students brainstorm a list of words they know from the topic; or

- Ask questions about the picture(s) on the page.

Present the vocabulary

Once you've discovered which words your students already know, you are ready to focus on presenting the words they need. Introducing 10–15 new words in a lesson allows students to really learn the new words. On pages where the word lists are longer, and students are unfamiliar with many of the words, you may wish to introduce the words by categories or sections, or simply choose the words you want in the lesson.

Here are four different presentation techniques. The techniques you choose will depend on the topic being studied and the level of your students.

- Say each new word and describe or define it within the context of the picture.

- Demonstrate verbs or verb sequences for the students, and have volunteers demonstrate the actions as you say them.

- Use Total Physical Response commands to build comprehension of the vocabulary: *Put the pencil on your book. Put it on your notebook. Put it on your desk.*

- Ask a series of questions to build comprehension and give students an opportunity to say the new words:

English / Russian
английский / русский

THE OXFORD
Picture
Dictionary

NORMA SHAPIRO AND JAYME ADELSON-GOLDSTEIN

Translated by Techno-Graphics & Translations, Inc.

Oxford University Press

Oxford University Press
198 Madison Avenue, New York, NY 10016 USA
Great Clarendon Street, Oxford OX2 6DP England

Oxford New York

Auckland Cape Town Dar es Salaam Hong Kong Karachi
Kuala Lumpur Madrid Melbourne Mexico City Nairobi
New Delhi Shanghai Taipei Toronto
With offices in
Argentina Austria Brazil Chile Czech Republic France Greece
Guatemala Hungary Italy Japan Poland Portugal Singapore
South Korea Switzerland Thailand Turkey Ukraine Vietnam

OXFORD is a trademark of Oxford University Press.

Library of Congress Cataloging-in-Publication Data

Shapiro, Norma.
     The Oxford picture dictionary: English/Russian =
     английский / русский
     Norma Shapiro and Jayme Adelson-Goldstein; translated
     by Techno-Graphics and Translations, Inc.
          p.   cm.
     Includes bibliographical references and index.
     ISBN : 978 0 19 435192 8

     1. English language—Dictionaries—Russian.   2. Picture
     dictionaries, Russian.   3. Picture dictionaries, English.
     I. Adelson-Goldstein, Jayme.   II. Title.
     PG2640.S45   1998   98-10026
     423'.9171—dc21   CIP

No unauthorized photocopying.

Translation reviewed by Cambridge Translation Resources
Editorial Manager: Susan Lanzano
Art Director: Lynn Luchetti
Senior Editor: Eliza Jensen
Senior Designer: Susan P. Brorein
Production Editor: Rita Chabot
Art Buyer: Tracy A. Hammond
Cover Design Production: Brett Sonnenschein
Production Services by: Techno-Graphics and Translations, Inc.
Production Manager: Abram Hall
Pronunciation Coordinator: Shanta Persand
Production Editor: Sharon Goldstein
Cover design by Silver Editions

Printing (last digit): 20 19 18 17 16 15 14 13 12 11

Printed in China.

Illustrations by: David Aikins, Doug Archer, Craig Attebery,
Garin Baker, Sally Bensusen, Eliot Bergman, Mark Bischel, Dan
Brown / Artworks NY, Roy Douglas Buchman, George Burgos /
Larry Dodge, Carl Cassler, Mary Chandler, Robert Crawford,
Jim DeLapine, Judy Francis, Graphic Chart and Map Co., Dale
Gustafson, Biruta Akerbergs Hansen, Marcia Hartsock, C.M.I.,
David Hildebrand, The Ivy League of Artists, Inc. / Judy
Degraffenreid, The Ivy League of Artists, Inc. / Tom Powers,
The Ivy League of Artists, Inc. / John Rice, Pam Johnson, Ed
Kurtzman, Narda Lebo, Scott A. MacNeill / MACNEILL &
MACINTOSH, Andy Lendway / Deborah Wolfe Ltd., Jeffrey
Mangiat, Suzanne Mogensen, Mohammad Mansoor, Tom
Newsom, Melodye Benson Rosales, Stacey Schuett, Rob
Schuster, James Seward, Larry Taugher, Bill Thomson, Anna
Veltfort, Nina Wallace, Wendy Wassink-Ackison, Michael
Wepplo, Don Wieland
Thanks to Mike Mikos for his preliminary architectural sketches
of several pieces.

References
Boyer, Paul S., Clifford E. Clark, Jr., joseph F. Kett, Thomas L.
Purvis, Harvard Sitkoff, Nancy Woloch *The Enduring Vision: A
History of the American People*, Lexington, Massachusetts:
D.C. Heath and Co., 1990.

Grun, Bernard, *The Timetables of History: A Horizontal Linkage
of People and Events*, (based on Werner Stein's Kulturfahrplan)
New York: A Touchstone Book, Simon and Schuster, 1946,
1963, 1975, 1979.

Statistical Abstract of the United States: 1996, 116th Edition,
Washington, DC: US Bureau of the Census, 1996.

The World Book Encyclopedia, Chicago: World Book Inc., a
Scott Fetzer Co., 1988 Edition.

Toff, Nancy, Editor-in-Chief, *The People of North America*
(Series), New York: Chelsea House Publishers, Main Line
Books, 1988.

Trager, James, *The People's Chronology, A Year-by-Year Record
of Human Events from Prehistory to the Present*, New York:
Henry Holt Reference Book, 1992.

- ▶ Begin with *yes/no* questions. *Is #16 chalk?* (yes)
- ▶ Progress to *or* questions. *Is #16 chalk or a marker?* (chalk)
- ▶ Finally ask *Wh* questions.

  What can I use to write on this paper? (a marker/ Use a marker.)

Check comprehension

Before moving on to the practice stage, it is helpful to be sure all students understand the target vocabulary. There are many different things you can do to check students' understanding. Here are two activities to try:

- Tell students to open their books and point to the items they hear you say. Call out target vocabulary at random as you walk around the room checking to see if students are pointing to the correct pictures.
- Make true/false statements about the target vocabulary. Have students hold up two fingers for true, three fingers for false. *You can write with a marker.* [two fingers] *You raise your notebook to talk to the teacher.* [three fingers]

Take a moment to review any words with which students are having difficulty before beginning the practice activities.

Practice the vocabulary

Guided practice activities give your students an opportunity to use the new vocabulary in meaningful communication. The exercises at the bottom of the pages are one source of guided practice activities.

- **Talk about...** This activity gives students an opportunity to practice the target vocabulary through sentence substitutions with meaningful topics.

  e.g. **Talk about your feelings.**

  I feel <u>happy</u> when I see my friends.

- **Practice...** This activity gives students practice using the vocabulary within common conversational functions such as making introductions, ordering food, making requests, etc.

  e.g. **Practice asking for things in the dining room.**

  Please pass <u>the platter</u>.

  May I have <u>the creamer</u>?

  Could I have <u>a fork</u>, please?

- **Use the new language.** This activity asks students to brainstorm words within various categories, or may

ask them to apply what they have learned to another topic in the dictionary. For example, on *Colors*, page 12, students are asked to look at *Clothing I*, pages 64–65, and name the colors of the clothing they see.

- **Share your answers.** These questions provide students with an opportunity to expand their use of the target vocabulary in personalized discussion. Students can ask and answer these questions in whole class discussions, pair or group work, or they can write the answers as journal entries.

Further guided and communicative practice can be found in the *Oxford Picture Dictionary Teacher's Book* and in *Classic Classroom Activities*. The *Oxford Picture Dictionary Beginning* and *Intermediate Workbooks* and *Read All About It 1* and *2* provide your students with controlled and communicative reading and writing practice.

We encourage you to adapt the materials to suit the needs of your classes, and we welcome your comments and ideas. Write to us at:

Oxford University Press
ESL Department
198 Madison Avenue
New York, NY 10016

Jayme Adelson-Goldstein
Norma Shapiro

A Letter to the Student

Dear Student of English,

Welcome to *The Oxford Picture Dictionary*. The more than 3,700 words in this book will help you as you study English.

Each page in this dictionary teaches about a specific topic. The topics are grouped together in units. All pages in a unit have the same color and symbol. For example, each page in the Food unit has this symbol:

On each page you will see pictures and words. The pictures have numbers or letters that match the numbers or letters in the word lists. Verbs (action words) are identified by letters and all other words are identified by numbers.

How to find words in this book

- Use the Table of Contents, pages ix–xi.
  Look up the general topic you want to learn about.

- Use the Index, pages 173–205.
  Look up individual words in alphabetical (A–Z) order.

- Go topic by topic.
  Look through the book until you find something that interests you.

How to use the Index

When you look for a word in the index this is what you will see:

the word   the number (or letter) in the word list

apples [ăp/əlz] **50**–4

the pronunciation   the page number

If the word is on one of the maps, pages 122–125, you will find it in the Geographical Index on pages 206–208.

How to use the Verb Guide

When you want to know the past form of a verb or its past participle form, look up the verb in the verb guide. The regular verbs and their spelling changes are listed on pages 170–171. The simple form, past form, and past participle form of irregular verbs are listed on page 172.

Workbooks

There are two workbooks to help you practice the new words:
The Oxford Picture Dictionary Beginning and *Intermediate Workbooks*.

As authors and teachers we both know how difficult English can be (and we're native speakers!). When we wrote this book, we asked teachers and students from the U.S. and other countries for their help and ideas. We hope their ideas and ours will help you. Please write to us with your comments or questions at:

Oxford University Press
ESL Department
198 Madison Avenue
New York, NY 10016

We wish you success!

Jayme Adelson-Goldstein   *Norma Shapiro*

Письмо изучающему английский язык

Дорогой студент,

Добро пожаловать в *The Oxford Picture Dictionary*. Более 3700 слов в этой книге помогут Вам при изучении английского языка.

Каждая страница данного словаря посвящена определённой теме. Темы сгруппированы по разделам. Страницы каждого раздела имеют определённую окраску и символ. Например, каждая страница раздела о пище имеет следующий символ:

На каждой странице Вы увидите иллюстрации и слова. Иллюстрации обозначены цифрами или буквами, которые соотвествуют цифрам или буквам в списках слов. Глаголы (слова действия) обозначены буквами, а все другие слова - цифрами.

Как найти нужное слово в словаре

- С помощью Содержания на стр. ix – xi.
  Найдите интресующую Вас тему.

- С помощью Указателя на стр. 173 – 205.
  Найдите отдельные слова, расположенные в алфавитном порядке (A – Z).

- Просматривая тему за темой.
  Найдите что-то для Вас интересное, пролистывая словарь.

Как пользоваться Указателем

При поисках слова в указателе Вы увидите следующее:

Если слово написано на одной из карт (стр. 122 – 125), его можно найти в Географическом указателе на страницах 206 – 208.

Как пользоваться Списком глаголов

Когда Вы захотите ознакомиться с прошедшей или причастной формой глагола, обратитесь к Списку глаголов. Правильные глаголы и изменения в их написании приведены на страницах 170 – 171. Простая, прошедшая и причастная формы неправильных глаголов приведены на странице 172.

Сборник упражнений

Также имеются два сборника упражнений, которые помогут Вам практиковаться в употреблении новых слов:
The Oxford Picture Dictionary Beginning и *Intermediate Workbooks.*

Будучи авторами и преподавателями, мы хорошо знаем, насколько сложным может быть английский (а это наш родной язык!). При составлении этой книги мы обратились за помощью и идеями к учителям и студентам из США и других стран. Надеемся, что наш совместный труд окажет Вам хорошую службу. Пожалуйста, отправляйте комментарии и вопросы по адресу:

Oxford University Press
ESL Department
198 Madison Avenue
New York, NY 10016

Желаем удачи!

Jayme Adelson-Goldstein   *Norma Shapiro*

Contents Содержание

1. Everyday Language Обиходная речь

A Classroom Класс — 2–3
Personal Information Личные данные — 4
School Школа — 5
Studying Занятия — 6–7
Everyday Conversation Разговор на бытовые темы — 8
The Telephone Телефон — 9
Weather Погода — 10
Describing Things Описание предметов — 11
Colors Цвета — 12
Prepositions Предлоги — 13
Numbers and Measurements Числа, цифры и системы мер — 14–15
Time Время — 16–17
The Calendar Календарь — 18–19
Money Деньги — 20
Shopping Покупки — 21

2. People Люди

Age and Physical Description Возраст и описание внешности — 22
Describing Hair Описание причёски — 23
Family Семья — 24–25
Daily Routines Распорядок дня — 26–27
Life Events События жизни — 28–29
Feelings Чувства — 30–31
A Graduation Окончание школы — 32–33

3. Housing Жилое помещение

Places to Live Жильё — 34
Finding a Home Поиск жилья — 35
Apartments Квартиры — 36–37
A House Дом — 38
A Yard Двор / участок — 39
A Kitchen Кухня — 40
A Dining Area Столовая — 41
A Living Room Гостиная — 42
A Bathroom Ванная — 43
A Bedroom Спальня — 44
A Children's Bedroom Детская — 45
Housework Работа по дому — 46
Cleaning Supplies Моющие средства — 47
Household Problems and Repairs Неполадки и ремонт в доме — 48–49

4. Food Пища

Fruit Фрукты — 50
Vegetables Овощи — 51
Meat and Poultry Мясо и птица — 52
Deli and Seafood Деликатесы и дары моря — 53
The Market Рынок — 54–55
Containers and Packaged Foods Упаковка и расфасованные продукты — 56
Weights and Measures Система мер и весов — 57
Food Preparation Приготовление пищи — 58
Kitchen Utensils Кухонная утварь — 59

Contents   Содержание

Fast Food   Блюда быстрого приготовления   60
A Coffee Shop Menu   Меню кафе   61
A Restaurant   Ресторан   62–63

5. Clothing   Одежда

Clothing I   Одежда I   64–65
Clothing II   Одежда II   66
Clothing III   Одежда III   67
Shoes and Accessories   Обувь и принадлежности туалета   68–69
Describing Clothes   Описание одежды   70–71
Doing the Laundry   Стирка белья   72
Sewing and Alterations   Шитьё и переделка одежды   73

6. Health   Здоровье

The Body   Тело   74–75
Personal Hygiene   Личная гигиена   76–77
Symptoms and Injuries   Симптомы заболеваний и травмы   78
Illnesses and Medical Conditions   Болезни и состояние здоровья   79
Health Care   Здравоохранение   80–81
Medical Emergencies   Травмы / несчастные случаи   82
First Aid   Первая медицинская помощь   83
Clinics   Клиники   84
Medical and Dental Exams   Медицинский и зубоврачебный осмотр   85
A Hospital   Больница   86–87

7. Community   Общество

City Streets   Улицы города   88–89
An Intersection   Перекрёсток   90–91
A Mall   Торговый центр   92–93
A Childcare Center   Ясли / десткий сад   94–95
U.S. Mail   Почта США   96
A Bank   Банк   97
A Library   Библиотека   98
The Legal System   Правовая система   99
Crime   Преступление   100
Public Safety   Общественная безопасность   101
Emergencies and Natural Disasters   Несчастные случаи и
    стихийные бедствия   102–103

8. Transportation   Транспорт

Public Transportation   Общественный транспорт   104
Prepositions of Motion   Предлоги, относящиеся к движению   105
Cars and Trucks   Легковые и грузовые автомобили   106
Directions and Traffic Signs   Указатели и дорожные знаки   107
Parts of a Car and Car Maintenance   Детали автомобиля и его
    обслуживание   108–109
An Airport   Аэропорт   110
A Plane Trip   Полёт на самолёте   111

9. Areas of Study   Предметы изучения

Types of Schools   Типы школ   112
English Composition   Сочинение на английском языке   113
U.S. History   История США   114–115

x

Содержание   Contents

U.S. Government and Citizenship   Правительство и гражданство США   116
Geography   География   117
Mathematics   Математика   118
Science   Наука   119
Music   Музыка   120
More School Subjects   Школьные предметы (продолжение)   121
North America and Central America   Северная и Центральная
    Америка   122–123
The World   Мир   124–125
Energy and the Environment   Энергия и окружающая среда   126
The Universe   Вселенная   127

10. Plants and Animals   Растения и животные

Trees and Plants   Деревья и растения   128
Flowers   Цветы   129
Marine Life, Amphibians, and Reptiles   Морская фауна, амфибии
    и пресмыкающиеся   130–131
Birds, Insects, and Arachnids   Птицы, насекомые и паукообразные   132
Domestic Animals and Rodents   Домашние животные и грызуны   133
Mammals   Млекопитающие   134–135

11. Work   Работа

Jobs and Occupations, A–H   Должности и профессии   136–137
Jobs and Occupations, H–W   Должности и профессии   138–139
Job Skills   Профессиональные навыки   140
Job Search   Поиск работы   141
An Office   Офис   142–143
Computers   Компьютеры   144
A Hotel   Гостиница   145
A Factory   Завод   146
Job Safety   Безопасность труда   147
Farming and Ranching   Земледелие и скотоводство   148
Construction   Строительство   149
Tools and Building Supplies   Инструменты и стройматериалы   150–151

12. Recreation   Отдых

Places to Go   Места проведения досуга   152
The Park and Playground   Парк и игровая площадка   153
Outdoor Recreation   Развлечения на открытом воздухе   154
The Beach   Пляж   155
Sports Verbs   Глаголы, относящиеся к спорту   156–157
Team Sports   Командные виды спорта   158
Individual Sports   Индивидуальные виды спорта   159
Winter Sports and Water Sports   Зимние и водные виды спорта   160
Sports Equipment   Спротивное оборудование   161
Hobbies and Games   Хобби и игры   162–163
Electronics and Photography   Электроника и фотография   164–165
Entertainment   Развлечения   166–167
Holidays   Праздники   168
A Party   Вечеринка   169
Verb Guide   Список глаголов   170
Index   Указатель   173
Geographical Index   Географический указатель   206
Russian Index   Указатель на русском языке   209

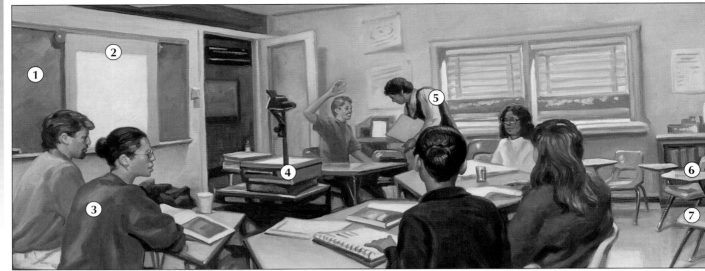

1. **chalkboard**
   доска

2. **screen**
   экран

3. **student**
   ученик / ученица

4. **overhead projector**
   проектор

5. **teacher**
   учитель / учительница

6. **desk**
   парта

7. **chair / seat**
   стул / сиденье / место

A. Raise your hand.
Поднимите руку.

B. Talk to the teacher.
Говорите с учителем.

C. Listen to a cassette.
Прослушайте кассету.

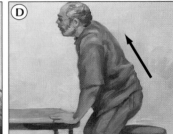

D. Stand up.
Встаньте.

E. Sit down. / Take a seat.
Садитесь. / Займите своё место.

F. Point to the picture.
Укажите на рисунок.

G. Write on the board.
Пишите на доске.

H. Erase the board.
Вытрите доску.

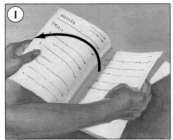

I. Open your book.
Откройте книгу.

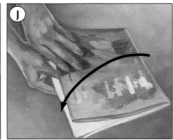

J. Close your book.
Закройте книгу.

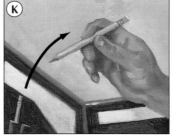

K. Take out your pencil.
Достаньте карандаш.

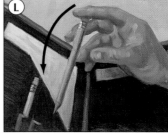

L. Put away your pencil.
Уберите карандаш.

8. bookcase
книжный шкаф

9. globe
глобус

10. clock
часы

11. cassette player
плейер

12. map
карта

13. pencil sharpener
точилка для карандашей

14. bulletin board
доска объявлений

15. computer
компьютер

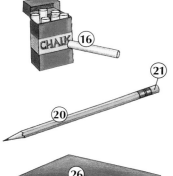

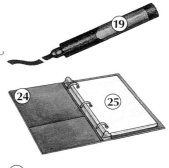

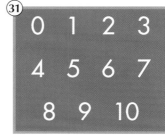

16. chalk
мел

17. chalkboard eraser
губка

18. pen
ручка

19. marker
фломастер

20. pencil
карандаш

21. pencil eraser
стерательная резинка

22. textbook
учебник

23. workbook
тетрадь

24. binder/notebook
скоросшиватель /
тетрадь

25. notebook paper
линованная бумага

26. spiral notebook
блокнот

27. ruler
линейка

28. dictionary
словарь

29. picture dictionary
словарь в картинках

30. the alphabet
алфавит

31. numbers
номера / цифры

Use the new language.

1. Name three things you can open.

2. Name three things you can put away.

3. Name three things you can write with.

Share your answers.

1. Do you like to raise your hand?

2. Do you ever listen to cassettes in class?

3. Do you ever write on the board?

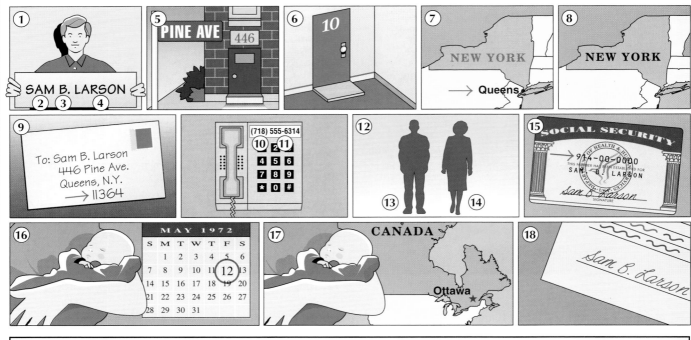

School Registration Form   Бланк о зачислении в школу

1. name _____

    имя   **2.** first name   **3.** middle initial   **4.** last name

               имя   второй инициал   фамилия

5. address _____   **6.** apt. # * _____

    адрес   № квартиры

7. city _____   **8.** state _____   **9.** ZIP code _____

   город   штат   индекс

   (   )   ___ __ ___

10. area code   **11.** telephone number   **12.** sex: **13.** ☐ male   **15.** Social Security number

    код города   номер телефона   пол: мужской   номер социального

                                   14. ☐ female   обеспечения

                                       женский

16. date of birth _____   **17.** place of birth _____

    дата   (month) (date) (year)   место рождения

    рождения (месяц) (число) (год)

                                         18. signature _____

                                          подпись

* apt. # = apartment number

A. **Spell** your name.
Произнесите своё имя
по буквам.

B. **Fill out** a form.
Заполните бланк.

C. **Print** your name.
Напишите своё имя
печатными буквами.

D. **Sign** your name.
Распишитесь.

Talk about yourself.

My first name is <u>Sam</u>.
My last name is spelled <u>L-A-R-S-O-N</u>.
I come from <u>Ottawa</u>.

Share your answers.

1. Do you like your first name?
2. Is your last name from your mother? father? husband?
3. What is your middle name?

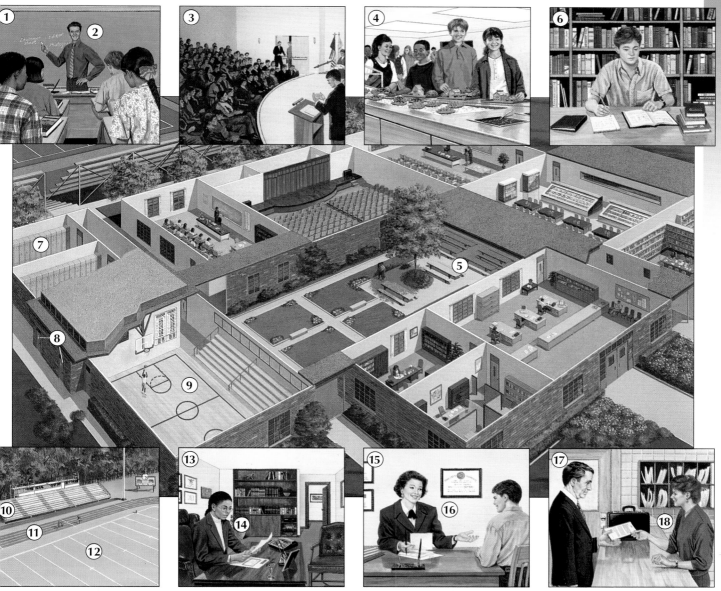

1. **classroom**
   класс
2. **teacher**
   учитель / преподаватель
3. **auditorium**
   актовый зал
4. **cafeteria**
   кафетерий
5. **lunch benches**
   скамейки
6. **library**
   библиотека

7. **lockers**
   запирающиеся шкафчики
8. **rest rooms**
   туалеты
9. **gym**
   спортзал
10. **bleachers**
    трибуны
11. **track**
    беговая дорожка
12. **field**
    поле

13. **principal's office**
    кабинет директора
14. **principal**
    директор
15. **counselor's office**
    кабинет завуча
16. **counselor**
    завуч
17. **main office**
    приёмная
18. **clerk**
    клерк / служащий

More vocabulary

instructor: teacher

coach: gym teacher

administrator: principal or other school supervisor

Share your answers.

1. Do you ever talk to the principal of your school?
2. Is there a place for you to eat at your school?
3. Does your school look the same as or different from the one in the picture?

5

Dictionary work   Работа со словарём

A. Look up a word.
Найдите слово в словаре.

B. Read the word.
Прочитайте слово.

C. Say the word.
Произнесите слово.

D. Repeat the word.
Повторите слово.

E. Spell the word.
Произнесите слово по буквам.

F. Copy the word.
Выпишите слово.

Work with a partner   Работа в паре

G. Ask a question.
Задайте вопрос.

H. Answer a question.
Ответьте на вопрос.

I. Share a book.
Поделитесь книгой.

J. Help your partner.
Помогите товарищу.

Work in a group   Работа в группе

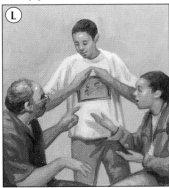

K. Brainstorm a list.
Составьте список.

L. Discuss the list.
Обсудите список.

M. Draw a picture.
Нарисуйте картинку.

N. Dictate a sentence.
Продиктуйте предложение.

Class work   Работа в классе

O. Pass out the papers.
Раздайте письменные работы.

P. Talk with each other.
Поговорите друг с другом.

Q. Collect the papers.
Соберите работы.

Follow directions   Следование инструкции

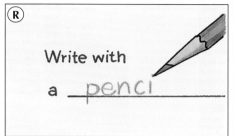

R. Fill in the blank.
Вставьте пропущенное слово.

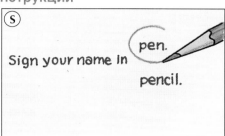

S. Circle the answer.
Обведите правильный ответ.

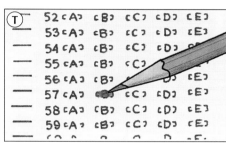

T. Mark the answer sheet.
Отметьте правильный ответ
в экзаменационном листе.

U. Cross out the word.
Вычеркните слово.

V. Underline the word.
Подчеркните слово.

W. Put the words **in order.**
Восстановите правильный
порядок слов.

X. Match the items.
Найдите пары.

Y. Check your work.
Проверьте свою работу.

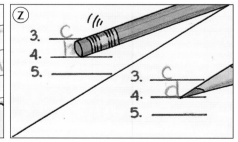

Z. Correct the mistake.
Исправьте ошибку.

Share your answers.

1. Do you like to work in groups?
2. Do you like to share books?
3. Do you like to answer questions?
4. Is it easy for you to talk with your classmates?
5. Do you always check your work?
6. Do you cross out your mistakes or erase them?

A. greet someone
поздороваться

B. begin a conversation
начать разговор

C. end the conversation
закончить разговор

D. introduce yourself
представиться

E. make sure you **understand**
убедиться, что вы правильно
поняли

F. introduce your friend
представить своего друга

G. compliment your friend
сделать комплимент
другу

H. thank your friend
поблагодарить друга

I. apologize
извиниться

Practice introductions.

Hi, I'm Sam Jones and this is my friend, Pat Green.

  Nice to meet you. I'm Tomas Garcia.

Practice giving compliments.

That's a great sweater, Tomas.

  Thanks Pat. I like your shoes.

Look at **Clothing I,** pages **64–65** for more ideas.

 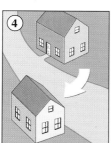 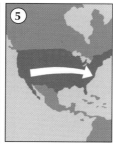 

  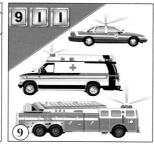

 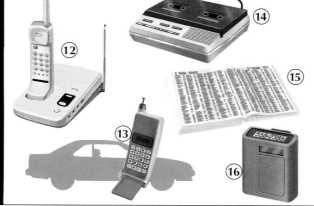

1. telephone / phone
   телефон
2. receiver
   трубка
3. cord
   шнур
4. local call
   местный звонок
5. long-distance call
   междугородний звонок
6. international call
   международный звонок
7. operator
   оператор
8. directory assistance (411)
   справочная
9. emergency service (911)
   пожарная / скорая / милиция
10. phone card
    телефонная карточка
11. pay phone
    телефон-автомат
12. cordless phone
    переносной телефон
13. cellular phone
    сотовый телефон
14. answering machine
    автоответчик
15. telephone book
    телефонная книга
16. pager
    пейджер

Using a pay phone Пользование телефоном-автоматом

A. **Pick up** the receiver.
   Снимите трубку.
B. **Listen** for the dial tone.
   Дождитесь гудка.
C. **Deposit** coins.
   Опустите монеты.
D. **Dial** the number.
   Наберите номер.
E. **Leave** a message.
   Оставьте сообщение.
F. **Hang up** the receiver.
   Повесьте трубку.

More vocabulary
When you get a person or place that you didn't want to call, we say you have the **wrong number.**

Share your answers.
1. What kinds of calls do you make?
2. How much does it cost to call your country?
3. Do you like to talk on the telephone?

9

Weather   Погода

Temperature
Температура

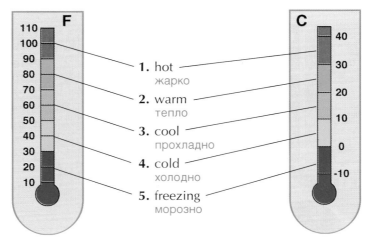

Degrees
Fahrenheit

Degrees
Celcius

1. hot
жарко

2. warm
тепло

3. cool
прохладно

4. cold
холодно

5. freezing
морозно

6. sunny / clear
солнечно / ясно

7. cloudy
облачно

8. raining
идёт дождь

9. snowing
идёт снег

10. windy
ветренно

11. foggy
туманно

12. humid
влажно

13. icy
гололёд

14. smoggy
смог

15. heat wave
жара

16. thunderstorm
гроза

17. lightning
молния

18. hailstorm
гроза с градом

19. hail
град

20. snowstorm
снежная буря / метель

21. dust storm
пыльная буря

Language note: *it is, there is*

For **1–14** we use,   *It's <u>cloudy</u>.*

For **15–21** we use,   *There's <u>a heat wave</u>.*
There's <u>lightning</u>.

Talk about the weather.

Today it's <u>hot</u>. It's <u>98 degrees</u>.

Yesterday it was <u>warm</u>. It was <u>85 degrees</u>.

1. **little** hand
   маленькая
   рука/ручка
2. **big** hand
   большая рука

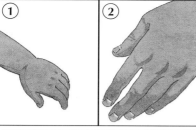

3. **fast** driver
   лихой
   водитель
4. **slow** driver
   осторожный
   водитель

5. **hard** chair
   жёсткий стул
6. **soft** chair
   мягкий стул

7. **thick** book/
   fat book
   толстая книга
8. **thin** book
   тонкая книга

9. **full** glass
   полный стакан
10. **empty** glass
    пустой стакан

11. **noisy** children/
    loud children
    шумные дети
12. **quiet** children
    спокойные/
    тихие дети

13. **heavy** box
    тяжёлый ящик
14. **light** box
    лёгкий ящик

15. **neat** closet
    опрятный шкаф
16. **messy** closet
    неопрятный шкаф

17. **good** dog
    хорошая собака
18. **bad** dog
    плохая собака

19. **expensive** ring
    дорогое кольцо
20. **cheap** ring
    дешёвое кольцо

$950

25¢

21. **beautiful** view
    красивый вид
22. **ugly** view
    безобразный вид

23. **easy** problem
    лёгкая задача
24. **difficult** problem/
    hard problem
    трудная задача

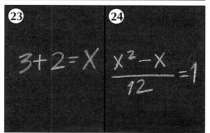

$3+2=X$ $\dfrac{x^2-x}{12}=1$

Use the new language.

1. Name three things that are thick.
2. Name three things that are soft.
3. Name three things that are heavy.

Share your answers.

1. Are you a slow driver or a fast driver?
2. Do you have a neat closet or a messy closet?
3. Do you like loud or quiet parties?

Colors   Цвета

1. blue
голубой

2. dark blue
синий

3. light blue
светло-голубой

4. turquoise
бирюзовый

5. gray
серый

6. orange
оранжевый

7. purple
лиловый

8. green
зелёный

9. beige
бежевый

10. pink
розовый

11. brown
коричневый

12. yellow
жёлтый

13. red
красный

14. white
белый

15. black
чёрный

Use the new language.
Look at **Clothing I**, pages **64–65**.
Name the colors of the clothing you see.
That's a dark blue suit.

Share your answers.
1. What colors are you wearing today?
2. What colors do you like?
3. Is there a color you don't like? What is it?

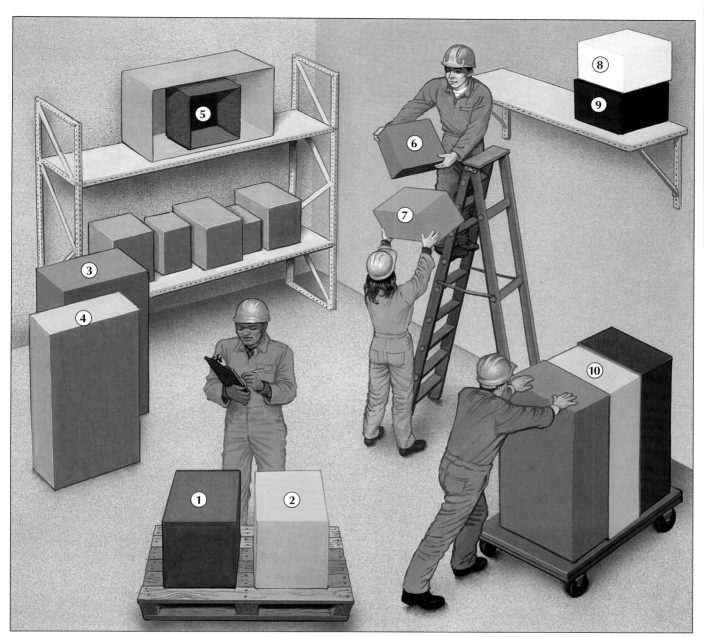

1. The red box is **next to** the yellow box, **on the left.**
Красная коробка находится **рядом с** жёлтой, **слева от** жёлтой.

2. The yellow box is **next to** the red box, **on the right.**
Жёлтая коробка находится **рядом с** красной коробкой, **справа от** красной.

3. The turquoise box is **behind** the gray box.
Бирюзовая коробка находится **за** серой коробкой.

4. The gray box is **in front of** the turquoise box.
Серая коробка находится **перед** бирюзовой коробкой.

5. The dark blue box is **in** the beige box.
Синяя коробка находится **в** бежевой коробке.

6. The green box is **above** the orange box.
Зелёная коробка находится **над** оранжевой коробкой.

7. The orange box is **below** the green box.
Оранжевая коробка находится **под** зелёной коробкой.

8. The white box is **on** the black box.
Белая коробка находится **на** чёрной коробке.

9. The black box is **under** the white box.
Чёрная коробка находится **под** белой коробкой.

10. The pink box is **between** the purple box and the brown box.
Розовая коробка находится **между** лиловой и коричневой коробками.

More vocabulary

near: in the same area
*The white box is **near** the black box.*

far from: not near
*The red box is **far from** the black box.*

Numbers and Measurements   Числа, цифры и системы мер

HOME	1	8
VISITOR	2	2

SAN DIEGO
235 miles

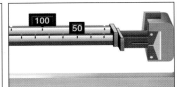

Cardinals   Количественные числительные

0 zero
   ноль

1 one
   один

2 two
   два

3 three
   три

4 four
   четыре

5 five
   пять

6 six
   шесть

7 seven
   семь

8 eight
   восемь

9 nine
   девять

10 ten
    десять

11 eleven
    одиннадцать

12 twelve
    двенадцать

13 thirteen
    тринадцать

14 fourteen
    четырнадцать

15 fifteen
    пятнадцать

16 sixteen
    шестнадцать

17 seventeen
    семнадцать

18 eighteen
    восемнадцать

19 nineteen
    девятнадцать

20 twenty
    двадцать

21 twenty-one
    двадцать один

22 twenty-two
    двадцать два

30 thirty
    тридцать

40 forty
    сорок

50 fifty
    пятьдесят

60 sixty
    шестьдесят

70 seventy
    семьдесят

80 eighty
    восемьдесят

90 ninety
    девяносто

100 one hundred
     сто

101
    one hundred one
    сто один

1,000
    one thousand
    тысяча

1,001
    one thousand one
    тысяча один

10,000
    ten thousand
    десять тысяч

100,000
    one hundred thousand
    сто тысяч

1,000,000
    one million
    миллион

1,000,000,000
    one billion
    миллиард

Ordinals   Порядковые   числительные

FINISH

1st first
     первый

2nd second
     второй

3rd third
     третий

4th fourth
     четвёртый

5th fifth
     пятый

6th sixth
     шестой

7th seventh
     седьмой

8th eighth
     восьмой

9th ninth
     девятый

10th tenth
      десятый

11th eleventh
      одиннадцатый

12th twelfth
      двенадцатый

13th thirteenth
      тринадцатый

14th fourteenth
      четырнадцатый

15th fifteenth
      пятнадцатый

16th sixteenth
      шестнадцатый

17th seventeenth
      семнадцатый

18th eighteenth
      восемнадцатый

19th nineteenth
      девятнадцатый

20th twentieth
      двадцатый

Roman numerals   Римские цифры

I	=	1	VII	=	7	XXX	=	30
II	=	2	VIII	=	8	XL	=	40
III	=	3	IX	=	9	L	=	50
IV	=	4	X	=	10	C	=	100
V	=	5	XV	=	15	D	=	500
VI	=	6	XX	=	20	M	=	1,000

14

Fractions   Дроби

1. 1/8   one-eighth
одна восьмая

2. 1/4   one-fourth
одна
четвёртая

3. 1/3   one-third
одна третья

4. 1/2   one-half
одна вторая

5. 3/4   three-fourths
три четвёртых

6. 1   whole
целое

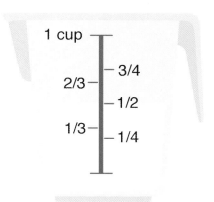

Percents   Проценты

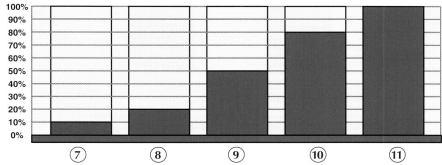

7. 10%   ten percent
10%   десять процентов

8. 20%   twenty percent
20%   двадцать процентов

9. 50%   fifty percent
50%   пятьдесят процентов

10. 80%   eighty percent
80%   восемьдесят процентов

11. 100%   one hundred percent
100%   сто процентов

Measurement   Система мер

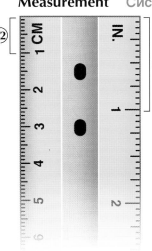

12. centimeter [cm]
сантиметр [см]

13. inch [in.]
дюйм

Equivalencies   Таблица
перевода единиц
измерений

1 inch	= 2.54 centimeters
1 yard	= .91 meters
1 mile	= 1.6 kilometers
12 inches	= 1 foot
3 feet	= 1 yard
1,760 yards	= 1 mile

Dimensions   Размеры

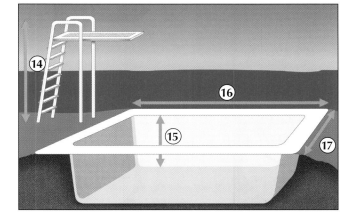

14. height
высота

16. length
длина

15. depth
глубина

17. width
ширина

More vocabulary

measure: to find the size or amount of something

count: to find the total number of something

Share your answers.

1. How many students are in class today?

2. Who was the first person in class today?

3. How far is it from your home to your school?

Time Время

A.M.

P.M.

1. second
секунда

2. minute
минута

3. hour
час

4. 1:00
one o'clock
час (дня / ночи)

5. 1:05
one-oh-five
час пять (минут)
five after one
пять минут второго

6. 1:10
one-ten
час десять
ten after one
десять минут второго

7. 1:15
one-fifteen
час пятнадцать
a quarter after one
четверть второго

8. 1:20
one-twenty
час двадцать
twenty after one
двадцать минут второго

9. 1:25
one twenty-five
час двадцать пять
twenty-five after one
двадцать пять минут
второго

10. 1:30
one-thirty
час тридцать
half past one
половина второго

11. 1:35
one thirty-five
час тридцать пять
twenty-five to two
без двадцати пяти два

12. 1:40
one-forty
час сорок
twenty to two
без двадцати два

13. 1:45
one forty-five
час сорок пять
a quarter to two
без четверти два

14. 1:50
one-fifty
час пятьдесят
ten to two
без десяти два

15. 1:55
one fifty-five
час пятьдесят пять
five to two
без пяти два

Talk about the time.

What time is it? It's <u>10:00 a.m.</u>

What time do you wake up on weekdays? At <u>6:30 a.m.</u>

What time do you wake up on weekends? At <u>9:30 a.m.</u>

Share your answers.

1. How many hours a day do you study English?

2. You are meeting friends at 1:00. How long will you wait for them if they are late?

16. morning
утро

17. noon
полдень

18. afternoon
день

19. evening
вечер

20. night
ночь

21. midnight
полночь

22. early
рано

23. late
поздно

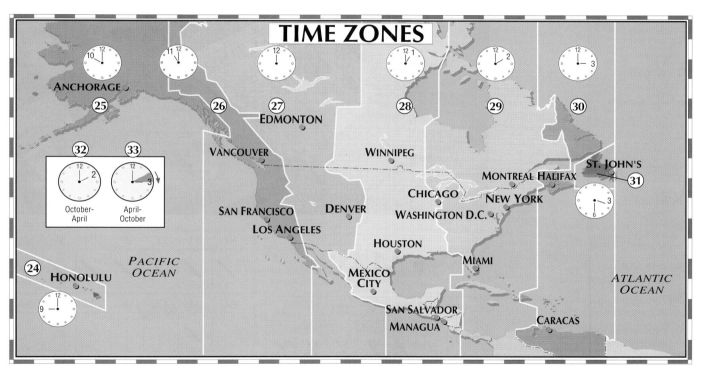

TIME ZONES

24. Hawaii-Aleutian time
время на Гаваях

25. Alaska time
время на Аляске

26. Pacific time
время на Тихоокеанском
побережье

27. mountain time
время в районе
Скалистых гор

28. central time
время в Центральной
части США

29. eastern time
время в восточной
части США

30. Atlantic time
время на Атлантическом
побережье

31. Newfoundland time
время в районе
Ньюфаундленда

32. standard time
стандартное время

33. daylight saving time
летнее время

More vocabulary

on time: not early and not late
*He's **on time**.*

Share your answers.

1. When do you watch television? study?
   do housework?

2. Do you come to class on time? early? late?

Days of the week
Дни недели

1. Sunday
   воскресенье

2. Monday
   понедельник

3. Tuesday
   вторник

4. Wednesday
   среда

5. Thursday
   четверг

6. Friday
   пятница

7. Saturday
   суббота

8. year
   год

9. month
   месяц

10. day
    день

11. week
    неделя

12. weekdays
    будни

13. weekend
    выходные (дни)

14. date
    число

15. today
    сегодня

16. tomorrow
    завтра

17. yesterday
    вчера

18. last week
    прошлая неделя

19. this week
    эта неделя

20. next week
    следующая неделя

21. every day
    каждый день

22. once a week
    раз в неделю

23. twice a week
    два раза в неделю

24. three times a week
    три раза в неделю

2001 ⑧ ⑨ **JANUARY** **2001**

① SUN	② MON	③ TUE	④ WED	⑤ THU	⑥ FRI	⑦ SAT
	⑩ 1	2	3	4	5	6
7	8	9	10	11	12	13
14	15	16	⑪ 17	18	19	20
21	22	23	⑫ 24	25	26	⑬ 27
28	29	30	31			

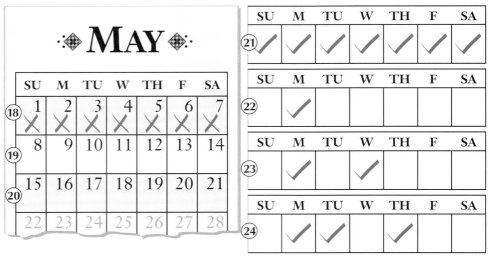

Talk about the calendar.

What's today's date? It's March 10th.

What day is it? It's Tuesday.

What day was yesterday? It was Monday.

Share your answers.

1. How often do you come to school?
2. How long have you been in this school?

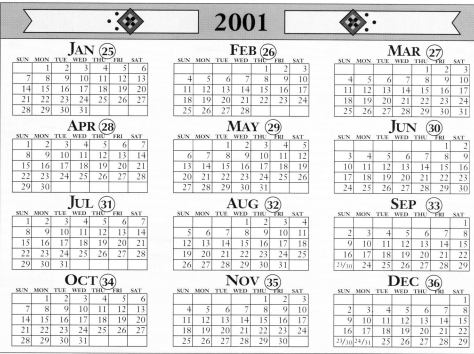

2001

JAN (25)
SUN	MON	TUE	WED	THU	FRI	SAT
	1	2	3	4	5	6
7	8	9	10	11	12	13
14	15	16	17	18	19	20
21	22	23	24	25	26	27
28	29	30	31			

FEB (26)
SUN	MON	TUE	WED	THU	FRI	SAT
				1	2	3
4	5	6	7	8	9	10
11	12	13	14	15	16	17
18	19	20	21	22	23	24
25	26	27	28			

MAR (27)
SUN	MON	TUE	WED	THU	FRI	SAT
				1	2	3
4	5	6	7	8	9	10
11	12	13	14	15	16	17
18	19	20	21	22	23	24
25	26	27	28	29	30	31

APR (28)
SUN	MON	TUE	WED	THU	FRI	SAT
1	2	3	4	5	6	7
8	9	10	11	12	13	14
15	16	17	18	19	20	21
22	23	24	25	26	27	28
29	30					

MAY (29)
SUN	MON	TUE	WED	THU	FRI	SAT
		1	2	3	4	5
6	7	8	9	10	11	12
13	14	15	16	17	18	19
20	21	22	23	24	25	26
27	28	29	30	31		

JUN (30)
SUN	MON	TUE	WED	THU	FRI	SAT
					1	2
3	4	5	6	7	8	9
10	11	12	13	14	15	16
17	18	19	20	21	22	23
24	25	26	27	28	29	30

JUL (31)
SUN	MON	TUE	WED	THU	FRI	SAT
1	2	3	4	5	6	7
8	9	10	11	12	13	14
15	16	17	18	19	20	21
22	23	24	25	26	27	28
29	30	31				

AUG (32)
SUN	MON	TUE	WED	THU	FRI	SAT
			1	2	3	4
5	6	7	8	9	10	11
12	13	14	15	16	17	18
19	20	21	22	23	24	25
26	27	28	29	30	31	

SEP (33)
SUN	MON	TUE	WED	THU	FRI	SAT
						1
2	3	4	5	6	7	8
9	10	11	12	13	14	15
16	17	18	19	20	21	22
23/30	24	25	26	27	28	29

OCT (34)
SUN	MON	TUE	WED	THU	FRI	SAT
	1	2	3	4	5	6
7	8	9	10	11	12	13
14	15	16	17	18	19	20
21	22	23	24	25	26	27
28	29	30	31			

NOV (35)
SUN	MON	TUE	WED	THU	FRI	SAT
				1	2	3
4	5	6	7	8	9	10
11	12	13	14	15	16	17
18	19	20	21	22	23	24
25	26	27	28	29	30	

DEC (36)
SUN	MON	TUE	WED	THU	FRI	SAT
						1
2	3	4	5	6	7	8
9	10	11	12	13	14	15
16	17	18	19	20	21	22
23/30	24/31	25	26	27	28	29

Months of the year
Месяцы года

25. January
января

26. February
февраль

27. March
март

28. April
апрель

29. May
май

30. June
июнь

31. July
июль

32. August
август

33. September
сентябрь

34. October
октябрь

35. November
ноябрь

36. December
декабрь

Seasons
Времена года

MARCH 21 (37)
JUNE 21 (38)
SEPT. 21 (39)
DEC. 21 (40)

37. spring
весна

38. summer
лето

39. fall
осень

40. winter
зима

JUNE **5** — TIM! (41)
MARCH **2** — ANNIVERSARY (42)
JULY **4** — INDEPENDENCE DAY — STATE BANK — CLOSED-JULY4 (43)

41. birthday
день рождения

42. anniversary
годовщина

43. legal holiday
государственный праздник

APRIL **4** — EASTER SUNDAY (44)
MAY **17** — DOCTOR 4:30 (45)
AUGUST (46)

44. religious holiday
церковный праздник

45. appointment
приём у врача

46. vacation
отпуск

Use the new language.
Look at the **ordinal numbers** on page **14.**
Use ordinal numbers to say the date.
It's June 5th. It's the fifth.

Talk about your birthday.
My birthday is in the winter.
My birthday is in January.
My birthday is on January twenty-sixth.

Money Деньги

Coins Монеты

1. $.01 = 1¢
a penny/1 cent
один цент/1 цент

2. $.05 = 5¢
a nickel/5 cents
пять центов/5 центов

3. $.10 = 10¢
a dime/10 cents
десять центов/10 центов

4. $.25 = 25¢
a quarter/25 cents
двадцать пять центов/25 центов

5. $.50 = 50¢
a half dollar
пятьдесят центов/50 центов

6. $1.00
a silver dollar
серебряный доллар

Bills Счета

7. $1.00
a dollar
доллар

8. $5.00
five dollars
пять долларов

9. $10.00
ten dollars
десять долларов

10. $20.00
twenty dollars
двадцать долларов

11. $50.00
fifty dollars
пятьдесят долларов

12. $100.00
one hundred dollars
сто долларов

Ways to pay Способы оплаты

13. cash
наличные (деньги)

14. personal check
(личный) чек

15. credit card
кредитная карточка

16. money order
денежный перевод

17. traveler's check
дорожный чек

More vocabulary

borrow: to get money from someone and return it later

lend: to give money to someone and get it back later

pay back: to return the money that you borrowed

Other ways to talk about money:

a dollar bill or *a one*

a five-dollar bill or *a five*

a ten-dollar bill or *a ten*

a twenty-dollar bill or *a twenty*

A. shop for
покупать

B. sell
продавать

C. pay for / **buy**
платить / купить

D. give
дать (сдачу)

E. keep
оставить

F. return
вернуть

G. exchange
обменять

1. price tag
ценник

2. regular price
(обычная) цена

3. sale price
цена во время распро-
дажи / цена со скидкой

4. bar code
штриховой код

5. receipt
чек

6. price / cost
цена / стоимость

7. sales tax
налог на продажу

8. total
итого / общая сумма

9. change
сдача

More vocabulary

When you use a credit card to shop, you get a **bill** in the mail. Bills list, in writing, the items you bought and the total you have to pay.

Share your answers.

1. Name three things you pay for every month.
2. Name one thing you will buy this week.
3. Where do you like to shop?

1. **children**
   дети

2. **baby**
   ребёнок / малыш

3. **toddler**
   ребёнок, начинающий
   ходить

4. **6-year-old boy**
   шестилетний мальчик

5. **10-year-old girl**
   десятилетняя девочка

6. **teenagers**
   подростки

7. **13-year-old boy**
   тринадцатилетний
   мальчик

8. **19-year-old girl**
   девятнадцатилетняя
   девушка

9. **adults**
   взрослые

10. **woman**
    женщина

11. **man**
    мужчина

12. **senior citizen**
    пожилой человек

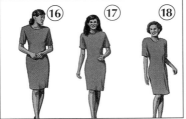

13. **young**
    молодой / молодая

14. **middle-aged**
    средних лет

15. **elderly**
    пожилой / пожилая

16. **tall**
    высокий / высокая

17. **average height**
    среднего роста

18. **short**
    небольшого роста

19. **pregnant**
    беременная

20. **heavyset**
    полный / полная

21. **average weight**
    средней комплекции

22. **thin / slim**
    худой / худая /
    стройный / стройная

23. **attractive**
    привлекательный /
    привлекательная

24. **cute**
    милый / милая

25. **physically challenged**
    с физическими
    недостатками

26. **sight impaired / blind**
    с плохим зрением /
    слепой / слепая

27. **hearing impaired / deaf**
    с плохим слухом /
    глухой / глухая

Talk about yourself and your teacher.

I am young, average height, and average weight.

My teacher is a middle-aged, tall, thin man.

Use the new language.

Turn to **Hobbies and Games**, pages **162–163.**

Describe each person on the page.

He's a heavy-set, short, senior citizen.

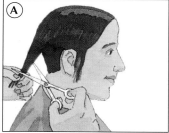 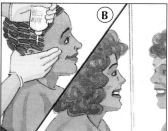  

1. short hair
короткие волосы

2. shoulder-length hair
волосы до плеч

3. long hair
длинные волосы

4. part
пробор

5. mustache
усы

6. beard
борода

7. sideburns
бакенбарды

8. bangs
чёлка

9. straight hair
прямые волосы

10. wavy hair
волнистые волосы

11. curly hair
вьющиеся / кудрявые
волосы

12. bald
лысина

13. gray hair
седые волосы

14. red hair
рыжие волосы

15. black hair
брюнет / брюнетка

16. blond hair
блондин / блондинка

17. brown hair
шатен / шатенка

18. brush
щётка

19. scissors
ножницы

20. blow dryer
фен

21. rollers
бигуди

22. comb
расчёска

A. **cut** hair
делать стрижку /
стричься

B. **perm** hair
делать химическую
завивку

C. **set** hair
делать укладку

D. **color** hair / **dye** hair
красить волосы

More vocabulary

hair stylist: a person who cuts, sets, and perms hair
hair salon: the place where a hair stylist works

Talk about your hair.

My hair is long, straight, and brown.
I have long, straight, brown hair.
When I was a child my hair was short, curly, and blond.

Tom Lee's Family

1. grandparents
бабушка и дедушка

Min

Lu

2. grandmother
бабушка

3. grandfather
дедушка

4. parents
родители

Rose

Chang

Helen

Daniel

5. mother
мать

6. father
отец

10. aunt
тётя

11. uncle
дядя

Tom

Lily

Alex

Emily

8. sister
сестра

9. brother
брат

12. cousin
двоюродн
ая сестра

7. (Min and Lu's)
grandson
внук Мины и Лу

Berta

Mario

Ana Garcia's Family

Ana

13. mother-in-law
свекровь / тёща

14. father-in-law
свёкр / тесть

Marta

Carlos

Tito

20. (Tito's) wife
жена (Тито)

15. sister-in-law золовка/
невестка / свояченница

16. brother-in-law
зять / шурин / свояк / деверь

19. husband
муж

Alice

Eddie

Sara

Felix

17. niece
племянница

18. nephew
племянник

21. daughter
дочь

22. son
сын

More vocabulary

Lily and Emily are Min and Lu's **granddaughters.**

Daniel is Min and Lu's **son-in-law.**

Ana is Berta and Mario's **daughter-in-law.**

Share your answers.

1. How many brothers and sisters do you have?
2. What number son or daughter are you?
3. Do you have any children?

Lisa Smith's Family

23. married
женатый / замужняя

Carol

Dan

Lisa

24. divorced
разведённый / разведённая

25. single mother
мать-одиночка

26. single father
отец-одиночка

27. remarried
вторично женатый / вышедшая замуж

Rick

Carol

Dan

Sue

Rick

Carol

Lisa

Dan

Sue

28. stepfather
отчим

31. stepmother
мачеха

David

Mary

Kim

Bill

29. half brother
сводный брат

30. half sister
сводная сестра

32. stepsister
сводная сестра

33. stepbrother
сводный брат

More vocabulary

Carol is Dan's **former wife**.
Sue is Dan's **wife**.
Dan is Carol's **former husband**.

Rick is Carol's **husband**.
Lisa is the **stepdaughter** of both Rick and Sue.

Daily Routines Распорядок дня

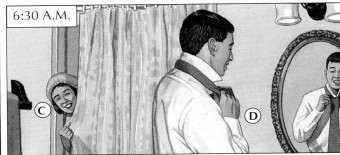

A. wake up
просыпаться

B. get up
вставать

C. take a shower
принимать душ

D. get dressed
одеваться

E. eat breakfast
завтракать

F. make lunch
готовить обед

G. take the children to school
отвозить детей в школу

H. take the bus to school
ехать в школу **на автобусе**

I. drive to work / **go** to work
ехать на работу **на машине** / **идти**
на работу

J. be in school
быть в школе

K. work
работать

L. go to the market
идти на рынок

M. leave work
уходить с работы

Grammar point: 3rd person singular

For **he** and **she**, we add **-s** or **-es** to the verb.

*He/She wak**es** up.*

*He/She watch**es** TV.*

These verbs are different (irregular):

be   *He/She **is** in school at 10:00 a.m.*

have   *He/She **has** dinner at 6:30 p.m.*

5:30 P.M. — N, O

6:00 P.M. — P, Q

6:30 P.M. — R

7:30 P.M. — S, T

8:00 P.M. — U, V

8:30 P.M. — W

10:30 P.M. — X

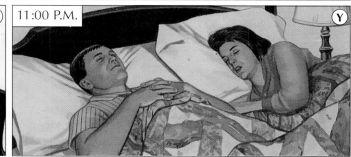

11:00 P.M. — Y

N. clean the house
убирать дом

O. pick up the children
забрать детей

P. cook dinner
готовить ужин

Q. come home / **get** home
придти домой / попасть домой

R. have dinner
ужинать

S. watch TV
смотреть телевизор

T. do homework
делать домашнюю работу

U. relax
отдыхать

V. read the paper
читать газету

W. exercise
делать гимнастику

X. go to bed
ложиться спать

Y. go to sleep
идти спать

Talk about your daily routine.

I take a shower in the morning.

I go to school in the evening.

I go to bed at 11 o'clock.

Share your answers.

1. Who makes dinner in your family?
2. Who goes to the market?
3. Who goes to work?

Life Events   События жизни

A. be born
родиться

B. start school
пойти в школу

C. immigrate
иммигрировать

D. graduate
закончить школу / вуз

E. learn to drive
учиться водить машину

F. join the army
пойти в армию

G. get a job
найти работу

H. become a citizen
получить гражданство /
стать гражданином

I. rent an apartment
снять квартиру

J. go to college
поступить в колледж

K. fall in love
влюбиться

L. get married
жениться / выйти замуж

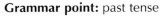

Grammar point: past tense

start learn join rent travel	+ed	immigrate graduate move retire die	+d

These verbs are different (irregular):

be	— was	have	— had
get	— got	buy	— bought
become	— became		
go	— went		
fall	— fell		

28

1960

1967

M. have a baby
родить ребёнка

N. travel
путешествовать

1971

1971

O. buy a house
купить дом

P. move
переехать

1985

1997

Q. have a grandchild
иметь внука / внучку

R. die
умереть

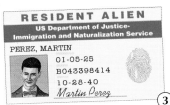

1. birth certificate
свидетельство о рождении

2. diploma
диплом

3. Resident Alien card
вид на жительство

4. driver's license
водительские права

5. Social Security card
карточка с номером
социального обеспечения

6. Certificate of Naturalization
свидетельство о получении
гражданства

7. college degree
диплом колледжа

8. marriage license
свидетельство о браке

9. passport
паспорт

More vocabulary

When a husband dies, his wife becomes a **widow**.
When a wife dies, her husband becomes a **widower**.
When older people stop working, we say they **retire**.

Talk about yourself.

I was born in 1968.
I learned to drive in 1987.
I immigrated in 1990.

Feelings   Чувства

1. **hot**
   жарко

2. **thirsty**
   хотеть пить

3. **sleepy**
   хотеть спать

4. **cold**
   холодно

5. **hungry**
   голоден / голодна

6. **full**
   сыт / сыта

7. **comfortable**
   удобно

8. **uncomfortable**
   неудобно

9. **disgusted**
   испытывающий / испы-
   тывающая отвращение

10. **calm**
    спокойный / спокойная

11. **nervous**
    нервный / нервная

12. **in pain**
    испытывающий /
    испытывающая боль

13. **worried**
    обеспокоенный /
    обеспокоенная

14. **sick**
    больной / больная

15. **well**
    хорошо

16. **relieved**
    легче

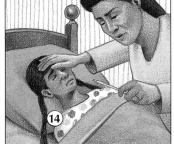

17. **hurt**
    обиженный / обиженная

18. **lonely**
    одинокий / одинокая

19. **in love**
    влюблённый /
    влюблённая

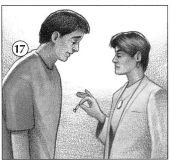
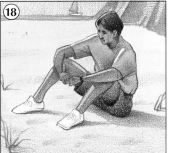

More vocabulary
furious: very angry
terrified: very scared
overjoyed: very happy

exhausted: very tired
starving: very hungry
humiliated: very embarrassed

Talk about your feelings.
I feel <u>happy</u> when I see <u>my friends</u>.
I feel <u>homesick</u> when I think about <u>my family</u>.

20. sad
грустный / грустная

21. homesick
чувство ностальгии / тоски по родине / по дому

22. proud
гордый / гордая

23. excited
взволнованный / взволнованная

24. scared
испуганный / испуганная

25. embarrassed
испытывающий / испытывающая неловкость

26. bored
скучающий / скучающая

27. confused
смущённый / смущённая

28. frustrated
расстроенный / расстроенная

29. angry
сердитый / сердитая

30. upset
огорчённый / огорчённая

31. surprised
удивлённый / удивлённая

32. happy
счастливый / счастливая

33. tired
усталый / усталая

Use the new language.
Look at **Clothing I,** page **64,** and answer the questions.

1. How does the runner feel?

2. How does the man at the bus stop feel?

3. How does the woman at the bus stop feel?

4. How do the teenagers feel?

5. How does the little boy feel?

1. **graduating class**
   выпускной класс / курс

2. **gown**
   мантия

3. **cap**
   шапка / головной убор

4. **stage**
   сцена

5. **podium**
   кафедра

6. **graduate**
   выпускник

7. **diploma**
   аттестат зрелости

8. **valedictorian**
   выпускник,
   отличившийся в учёбе

9. **guest speaker**
   приглашённый оратор

10. **audience**
    аудитория

11. **photographer**
    фотограф

A. **graduate**
   окончить школу /
   колледж

B. **applaud / clap**
   аплодировать / хлопать
   в ладоши

C. **cry**
   плакать

D. **take** a picture
   делать снимок /
   фотографировать

E. **give** a speech
   выступать с речью

Talk about what the people in the pictures are doing.

She is ⎡ *tak**ing** a picture.*
⎢ *giv**ing** a speech.*
⎢ *smil**ing**.*
⎣ *laugh**ing**.*

He is ⎡ *mak**ing** a toast.*
⎣ *clap**ping**.*

They are ⎡ *graduat**ing**.*
⎢ *hug**ging**.*
⎢ *kiss**ing**.*
⎣ *applaud**ing**.*

12. caterer
организатор банкета

13. buffet
буфет / шведский стол

14. guests
гости

15. banner
знамя

16. dance floor
танцплощадка

17. DJ (disc jockey)
диск-жокей

18. gifts
подарки

F. kiss
целовать / целоваться

G. hug
обнимать / обниматься

H. laugh
смеяться

I. make a toast
произносить тост

J. dance
танцевать

Share your answers.

1. Did you ever go to a graduation? Whose?

2. Did you ever give a speech? Where?

3. Did you ever hear a great speaker? Where?

4. Did you ever go to a graduation party?

5. What do you like to eat at parties?

6. Do you like to dance at parties?

Places to Live   Жильё

1. the city/an urban area
город/городской район

2. the suburbs
пригород

3. a small town
небольшой город

4. the country/a rural area
деревня/сельская
местность

5. apartment building
многоквартирный дом

6. house
дом

7. townhouse
дом ленточной застройки

8. mobile home
передвижной/сборный дом

9. college dormitory
студенческое общежитие

10. shelter
приют

11. nursing home
дом для престарелых

12. ranch
ранчо

13. farm
ферма

More vocabulary

duplex house: a house divided into two homes

condominium: an apartment building where each apartment is owned separately

co-op: an apartment building owned by the residents

Share your answers.

1. Do you like where you live?

2. Where did you live in your country?

3. What types of housing are there near your school?

Renting an apartment Съём квартиры

A. look for a new apartment
искать новую квартиру

> Utilities?

> Utilities are included.

B. talk to the manager
говорить с менеджером

C. sign a rental agreement
подписать договор об аренде

D. move in
въехать в (квартиру)

E. unpack
распаковать вещи

F. pay the rent
платить за квартиру

Buying a house Покупка дома

G. talk to the Realtor
говорить с агентом по продаже недвижимости

> $$$$$$

H. make an offer
сделать предложение

> Congratulations!

I. get a loan
получить ссуду (в банке)

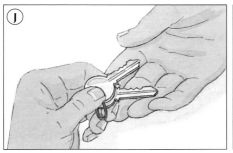

J. take ownership
вступить во владение собственностью

K. arrange the furniture
расставить мебель

L. pay the mortgage
выплачивать ссуду

More vocabulary

lease: a rental agreement for a specific period of time

utilities: gas, water, and electricity for the home

Practice talking to an apartment manager.

How much is the rent?

Are utilities included?

When can I move in?

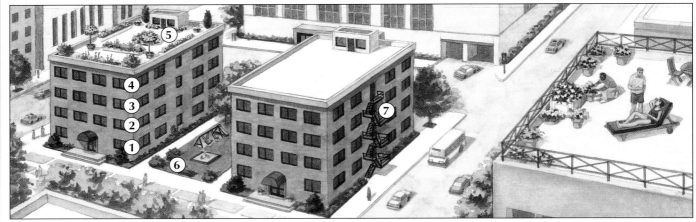

Entrance

Laundry Room

Recreation Room

Garage

1. first floor
первый этаж

2. second floor
второй этаж

3. third floor
третий этаж

4. fourth floor
четвёртый этаж

5. roof garden
сад на крыше

6. playground
детская площадка

7. fire escape
пожарный выход

8. intercom/speaker
переговорное устройство/
интерком

9. security system
система безопасности

10. doorman
портье

11. vacancy sign
вывеска о сдаче квартиры в аренду

12. manager/superintendent
менеджер/комендант

13. security gate
запирающиеся ворота

14. storage locker
кладовка

15. parking space
стоянка

More vocabulary

rec room: a short way of saying **recreation room**

basement: the area below the street level of an apartment
or a house

Talk about where you live.

I live in Apartment 3 near the entrance.

*I live in Apartment 11 on the second floor near the fire
escape.*

Hallway

FIRE EXIT

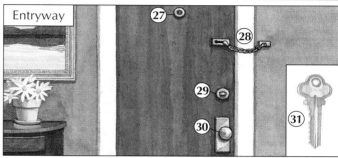

Entryway

Office

Lobby

16. **swimming pool**
бассейн

17. **balcony**
балкон

18. **courtyard**
внутренний дворик

19. **air conditioner**
кондиционер

20. **trash bin**
мусорное ведро

21. **alley**
переулок

22. **neighbor**
сосед

23. **fire exit**
пожарный выход

24. **trash chute**
мусоропровод

25. **smoke detector**
дымоуловитель

26. **stairway**
лестничная клетка

27. **peephole**
глазок

28. **door chain**
дверная цепочка

29. **dead-bolt lock**
засов / замок с засовом

30. **doorknob**
дверная ручка

31. **key**
ключ

32. **landlord**
хозяин (квартиры / дома) /
домовладелец

33. **tenant**
квартиросъёмщик

34. **elevator**
лифт

35. **stairs**
лестница / ступеньки

36. **mailboxes**
почтовые ящики

Grammar point: *there is, there are*

singular: *there is*   plural: *there are*

There is a fire exit in the hallway.

There are mailboxes in the lobby.

Talk about apartments.

My apartment has <u>an elevator</u>, <u>a lobby</u>, and <u>a rec room</u>.

My apartment doesn't have <u>a pool</u> or <u>a garage</u>.

My apartment needs <u>air conditioning</u>.

A House   Дом

1. **floor plan**
   план этажа

2. **backyard**
   задний двор

3. **fence**
   забор

4. **mailbox**
   почтовый ящик

5. **driveway**
   проезд / подъездная
   дорога

6. **garage**
   гараж

7. **garage door**
   гаражная дверь

8. **screen door**
   дверь с сеткой

9. **porch light**
   фонарь на крыльце

10. **doorbell**
    звонок

11. **front door**
    входная дверь

12. **storm door**
    внешняя дверь

13. **steps**
    ступеньки

14. **front walk**
    дорожка перед домом

15. **front yard**
    передний двор

16. **deck**
    веранда с деревянным
    настилом

17. **window**
    окно

18. **shutter**
    ставень

19. **gutter**
    водосточный жёлоб

20. **roof**
    крыша

21. **chimney**
    труба

22. **TV antenna**
    телевизионная антена

More vocabulary

two-story house: a house with two floors

downstairs: the bottom floor

upstairs: the part of a house above the bottom floor

Share your answers.

1. What do you like about this house?

2. What's something you don't like about the house?

3. Describe the perfect house.

1. hedge
живая изгородь

2. hammock
гамак

3. garbage can
мусорный бак

4. leaf blower
воздуходувка для
уборки листьев

5. patio furniture
садовая мебель

6. patio
патио

7. barbecue grill
гриль

8. sprinkler
разбрызгиватель воды

9. hose
шланг

10. compost pile
куча удобрений

11. rake
грабли

12. hedge clippers
садовые ножницы

13. shovel
лопата

14. trowel
мастерок

15. pruning shears
секатор

16. wheelbarrow
тачка

17. watering can
лейка

18. flowerpot
цветочный горшок

19. flower
цветок

20. bush
куст

21. lawn
газон

22. lawn mower
газонокосилка

A. **weed** the flower bed
полоть клумбу

B. **water** the plants
поливать цветы

C. **mow** the lawn
косить траву

D. **plant** a tree
сажать дерево

E. **trim** the hedge
подрезать кусты

F. **rake** the leaves
сгребать листья

Talk about your yard and gardening.

I like to _plant trees_.

I don't like to _weed_.

I like / don't like to work in the yard/garden.

Share your answers.

1. What flowers, trees, or plants do you see in the picture? (Look at **Trees, Plants, and Flowers,** pages **128–129** for help.)

2. Do you ever use a barbecue grill to cook?

A Kitchen Кухня

1. **cabinet**
   кухонный шкаф

2. **paper towels**
   бумажные полотенца

3. **dish drainer**
   сушилка для посуды

4. **dishwasher**
   посудомоечная машина

5. **garbage disposal**
   электромусоропровод

6. **sink**
   мойка

7. **toaster**
   тостер

8. **shelf**
   полка

9. **refrigerator**
   холодильник

10. **freezer**
    морозилка

11. **coffeemaker**
    кофеварка

12. **blender**
    блендер

13. **microwave oven**
    микроволновая печь

14. **electric can opener**
    электрическая
    открывалка

15. **toaster oven**
    духовка-тостер

16. **pot**
    кастрюля

17. **teakettle**
    чайник

18. **stove**
    плита

19. **burner**
    горелка

20. **oven**
    духовка

21. **broiler**
    бройлер

22. **counter**
    кухонный стол

23. **drawer**
    выдвижной ящик

24. **pan**
    кастрюля

25. **electric mixer**
    электрический миксер

26. **food processor**
    кухонный комбайн

27. **cutting board**
    доска

Talk about the location of kitchen items.

The toaster oven is *on the counter* *near the stove*.
The microwave is *above the stove*.

Share your answers.

1. Do you have a garbage disposal? a dishwasher?
   a microwave?

2. Do you eat in the kitchen?

1. china cabinet
сервант / буфет

2. set of dishes
сервиз

3. platter
блюдо

4. ceiling fan
потолочный
вентилятор

5. light fixture
светильник

6. serving dish
блюдо

7. candle
свеча

8. candlestick
подсвечник

9. vase
ваза

10. tray
поднос

11. teapot
чайник

12. sugar bowl
сахарница

13. creamer
молочник

14. saltshaker
солонка

15. pepper shaker
перечница

16. dining room chair
стул от обеденного
гарнитура

17. dining room table
обеденный стол

18. tablecloth
скатерть

19. napkin
салфетка

20. place mat
салфетка под
столовый прибор

21. fork
вилка

22. knife
нож

23. spoon
ложка

24. plate
тарелка

25. bowl
миска / глубокая
тарелка

26. glass
стакан

27. coffee cup
кофейная чашка

28. mug
кружка

Practice asking for things in the dining room.

Please pass the platter.

May I have the creamer?

Could I have a fork, please?

Share your answers.

1. What are the women in the picture saying?

2. In your home, where do you eat?

3. Do you like to make dinner for your friends?

A Living Room   Гостиная

1. bookcase книжный шкаф	**8.** mantel каминная полка	**15.** floor lamp торшер	**22.** magazine holder подставка для журналов и газет
2. basket корзина	**9.** fireplace камин	**16.** drapes шторы	**23.** coffee table журнальный столик
3. track lighting направленное освещение	**10.** fire огонь	**17.** window окно	**24.** armchair/easy chair кресло
4. lightbulb лампочка	**11.** fire screen заслонка	**18.** plant цветок	**25.** love seat диван на двоих
5. ceiling потолок	**12.** logs поленья	**19.** sofa/couch софа/диван	**26.** TV (television) телевизор
6. wall стена	**13.** wall unit стенка	**20.** throw pillow декоративные подушки	**27.** carpet ковёр
7. painting картина	**14.** stereo system стереосистема	**21.** end table приставной столик	

Use the new language.

Look at **Colors**, page **12**, and describe this room.

There is a gray sofa and a gray armchair.

Talk about your living room.

In my living room I have a sofa, two chairs, and a coffee table.

I don't have a fireplace or a wall unit.

1. hamper
корзина для грязного белья

2. bathtub
ванна

3. rubber mat
резиновый коврик

4. drain
слив

5. hot water
горячая вода

6. faucet
кран

7. cold water
холодная вода

8. towel rack
вешалка для полотенец

9. tile
кафель

10. showerhead
душ

11. (mini)blinds
жалюзи

12. bath towel
банное полотенце

13. hand towel
полотенце для рук

14. washcloth
мочалка из махровой ткани

15. toilet paper
туалетная бумага

16. toilet brush
щётка для унитаза

17. toilet
унитаз

18. mirror
зеркало

19. medicine cabinet
аптечка

20. toothbrush
зубная щётка

21. toothbrush holder
подставка для зубных щёток

22. sink
умывальник / раковина

23. soap
мыло

24. soap dish
мыльница

25. wastebasket
корзина для мусора

26. scale
весы

27. bath mat
коврик для ванной

More vocabulary

half bath: a bathroom without a shower or bathtub
linen closet: a closet or cabinet for towels and sheets
stall shower: a shower without a bathtub

Share your answers.

1. Do you turn off the water when you brush your teeth? wash your hair? shave?
2. Does your bathroom have a bathtub or a stall shower?

1. mirror зеркало	**8. bed** кровать	**15. headboard** спинка кровати	**22. dust ruffle** простыня с подзором
2. dresser/bureau комод	**9. pillow** подушка	**16. clock radio** радио с часами	**23. rug** половик / ковёр
3. drawer выдвижной ящик	**10. pillowcase** наволочка	**17. lamp** лампа	**24. floor** пол
4. closet шкаф	**11. bedspread** покрывало	**18. lampshade** абажур	**25. mattress** матрас
5. curtains шторы	**12. blanket** одеяло	**19. light switch** выключатель	**26. box spring** пружины кровати
6. window shade занавески	**13. flat sheet** простыня	**20. outlet** розетка	**27. bed frame** рама
7. photograph фотография	**14. fitted sheet** простыня-наматрасник	**21. night table** ночной столик	

Use the new language.

Describe this room. (See **Describing Things**, page 11, for help.)

I see a soft pillow and a beautiful bedspread.

Share your answers.

1. What is your favorite thing in your bedroom?

2. Do you have a clock in your bedroom? Where is it?

3. Do you have a mirror in your bedroom? Where is it?

1. bunk bed
двухэтажная кровать

2. comforter
одеяло

3. night-light
ночник

4. mobile
подвесная игрушка над
кроватью ребёнка

5. wallpaper
обои

6. crib
детская кроватка

7. bumper pad
бордюр из подушек

8. chest of drawers
комод

9. baby monitor
монитор «электронная
няня»

10. teddy bear
мишка

11. smoke detector
дымоуловитель

12. changing table
пеленальный стол

13. diaper pail
ведро для
использованных
подгузников

14. dollhouse
игрушечный дом

15. blocks
кубики

16. ball
мяч

17. picture book
книжка с картинками

18. doll
кукла

19. cradle
колыбель

20. coloring book
книжка для
раскрашивания

21. crayons
цветные карандаши

22. puzzle
головоломка

23. stuffed animals
мякие игрушки

24. toy chest
ящик для игрушек

Talk about where items are in the room.

The dollhouse is near the coloring book.

The teddy bear is on the chest of drawers.

Share your answers.

1. Do you think this is a good room for children? Why?

2. What toys did you play with when you were a child?

3. What children's stories do you know?

A. dust the furniture
вытирать пыль с мебели

B. recycle the newspapers
сдавать газеты **в макулатуру**

C. clean the oven
мыть духовку

D. wash the windows
мыть окна

E. sweep the floor
подметать пол

F. empty the wastebasket
выбрасывать мусор из корзины

G. make the bed
застилать постель

H. put away the toys
убирать игрушки

I. vacuum the carpet
пылесосить ковёр

J. mop the floor
мыть пол

K. polish the furniture
полировать мебель

L. scrub the floor
мыть пол щёткой

M. wash the dishes
мыть посуду

N. dry the dishes
вытирать посуду

O. wipe the counter
вытирать кухонный стол

P. change the sheets
менять постельное бельё

Q. take out the garbage
выносить мусор

Talk about yourself.

I wash <u>the dishes</u> every day.

I change <u>the sheets</u> every week.

I never <u>dry the dishes</u>.

Share your answers.

1. Who does the housework in your family?

2. What is your favorite cleaning job?

3. What is your least favorite cleaning job?

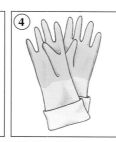

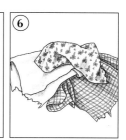

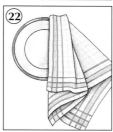

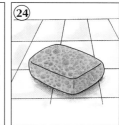

1. **feather duster**
метёлка из перьев для смахивания пыли

2. **recycling bin**
ведро для сбора вторсырья

3. **oven cleaner**
средство для мытья духовки

4. **rubber gloves**
резиновые перчатки

5. **steel-wool soap pads**
металлические-войлочные губки, пропитанные моющим средством

6. **rags**
тряпки

7. **stepladder**
стремянка

8. **glass cleaner**
жидкость для мытья окон

9. **squeegee**
резиновая швабра для мытья окон

10. **broom**
метла / веник

11. **dustpan**
совок для мусора

12. **trash bags**
пакеты для мусора

13. **vacuum cleaner**
пылесос

14. **vacuum cleaner attachments**
насадки для пылесоса

15. **vacuum cleaner bag**
бумажные мешки для пылесоса

16. **wet mop**
швабра для мытья

17. **dust mop**
швабра для пыли

18. **furniture polish**
полироль

19. **scrub brush**
жёсткая щётка

20. **bucket / pail**
ведро

21. **dishwashing liquid**
жидкость для мытья посуды

22. **dish towel**
кухонное полотенце

23. **cleanser**
моющее средство

24. **sponge**
губка

Practice asking for the items.

I want to _wash the windows_.
Please hand me _the squeegee_.

I have to _sweep the floor_.
Can you get me _the broom_, please?

47

1. The water heater is **not working**.
Нагреватель воды **не работает**.

2. The power is **out**.
Электричества **нет**.

3. The roof is **leaking**.
Крыша **течёт**.

4. The wall is **cracked**.
Стена **потрескалась**.

5. The window is **broken**.
Окно **разбито**.

6. The lock is **broken**.
Замок **сломан**.

7. The steps are **broken**.
Ступеньки **сломаны**.

8. roofer
кровельщик

9. electrician
электрик

10. repair person
мастер

11. locksmith
слесарь

12. carpenter
плотник

13. fuse box
блок предохранителей

14. gas meter
газовый счётчик

Use the new language.
Look at **Tools and Building Supplies,** pages **150–151.**
Name the tools you use for household repairs.

I use a hammer and nails to fix a broken step.
I use a wrench to repair a dripping faucet.

15. The furnace is **broken**.
Печка **сломана**.

16. The faucet is **dripping**.
Кран **течёт**.

17. The sink is **overflowing**.
Раковина **засорилась**.

18. The toilet is **stopped up**.
Унитаз **засорился**.

19. The pipes are **frozen**.
Трубы **замерзли**.

20. plumber
водопроводчик

21. exterminator
дезинсектор

Household pests
домашние паразиты /
вредители

22. termite(s)
термит (термиты)

23. flea(s)
блоха (блохи)

24. ant(s)
муравей (муравьи)

25. cockroach(es)
таракан (тараканы)

26. mice*
мышь (мыши)

27. rat(s)
крыса (крысы)

*Note: *one mouse, two mice*

More vocabulary

fix: to repair something that is broken

exterminate: to kill household pests

pesticide: a chemical that is used to kill household pests

Share your answers.

1. Who does household repairs in your home?

2. What is the worst problem a home can have?

3. What is the most expensive problem a home can have?

1. grapes
виноград

2. pineapples
ананасы

3. bananas
бананы

4. apples
яблоки

5. peaches
персики

6. pears
груши

7. apricots
абрикосы

8. plums
сливы

9. grapefruit
грейпфрут

10. oranges
апельсины

11. lemons
лимоны

12. limes
лаймы

13. tangerines
мандарины

14. avocadoes
авокадо

15. cantaloupes
канталупа / мускусная
дыня

16. cherries
вишни

17. strawberries
клубника

18. raspberries
малина

19. blueberries
черника

20. papayas
папайя

21. mangoes
манго

22. coconuts
кокосовые орехи

23. nuts
орехи

24. watermelons
арбузы

25. dates
финики

26. prunes
чернослив

27. raisins
изюм

28. not ripe
неспелый / ая / ое
зелёный / ая / ое

29. ripe
спелый / ая / ое

30. rotten
гнилой / ая / ое

Language note: *a bunch of*

We say *a bunch of grapes* and *a bunch of bananas*.

Share your answers.

1. Which fruits do you put in a fruit salad?

2. Which fruits are sold in your area in the summer?

3. What fruits did you have in your country?

1. lettuce
   салат-латук

2. cabbage
   капуста

3. carrots
   морковь

4. zucchini
   цуккини

5. radishes
   редис

6. beets
   свёкла

7. sweet peppers
   сладкий перец

8. chili peppers
   острый перец

9. celery
   сельдерей

10. parsley
    петрушка

11. spinach
    шпинат

12. cucumbers
    огурцы

13. squash
    кабачок / тыква

14. turnips
    репа / брюква

15. broccoli
    брокколи / спаржевая
    капуста

16. cauliflower
    цветная капуста

17. scallions
    зелёный лук

18. eggplants
    баклажаны

19. peas
    горох

20. artichokes
    артишоки

21. potatoes
    картофель

22. yams
    ямс / батат

23. tomatoes
    помидоры

24. asparagus
    спаржа

25. string beans
    стручковая фасоль

26. mushrooms
    грибы

27. corn
    кукуруза

28. onions
    лук

29. garlic
    чеснок

Language note: *a bunch of, a head of*

We say *a bunch of carrots, a bunch of celery,* and *a bunch of spinach.*

We say *a head of lettuce, a head of cabbage,* and *a head of cauliflower.*

Share your answers.

1. Which vegetables do you eat raw? cooked?

2. Which vegetables need to be in the refrigerator?

3. Which vegetables don't need to be in the refrigerator?

Meat and Poultry Мясо и птица

Beef Говядина

1. roast beef
   ростбиф
2. steak
   бифштекс
3. stewing beef
   тушёная говядина
4. ground beef
   говяжий фарш

5. beef ribs
   говяжьи рёбрышки
6. veal cutlets
   телячьи отбивные
7. liver
   печёнка
8. tripe
   требуха

Pork Свинина

9. ham
   ветчина
10. pork chops
    свиные отбивные
11. bacon
    бекон / копчёная
    грудинка
12. sausage
    колбаса

Lamb Баранина

13. lamb shanks
    крупные куски
    баранины
14. leg of lamb
    баранья нога
15. lamb chops
    бараньи отбивные

16. chicken
    курица
17. turkey
    индейка
18. duck
    утка

19. breasts
    грудки
20. wings
    крылышки
21. thighs
    куриные окорочка

22. drumsticks
    куриные ножки
23. gizzards
    желудки

24. **raw** chicken
    сырая курица
25. **cooked** chicken
    приготовленная
    курица

More vocabulary

vegetarian: a person who doesn't eat meat
Meat and poultry without bones are called **boneless**.
Poultry without skin is called **skinless**.

Share your answers.

1. What kind of meat do you eat most often?
2. What kind of meat do you use in soup?
3. What part of the chicken do you like the most?

1. white bread
белый хлеб

2. wheat bread
пшеничный хлеб

3. rye bread
ржаной хлеб

4. smoked turkey
копчёная индейка

5. salami
салями

6. pastrami
пастрами

7. roast beef
ростбиф

8. corned beef
солонина

9. American cheese
американский сыр

10. cheddar cheese
сыр чедер

11. Swiss cheese
швейцарский сыр

12. jack cheese
сыр жак

13. potato salad
картофельный салат

14. coleslaw
американский салат
из свежей капусты

15. pasta salad
салат из макарон

Fish   Рыба

16. trout
форель

17. catfish
сом

18. whole salmon
лосось / горбуша
целиком

19. salmon steak
кусок лосося / горбуши

20. halibut
палтус

21. filet of sole
филе камбалы

Shellfish   Ракушки

22. crab
краб

23. lobster
омар

24. shrimp
креветка

25. scallops
гребешки

26. mussels
мидии

27. oysters
устрицы

28. clams
моллюски

29. **fresh** fish
свежая рыба

30. **frozen** fish
мороженая рыба

Practice ordering a sandwich.

I'd like <u>roast beef</u> and <u>American cheese</u> on <u>rye bread</u>.

Tell what you want on it.

Please put <u>tomato</u>, <u>lettuce</u>, <u>onions</u>, and <u>mustard</u> on it.

Share your answers.

1. Do you like to eat fish?

2. Do you buy fresh or frozen fish?

The Market   Рынок

1. bottle return
пункт сбора
стеклотары

**2. meat and poultry
section**
отдел «Мясо-птица»

3. shopping cart
тележка для покупок

4. canned goods
консервы

5. aisle
проход между полками
в магазине

6. baked goods
хлебо-булочные
изделия

7. shopping basket
корзина для покупок

8. manager
заведующий отделом

9. dairy section
молочный отдел

10. pet food
продукты для животных

11. produce section
сельскохозяйственные
продукты

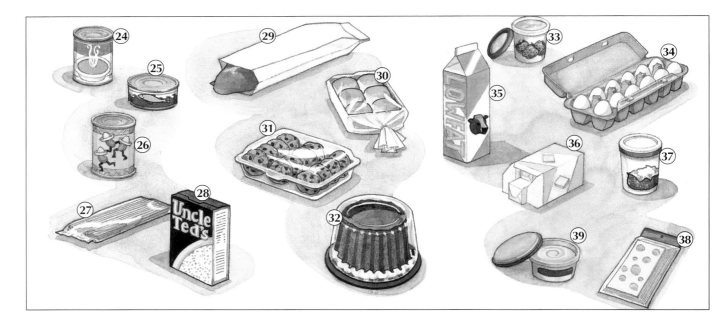

24. soup
суп

25. tuna
тунец

26. beans
бобы / фасоль

27. spaghetti
спагетти / макароны

28. rice
рис

29. bread
хлеб

30. rolls
булочки

31. cookies
печенье

32. cake
кекс / торт

33. yogurt
йогурт

34. eggs
яйца

35. milk
молоко

36. butter
масло

37. sour cream
сметана

38. cheese
сыр

39. margarine
маргарин

12. frozen foods
мороженые продукты

13. baking products
хлебо-булочные
изделия

14. paper products
бумажные изделия

15. beverages
напитки

16. snack foods
закуски

17. checkstand
кассовая стойка

18. cash register
касса

19. checker
кассир

20. line
очередь

21. bagger
упаковщик

22. paper bag
бумажный пакет

23. plastic bag
целлофановый пакет

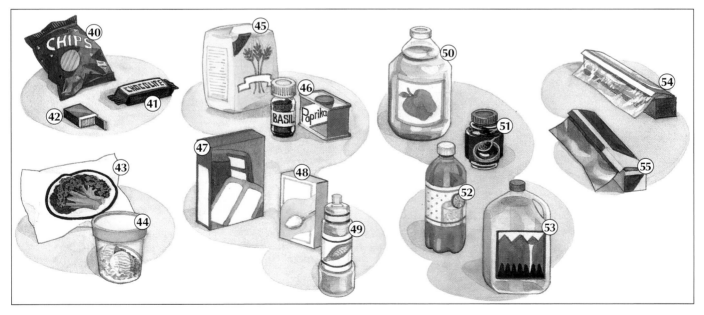

40. potato chips
картофельные чипсы

41. candy bar
конфета / батончик

42. gum
жвачка

43. frozen vegetables
мороженые овощи

44. ice cream
мороженое

45. flour
мука

46. spices
специи / пряности

47. cake mix
кондитерская смесь /
порошок для
приготовления торта

48. sugar
сахар

49. oil
растительное масло

50. apple juice
яблочный сок

51. instant coffee
растворимый кофе

52. soda
газированная вода

53. bottled water
вода в бутылке

54. plastic wrap
упаковочная плёнка

55. aluminum foil
фольга

Containers and Packaged Foods   Упаковка и расфасованные продукты

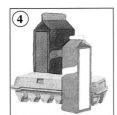

1. bottle
бутылка

2. jar
стеклянная
банка

3. can
консервная
банка

4. carton
коробка /
пакет

5. container
ёмкость /
упаковка

6. box
ящик /
коробка

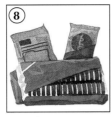

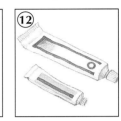

7. bag
мешок / пакет

8. package
упаковка

9. six-pack
упаковка из
6 предметов

10. loaf
буханка

11. roll
булочка

12. tube
тюбик

13. a bottle of soda
бутылка газированной воды

14. a jar of jam
банка варенья / джема / повидла

15. a can of soup
банка супа

16. a carton of eggs
коробка яиц

17. a container of cottage cheese
банка творога

18. a box of cereal
пачка хлопьев / овсянки

19. a bag of flour
пакет муки

20. a package of cookies
коробка печенья

21. a six-pack of soda
упаковка из шести банок /
бутылок газированной воды

22. a loaf of bread
буханка хлеба

23. a roll of paper towels
рулон бумажного полотенца

24. a tube of toothpaste
тюбик зубной пасты

Grammar point: *How much? How many?*

Some foods can be counted: *one apple, two apples.*

How many *apples do you need? I need **two** apples.*

Some foods cannot be counted, like liquids, grains, spices, or dairy foods. For these, count containers: *one box of rice, two boxes of rice.*

How much *rice do you need? I need **two** boxes.*

56

Система мер и весов **Weights and Measures**

A. Measure the ingredients.
Измерять ингредиенты.

B. Weigh the food.
Взвешивать продукты.

C. Convert the measurements.
Перевести из одной системы мер в другую.

1 cup = 237 milliliters

Liquid measures Меры жидкостей

1 fl. oz.
1 c.
1 pt.
1 qt.
1 gal.

Dry measures Меры сыпучих тел

1 tsp.
1 TBS.
1/4 c.
1/2 c.
1 c.

Weight Вес

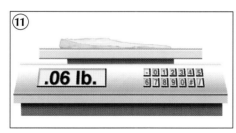 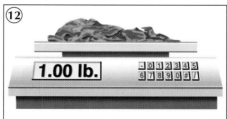

.06 lb.
1.00 lb.

1. a fluid ounce of water
   жидкая унция воды
2. a cup of oil
   чашка масла
3. a pint of yogurt
   пинта йогурта
4. a quart of milk
   кварта молока

5. a gallon of apple juice
   галлон яблочного сока
6. a teaspoon of salt
   чайная ложка соли
7. a tablespoon of sugar
   столовая ложка сахара
8. a 1/4 cup of brown sugar
   четверть чашки неочищенного сахара

9. a 1/2 cup of raisins
   полчашки изюма
10. a cup of flour
    чашка муки
11. an ounce of cheese
    унция сыра
12. a pound of roast beef
    фунт говяжьей вырезки

VOLUME
1 fl. oz. = 30 milliliters (ml.)
1 c. = 237 ml.
1 pt. = .47 liters (l.)
1 qt. = .95 l.
1 gal. = 3.79 l.

EQUIVALENCIES
3 tsp. = 1 TBS. | 2 c. = 1 pt.
2 TBS. = 1 fl. oz. | 2 pt. = 1 qt.
8 fl. oz. = 1 c. | 4 qt. = 1 gal.

WEIGHT
1 oz. = 28.35 grams (g.)
1 lb. = 453.6 g.
2.205 lbs. = 1 kilogram
1 lb. = 16 oz.

Scrambled eggs   Яичница-болтунья

A. Break 3 eggs.
Разбейте 3 яйца.

B. Beat well.
Хорошо **взбейте.**

C. Grease the pan.
Смажьте
сковородку маслом.

D. Pour the eggs into the pan.
Вылейте яйца в сковородку.

E. Stir.
Перемешайте.

F. Cook until done.
Жарьте до готовности.

Vegetable casserole   Тушёные овощи

G. Chop the onions.
Нарежьте лук.

H. Sauté the onions.
Обжарьте лук.

I. Steam the broccoli.
Приготовьте на пару брокколи.

J. Grate the cheese.
Натрите сыр на тёрке.

K. Mix the ingredients.
Перемешайте ингредиенты.

L. Bake at 350° for 45 minutes.
Готовьте в духовке 45 минут при температуре 350° по Фаренгейту.

Chicken soup   Куриный суп

M. Cut up the chicken.
Разделайте курицу.

N. Peel the carrots.
Почистите морковь.

O. Slice the carrots.
Нарежьте морковь.

P. Boil the chicken.
Сварите курицу.

Q. Add the vegetables.
Добавьте овощи.

R. Simmer for 1 hour.
Варите 1 час на медленном огне.

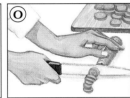

Five ways to cook chicken   Пять способов приготовления курицы

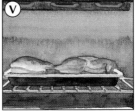
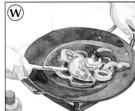

S. fry
жарить на сковородке

T. barbecue / grill
жарить на углях / готовить на гриле

U. roast
готовить (мясо) на медленном огне

V. broil
печь в духовке при высокой температуре

W. stir-fry
жарить переворачивая

Talk about the way you prepare these foods.

I _fry_ eggs.

I _bake_ potatoes.

Share your answers.

1. What are popular ways in your country to make rice? vegetables? meat?

2. What is your favorite way to cook chicken?

1. can opener
открывалка для консервов

2. grater
тёрка

3. plastic storage container
пластмассовый контейнер для хранения

4. steamer
пароварка

5. frying pan
сковородка

6. pot
кастрюля

7. ladle
половник

8. double boiler
двойная пароварка

9. wooden spoon
деревянная ложка

10. garlic press
чеснокодавилка

11. casserole dish
кастрюля для тушения

12. carving knife
разделочный нож

13. roasting pan
жаровня

14. roasting rack
решётка для жарки

15. vegetable peeler
нож для чистки овощей

16. paring knife
нож для чистки фруктов и овощей

17. colander
дуршлаг

18. kitchen timer
кухонный таймер

19. spatula
лопатка

20. eggbeater
сбивалка для яиц

21. whisk
веничек

22. strainer
ситечко

23. tongs
щипцы

24. lid
крышка

25. saucepan
кастрюля

26. cake pan
форма для торта/кекса

27. cookie sheet
противень

28. pie pan
форма для пирога

29. pot holders
прихватки

30. rolling pin
скалка

31. mixing bowl
глубокая миска

Talk about how to use the utensils.

You use a peeler to peel potatoes.

You use a pot to cook soup.

Use the new language.

Look at **Food Preparation,** page **58.**

Name the different utensils you see.

1. **hamburger**
   гамбургер

2. **french fries**
   жареный картофель

3. **cheeseburger**
   гамбургер с сыром

4. **soda**
   газированная вода

5. **iced tea**
   чай со льдом

6. **hot dog**
   булочка с горячей сосиской

7. **pizza**
   пицца

8. **green salad**
   салат из свежих овощей

9. **taco**
   тако

10. **nachos**
    начос

11. **frozen yogurt**
    мороженое из йогурта

12. **milk shake**
    молочный коктейль

13. **counter**
    стойка

14. **muffin**
    сдобная булочка

15. **doughnut**
    пончик

16. **salad bar**
    стойка с выбором салатов

17. **lettuce**
    салат-латук

18. **salad dressing**
    заправка для салата

19. **booth**
    киоск / палатка

20. **straw**
    соломка

21. **sugar**
    сахар

22. **sugar substitute**
    сахарин / заменитель сахара

23. **ketchup**
    кетчуп

24. **mustard**
    горчица

25. **mayonnaise**
    майонез

26. **relish**
    приправа из маринованных овощей

A. **eat**
   есть

B. **drink**
   пить

More vocabulary

donut: doughnut (spelling variation)

condiments: relish, mustard, ketchup, mayonnaise, etc.

Share your answers.

1. What would you order at this restaurant?

2. Which fast foods are popular in your country?

3. How often do you eat fast food? Why?

Breakfast

Lunch

Dinner

Desserts

Beverages

1. scrambled eggs
   яичница-болтунья

2. sausage
   колбаса

3. toast
   тост

4. waffles
   вафли

5. syrup
   сироп

6. pancakes
   блины / оладьи

7. bacon
   бекон

8. grilled cheese sandwich
   тост с сыром

9. chef's salad
   фирменный салат

10. soup of the day
    дежурный суп

11. mashed potatoes
    картофельное пюре

12. roast chicken
    курица, зажаренная в духовке

13. steak
    бифштекс

14. baked potato
    печёный картофель

15. pasta
    макароны

16. garlic bread
    горячий хлеб с чесноком и маслом

17. fried fish
    жареная рыба

18. rice pilaf
    плов

19. cake
    торт / кекс

20. pudding
    пудинг

21. pie
    пирог

22. coffee
    кофе

23. decaf coffee
    кофе без кофеина

24. tea
    чай

Practice ordering from the menu.

I'd like a grilled cheese sandwich and some soup.
I'll have the chef's salad and a cup of decaf coffee.

Use the new language.

Look at **Fruit**, page **50**.

Order a slice of pie using the different fruit flavors.

Please give me a slice of apple pie.

61

A Restaurant   Ресторан

1. hostess
метрдотель

2. dining room
обеденный зал

3. menu
меню

4. server / waiter
подавальщик / официант

5. patron / diner
посетитель / обедающий

A. set the table
накрыть на стол

B. seat the customer
проводить посетителя
к столу

C. pour the water
налить воды

D. order from the menu
заказать блюдо из
меню

E. take the order
принять заказ

F. serve the meal
подать на стол

G. clear the table
убрать со стола

H. carry the tray
нести поднос

I. pay the check
оплатить счёт

J. leave a tip
оставить чаевые

More vocabulary

eat out: to go to a restaurant to eat

take out: to buy food at a restaurant and take it home
to eat

Practice giving commands.

Please <u>set the table</u>.

I'd like you to <u>clear the table</u>.

It's time to <u>serve the meal</u>.

6. server / waitress
подавальщица /
официанка

7. dessert tray
поднос с десертом

8. bread basket
корзинка с хлебом

9. busperson
помощник / помощница
официанта

10. kitchen
кухня

11. chef
шеф-повар

12. dishroom
посудомоечная

13. dishwasher
посудомоечная машина

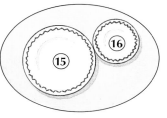

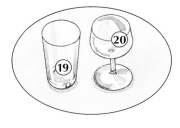

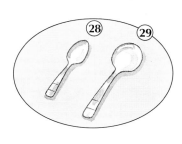

14. place setting
столовый прибор

15. dinner plate
мелкая тарелка

16. bread-and-butter plate
тарелка с хлебом и
маслом

17. salad plate
тарелка для салата

18. soup bowl
суповая тарелка

19. water glass
стакан для воды

20. wine glass
фужер / бокал

21. cup
чашка

22. saucer
блюдце

23. napkin
салфетка

24. salad fork
вилка для салата

25. dinner fork
столовая вилка

26. steak knife
нож для мяса

27. knife
нож

28. teaspoon
чайная ложка

29. soupspoon
столовая ложка

Talk about how you set the table in your home.

The glass is on the right.

The fork goes on the left.

The napkin is next to the plate.

Share your answers.

1. Do you know anyone who works in a restaurant? What does he or she do?

2. In your opinion, which restaurant jobs are hard? Why?

Clothing I Одежда I

1. **three-piece suit**
костюм-тройка

2. **suit**
костюм

3. **dress**
платье

4. **shirt**
рубашка

5. **jeans**
джинсы

6. **sports coat**
спортивный пиджак

7. **turtleneck**
водолазка

8. **slacks/pants**
брюки/штаны

9. **blouse**
блузка

10. **skirt**
юбка

11. **pullover sweater**
пуловер/свитер

12. **T-shirt**
футболка

13. **shorts**
шорты

14. **sweatshirt**
спортивная кофта с начёсом

15. **sweatpants**
спортивные штаны с начёсом

More vocabulary:

outfit: clothes that look nice together

When clothes are popular, they are **in fashion.**

Talk about what you're wearing today and what you wore yesterday.

I'm wearing <u>a gray sweater</u>, <u>a red T-shirt</u>, and <u>blue jeans</u>.

Yesterday I wore <u>a green pullover sweater</u>, <u>a white shirt</u>, and <u>black slacks</u>.

16. jumpsuit
комбинезон / спортивный
костюм

17. uniform
униформа

18. jumper
джемпер

19. maternity dress
платье для беременной

20. knit shirt
трикотажная рубашка

21. overalls
комбинезон

22. tunic
туника

23. leggings
рейтузы / леггинсы

24. vest
безрукавка / жилет

25. split skirt
юбка с разрезом

26. sports shirt
спортивная рубашка

27. cardigan sweater
кардиган

28. tuxedo
смокинг

29. evening gown
вечернее платье

Use the new language.

Look at **A Graduation**, pages **32–33**.

Name the clothes you see.

The man at the podium is wearing <u>a suit</u>.

Share your answers.

1. Which clothes in this picture are in fashion now?

2. Who is the best-dressed person in this line? Why?

3. What do you wear when you go to the movies?

1. hat
шляпа

2. overcoat
пальто

3. leather jacket
кожаная куртка

4. wool scarf / muffler
шерстяной
шарф/кашне

5. gloves
перчатки

6. cap
кепка

7. jacket
куртка

8. parka
парка

9. mittens
варежки

10. ski cap
лыжная шапочка

11. tights
рейтузы

12. earmuffs
меховые наушники

13. down vest
пуховая безрукавка

14. ski mask
лыжная маска

15. down jacket
пуховик / пуховая
куртка

16. umbrella
зонтик

17. raincoat
плащ

18. poncho
пончо

19. rain boots
резиновые сапоги

20. trench coat
полупальто

21. sunglasses
солнечные очки

22. swimming trunks
плавки

23. straw hat
соломенная шляпа

24. windbreaker
ветровка

25. cover-up
купальный халат

26. swimsuit / bathing suit
купальник / купальный костюм

27. baseball cap
бейсбольная кепка

Use the new language.
Look at **Weather, page 10.**
Name the clothing for each weather condition.
Wear a jacket when it's windy.

Share your answers.
1. Which is better in the rain, an umbrella or a poncho?
2. Which is better in the cold, a parka or a down jacket?
3. Do you have more summer clothes or winter clothes?

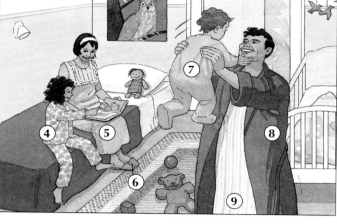

1. leotard
трико

2. tank top
майка

3. bike shorts
велосипедные шорты

4. pajamas
пижама

5. nightgown
ночная рубашка

6. slippers
шлёпанцы

7. blanket sleeper
конверт для младенца

8. bathrobe
халат

9. nightshirt
ночная сорочка

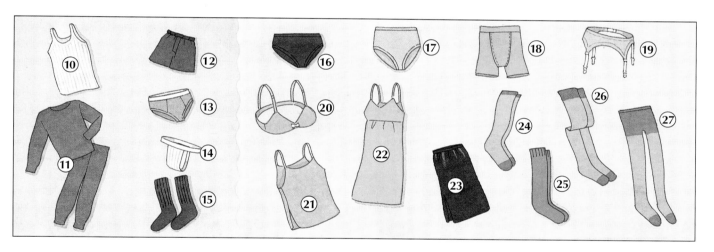

10. undershirt
майка

11. long underwear
нижнее бельё / фуфайка / кальсоны

12. boxer shorts
боксёрские трусы

13. briefs
мужские трусы

14. athletic supporter / jockstrap
защитная раковина спортсмена

15. socks
носки

16. (bikini) panties
женские трусики / бикини

17. briefs / underpants
мужские трусы

18. girdle
пояс / корсет

19. garter belt
пояс с резинками

20. bra
бюстгальтер / лифчик

21. camisole
грация

22. full slip
комбинация

23. half slip
нижняя юбка

24. knee-highs
гольфы

25. kneesocks
длинные носки

26. stockings
чулки

27. pantyhose
колготки

More vocabulary

lingerie: underwear or sleepwear for women

loungewear: clothing (sometimes sleepwear) people wear around the home

Share your answers.

1. What do you wear when you exercise?

2. What kind of clothing do you wear for sleeping?

Shoes and Accessories   Обувь и принадлежности туалета

1. **salesclerk**
   продавец
2. **suspenders**
   подтяжки

3. **shoe department**
   обувной отдел
4. **silk scarves***
   шёлковые шарфы

5. **hats**
   шляпы

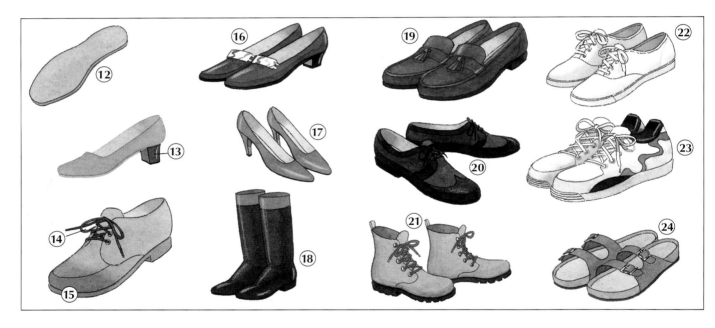

12. **sole**
    подошва
13. **heel**
    каблук
14. **shoelace**
    шнурок
15. **toe**
    носок
16. **pumps**
    лодочки

17. **high heels**
    высокие каблуки / шпильки
18. **boots**
    сапоги
19. **loafers**
    мокасины
20. **oxfords**
    полуботинки
21. **hiking boots**
    туристкие ботинки

22. **tennis shoes**
    теннисные туфли
23. **athletic shoes**
    кроссовки
24. **sandals**
    босоножки / сандалии

***Note:** one scarf, two scarves*

Talk about the shoes you're wearing today.

I'm wearing a pair of <u>white sandals</u>.

Practice asking a salesperson for help.

Could I try on these <u>sandals</u> in size <u>10</u>?

Do you have any <u>silk scarves</u>?

Where are <u>the hats</u>?

6. purses / handbags
дамские сумки

7. display case
витрина

8. jewelry
украшения / драгоценности

9. necklaces
бусы

10. ties
галстуки

11. belts
пояса / ремни

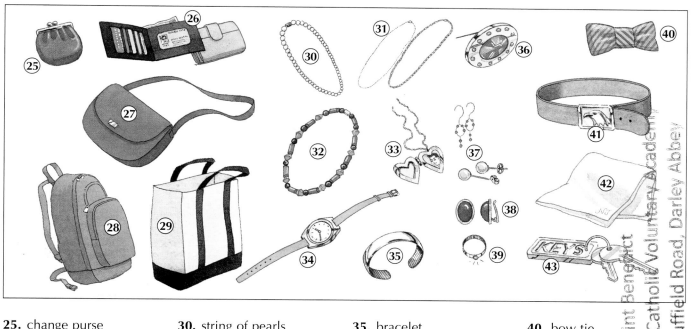

25. change purse
кошелёк

26. wallet
бумажник

27. shoulder bag
сумка через плечо

28. backpack / bookbag
рюкзак / ранец

29. tote bag
авоська / сетка

30. string of pearls
нитка жемчуга

31. chain
цепочка

32. beads
бисер

33. locket
медальон

34. (wrist)watch
(наручные) часы

35. bracelet
браслет

36. pin
брошь

37. pierced earrings
серьги

38. clip-on earrings
клипсы

39. ring
кольцо

40. bow tie
галстук «бабочка»

41. belt buckle
пряжка на ремне

42. handkerchief
носовой платок

43. key chain
цепочка / брелок для
ключей

Share your answers.

1. Which of these accessories are usually worn by women? by men?

2. Which of these do you wear every day?

3. Which of these would you wear to a job interview? Why?

4. Which accessory would you like to receive as a present? Why?

Describing Clothes   Описание одежды

Sizes   Размеры

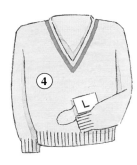

1. extra small
очень маленький

2. small
маленький

3. medium
средний

4. large
большой

5. extra large
очень большой

Patterns   Образцы тканей

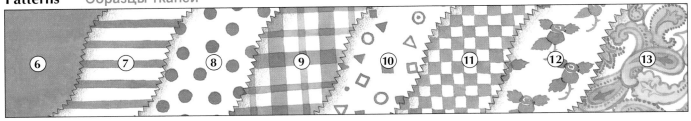

6. solid green
однотонная зелёная
ткань

7. striped
в полоску

8. polka-dotted
в горошек / в крапинку

9. plaid
шотландка

10. print
набивная ткань

11. checked
в клетку

12. floral
в цветочек

13. paisley
пёстрая ткань

Types of material   Типы тканей / материала

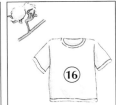

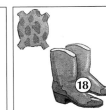
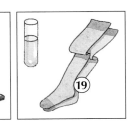

14. **wool** sweater
шерстяной свитер

15. **silk** scarf
шёлковый шарф

16. **cotton** T-shirt
хлопчатобумажная футболка

17. **linen** jacket
льняная куртка

18. **leather** boots
кожаные сапоги

19. **nylon** stockings*
нейлоновые чулки

Problems   Проблемы

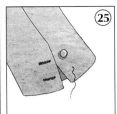

20. too small
мал/а/о

21. too big
велик/а/о

22. stain
пятно

23. rip / tear
порван/а/о /
распорот/а/о

24. **broken** zipper
молния **сломана**

25. **missing** button
не хватает пуговицы

*****Note:** Nylon, polyester, rayon, and plastic are synthetic materials.

70

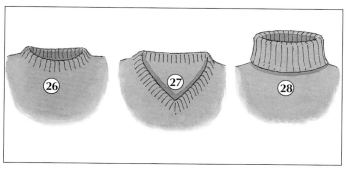

26. **crewneck** sweater
свитер **под горло**

27. **V-neck** sweater
пуловер

28. **turtleneck** sweater
водолазка

29. **sleeveless** shirt
рубашка **без рукавов**

30. **short-sleeved** shirt
рубашка **с короткими рукавами**

31. **long-sleeved** shirt
рубашка **с длинными рукавами**

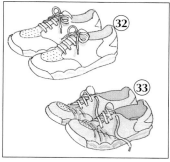

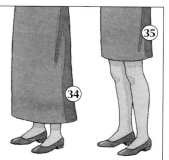

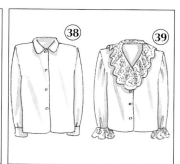

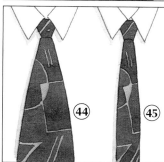

32. **new** shoes
новые туфли

33. **old** shoes
старые туфли

34. **long** skirt
длинная юбка

35. **short** skirt
короткая юбка

36. **formal** dress
выходное / нарядное платье

37. **casual** dress
повседневное платье

38. **plain** blouse
обычная блузка

39. **fancy** blouse
нарядная блузка

40. **light** jacket
лёгкая куртка

41. **heavy** jacket
тёплая куртка

42. **loose** pants / **baggy** pants
свободные брюки /
мешковатые брюки

43. **tight** pants
узкие брюки

44. **wide** tie
широкий галстук

45. **narrow** tie
узкий галстук

46. **low** heels
низкие каблуки

47. **high** heels
высокие каблуки

Talk about yourself.

I like <u>long-sleeved</u> shirts and <u>baggy</u> pants.

I like <u>short skirts</u> and <u>high heels</u>.

I usually wear <u>plain</u> clothes.

Share your answers.

1. What type of material do you usually wear in the summer? in the winter?

2. What patterns do you see around you?

3. Are you wearing casual or formal clothes?

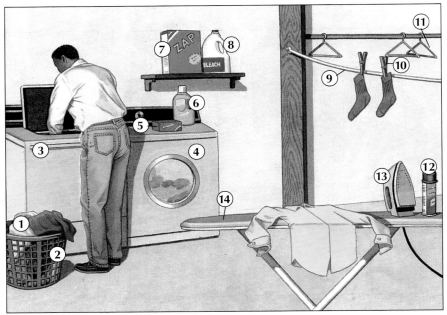

1. **laundry**
   стирка / грязное бельё

2. **laundry basket**
   корзина для грязного белья

3. **washer**
   стиральная машина

4. **dryer**
   сушилка

5. **dryer sheets**
   ароматизирующие салфетки для сушки

6. **fabric softener**
   смягчитель тканей

7. **laundry detergent**
   стиральный порошок

8. **bleach**
   отбеливатель

9. **clothesline**
   бельевая верёвка

10. **clothespin**
    прищепка

11. **hanger**
    вешалка

12. **spray starch**
    жидкий крахмал в распылителе

13. **iron**
    утюг

14. **ironing board**
    гладильная доска

15. **dirty** T-shirt
    грязная футболка

16. **clean** T-shirt
    чистая футболка

17. **wet** T-shirt
    мокрая футболка

18. **dry** T-shirt
    сухая футболка

19. **wrinkled** shirt
    мятая рубашка

20. **ironed** shirt
    глаженная рубашка

A. **Sort** the laundry.
   Рассортировать бельё.

B. **Add** the detergent.
   Добавить стиральный порошок.

C. **Load** the washer.
   Загрузить стиральную машину.

D. **Clean** the lint trap.
   Вычистить фильтр в сушилке.

E. **Unload** the dryer.
   Вынуть бельё из сушилки.

F. **Fold** the laundry.
   Сложить бельё.

G. **Iron** the clothes.
   Выгладить одежду.

H. **Hang up** the clothes.
   Развесить одежду.

More vocabulary

dry cleaners: a business that cleans clothes using chemicals, not water and detergent

 wash in cold water only

 no bleach

line dry

dry-clean only, do not wash

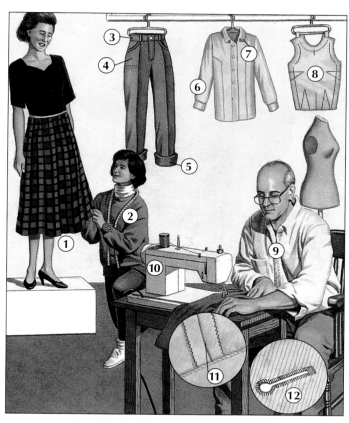

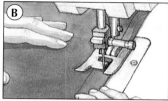

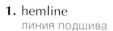

A. **sew** by hand
шить на руках / руками

B. **sew** by machine
шить на машинке

C. **lengthen**
удлинять

D. **shorten**
укорачивать

E. **take in**
ушивать

F. **let out**
выпускать / надставлять

1. hemline
   линия подшива
2. dressmaker
   портной
3. waistband
   пояс / корсаж

4. pocket
   карман
5. cuff
   манжета / отворот
6. sleeve
   рукав

7. collar
   воротник
8. pattern
   выкройка
9. tailor
   портной

10. sewing machine
    швейная машинка
11. seam
    шов
12. buttonhole
    петля / петлица

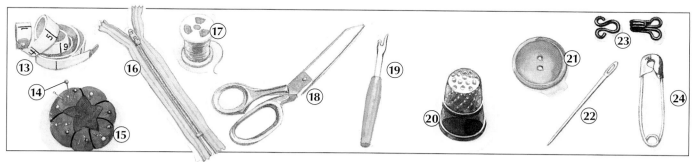

13. tape measure
    сантиметр
14. pin
    булавка
15. pin cushion
    подушечка для
    иголок / булавок

16. zipper
    молния
17. spool of thread
    катушка ниток
18. (pair of) scissors
    ножницы

19. seam ripper
    нож для порки швов
20. thimble
    напёрсток
21. button
    пуговица

22. needle
    игла
23. hook and eye
    крючок и петелька
24. safety pin
    английская булавка

More vocabulary

pattern maker: a person who makes patterns

garment worker: a person who works in a clothing factory

fashion designer: a person who makes original clothes

Share your answers.

1. Do you know how to use a sewing machine?

2. Can you sew by hand?

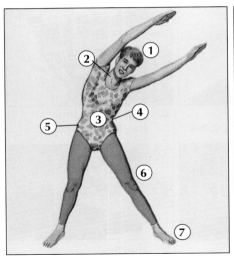

1. head
голова

2. neck
шея

3. abdomen
живот

4. waist
талия / пояс

5. hip
бедро

6. leg
нога

7. foot
ступня

8. hand
рука / кисть руки

9. arm
рука

10. shoulder
плечо

11. back
спина

12. buttocks
ягодицы

13. chest
грудь

14. breast
груди

15. elbow
локоть

16. thigh
бедро

17. knee
колено

18. calf
икра

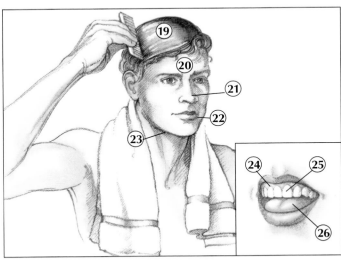

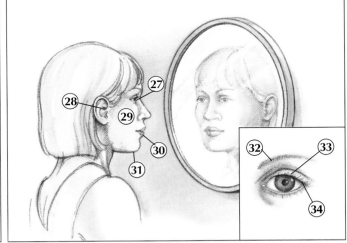

The face
Лицо

19. hair
волосы

20. forehead
лоб

21. nose
нос

22. mouth
рот

23. jaw
челюсть

24. gums
дёсны

25. teeth
зубы

26. tongue
язык

27. eye
глаз

28. ear
ухо

29. cheek
щека

30. lip
губа

31. chin
подбородок

32. eyebrow
бровь

33. eyelid
веко

34. eyelashes
ресницы

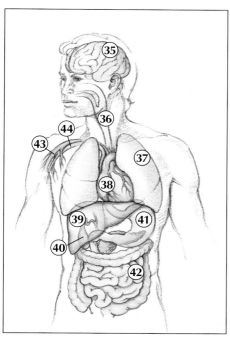

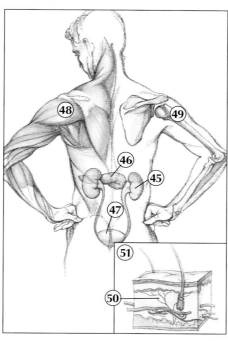

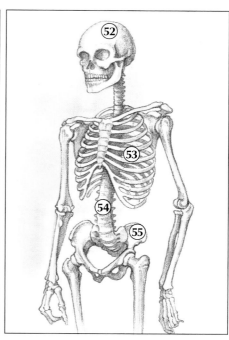

Inside the body
Внутренние органы

35. brain
мозг

36. throat
горло

37. lung
лёгкое

38. heart
сердце

39. liver
печень

40. gallbladder
жёлчный пузырь

41. stomach
желудок

42. intestines
кишечник

43. artery
артерия

44. vein
вена

45. kidney
почка

46. pancreas
поджелудочная железа

47. bladder
мочевой пузырь

48. muscle
мышца

49. bone
кость

50. nerve
нерв

51. skin
кожа

The skeleton
Скелет

52. skull
череп

53. rib cage
грудная клетка

54. spinal column
позвоночник

55. pelvis
таз

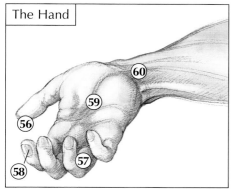

The Hand

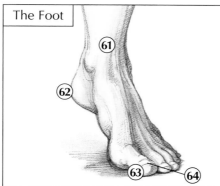

The Foot

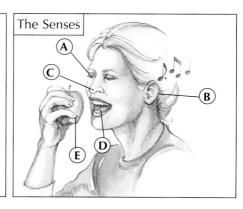

The Senses

56. thumb
большой палец

57. fingers
пальцы

58. fingernail
ноготь

59. palm
ладонь

60. wrist
запястье

61. ankle
лодыжка /
голеностопный сустав

62. heel
пятка

63. toe
палец ноги

64. toenail
ноготь на пальце ноги

A. see
видеть

B. hear
слышать

C. smell
нюхать

D. taste
пробовать

E. touch
трогать

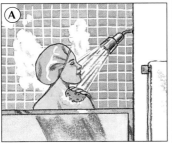  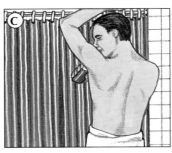 

A. **take** a shower
принимать душ

B. **bathe / take** a bath
принимать
ванну / **купаться**

C. **use** deodorant
использовать
дезодорант

D. **put on** sunscreen
намазаться кремом от
загара

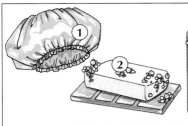      

1. shower cap
купальная шапочка

2. soap
мыло

3. bath powder / talcum powder
присыпка / тальк

4. deodorant
дезодорант

5. perfume / cologne
духи/одеколон

6. sunscreen
крем от загара

7. body lotion
лосьон для тела

8. moisturizer
увлажняющий крем

 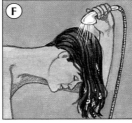  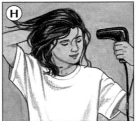 

E. **wash**…hair
мыть…голову

F. **rinse**…hair
ополаскивать…
волосы

G. **comb**…hair
расчёсывать…
волосы

H. **dry**…hair
сушить…
волосы

I. **brush**…hair
причёсывать…
волосы щёткой

      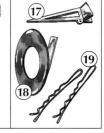

9. shampoo
шампунь

10. conditioner
кондиционер для волос

11. hair gel
гель для волос

12. hair spray
лак для волос

13. comb
расчёска

14. brush
щётка

15. curling iron
щипцы для завивки

16. blow dryer
фен

17. hair clip
зажим для волос

18. barrette
заколка

19. bobby pins
невидимки

J. brush…teeth
чистить…зубы

K. floss…teeth
чистить ниткой
…между зубами

L. gargle
полоскать рот

M. shave
бриться

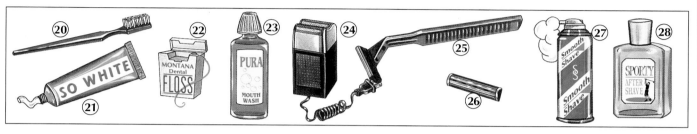

20. toothbrush
зубная щётка

21. toothpaste
зубная паста

22. dental floss
нитка для зубов

23. mouthwash
жидкость для полоскания рта

24. electric shaver
электробритва

25. razor
бритва (станок)

26. razor blade
лезвие

27. shaving cream
крем для бритья

28. aftershave
лосьон для бритья

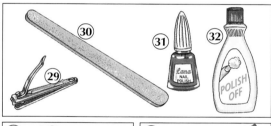

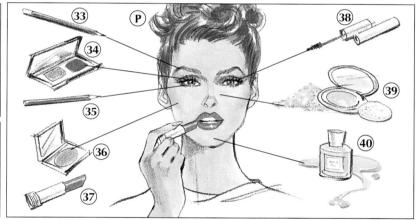

N. cut…nails
стричь…ногти

O. polish…nails
покрывать лаком /
красить…ногти

P. put on…makeup
накладывать…макияж / **краситься**

29. nail clipper
щипчики для ногтей

30. emery board
пилочка для ногтей

31. nail polish
лак для ногтей

32. nail polish remover
жидкость для снятия лака

33. eyebrow pencil
карандаш для бровей

34. eye shadow
тени для век

35. eyeliner
карандаш / кисточка для век

36. blush / rouge
румяна

37. lipstick
помада

38. mascara
тушь

39. face powder
пудра

40. foundation
тон

More vocabulary

A product without perfume or scent is **unscented.**

A product that is better for people with allergies is **hypoallergenic.**

Share your answers.

1. What is your morning routine if you stay home? if you go out?

2. Do women in your culture wear makeup? How old are they when they begin to use it?

Symptoms and Injuries   Симптомы заболеваний и травмы

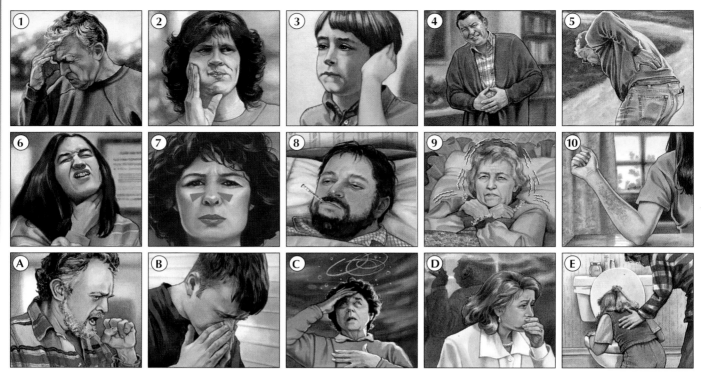

1. headache
   головная боль

2. toothache
   зубная боль

3. earache
   боль в ухе

4. stomachache
   боль в желудке

5. backache
   боль в спине

6. sore throat
   ангина

7. nasal congestion
   насморк

8. fever / temperature
   жар / температура

9. chills
   озноб

10. rash
    сыпь

A. **cough**
   кашлять

B. **sneeze**
   чихать

C. **feel** dizzy
   испытывать головокружение

D. **feel** nauseous
   испытывать тошноту

E. **throw up / vomit**
   рвать

11. insect bite
    укус насекомого

12. bruise
    синяк

13. cut
    порез

14. sunburn
    солнечный ожог

15. blister
    волдырь

16. **swollen** finger
    опухший палец

17. **bloody** nose
    кровотечение из носа

18. **sprained** ankle
    растяжение лодыжки / голеностопного сустава

Use the new language.

Look at **Health Care**, pages **80–81**.

Tell what medication or treatment you would use for each health problem.

Share your answers.

1. For which problems would you go to a doctor? use medication? do nothing?

2. What do you do for a sunburn? for a headache?

78

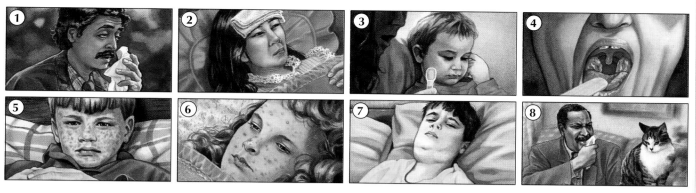

Common illnesses and childhood diseases   Распространённые заболевания и детские болезни

1. cold
простуда

2. flu
грипп

3. ear infection
воспаление уха

4. strep throat
стрептококковая ангина

5. measles
корь

6. chicken pox
ветрянка

7. mumps
свинка

8. allergies
аллергия

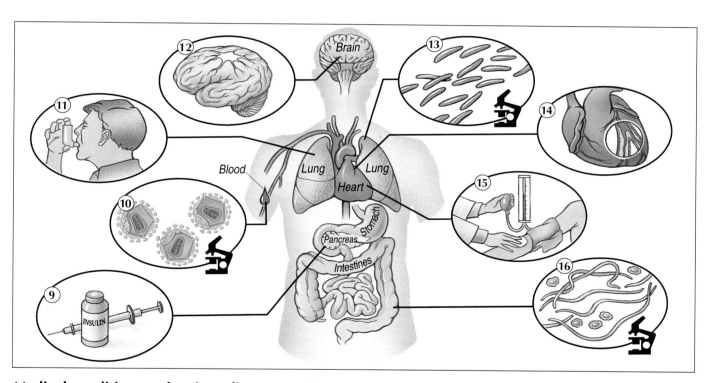

Medical conditions and serious diseases   Состояние здоровья и тяжёлые заболевания

9. diabetes
диабет

10. HIV (human immunodeficiency virus)
ВИЧ вирус иммунодефицита человека (возбудитель СПИДа)

11. asthma
астма

12. brain cancer
рак мозга

13. TB (tuberculosis)
туберкулёз

14. heart disease
болезнь сердца

15. high blood pressure
высокое кровяное давление

16. intestinal parasites
кишечные паразиты

More vocabulary

AIDS (acquired immunodeficiency syndrome): a medical condition that results from contracting the HIV virus

influenza: flu

hypertension: high blood pressure

infectious disease: a disease that is spread through air or water

Share your answers.

Which diseases on this page are infectious?

Health Care Здравоохранение

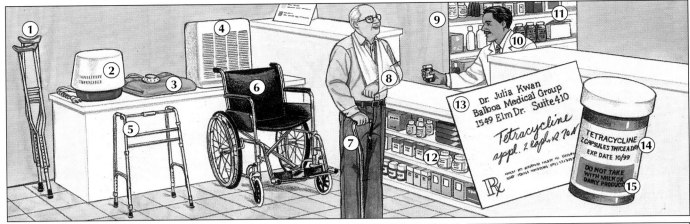

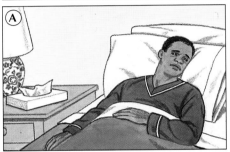  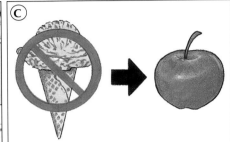

  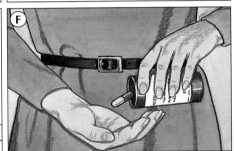

1. crutches
костыли

2. humidifier
увлажнитель воздуха

3. heating pad
горячий компресс

4. air purifier
очиститель воздуха

5. walker
ходунок (для больных /
пожилых людей)

6. wheelchair
инвалидное кресло

7. cane
трость

8. sling
перевязь

9. pharmacy
аптека

10. pharmacist
аптекарь / фармацевт

11. prescription medication
лекарства по рецепту

12. over-the-counter medication
лекарства, отпускаемые без
рецепта

13. prescription
рецепт

14. prescription label
этикетка с названием лекарства,
фамилией врача и пациента

15. warning label
этикетка с предупредительной
надписью

A. **Get** bed rest.
Соблюдайте постельный режим.

B. **Drink** fluids.
Пейте много жидкости.

C. **Change** your diet.
Измените режим питания.

D. **Exercise.**
Делайте упражнения.

E. **Get** an injection.
Сделайте укол.

F. **Take** medicine.
Примите лекарство.

More vocabulary

dosage: how much medicine you take and how many times a day you take it

expiration date: the last day the medicine can be used

treatment: something you do to get better

Staying in bed, drinking fluids, and getting physical therapy are treatments.

An injection that stops a person from getting a serious disease is called **an immunization** or **a vaccination.**

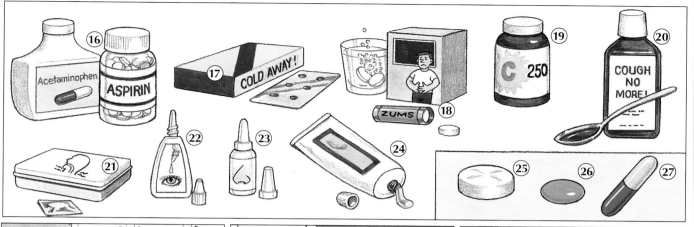

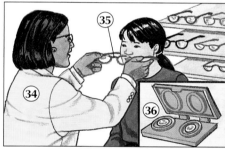

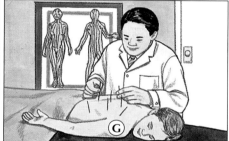

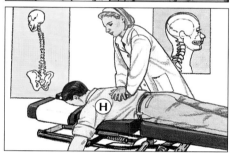

16. pain reliever
болеутоляющее

17. cold tablets
таблетки от простуды

18. antacid
антацидное средство

19. vitamins
витамины

20. cough syrup
микстура от кашля

21. throat lozenges
леденцы от боли в горле

22. eyedrops
глазные капли

23. nasal spray
аэрозоль от насморка

24. ointment
мазь

25. tablet
таблетка

26. pill
пилюля

27. capsule
капсула

28. orthopedist
ортопед

29. cast
гипс

30. physical therapist
физиотерапевт

31. brace
шина

32. audiologist
аудиолог

33. hearing aid
слуховой аппарат

34. optometrist
оптик

35. (eye)glasses
очки

36. contact lenses
контактные линзы

G. Get acupuncture.
Сделайте акупунктуру.

H. Go to a chiropractor.
Обратитесь к хиропрактику.

Share your answers.

1. What's the best treatment for a headache? a sore throat? a stomachache? a fever?

2. Do you think vitamins are important? Why or why not?

3. What treatments are popular in your culture?

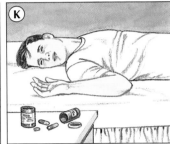

A. **be** injured / **be** hurt
получить травму /
быть раненным

B. **be** unconscious
быть без сознания

C. **be** in shock
быть в шоке

D. **have** a heart attack
получить инфаркт

E. **have** an allergic reaction
получить аллергическую
реакцию

F. **get** an electric shock
получить удар электричеством /
электрошок

G. **get** frostbite
обморозиться

H. **burn** (your)self
обжечься

I. **drown**
утонуть

J. **swallow** poison
проглотить яд

K. **overdose** on drugs
превысить дозу / получить
передозировку
лекарств / наркотиков

L. **choke**
подавиться

M. **bleed**
кровоточить

N. **can't breathe**
задыхаться

O. **fall**
упасть

P. **break** a bone
сломать кость

Grammar point: past tense

burn	—	burned	choke	—	choked	bleed	—	bled
drown	—	drowned	be	—	was, were	can't	—	couldn't
swallow	—	swallowed	have	—	had	fall	—	fell
overdose	—	overdosed	get	—	got	break	—	broke

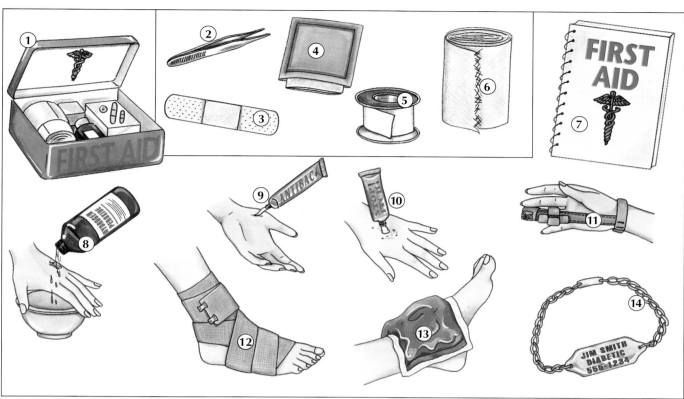

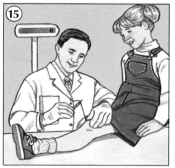
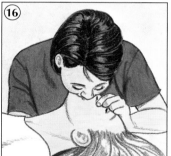
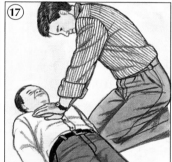

1. first aid kit
аптечка первой медицинской помощи

2. tweezers
пинцет

3. adhesive bandage
лейкопластырь

4. sterile pad
стерильная прокладка /
стерильный тампон

5. tape
пластырь / клейкая лента

6. gauze
марля

7. first aid manual
справочник / пособие по оказанию
первой медицинской помощи

8. hydrogen peroxide
перекись водорода

9. antibacterial ointment
бактерицидная мазь

10. antihistamine cream
антигистаминный крем

11. splint
шина

12. elastic bandage
эластичный бинт

13. ice pack
пакет со льдом

14. medical emergency bracelet
медицинский браслет / бирка

15. stitches
швы

16. rescue breathing
искусственное дыхание

17. CPR (cardiopulmonary resuscitation)
сердечно-лёгочная реанимация /
искусственный массаж сердца
и искусственное дыхание

18. Heimlich maneuver
приём Хаймлиха

Important Note: Only people who are properly trained should give stitches or do CPR.

Share your answers.

1. Do you have a First Aid kit in your home? Where can you buy one?

2. When do you use hydrogen peroxide? an elastic support bandage? antihistamine cream?

3. Do you know first aid? Where did you learn it?

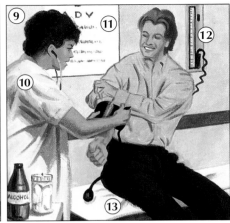

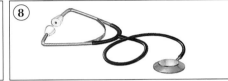

Medical clinic   Поликлиника

1. waiting room
приёмная

2. receptionist
регистратор

3. patient
пациент

4. insurance card
карточка страховой компании

5. insurance form
бланк страховки

6. doctor
врач / доктор

7. scale
весы

8. stethoscope
стетоскоп

9. examining room
смотровой кабинет

10. nurse
медсестра

11. eye chart
таблица для проверки зрения

12. blood pressure gauge
аппарат для измерения
кровяного давления

13. examination table
кушетка для осмотра

14. syringe
шприц

15. thermometer
термометр

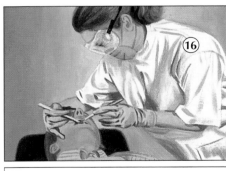
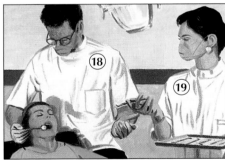
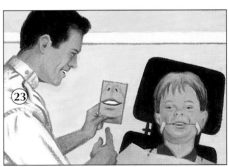

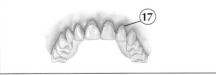

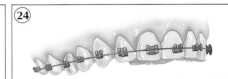

Dental clinic   Зубная поликлиника

16. dental hygienist
гигиенист

17. tartar
зубной камень

18. dentist
зубной врач / дантист

19. dental assistant
ассистент дантиста

20. cavity
дупло (в зубе)

21. drill
сверло

22. filling
пломба

23. orthodontist
стоматолог-ортодонт

24. braces
ортодонтические скобы

Can I come in on the 5th?

Yes. Come in at 2:00.

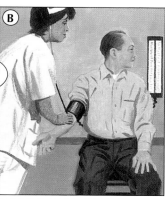

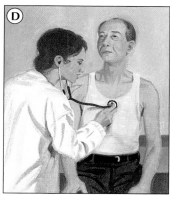

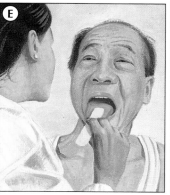

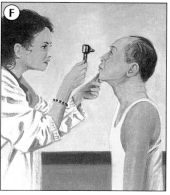

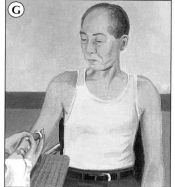

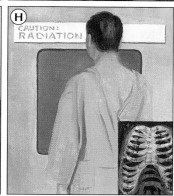

CAUTION: RADIATION

A. **make** an appointment
записаться...на приём к врачу

B. **check**...blood pressure
проверить...кровяное давление

C. **take**...temperature
измерить...температуру

D. **listen** to...heart
прослушать...сердце

E. **look** in...throat
осмотреть...горло

F. **examine**...eyes
проверить...глаза

G. **draw**...blood
брать...кровь

H. **get** an X ray
сделать рентген

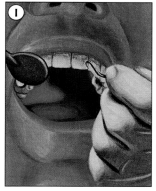

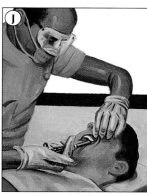

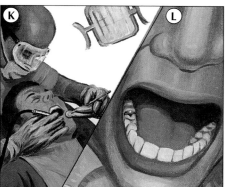

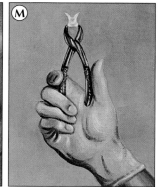

I. **clean**...teeth
снять...камень с зубов

J. **give**...a shot of anesthetic
сделать...обезболивающий укол / заморозку

K. **drill** a tooth
сверлить зуб

L. **fill** a cavity
запломбировать зуб / дупло в зубе

M. **pull** a tooth
удалить зуб

More vocabulary

get a checkup: to go for a medical exam

extract a tooth: to pull out a tooth

Share your answers.

1. What is the average cost of a medical exam in your area?

2. Some people are nervous at the dentist's office. What can they do to relax?

A Hospital   Больница

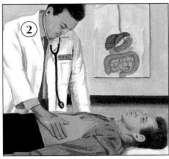

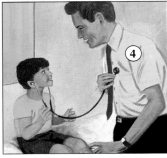
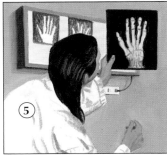

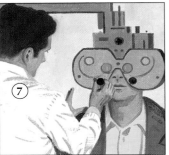
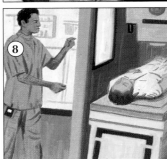

Hospital staff   Медперсонал больницы

1. obstetrician
акушер-гинеколог

2. internist
врач-терапевт

3. cardiologist
кардиолог

4. pediatrician
педиатр

5. radiologist
рентгенолог

6. psychiatrist
психиатр

7. ophthalmologist
офтальмолог / окулист

8. X-ray technician
техник-рентгенолог

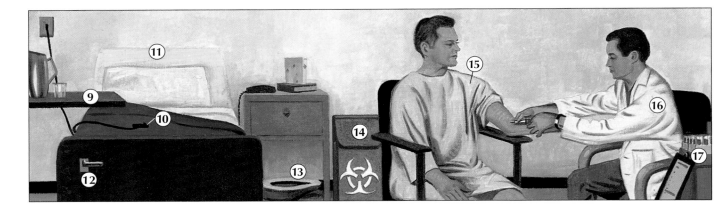

Patient's room   Палата пациента

9. bed table
прикроватный столик

10. call button
кнопка для вызова медперсонала

11. hospital bed
больничная койка

12. bed control
ручка / кнопка регулирования
положения высоты койки

13. bedpan
подкладное судно

14. medical waste disposal
контейнер для медицинских
отходов

15. hospital gown
больничная пижама /
больничный халат

16. lab technician
лаборант

17. blood work / blood test
анализ крови

More vocabulary

nurse practitioner: a nurse licensed to give medical exams

specialist: a doctor who only treats specific medical problems

gynecologist: a specialist who examines and treats women

nurse midwife: a nurse practitioner who examines pregnant women and delivers babies

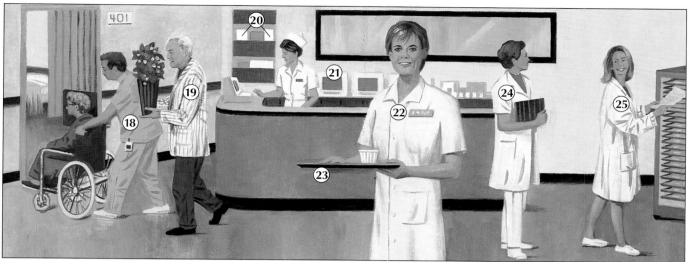

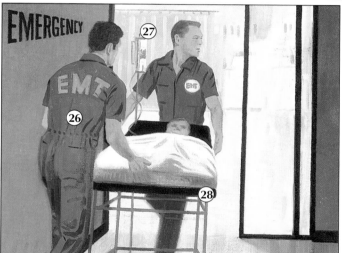

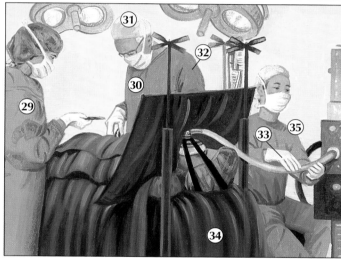

Nurse's station
Пост медсестры

18. orderly
санитар

19. volunteer
доброволец

20. medical charts
истории болезней

21. vital signs monitor
датчики давления /
дыхания / пульса

22. RN (registered nurse)
дипломированная медсестра

23. medication tray
поднос с ячейками для лекарств

24. LPN (licensed practical nurse) /
LVN (licensed vocational nurse)
дипломированная практикующая
медсестра / медсестра помощи на
дому

25. dietician
диетолог

Emergency room
Реанимация

26. emergency medical technician
(EMT)
медицинский техник по оказанию
первой помощи

27. IV (intravenous drip)
капельница / внутривенное
капельное введение

28. stretcher/gurney
каталка / носилки

Operating room
Операционная

29. surgical nurse
операционная сестра

30. surgeon
хирург

31. surgical cap
хирургическая шапочка

32. surgical gown
хирургический халат

33. latex gloves
резиновые перчатки

34. operating table
операционный стол

35. anesthesiologist
анестезиолог

Practice asking for the hospital staff.

Please get the nurse. I have a question for her.
Where's the anesthesiologist? I need to talk to her.
I'm looking for the lab technician. Have you seen him?

Share your answers.

1. Have you ever been to an emergency room? Who helped you?

2. Have you ever been in the hospital? How long did you stay?

City Streets Улицы города

1. fire station
пожарная станция

2. coffee shop
кафе

3. bank
банк

4. car dealership
автосалон и автосервис

5. hotel
гостиница

6. church
церковь

7. hospital
больница

8. park
парк

9. synagogue
синагога

10. theater
театр

11. movie theater
кинотеатр

12. gas station
бензозаправочная станция

13. furniture store
мебельный магазин

14. hardware store
магазин скобяных изделий

15. barber shop
парикмахерская

More vocabulary

skyscraper: a very tall office building

downtown/city center: the area in a city with the city hall, courts, and businesses

Practice giving your destination.

I'm going to go <u>downtown</u>.

I have to go to <u>the post office</u>.

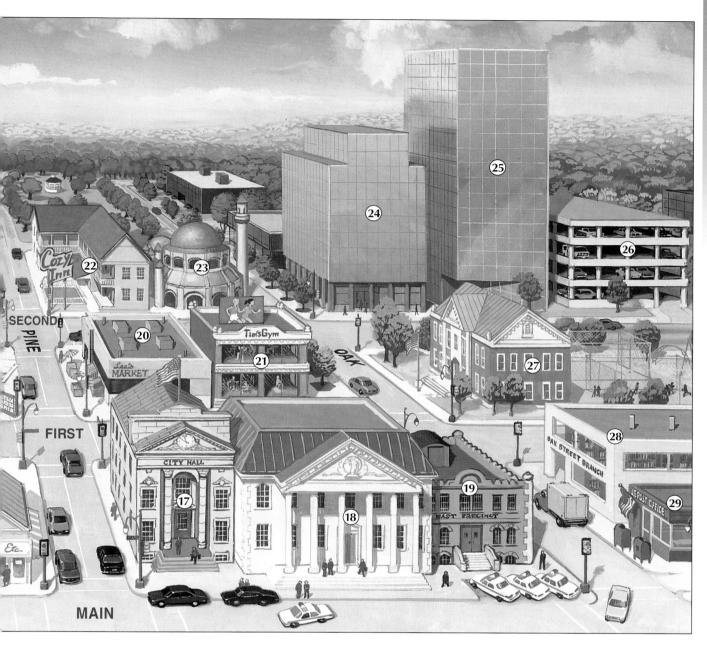

16. bakery
пекарня

17. city hall
здание муниципалитета

18. courthouse
здание суда

19. police station
полиция / полицейский участок

20. market
рынок

21. health club
клуб здоровья

22. motel
мотель

23. mosque
мечеть

24. office building
административное здание

25. high-rise building
высотное здание / небоскрёб

26. parking garage
гараж

27. school
школа

28. library
библиотека

29. post office
почта

Practice asking for and giving the locations of buildings.

Where's <u>the post office</u>?

  It's on <u>Oak Street</u>.

Share your answers.

1. Which of the places in this picture do you go to every week?

2. Is it good to live in a city? Why or why not?

3. What famous cities do you know?

1. **Laundromat**
   прачечная

2. **drugstore / pharmacy**
   промтоварный магазин / аптека
   (американского образца)

3. **convenience store**
   магазин удобства

4. **photo shop**
   магазин фототоваров

5. **parking space**
   стоянка

6. **traffic light**
   светофор

7. **pedestrian**
   пешеход

8. **crosswalk**
   переход

9. **street**
   улица

10. **curb**
    обочина / край тротуара

11. **newsstand**
    газетный киоск

12. **mailbox**
    почтовый ящик

13. **drive-thru window**
    окно выдачи на вынос для
    водителей за рулём

14. **fast food restaurant**
    ресторан быстрого
    обслуживания

15. **bus**
    автобус

A. **cross** the street
   переходить дорогу

B. **wait** for the light
   ждать сигнала светофора

C. **drive** a car
   водить машину

More vocabulary

neighborhood: the area close to your home

do errands: to make a short trip from your home to buy
or pick up something

Talk about where to buy things.

You can buy newspapers at a newsstand.

You can buy donuts at a donut shop.

You can buy food at a convenience store.

16. bus stop	22. copy center/print shop	28. fire hydrant
остановка автобуса	копировальный/печатный центр	пожарный кран
17. corner	23. streetlight	29. sign
угол	уличный фонарь	вывеска/знак
18. parking meter	24. dry cleaners	30. street vendor
счётчик парковки автомобилей	химчистка	уличный торговец
19. motorcycle	25. nail salon	31. cart
мотоцикл	маникюрный салон	тележка
20. donut shop	26. sidewalk	D. **park** the car
пончиковая	тротуар	**парковать** машину
21. public telephone	27. garbage truck	E. **ride** a bicycle
телефон-автомат	мусоровоз	**ехать** на велосипеде

Share your answers.

1. Do you like to do errands?

2. Do you always like to go to the same stores?

3. Which businesses in the picture are also in your neighborhood?

4. Do you know someone who has a small business? What kind?

5. What things can you buy from a street vendor?

A Mall   Торговый центр

1. **music store**
   музыкальный магазин

2. **jewelry store**
   ювелирный магазин

3. **candy store**
   кондитерский магазин

4. **bookstore**
   книжный магазин

5. **toy store**
   магазин игрушек

6. **pet store**
   зоомагазин

7. **card store**
   магазин открыток

8. **optician**
   оптика

9. **travel agency**
   туристическое агентство /
   бюро путешествий

10. **shoe store**
    обувной магазин

11. **fountain**
    фонтан

12. **florist**
    цветочный магазин

More vocabulary

beauty shop: hair salon

men's store: a store that sells men's clothing

dress shop: a store that sells women's clothing

Talk about where you want to shop in this mall.

Let's go to <u>the card store</u>.

I need to buy <u>a card</u> for Maggie's birthday.

13. department store
универмаг

14. food court
центр общественного питания в
торговом центре

15. video store
магазин видеотоваров

16. hair salon
салон-парикмахерская

17. maternity shop
магазин для будущих матерей

18. electronics store
магазин электронных товаров

19. directory
информационная схема

20. ice cream stand
киоск «мороженое»

21. escalator
эскалатор

22. information booth
справочное бюро

Practice asking for and giving the location of different shops.

Where's the maternity shop?

   It's on the first floor, next to the hair salon.

Share your answers.

1. Do you like shopping malls? Why or why not?

2. Some people don't go to the mall to shop.
   Name some other things you can do in a mall.

A Childcare Center   Ясли/детский сад

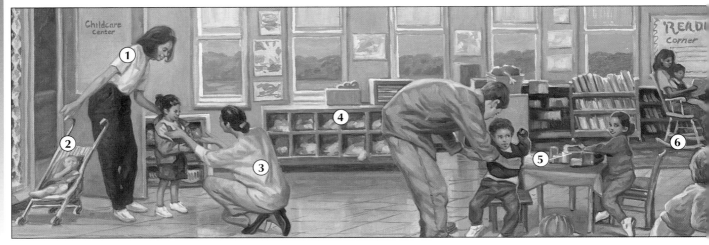

1. parent
родитель

2. stroller
прогулочная коляска

3. childcare worker
работник / воспитатель
яслей / сада

4. cubby
домик для игр

5. toys
игрушки

6. rocking chair
кресло-качалка

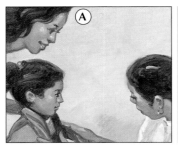

A. drop off
ронять

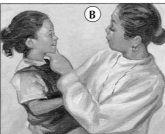

B. hold
держать

C. nurse
кормить грудью

D. feed
кормить

E. change diapers
менять пеленки

F. read a story
читать рассказ

G. pick up
поднимать

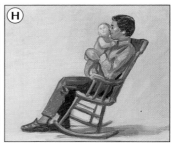

H. rock
качать

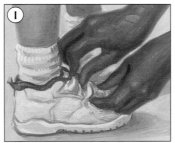

I. tie shoes
завязывать ботинки

J. dress
одевать

K. play
играть

L. take a nap
спать

7. high chair
детский стул с
высоким сиденьем

8. bib
слюнявчик

9. changing table
стол для пеленания

10. potty seat
сиденье для горшка

11. playpen
манеж

12. walker
ходунок

13. car safety seat
детское сиденье для автомобиля

14. baby carrier
переносная люлька

15. baby backpack
рюкзак для ношения ребёнка

16. carriage
детская коляска

17. wipes
салфетки с пропиткой

18. baby powder
детская присыпка / тальк

19. disinfectant
дезинфицирующее средство

20. disposable diapers
одноразовые подгузники

21. cloth diapers
матерчатые пелёнки

22. diaper pins
булавки для пелёнок

23. diaper pail
ведро для грязных подгузников

24. training pants
тренировочные штаны

25. formula
детское сухое молоко

26. bottle
бутылка

27. nipple
соска

28. baby food
детское питание

29. pacifier
пустышка

30. teething ring
кольцо для прорезывания зубов

31. rattle
погремушка

1. envelope
   конверт

2. letter
   письмо

3. postcard
   почтовая открытка

4. greeting card
   поздравительная
   открытка

5. package
   посылка

6. letter carrier
   почтальон

7. return address
   обратный адрес

8. mailing address
   почтовый адрес

9. postmark
   почтовый штемпель

10. stamp / postage
    марка / почтовый сбор

11. certified mail
    заказная почта

12. priority mail
    срочная почта

13. air letter / aerogramme
    письмо, доставляемое
    авиапочтой / радиограмма

14. ground post /
    parcel post
    почта, доставляемая
    наземным транспортом /
    посылочный отдел

15. Express Mail /
    overnight mail
    Экспресс-почта/почта,
    доставляемая на
    следующий день

A. **address** a postcard
   написать адрес на
   почтовой открытке

B. **send** it / **mail** it
   отправить / **послать**
   по почте

C. **deliver** it
   доставить

D. **receive** it
   получить

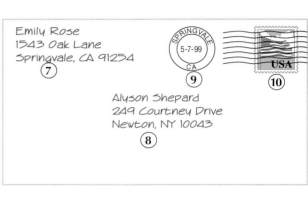

1. teller
кассир

2. vault
сейф

3. ATM (automated
teller machine)
банкомат

4. security guard
охранник

*Saint Benedict
A Catholic Voluntary Academy
Duffield Road, Darley Abbey
Derby
DE22 1JD*

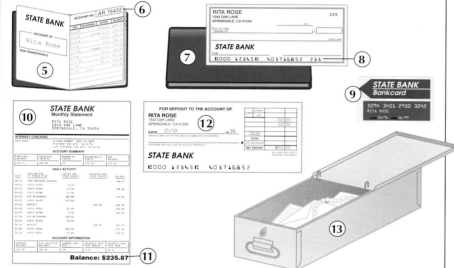

5. passbook
отчётная банковская книжка

6. savings account number
номер сберегательного счёта

7. checkbook
чековая книжка

8. checking account number
номер чекового счёта

9. ATM card
банкоматная карточка

10. monthly statement
ежемесячный банковский отчёт

11. balance
баланс

12. deposit slip
депозитная квитанция

13. safe-deposit box
личный банковский сейф

Using the ATM machine   Пользование банкоматом

A. **Insert** your ATM card.
Вставьте карточку в банкомат.

B. **Enter** your PIN number.*
Наберите личный код.

C. **Make** a deposit.
Сделайте вклад.

D. **Withdraw** cash.
Снимите деньги со счёта.

E. **Transfer** funds.
Переведите деньги.

F. **Remove** your ATM card.
Выньте карточку из банкомата.

*PIN: personal identification number

More vocabulary

overdrawn account: When there is not enough money in an account to pay a check, we say the account is overdrawn.

Share your answers.

1. Do you use a bank?
2. Do you use an ATM card?
3. Name some things you can put in a safe-deposit box.

1. reference librarian
библиотекарь справочного стола

2. reference desk
справочный стол

3. atlas
атлас

4. microfilm reader
считыватель микрофильма

5. microfilm
микрофильм

6. periodical section
отдел периодических изданий

7. magazine
журнал

8. newspaper
газета

9. online catalog
компьютерный каталог

10. card catalog
картотека

11. media section
отдел средств массовой информации

12. audiocassette
аудиокассета

13. videocassette
видеокассета

14. CD (compact disc)
компакт-диск

15. record
пластинка

16. checkout desk
отдел выдачи

17. library clerk
библиотекарь

18. encyclopedia
энциклопедия

19. library card
библиотечная карточка

20. library book
библиотечная книга

21. title
название

22. author
автор

More vocabulary

check a book out: to borrow a book from the library

nonfiction: real information, history or true stories

fiction: stories from the author's imagination

Share your answers.

1. Do you have a library card?

2. Do you prefer to buy books or borrow them from the library?

A. **arrest** a suspect
арестовать подозреваемого

1. police officer
полицейский

2. handcuffs
наручники

B. **hire** a lawyer / **hire** an attorney
нанять адвоката / юриста

3. guard
охранник

4. defense attorney
защитник

C. **appear** in court
явиться в суд

5. defendant
обвиняемый

6. judge
судья

D. **stand trial**
предстать перед судом

7. courtroom
зал суда

8. jury
присяжные

9. evidence
улики

10. prosecuting attorney
прокурор

11. witness
свидетель

12. court reporter
судебная стенографистка

13. bailiff
судебный исполнитель

E. **give** the verdict*
вынести приговор

F. **sentence** the defendant
приговорить обвиняемого

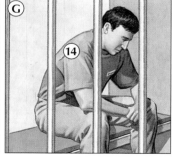

G. **go** to jail / **go** to prison
сесть в тюрьму

14. convict
осуждённый

H. **be released**
освободиться / выйти из заключения

*Note: There are two possible verdicts, "guilty" and "not guilty."

Share your answers.

1. What are some differences between the legal system in the United States and the one in your country?

2. Do you want to be on a jury? Why or why not?

Crime Преступление

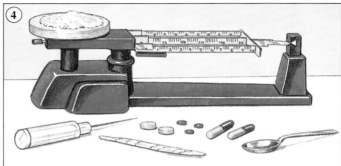

1. vandalism
вандализм

2. gang violence
групповое насилие

3. drunk driving
вождение машины в нетрезвом состоянии

4. illegal drugs
запрещённые наркотики

5. mugging
ограбление на улице

6. burglary
ограбление со взломом

7. assault
нападение

8. murder
убийство

9. gun
пистолет / ружьё

More vocabulary

commit a crime: to do something illegal

criminal: someone who commits a crime

victim: someone who is hurt or killed by someone else

Share your answers.

1. Is there too much crime on TV? in the movies?

2. Do you think people become criminals from watching crime on TV?

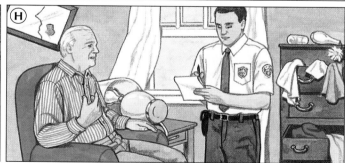

A. **Walk** with a friend.
Ходите в сопровождении друга.

B. **Stay** on well-lit streets.
Оставайтесь на хорошо освещённых улицах.

C. **Hold** your purse close to your body.
Прижимайте сумку к себе.

D. **Protect** your wallet.
Оберегайте кошелёк.

E. **Lock** your doors.
Запирайте двери.

F. **Don't open** your door to strangers.
Не открывайте дверь незнакомым людям.

G. **Don't drink** and **drive**.
Не пейте за рулём.

H. **Report** crimes to the police.
Сообщайте о преступлениях в полицию.

More vocabulary

Neighborhood Watch: a group of neighbors who watch for criminals in their neighborhood

designated drivers: people who don't drink alcoholic beverages so that they can drive drinkers home

Share your answers.

1. Do you feel safe in your neighborhood?

2. Look at the pictures. Which of these things do you do?

3. What other things do you do to stay safe?

1. lost child
потерявшийся ребёнок

2. car accident
автомобильная авария

3. airplane crash
авиакатастрофа

4. explosion
взрыв

5. earthquake
землетрясение

6. mudslide
оползень

7. fire
пожар

8. firefighter
пожарник

9. fire truck
пожарная машина

Practice reporting a fire.

This is <u>Lisa Broad</u>. There is a fire.

The address is <u>323 Oak Street.</u>

Please send someone quickly.

Share your answers.

1. Can you give directions to your home if there is a fire?

2. What information do you give to the other driver if you are in a car accident?

10. drought
засуха

11. blizzard
метель / снежная буря / буран

12. hurricane
ураган

13. tornado
торнадо / смерч

14. volcanic eruption
извержение вулкана

15. tidal wave
приливная волна

16. flood
наводнение

17. search and rescue team
поисково-спасательная группа

Share your answers.

1. Which disasters are common in your area? Which never happen?

2. What can you do to prepare for emergencies?

3. Do you have emergency numbers near your telephone?

4. What organizations will help you in an emergency?

Public Transportation   Общественный транспорт

1. **bus stop**
автобусная остановка

2. **route**
маршрут

3. **schedule**
расписание

4. **bus**
автобус

5. **fare**
плата за проезд

6. **transfer**
пересадка

7. **passenger**
пассажир

8. **bus driver**
водитель автобуса

9. **subway**
метро

10. **track**
железнодорожные
пути / рельсы

11. **token**
жетон

12. **fare card**
проездной билет

13. **train station**
железнодорожная
станция

14. **ticket**
билет

15. **platform**
платформа

16. **conductor**
кондуктор

17. **train**
поезд

18. **taxi / cab**
такси

19. **taxi stand**
стоянка такси

20. **taxi driver**
водитель такси

21. **meter**
счётчик

22. **taxi license**
удостоверение / лицензия
водителя такси

23. **ferry**
паром

More vocabulary

hail a taxi: to get a taxi driver's attention by raising your hand

miss the bus: to arrive at the bus stop late

Talk about how you and your friends come to school.

I take the bus to school.
You take the train.
We take the subway.

He drives to school.
She walks to school.
They ride bikes.

104

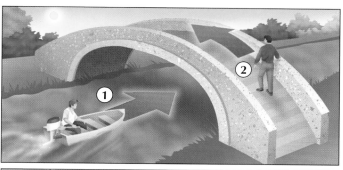

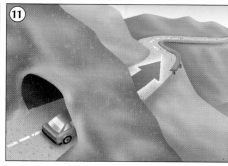

1. **under** the bridge
   под мост / под мостом

2. **over** the bridge
   через мост

3. **across** the water
   по воде / водным транспортом

4. **into** the taxi
   в такси

5. **out of** the taxi
   из такси

6. **onto** the highway
   на шоссе

7. **off** the highway
   с магистрали

8. **down** the stairs
   вниз по лестнице

9. **up** the stairs
   вверх по лестнице

10. **around** the corner
    за угол

11. **through** the tunnel
    через туннель

Grammar point: *into, out of, on, off*

We say, *get **into** a taxi or a car.*

But we say, *get **on** a bus, a train, or a plane.*

We say, *get **out of** a taxi or a car.*

But we say, *get **off** a bus, a train, or a plane.*

Cars and Trucks   Легковые и грузовые автомобили

1. **subcompact**
мини-автомобиль

2. **compact**
малогабаритный автомобиль

3. **midsize car**
среднегабаритный автомобиль

4. **full-size car**
крупногабаритный автомобиль

5. **convertible**
машина с откидным верхом

6. **sports car**
спортивная машина

7. **pickup truck**
пикап / грузовой автомобиль на легковом шасси

8. **station wagon**
грузо-пассажирский автофургон (на шасси легкового автомобиля)

9. **SUV (sports utility vehicle)**
спортивный автомобиль общего назначения

10. **minivan**
микроавтобус

11. **camper**
туристический автомобиль / дом на колёсах

12. **dump truck**
самосвал

13. **tow truck**
грузовой автомобиль-тягач

14. **moving van**
крытый грузовик-фургон для перевозки мебели

15. **tractor trailer / semi**
прицеп тягача / тракторный прицеп

16. **cab**
кабина

17. **trailer**
прицеп

More vocabulary

make: the name of the company that makes the car

model: the style of car

Share your answers.

1. What is your favorite kind of car?

2. What kind of car is good for a big family? for a single person?

Directions   Указатели

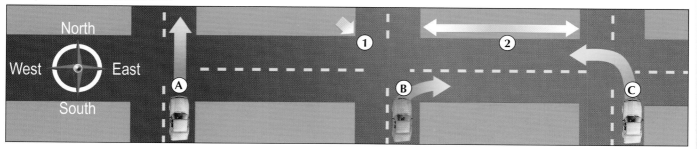

A. go straight
идите прямо

B. turn right
поверните направо

C. turn left
поверните налево

1. corner
угол

2. block
квартал

Signs   Дорожные знаки

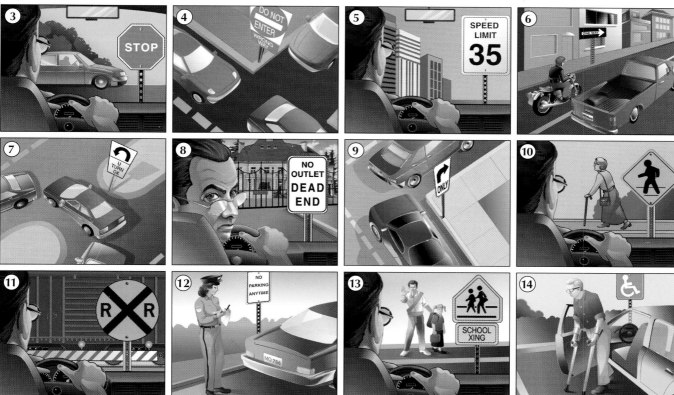

3. stop
стоп

4. do not enter/wrong way
проезд запрещён/встречное
движение

5. speed limit
ограничение скорости

6. one way
одностороннее движение

7. U-turn OK
разворот разрешён

8. no outlet/dead end
проезда нет/тупик

9. right turn only
только правый поворот

10. pedestrian crossing
пешеходный переход

11. railroad crossing
железнодорожный переезд

12. no parking
парковка запрещена

13. school crossing
осторожно, дети

14. handicapped parking
парковка для инвалидов

More vocabulary

right-of-way: the right to go first

yield: to give another person or car the right-of-way

Share your answers.

1. Which traffic signs are the same in your country?

2. Do pedestrians have the right-of-way in your city?

3. What is the speed limit in front of your school?
   your home?

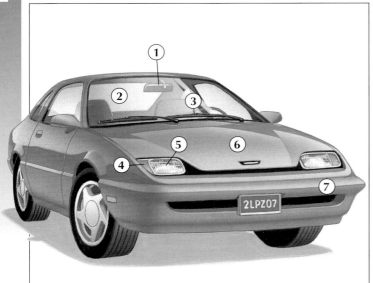
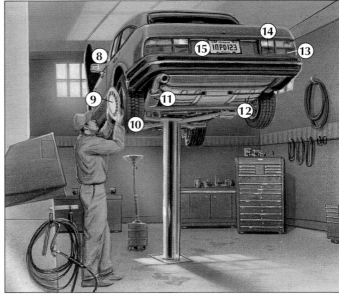

1. **rearview mirror**
зеркало заднего вида

2. **windshield**
ветровое стекло

3. **windshield wipers**
дворники

4. **turn signal**
сигнал поворота

5. **headlight**
передняя фара

6. **hood**
капот

7. **bumper**
бампер

8. **sideview mirror**
зеркало бокового вида

9. **hubcap**
колпак ступицы колеса

10. **tire**
шина

11. **muffler**
глушитель

12. **gas tank**
бензобак

13. **brake light**
тормозные фары

14. **taillight**
задняя фара

15. **license plate**
номерной знак

16. **air bag**
воздушная подушка

17. **dashboard**
приборный щиток

18. **turn signal**
сигнал поворота

19. **oil gauge**
масляный манометр /
измеритель уровня
масла

20. **speedometer**
спидометр

21. **odometer**
одометр / счётчик
пробега

22. **gas gauge**
бензиномер / указатель
уровня бензина

23. **temperature gauge**
индикатор
температуры

24. **horn**
звуковой сигнал

25. **ignition**
зажигание

26. **steering wheel**
руль

27. **gearshift**
механизм переключения
передач

28. **air conditioning**
кондиционер

29. **heater**
печка

30. **tape deck**
встроенный кассетный
магнитофон

31. **radio**
радио

32. **cigarette lighter**
зажигалка

33. **glove compartment**
бардачок

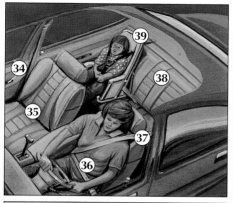
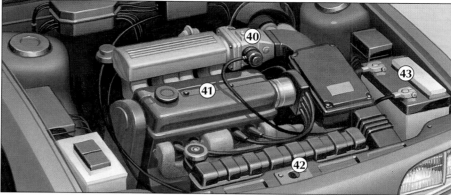
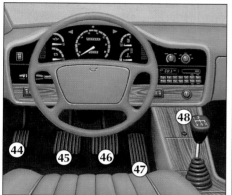

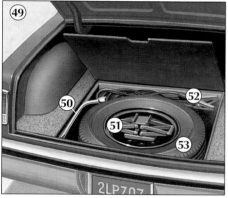

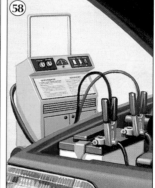

34. lock
замок

35. front seat
переднее сиденье

36. seat belt
предохранительный ремень безопасности

37. shoulder harness
плечевые предохранительные ремни

38. backseat
заднее сиденье

39. child safety seat
детское сиденье безопасности

40. fuel injection system
система подачи топлива

41. engine
двигатель / мотор

42. radiator
радиатор

43. battery
батарея

44. emergency brake
аварийный тормоз

45. clutch*
сцепление

46. brake pedal
педаль тормоза

47. accelerator / gas pedal
педаль акселератора газа

48. stick shift
рычаг ручного переключения передач

49. trunk
багажник

50. lug wrench
разводной ключ

51. jack
домкрат

52. jumper cables
кабели аварийного пуска двигателя

53. spare tire
запасное колесо

54. The car needs **gas**.
Нужно **заправить** машину.

55. The car needs **oil**.
Нужно **залить масло** в машину.

56. The radiator needs **coolant**.
Нужно **залить антифриз** в радиатор.

57. The car needs **a smog check**.
Нужно проверить **выхлопные газы на содержание загрязняющих веществ**.

58. The battery needs **recharging**.
Нужно **подзарядить** батарею.

59. The tires need **air**.
Нужно **подкачать** шины.

*Note: Standard transmission cars have a clutch; automatic transmission cars do not.

1. airline terminal
аэровокзал авиакомпании в аэропорту

2. airline representative
представитель авиакомпании

3. check-in counter
регистрационная стойка

4. arrival and departure monitors
мониторы прилёта и отлёта

5. gate
выход на посадку

6. boarding area
место сбора пассажиров для выхода на посадку

7. control tower
диспетчерская башня

8. helicopter
вертолёт

9. airplane
самолёт

10. overhead compartment
отделение для ручной клади, расположенное над сиденьями

11. cockpit
кабина пилота

12. pilot
пилот

13. flight attendant
стюард/стюардесса

14. oxygen mask
кислородная маска

15. airsickness bag
санитарный пакет

16. tray table
откидной столик

17. baggage claim area
отделение получения багажа

18. carousel
подвижная лента выдачи багажа

19. luggage carrier
багажная тележка

20. customs
таможня

21. customs officer
таможенник

22. declaration form
декларация

23. passenger
пассажир

A. **buy** your ticket
купить билет

B. **check** your bags
сдать багаж

C. **go through** security
пройти контроль

D. **check in** at the gate
пройти регистрацию у выхода
на посадку

E. **get** your boarding pass
получить посадочный талон

F. **board** the plane
сесть в самолёт

G. **find** your seat
занять своё место

H. **stow** your carry-on bag
уложить ручную кладь

I. **fasten** your seat belt
пристегнуть привязные ремни

J. **look for** the emergency exit
ознакомиться с расположением
аварийного выхода

K. **look at** the emergency card
ознакомиться с планом выхода
при аварии

L. **take off/leave**
взлететь/отправиться

M. **request** a blanket
попросить одеяло

N. **experience** turbulence
испытывать болтанку

O. **land/arrive**
произвести посадку/прибыть

P. **claim** your baggage
получить свой багаж

More vocabulary

destination: the place the passenger is going
departure time: the time the plane takes off
arrival time: the time the plane lands

direct flight: a plane trip between two cities with no stops
stopover: a stop before reaching the destination,
sometimes to change planes

1. public school
государственная школа

2. private school
частная школа

3. parochial school
приходская школа

4. preschool
дошкольное учебное
заведение

5. elementary school
начальная школа

6. middle school/
junior high school
младшие классы
средней школы

7. high school
старшие классы
средней школы

8. adult school
школа для взрослых

9. vocational school/trade school
ремесленное училище/
профессионально-техническое
училище

10. college/university
колледж/университет

Note: In the U.S. most children begin school at age 5 (in kindergarten)
and graduate from high school at 17 or 18.

More vocabulary

When students graduate from a college or university
they receive a **degree**:

Bachelor's degree—usually 4 years of study

Master's degree—an additional 1–3 years of study

Doctorate—an additional 3–5 years of study

community college: a two-year college where students
can get an Associate of Arts degree

graduate school: a school in a university where students
study for their master's and doctorates

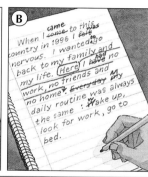

1. writing assignment
письменное задание

A. Write a first draft.
Напишите на черновике.

B. Edit your paper.
Проверьте работу.

C. Get feedback.
Выслушайте мнение о своей работе.

D. Rewrite your paper.
Перепишите работу.

E. Turn in your paper.
Сдайте работу.

2. paper / composition
работа / сочинение

③ *My life in the U.S.*

④ I arrived in this country in 1996. My family did not come with me. I was homesick, nervous, and a little excited. I had no job and no friends here. I lived with my aunt and my daily routine ⑤ was always the same: get up, look for a job, go to bed. At night I remembered my mother's words to me, "Son, you can always come home!" I was homesick and scared, but I did not go home.

I started to study English at night. English is a difficult language and many times I was too tired to study. One teacher, Mrs. Armstrong, was very kind to me. She showed me many

3. title
название

4. sentence
предложение

5. paragraph
абзац

Punctuation   Пунктуация

6. period
точка

7. question mark
вопросительный знак

8. exclamation mark
восклицательный знак

9. quotation marks
кавычки

10. comma
запятая

11. apostrophe
апостроф

12. colon
двоеточие

13. semicolon
точка с запятой

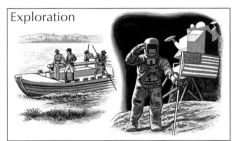

Exploration

War

Immigration

Historical and Political Events Исторические и политические события	**1492 →** French, Spanish, English explorers французские, испанские, английские исследователи	**1607–1750** Colonies along Atlantic coast founded by Northern Europeans колонии на атлантическом побережье, основанные северо-европейцами	**1619** 1st African slave sold in Virginia первый африканский раб продан в Виргинии **1653** 1st Indian reservation in Virginia первая индейская резервация в Виргинии
	Before 1700		1700
Immigration* Иммиграция	**1607** 1st English in Virginia первые англичане в Виргинии	**1610** Spanish at Santa Fe испанцы в Санта-Фе	
Population** Население	Before 1700: Native American: 1,000,000+ Коренные американцы: 1,000,000+		1700: colonists: 250,000 колонисты: 250,000

1803 Louisiana Purchase покупка Луизианы	**1812** War of 1812 война 1812 года	**1820** Missouri Compromise Миссурийский компромисс	**1830** Indian Removal Act акт о выселении индейцев	**1835–1838** Cherokee Trail of Tears «тропа слёз»/ насильственное переселение индейцев Чироки	**1846–1848** U.S. war with Mexico война США с Мексикой
1800	1810	1820	1830	1840	

1815 →
Irish
ирландцы

1800: citizens and free blacks: 5,300,000   slaves: 450,000
граждане и свободные негры: 5,300,000   рабы: 450,000

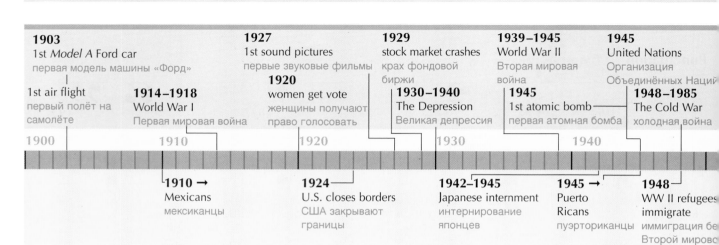

1903 1st *Model A* Ford car первая модель машины «Форд» 1st air flight первый полёт на самолёте	**1927** 1st sound pictures первые звуковые фильмы **1914–1918** World War I Первая мировая война **1920** women get vote женщины получают право голосовать	**1929** stock market crashes крах фондовой биржи **1930–1940** The Depression Великая депрессия	**1939–1945** World War II Вторая мировая война **1945** 1st atomic bomb первая атомная бомба	**1945** United Nations Организация Объединённых Наций **1948–1985** The Cold War холодная война
1900	1910	1920	1930	1940

1910 →
Mexicans
мексиканцы

1924
U.S. closes borders
США закрывают границы

1942–1945
Japanese internment
интернирование японцев

1945 →
Puerto Ricans
пуэрториканцы

1948
WW II refugees immigrate
иммиграция бе[...]
Второй мирово[...]

1900: 75,994,000

*Immigration dates indicate a time when large numbers of that group first began to immigrate to the U.S.
**All population figures before 1790 are estimates. Figures after 1790 are based on the official U.S. census.

Movement	Election	Invention
		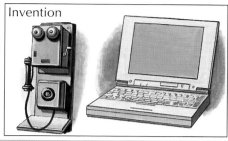

1754–1763
French and Indian War
Французско-индейская
война

1775–1783
Revolutionary War
Война за независимость

1776
Declaration of
Independence
Декларация
независимости

1788
U.S. Constitution
Конституция США
1789 Washington 1st President
Вашингтон 1-ый президент

1791
Bill of Rights
Билль о правах

1750   1760   1770   1780   1790

1750 →
Scots, Irish, Germans
шотландцы, ирландцы, немцы

1790 →
Haitians
Гаитянцы

1750: Native American: 1,000,000 +   colonists and free blacks: 1,171,000   slaves: 200,000
Коренные американцы: 1,000,000 +   колонисты и свободные негры: 1,171,000,   рабы: 200,000

1848
gold discovered
in California
в Калифорнии
найдено золото

1861–1865
Civil War
Гражданская
Война

1865
Lincoln assassinated
убийство Линкольна
1865
slavery abolished
отмена рабства

1867
U.S. buys Alaska
США покупают Аляску
1869
trans-continental railroad
трансконтинентальная
железная дорога

1879
lightbulb (Edison)
электрическая
лампочка (Эдисон)
1876
telephone (Bell)
телефон (Белл)

1898
Spanish American War
Испано-американская
война
1890
Battle of Wounded Knee
битва при Вундид-Ни

1850   1860   1870   1880   1890

1850 →
Chinese, Scandinavians
китайцы, скандинавы

1870 →
Hungarians
венгры

1885 →
Japanese
японцы

1890 →
Armenians, Southern and Eastern Europeans
армяне, иммигранты из Южной и
Восточной Европы

1850: 23,191,000

1950–1953
Korean War
война в Корее
1950
TV Popular
популярность телевидения

1954
civil rights movement
движение за
гражданские права
1963
Kennedy assassinated
убийство Кеннеди

1964–1973
war in Vietnam
война во
Вьетнаме
1968
King assassinated
убийство Кинга

1969
Armstrong on moon
Армстронг на луне

1979
computers popular
популярность компьютеров
1990
Internet popular
популярность интернета

1991
Persian Gulf War
Война в Персидском заливе

1950   1960   1970   1980   1990

1957
Hungarians
венгры

1960
Cubans
кубинцы

1965 →
Filipinos
филиппинцы

1968 →
Koreans
корейцы

1975 →
Southeast Asians
иммигранты из
Юго-восточной
Азии

1980 →
Middle Easterners
с Ближнего Востока
Central Americans
из Центральной Америки

1988 →
Russians
русские

1950: 150,697,000

1990: 248,700,000

BRANCHES OF GOVERNMENT

Legislative   Executive   Judicial

1. The House of Representatives
   Палата представителей

2. congresswoman/congressman
   женщина-конгрессмен/
   конгрессмен

3. The Senate
   Сенат

4. senator
   сенатор

5. The White House
   Белый дом

6. president
   президент

7. vice president
   вице-президент

8. The Supreme Court
   Верховный суд

9. chief justice
   главный судья

10. justices
    судьи

Citizenship application requirements
Требования при подаче заявления на гражданство

A. **be** 18 years old
   достичь 18-летнего возраста

B. **live** in the U.S. for five years
   жить в США в течение пяти лет

C. **take** a citizenship test
   сдать экзамен на получение гражданства

Rights and responsibilities
Права и обязанности

D. **vote**
   голосовать

E. **pay** taxes
   платить налоги

F. **register** with Selective Service*
   регистрироваться для прохождения выборочной службы

G. **serve** on a jury
   служить в качестве присяжного

H. **obey** the law
   соблюдать закон

*Note: All males 18 to 26 who live in the U.S. are required to register with Selective Service.

1. rain forest
   дождевой лес

2. waterfall
   водопад

3. river
   река

4. desert
   пустыня

5. sand dune
   песчаная дюна

6. ocean
   океан

7. peninsula
   полуостров

8. island
   остров

9. bay
   залив

10. beach
    пляж

11. forest
    лес

12. shore
    берег

13. lake
    озеро

14. mountain peak
    вершина горы

15. mountain range
    горный хребет

16. hills
    холмы

17. canyon
    каньон

18. valley
    долина

19. plains
    равнины

20. meadow
    луг

21. pond
    пруд

More vocabulary
a body of water: a river, lake, or ocean
stream/creek: a very small river

Talk about where you live and where you like to go.
I live in a valley. There is a lake nearby.
I like to go to the beach.

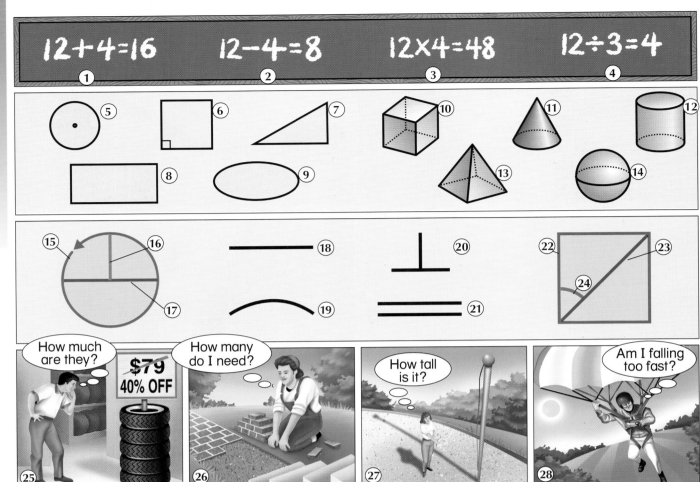

Operations
математические
действия

1. addition
сложение

2. subtraction
вычитание

3. multiplication
умножение

4. division
деление

Shapes
Геометрические
фигуры

5. circle
круг

6. square
квадрат

7. triangle
треугольник

8. rectangle
прямоугольник

9. oval / ellipse
овал / эллипс

Solids
Геометрические тела

10. cube
куб

11. cone
конус

12. cylinder
цилиндр

13. pyramid
пирамида

14. sphere
сфера

Parts of a circle
Части круга

15. circumference
окружность

16. radius
радиус

17. diameter
диаметр

Lines
Линии

18. straight
прямая

19. curved
волнистая

20. perpendicular
перпендикулярная

21. parallel
параллельная

Parts of a square
Части квадрата

22. side
сторона

23. diagonal
диагональ

24. angle
угол

Types of math
Разделы математики

25. algebra
алгебра

26. geometry
геометрия

27. trigonometry
тригонометрия

28. calculus
исчисление

More vocabulary

total: the answer to an addition problem

difference: the answer to a subtraction problem

product: the answer to a multiplication problem

quotient: the answer to a division problem

pi (π): the number when you divide the circumference of a circle by its diameter (approximately = 3.14)

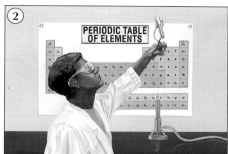

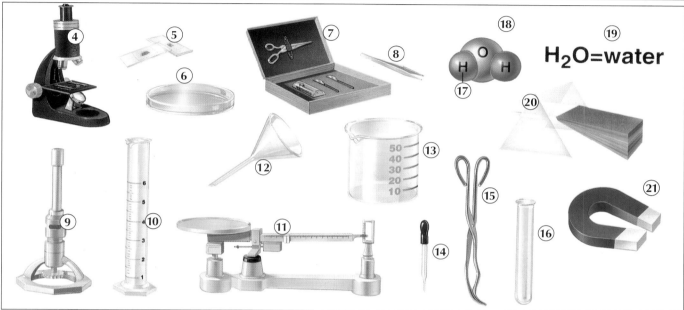

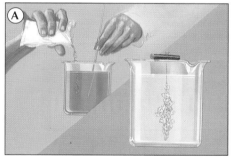

1. biology
   биология

2. chemistry
   химия

3. physics
   физика

4. microscope
   микроскоп

5. slide
   предметное стекло

6. petri dish
   чашка Петри

7. dissection kit
   набор для вскрытия

8. forceps
   зажим / пинцет

9. Bunsen burner
   горелка Бунзена

10. graduated cylinder
    цилиндрическая мензурка

11. balance
    противовес

12. funnel
    воронка

13. beaker
    мензурка / химический стакан

14. dropper
    сбрасыватель

15. crucible tongs
    щипцы

16. test tube
    пробирка

17. atom
    атом

18. molecule
    молекула

19. formula
    формула

20. prism
    призма

21. magnet
    магнит

A. **do** an experiment
   проводить эксперимент

B. **observe**
   наблюдать

C. **record** results
   записывать результаты

A. **play** an instrument
играть на музыкальном инструменте

B. **sing** a song
петь песню

1. orchestra
оркестр

2. rock band
рок-группа

Woodwinds

Strings

Brass

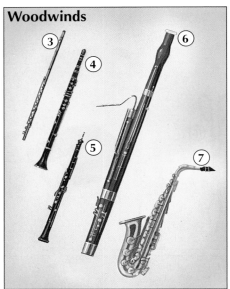

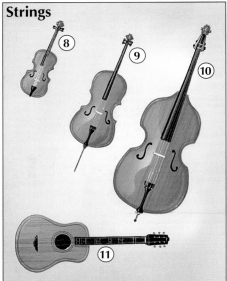

Percussion

Other Instruments

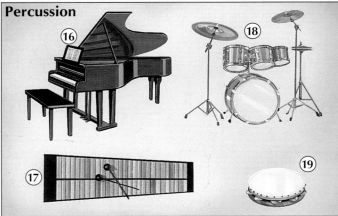

3. flute
флейта

4. clarinet
кларнет

5. oboe
гобой

6. bassoon
фагот

7. saxophone
саксофон

8. violin
скрипка

9. cello
виолончель

10. bass
контрабас

11. guitar
гитара

12. trombone
тромбон

13. trumpet / horn
труба / рожок

14. tuba
туба

15. French horn
валторна

16. piano
пианино

17. xylophone
ксилофон

18. drums
ударные инструменты

19. tambourine
тамбурин

20. electric keyboard
электрическая клавиатура

21. accordion
аккордеон

22. organ
орган

1. art
искусство

2. business education
бизнес

3. chorus
хоровое пение / хор

4. computer science
компьютерные науки

5. driver's education
вождение автомобиля

6. economics
экономика

7. English as a second language
английский как второй язык

8. foreign language
иностранный язык

9. home economics
домоводство

10. industrial arts / shop
промышленные
искусства / мастерская

11. PE (physical education)
физкультура

12. theater arts
театральное искусство

More vocabulary

core course: a subject students have to take
elective: a subject students choose to take

Share your answers.

1. What are your favorite subjects?

2. In your opinion, what subjects are most important? Why?

3. What foreign languages are taught in your school?

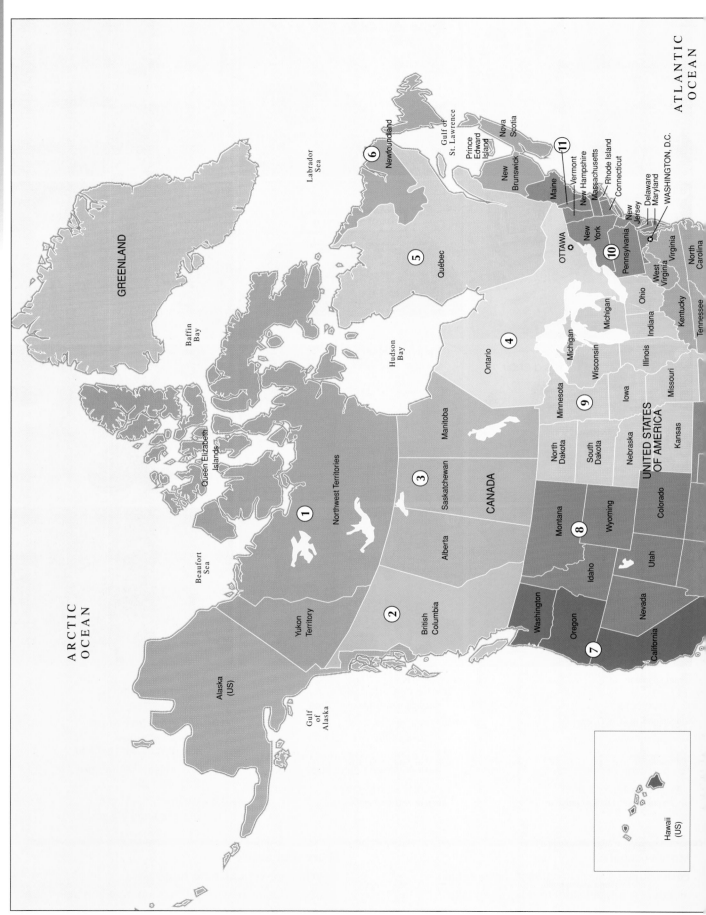

ARCTIC OCEAN

ATLANTIC OCEAN

GREENLAND

Labrador Sea

Baffin Bay

Hudson Bay

Beaufort Sea

Queen Elizabeth Islands

Newfoundland

Gulf of St. Lawrence

Prince Edward Island

Nova Scotia

New Brunswick

Maine

Vermont

New Hampshire

Massachusetts

Rhode Island

Connecticut

New Jersey

Delaware

Maryland

WASHINGTON, D.C.

Virginia

West Virginia

North Carolina

Pennsylvania

New York

OTTAWA

Québec

Ontario

Michigan

Michigan

Wisconsin

Ohio

Indiana

Kentucky

Tennessee

Illinois

Missouri

Iowa

Minnesota

North Dakota

South Dakota

Nebraska

Kansas

UNITED STATES OF AMERICA

Manitoba

Saskatchewan

Alberta

CANADA

British Columbia

Northwest Territories

Yukon Territory

Alaska (US)

Gulf of Alaska

Montana

Wyoming

Colorado

Idaho

Utah

Nevada

California

Washington

Oregon

Hawaii (US)

① ② ③ ④ ⑤ ⑥ ⑦ ⑧ ⑨ ⑩ ⑪

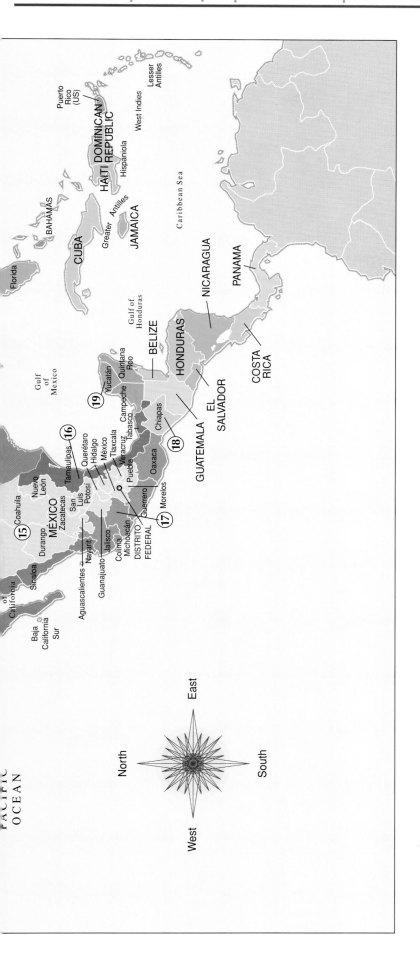

North

East

South

West

PACIFIC
OCEAN

Gulf
of
Mexico

Gulf of
Honduras

Caribbean Sea

Florida

BAHAMAS

CUBA

Greater Antilles

JAMAICA

HAITI

DOMINICAN REPUBLIC

Hispaniola

Puerto Rico (US)

West Indies

Lesser Antilles

BELIZE

HONDURAS

GUATEMALA

EL SALVADOR

NICARAGUA

COSTA RICA

PANAMA

Yucatán

Quintana Roo

Campeche

Tabasco

Chiapas

⑲

⑯

⑱

⑰

⑮

MÉXICO

Tamaulipas

Nuevo León

Coahuila

Zacatecas

San Luis Potosí

Querétaro

Hidalgo

México

Tlaxcala

Veracruz

Puebla

Oaxaca

Guerrero

Morelos

Durango

Sinaloa

Nayarit

Jalisco

Colima

Michoacán

DISTRITO FEDERAL

Aguascalientes

Guanajuato

Baja California Sur

Gulf of California

Regions of Canada
Регионы Канады

1. Northern Canada
Северная Канада

2. British Columbia
Британская Колумбия

3. The Prairie Provinces
Прерии

4. Ontario
Онтарио

5. Québec
Квебек

6. The Atlantic Provinces
Провинции побережья
Атлантического океана

Regions of the United States
Регионы Соединённых Штатов

7. The Pacific States/the West Coast
Тихоокеанские штаты / Западное побережье

8. The Rocky Mountain States
Штаты, расположенные на Скалистых горах

9. The Midwest
Средний Запад

10. The Mid-Atlantic States
Среднеатлантические штаты

11. New England
Новая Англия

12. The Southwest
Юго-Запад

13. The Southeast/the South
Юго-Восток / Юг

Regions of Mexico
Регионы Мексики

14. The Pacific Northwest
Тихоокеанский Северо-Запад

15. The Plateau of Mexico
Мексиканское плоскогорье

16. The Gulf Coastal Plain
Прибрежная равнина вдоль
Мексиканского залива

17. The Southern Uplands
Южная возвышенность

18. The Chiapas Highlands
Нагорье Чьяпас

19. The Yucatan Peninsula
Полуостров Юкатан

123

The World   Мир

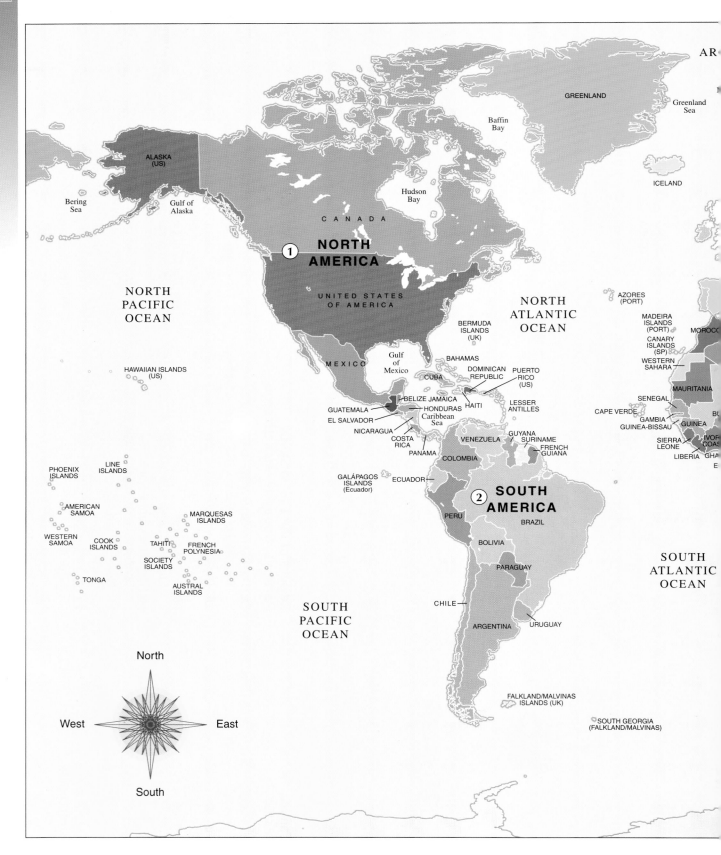

Continents
Континенты

1. North America
Северная Америка

2. South America
Южная Африка

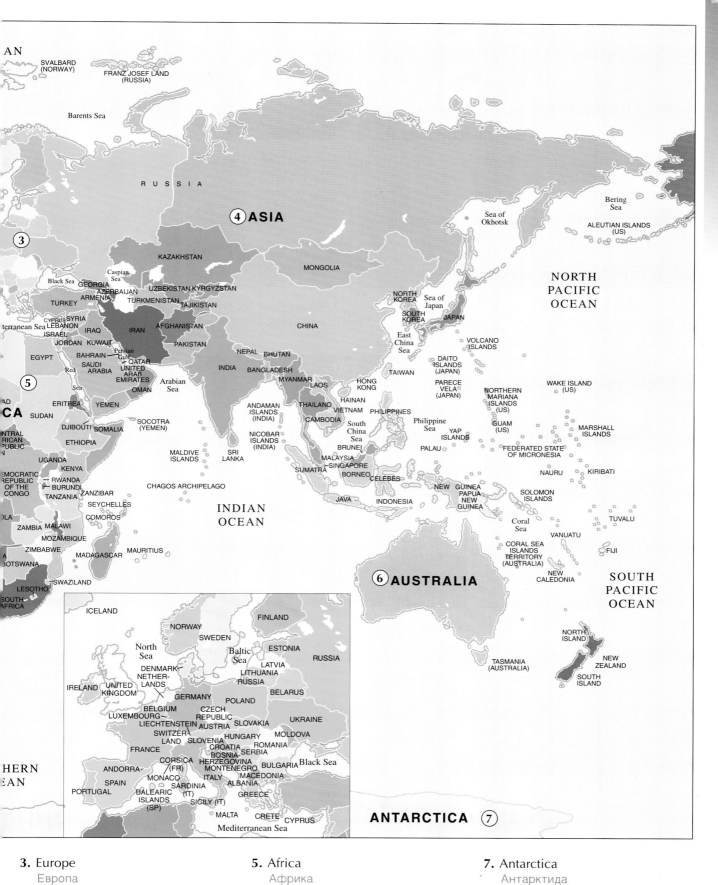

SVALBARD
(NORWAY)

FRANZ JOSEF LAND
(RUSSIA)

Barents Sea

R U S S I A

③

④ASIA

KAZAKHSTAN

MONGOLIA

Bering
Sea

ALEUTIAN ISLANDS
(US)

Sea of
Okhotsk

Caspian
Sea

Black Sea GEORGIA

AZERBAIJAN

ARMENIA

TURKEY

UZBEKISTAN KYRGYZSTAN

TURKMENISTAN

TAJIKISTAN

NORTH
KOREA

SOUTH
KOREA

Sea of
Japan

JAPAN

NORTH
PACIFIC
OCEAN

CYPRUS SYRIA

terranean Sea LEBANON

ISRAEL

JORDAN KUWAIT

IRAQ

IRAN

AFGHANISTAN

CHINA

East
China
Sea

TAIWAN

VOLCANO
ISLANDS

WAKE ISLAND
(US)

EGYPT

BAHRAIN

Persian
Gulf

QATAR

SAUDI
ARABIA

UNITED
ARAB
EMIRATES

OMAN

PAKISTAN

NEPAL BHUTAN

DAITO
ISLANDS
(JAPAN)

Red
Sea

⑤

Arabian
Sea

INDIA

BANGLADESH

MYANMAR

LAOS

HONG
KONG

HAINAN

PARECE
VELA
(JAPAN)

NORTHERN
MARIANA
ISLANDS
(US)

CA

ERITREA YEMEN

SUDAN

SOCOTRA
(YEMEN)

MALDIVE
ISLANDS

ANDAMAN
ISLANDS
(INDIA)

SRI
LANKA

THAILAND

VIETNAM

CAMBODIA

PHILIPPINES

South
China
Sea

Philippine
Sea

YAP
ISLANDS

GUAM
(US)

MARSHALL
ISLANDS

NTRAL
RICAN
N

DJIBOUTI SOMALIA

ETHIOPIA

NICOBAR
ISLANDS
(INDIA)

BRUNEI

MALAYSIA

PALAU

FEDERATED STATE
OF MICRONESIA

UGANDA

KENYA

EMOCRATIC
REPUBLIC
OF THE
CONGO

RWANDA

BURUNDI

TANZANIA

ZANZIBAR

SEYCHELLES

CHAGOS ARCHIPELAGO

SUMATRA

SINGAPORE

BORNEO

CELEBES

JAVA

INDONESIA

NEW GUINEA

PAPUA
NEW
GUINEA

NAURU KIRIBATI

SOLOMON
ISLANDS

LA

ZAMBIA MALAWI

MOZAMBIQUE

A

ZIMBABWE

BOTSWANA

MADAGASCAR

COMOROS

MAURITIUS

INDIAN
OCEAN

Coral
Sea

VANUATU

TUVALU

FIJI

CORAL SEA
ISLANDS
TERRITORY
(AUSTRALIA)

SOUTH
PACIFIC
OCEAN

LESOTHO

SWAZILAND

SOUTH
AFRICA

⑥AUSTRALIA

NEW
CALEDONIA

ICELAND

NORWAY

FINLAND

North
Sea

SWEDEN

Baltic
Sea

ESTONIA

LATVIA

RUSSIA

TASMANIA
(AUSTRALIA)

NORTH
ISLAND

NEW
ZEALAND

SOUTH
ISLAND

IRELAND

UNITED
KINGDOM

DENMARK

NETHER-
LANDS

LITHUANIA

RUSSIA

BELARUS

GERMANY

POLAND

BELGIUM

LUXEMBOURG

LIECHTENSTEIN

CZECH
REPUBLIC

AUSTRIA

SLOVAKIA

UKRAINE

SWITZER-
LAND

SLOVENIA

HUNGARY

MOLDOVA

FRANCE

CROATIA

BOSNIA
HERZEGOVINA

SERBIA

ROMANIA

ANDORRA

CORSICA
(FR)

MONTENEGRO

BULGARIA Black Sea

SPAIN

MONACO

ITALY

MACEDONIA

ALBANIA

PORTUGAL

BALEARIC
ISLANDS
(SP)

SARDINIA
(IT)

SICILY (IT)

GREECE

MALTA

CRETE

CYPRUS

Mediterranean Sea

HERN
AN

ANTARCTICA ⑦

3. Europe
Европа

5. Africa
Африка

7. Antarctica
Антарктида

4. Asia
Азия

6. Australia
Австралия

Energy and the Environment   Энергия и окружающая среда

Energy resources   Энергетические ресурсы

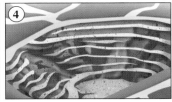

1. solar energy
солнечная энергия

2. wind
ветер

3. natural gas
природный газ

4. coal
уголь

5. hydroelectric power
гидроэлектроэнергия

6. oil/petroleum
нефть

7. geothermal energy
геотермическая
энергия

8. nuclear energy
атомная энергия

Pollution   Загрязнение окружающей среды

9. hazardous waste
опасные отходы

10. air pollution/smog
загрязнение
воздуха/смог

11. acid rain
кислотный дождь

12. water pollution
загрязнение воды

13. radiation
радиация

14. pesticide poisoning
отравление пестицидами

15. oil spill
разлив нефти

Conservation   Экономия энергии

A. recycle
рециркулировать

B. save water/**conserve** water
экономить/рационально
использовать воду

C. save energy/**conserve** energy
экономить/рационально
использовать энергию

Share your answers.

1. How do you heat your home?

2. Do you have a gas stove or an electric stove?

3. What are some ways you can save energy when it's cold?

4. Do you recycle? What products do you recycle?

5. Does your market have recycling bins?

The Solar System

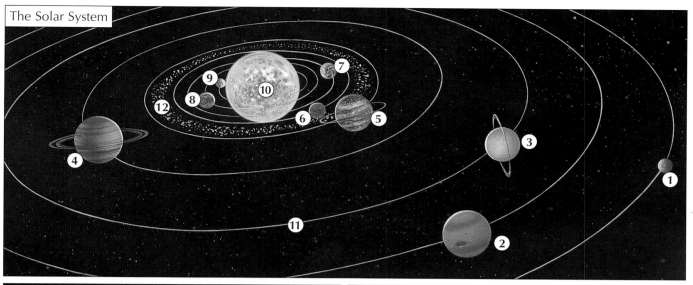

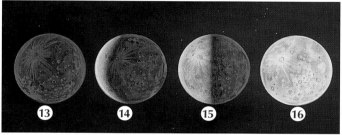

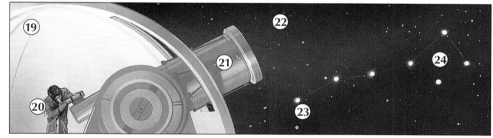

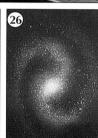

The planets
Планеты

1. Pluto
Плутон

2. Neptune
Нептун

3. Uranus
Уран

4. Saturn
Сатурн

5. Jupiter
Юпитер

6. Mars
Марс

7. Earth
Земля

8. Venus
Венера

9. Mercury
Меркурий

10. sun
солнце

11. orbit
орбита

12. asteroid belt
пояс астероидов

13. new moon
новолуние

14. crescent moon
месяц

15. quarter moon
четверть луны

16. full moon
полнолуние

17. astronaut
астронавт

18. space station
космическая станция

19. observatory
обсерватория

20. astronomer
астроном

21. telescope
телескоп

22. space
космос

23. star
звезда

24. constellation
созвездие

25. comet
комета

26. galaxy
галактика

More vocabulary

lunar eclipse: when the earth is between the sun and the moon

solar eclipse: when the moon is between the earth and the sun

Share your answers.

1. Do you know the names of any constellations?

2. How do you feel when you look up at the night sky?

3. Is the night sky in the U.S. the same as in your country?

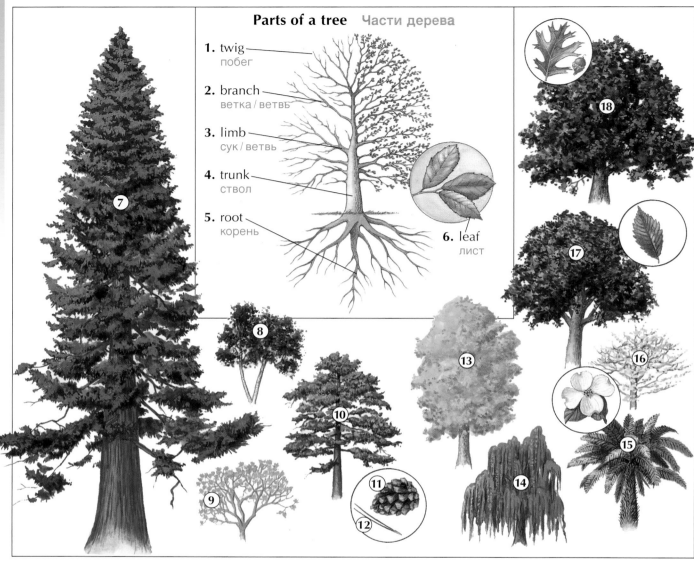

Parts of a tree Части дерева

1. twig
   побег
2. branch
   ветка / ветвь
3. limb
   сук / ветвь
4. trunk
   ствол
5. root
   корень
6. leaf
   лист

7. redwood секвойя	10. pine сосна	13. maple клён	16. dogwood кизил
8. birch берёза	11. pinecone сосновая шишка	14. willow ива	17. elm вяз
9. magnolia магнолия	12. needle иголка	15. palm пальма	18. oak дуб

Plants Растения

19. holly падуб / остролист	21. cactus кактус	23. poison oak сумах укореняющийся	25. poison ivy сумах укореняющийся
20. berries ягоды	22. vine вьющиеся растения	24. poison sumac сумах лаковый	

Parts of a flower

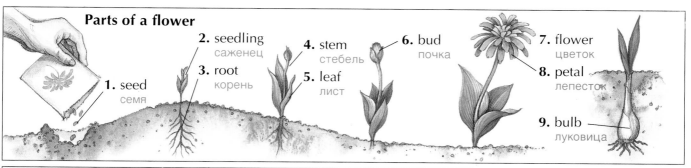

1. seed / семя
2. seedling / саженец
3. root / корень
4. stem / стебель
5. leaf / лист
6. bud / почка
7. flower / цветок
8. petal / лепесток
9. bulb / луковица

10. sunflower / подсолнух
11. tulip / тюльпан
12. hibiscus / гибискус
13. marigold / календула
14. daisy / маргаритка
15. rose / роза
16. gardenia / гардения
17. orchid / орхидея
18. carnation / гвоздика
19. chrysanthemum / хризантема
20. iris / ирис
21. jasmine / жасмин
22. violet / фиалка
23. poinsettia / молочай красивейший
24. lily / лилия
25. crocus / крокус
26. daffodil / нарцисс
27. bouquet / букет
28. thorn / шип
29. houseplant / комнатный цветок

Marine Life, Amphibians, and Reptiles

Морская фауна, амфибии и пресмыкающиеся

Parts of a fish Части рыбы   **Sea animals** Морские животные

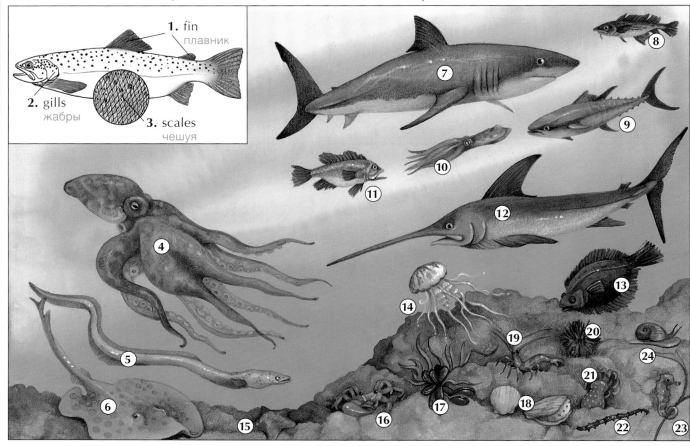

1. fin
   плавник
2. gills
   жабры
3. scales
   чешуя

4. octopus
осьминог

5. eel
угорь

6. ray
скат

7. shark
акула

8. cod
треска

9. tuna
тунец

10. squid
кальмар

11. bass
окунь

12. swordfish
рыба-меч

13. flounder
камбала

14. jellyfish
медуза

15. starfish
морская звезда

16. crab
краб

17. mussel
мидия

18. scallop
морской гребешок

19. shrimp
креветка

20. sea urchin
морской ёж

21. sea anemone
актиния

22. worm
червяк

23. sea horse
морской конёк

24. snail
улитка

Amphibians   Амфибии

25. frog
лягушка

26. newt
тритон

27. salamander
саламандра

28. toad
жаба

Sea mammals   Морские млекопитающие

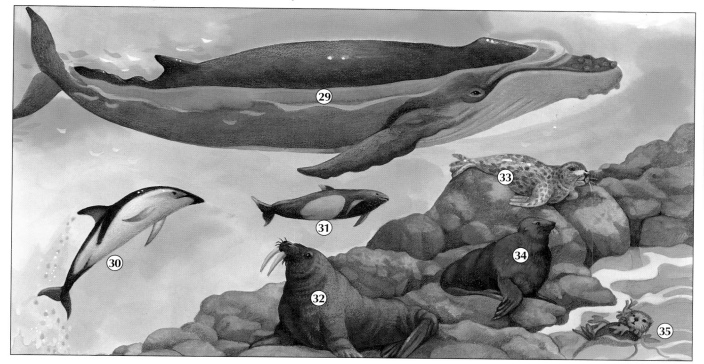

29. whale
кит

30. dolphin
дельфин

31. porpoise
морская свинья

32. walrus
морж

33. seal
тюлень

34. sea lion
морской лев

35. otter
выдра

Reptiles   Пресмыкающиеся

36. alligator
аллигатор

37. crocodile
крокодил

38. rattlesnake
гремучая змея

39. garter snake
уж

40. cobra
кобра

41. lizard
ящерица

42. turtle
черепаха

Birds, Insects, and Arachnids Птицы, насекомые и паукообразные

Parts of a bird Части птицы

1. beak/bill
клюв
2. wing
крыло
3. nest
гнездо
4. claw
коготь
5. feather
перо

6. owl сова	**9.** woodpecker дятел	**12.** penguin пингвин	**15.** peacock павлин
7. blue jay голубая сойка	**10.** eagle орёл	**13.** duck утка	**16.** pigeon голубь
8. sparrow воробей	**11.** hummingbird колибри	**14.** goose гусь	**17.** robin дрозд

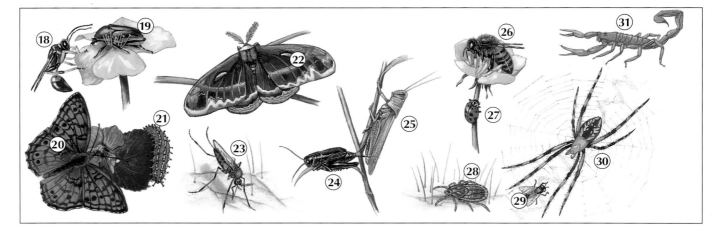

18. wasp оса	**22.** moth моль	**26.** honeybee медоносная пчела	**30.** spider паук
19. beetle жук	**23.** mosquito комар	**27.** ladybug божья коровка	**31.** scorpion скорпион
20. butterfly бабочка	**24.** cricket сверчок	**28.** tick клещ	
21. caterpillar гусеница	**25.** grasshopper кузнечик	**29.** fly муха	

Farm animals Сельскохозяйственные животные

1. goat
коза

2. donkey
осёл

3. cow
корова

4. horse
лошадь

5. hen
курица

6. rooster
петух

7. sheep
овца

8. pig
свинья

Pets Домашние животные

9. cat
кот / кошка

10. kitten
котёнок

11. dog
собака

12. puppy
щенок

13. rabbit
кролик

14. guinea pig
морская свинка

15. parakeet
попугай

16. goldfish
золотая рыбка

Saint Benedict
A Catholic Voluntary Academy
Duffield Road, Darley Abbey
Derby
DE22 1JD

Rodents Грызуны

17. mouse
мышь

18. rat
крыса

19. gopher
суслик

20. chipmunk
бурундук

21. squirrel
белка

22. prairie dog
луговая собачка

More vocabulary

Wild animals live, eat, and raise their young away from people, in the forests, mountains, plains, etc.

Domesticated animals work for people or live with them.

Share your answers.

1. Do you have any pets? any farm animals?

2. Which of these animals are in your neighborhood? Which are not?

Mammals   Млекопитающие

1. moose
лось

2. mountain lion
пума

3. coyote
койот

4. opossum
опоссум

5. wolf
волк

6. buffalo / bison
буйвол / бизон

7. bat
летучая мышь

8. armadillo
броненосец

9. beaver
бобр

10. porcupine
дикобраз

11. bear
медведь

12. skunk
скунс

13. raccoon
енот

14. deer
олень

15. fox
лиса

16. antler
олений рог

17. hoof
копыто

18. whiskers
усы

19. coat / fur
шерсть / мех

20. paw
лапа

21. horn
рог

22. tail
хвост

23. quill
игла

134

24. anteater муравьед	**30.** gorilla горилла	**36.** lion лев	**42.** elephant слон
25. leopard леопард	**31.** hyena гиена	**37.** tiger тигр	**43.** hippopotamus гиппопотам / бегемот
26. llama лама	**32.** baboon бабуин	**38.** camel верблюд	**44.** kangaroo кенгуру
27. monkey обезьяна	**33.** giraffe жираф	**39.** panther пантера	**45.** koala коала
28. chimpanzee шимпанзе	**34.** zebra зебра	**40.** orangutan орангутан	**46.** platypus утконос
29. rhinoceros носорог	**35.** antelope антилопа	**41.** panda панда	

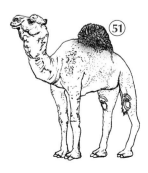

47. trunk туловище	**48.** tusk клык / бивень	**49.** mane грива	**50.** pouch сумка

51. hump
горб

Jobs and Occupations, A–H   Должности и профессии

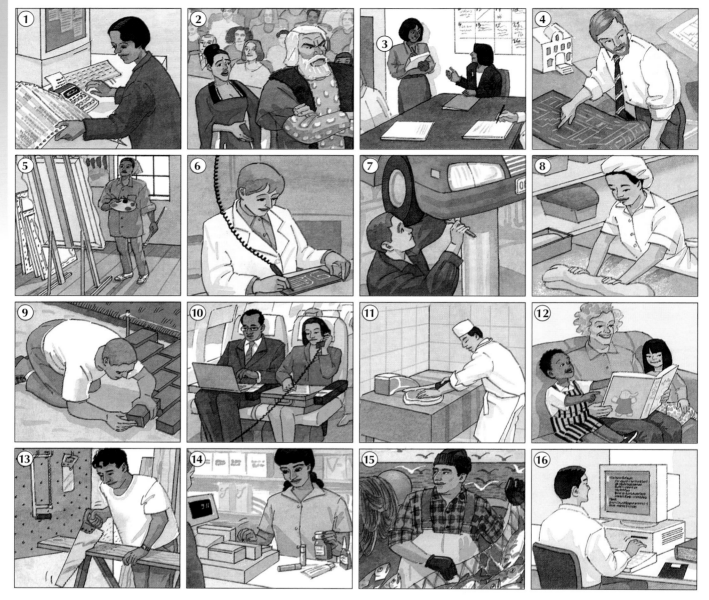

1. **accountant**
бухгалтер

2. **actor**
актёр

3. **administrative assistant**
помощник менеджера

4. **architect**
архитектор

5. **artist**
художник

6. **assembler**
сборщик

7. **auto mechanic**
автомеханик

8. **baker**
пекарь

9. **bricklayer**
каменщик

10. **businessman/businesswoman**
бизнесмен / деловая женщина

11. **butcher**
мясник

12. **caregiver/baby-sitter**
няня

13. **carpenter**
плотник

14. **cashier**
кассир

15. **commercial fisher**
рыбак

16. **computer programmer**
программист

Use the new language.

1. Who works outside?
2. Who works inside?
3. Who makes things?
4. Who uses a computer?
5. Who wears a uniform?
6. Who sells things?

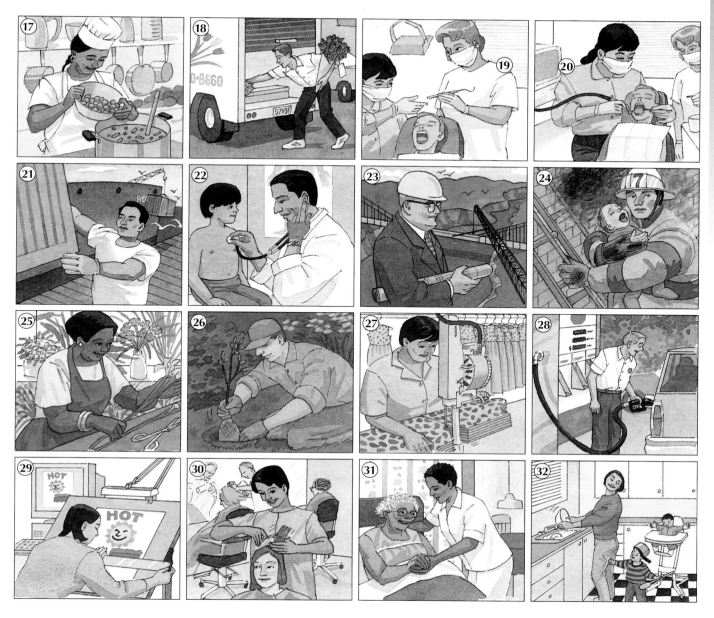

17. **cook**
повар

18. **delivery person**
разносчик / доставщик

19. **dental assistant**
ассистент дантиста / зубного
врача

20. **dentist**
дантист / зубной врач

21. **dockworker**
портовый рабочий

22. **doctor**
врач / доктор

23. **engineer**
инженер

24. **firefighter**
пожарник

25. **florist**
торговец цветами / цветочник

26. **gardener**
садовник

27. **garment worker**
швея

28. **gas station attendant**
работник заправочной станции

29. **graphic artist**
художник-график

30. **hairdresser**
парикмахер

31. **home attendant**
горничная

32. **homemaker**
домохозяйка

Share your answers.

1. Do you know people who have some of these jobs?
What do they say about their work?

2. Which of these jobs are available in your city?

3. For which of these jobs do you need special training?

33. housekeeper
экономка

34. interpreter/translator
переводчик

35. janitor/custodian
уборщик/дворник

36. lawyer
юрист

37. machine operator
рабочий-станочник

38. messenger/courier
посыльный/курьер

39. model
модель

40. mover
перевозчик

41. musician
музыкант

42. nurse
медсестра

43. painter
художник-живописец

44. police officer
полицейский

45. postal worker
почтальон

46. printer
печатник/работник типографии

47. receptionist
секретарь в приёмной/
регистратор

48. repair person
работник ремонтной мастерской

Talk about each of the jobs or occupations.

She's a housekeeper. She works in a hotel.
He's an interpreter. He works for the government.

She's a nurse. She works with patients.

49. reporter
репортёр

50. salesclerk / salesperson
продавец

51. sanitation worker
санитар

52. secretary
секретарь

53. server
подавальщик

54. serviceman / servicewoman
военнослужащий /
военнослужащая

55. stock clerk
работник фондовой биржи

56. store owner
владелец магазина

57. student
студент

58. teacher / instructor
учитель / преподаватель

59. telemarketer
работник телемаркетинга

60. travel agent
агент бюро путешествий

61. truck driver
водитель грузовика

62. veterinarian
ветеринар

63. welder
сварщик

64. writer / author
писатель / автор

Talk about your job or the job you want.

What do you do?

　I'm a salesclerk. I work in a store.

What do you want to do?

　I want to be a veterinarian. I want to work with animals.

A. **assemble** components
собирать детали

B. **assist** medical patients
помогать пациентам

C. **cook**
готовить

D. **do** manual labor
заниматься ручным трудом

E. **drive** a truck
водить машину

F. **operate** heavy machinery
управлять тяжёлым
оборудованием

G. **repair** appliances
чинить приборы

H. **sell** cars
продавать автомобили

I. **sew** clothes
шить одежду

J. **speak** another language
говорить на другом языке

K. **supervise** people
руководить людьми

L. **take care** of children
смотреть за детьми

M. **type**
печатать

N. **use** a cash register
работать в кассе

O. **wait on** customers
обслуживать посетителей

P. **work** on a computer
работать на компьютере

More vocabulary

act: to perform in a play, movie, or TV show

fly: to pilot an airplane

teach: to instruct, to show how to do something

Share your answers.

1. What job skills do you have? Where did you learn them?

2. What job skills do you want to learn?

A. talk to friends
говорить с друзьями

B. look at a job board
просматривать объявления о работе

C. look for a help wanted sign
искать объявления о предложении работы

D. look in the classifieds
просматривать раздел объявлений

E. call for information
обращаться за справкой по телефону

F. ask about the hours
спрашивать о рабочих часах

G. fill out an application
заполнять заявление

H. go on an interview
идти на собеседование

I. talk about your experience
рассказывать о своём опыте

J. ask about benefits
спрашивать о льготах

K. inquire about the salary
спрашивать о зарплате

L. get hired
устроиться на работу

141

1. **desk**
   письменный стол

2. **typewriter**
   пишущая машинка

3. **secretary**
   секретарь

4. **microcassette transcriber**
   микрокассетный аппарат для
   транскрибирования

5. **stacking tray**
   поднос для бумаг

6. **desk calendar**
   настольный календарь

7. **desk pad**
   подстилка на стол

8. **calculator**
   калькулятор

9. **electric pencil sharpener**
   электрическая точилка для
   карандашей

10. **file cabinet**
    шкаф-картотека

11. **file folder**
    папка

12. **file clerk**
    клерк по обслуживанию
    картотеки

13. **supply cabinet**
    шкаф для канцелярских
    принадлежностей

14. **photocopier**
    копировальная машина

A. **take** a message
   принять сообщение

B. **fax** a letter
   отправить письмо **по факсу**

C. **transcribe** notes
   транскрибировать заметки

D. **type** a letter
   печатать письмо

E. **make** copies
   делать копии

F. **collate** papers
   комплектовать листы

G. **staple**
   скреплять

H. **file** papers
   подшивать документы

Practice taking messages.

Hello. My name is <u>Sara Scott</u>. Is <u>Mr. Lee</u> in?

   Not yet. Would you like to leave a message?

Yes. Please ask <u>him</u> to call me at <u>555-4859</u>.

Share your answers.

1. Which office equipment do you know how to use?

2. Which jobs does a file clerk do?

3. Which jobs does a secretary do?

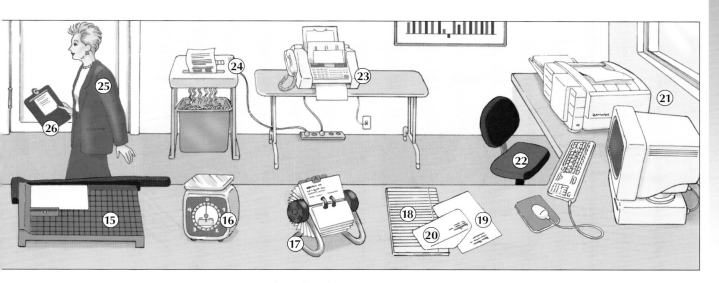

15. paper cutter
бумагорезатель

16. postal scale
почтовые весы

17. rotary card file
роторная настольная картотека

18. legal pad
бумага формата 35 на 42 см

19. letterhead paper
печатный фирменный бланк

20. envelope
конверт

21. computer workstation
компьютерная рабочая станция

22. swivel chair
вращающийся стул

23. fax machine
факс

24. paper shredder
бумагорежущая машина

25. office manager
менеджер офиса

26. clipboard
подставка для письма с зажимом

27. appointment book
журнал регистрации
посетителей

28. stapler
скобкосшиватель

29. staple
скобка

30. organizer
записная книжка

31. typewriter cartridge
кассета для пишущей
машинки

32. mailer
упаковочная коробка /
рекламная брошюра

33. correction fluid
жидкость для
исправления опечаток

34. Post-it notes
самоклеющаяся бумага
для заметок

35. label
наклейка с адресом

36. notepad
блокнот

37. glue
клей

38. rubber cement
резиновый клей

39. clear tape
прозрачная клейкая
лента

40. rubber stamp
резиновый штемпель

41. ink pad
штемпельная
подушечка

42. packing tape
упаковочная лента

43. pushpin
кнопка

44. paper clip
скрепка

45. rubber band
резинка

Use the new language.

1. Which items keep things together?

2. Which items are used to mail packages?

3. Which items are made of paper?

Share your answers.

1. Which office supplies do students use?

2. Where can you buy them?

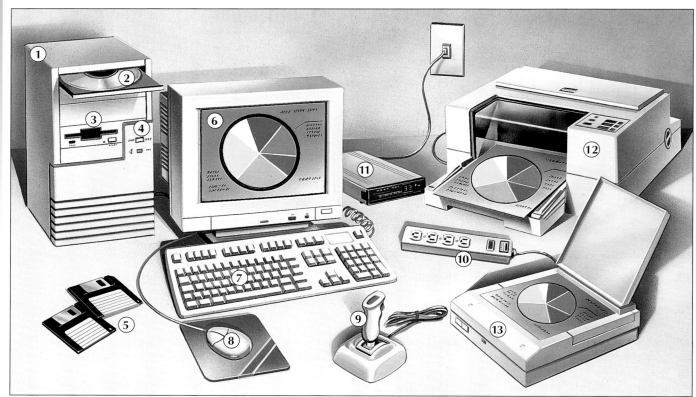

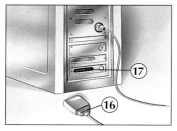

Hardware
Технические средства

1. CPU (central processing unit)
   ЦПУ (центральный процессор)

2. CD-ROM disc
   диск CD ROM

3. disk drive
   дисковод

4. power switch
   выключатель

5. disk / floppy
   гибкий диск / дискета

6. monitor / screen
   монитор / экран

7. keyboard
   клавиатура

8. mouse
   мышь

9. joystick
   джойстик

10. surge protector
    разрядник для защиты от перенапряжения

11. modem
    модем

12. printer
    принтер

13. scanner
    сканирующее устройство / сканер

14. laptop
    портативный компьютер

15. trackball
    шар трассировки

16. cable
    кабель / шнур

17. port
    порт

18. motherboard
    материнская плата

19. slot
    позиция

20. hard disk drive
    дисковод жёсткого диска

Software
программное обеспечение

21. program / application
    программа / прикладная программа

22. user's manual
    руководство пользователя

More vocabulary

data: information that a computer can read

memory: how much data a computer can hold

speed: how fast a computer can work with data

Share your answers.

1. Can you use a computer?

2. How did you learn? in school? from a book? by yourself?

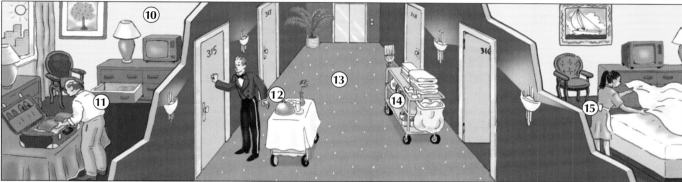

1. valet parking
служба парковки

2. doorman
швейцар

3. lobby
вестибюль

4. bell captain
старший коридорный

5. bellhop
коридорный

6. luggage cart
багажная тележка

7. gift shop
сувенирный магазин

8. front desk
стойка портье

9. desk clerk
портье

10. guest room
номер

11. guest
постоялец

12. room service
обслуживание в номере

13. hall
коридор

14. housekeeping cart
тележка горничной

15. housekeeper
горничная

16. pool
бассейн

17. pool service
обслуживание бассейна

18. ice machine
автомат со льдом

19. meeting room
конференц-зал

20. ballroom
бальный зал / танцевальный зал

More vocabulary

concierge: the hotel worker who helps guests find restaurants and interesting places to go

service elevator: an elevator for hotel workers

Share your answers.

1. Does this look like a hotel in your city? Which one?

2. Which hotel job is the most difficult?

3. How much does it cost to stay in a hotel in your city?

1. **front office**
   приёмная

2. **factory owner**
   владелец завода

3. **designer**
   проектировщик / конструктор

4. **time clock**
   табельные часы

5. **line supervisor**
   управляющий линией

6. **factory worker**
   рабочий завода

7. **parts**
   детали

8. **assembly line**
   сборочная линия

9. **warehouse**
   склад

10. **order puller**
    укладчик

11. **hand truck**
    ручная тележка

12. **conveyor belt**
    конвейерная лента / конвейер

13. **packer**
    упаковщик

14. **forklift**
    вилопогрузчик

15. **shipping clerk**
    заведующий отправкой

16. **loading dock**
    погрузочная платформа

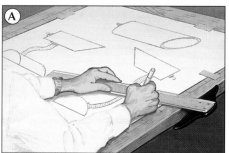

A. design
проектировать

B. manufacture
изготавливать / производить

C. ship
отправлять

  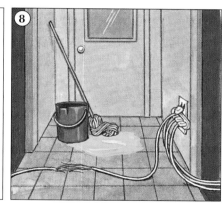

1. electrical hazard
осторожно, ток

2. flammable
огнеопасно

3. poison
яд

4. corrosive
корродирующее вещество

5. biohazard
биологически опасно

6. radioactive
радиоактивность

7. hazardous materials
опасные материалы

8. dangerous situation
опасная ситуация

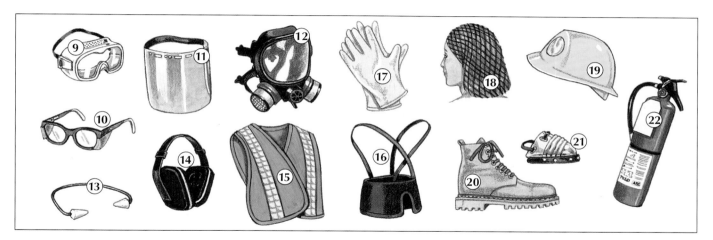

9. safety goggles
защитные очки

10. safety glasses
защитные очки

11. safety visor
защитный козырёк

12. respirator
респиратор

13. earplugs
ушные вкладыши

14. safety earmuffs
защитные наушники

15. safety vest
защитный жилет

16. back support
пояс

17. latex gloves
резиновые перчатки

18. hair net
сетка для волос

19. hard hat
каска

20. safety boot
защитный ботинок

21. toe guard
защитная вставка для пальцев ног

22. fire extinguisher
огнетушитель

23. careless
неосторожно

24. careful
осторожно

Crops Сельскохозяйственные культуры

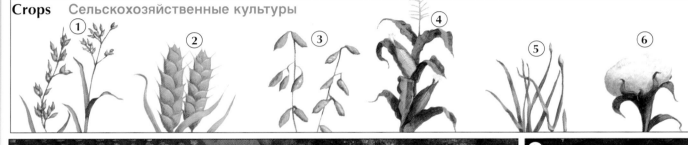

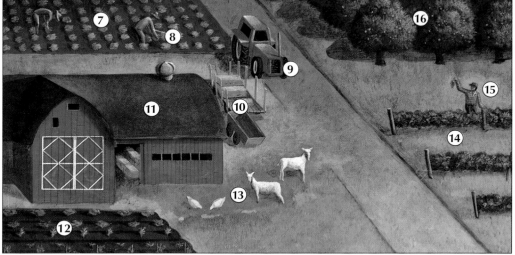

1. **rice**
   рис

2. **wheat**
   пшеница

3. **soybeans**
   соевые бобы

4. **corn**
   кукуруза

5. **alfalfa**
   люцерна

6. **cotton**
   хлопок

7. **field**
   поле

8. **farmworker**
   сельскохозяйственный
   рабочий

9. **tractor**
   трактор

10. **farm equipment**
    сельскохозяйственное
    оборудование

11. **barn**
    амбар

12. **vegetable garden**
    огород

13. **livestock**
    скот

14. **vineyard**
    виноградник

15. **farmer / grower**
    фермер

16. **orchard**
    фруктовый сад

17. **corral**
    загон

18. **hay**
    сено

19. **fence**
    ограда / забор

20. **hired hand**
    наёмный работник

21. **steers / cattle**
    волы / скот

22. **rancher**
    хозяин ранчо

A. **plant**
   сажать

B. **harvest**
   собирать урожай

C. **milk**
   доить

D. **feed**
   кормить

1. construction worker
строитель

2. ladder
стремянка

3. I beam/girder
балка / брус

4. scaffolding
строительные леса

5. cherry picker
кран-балка

6. bulldozer
бульдозер

7. crane
кран

8. backhoe
экскаватор

9. jackhammer/pneumatic drill
пневматический бурильный
молоток / пневматическая дрель

10. concrete
бетон

11. bricks
кирпичи

12. trowel
мастерок

13. insulation
изоляция

14. stucco
штукатурка

15. window pane
оконное стекло

16. plywood
фанера

17. wood/lumber
дерево / пиломатериал

18. drywall
сухая штукатурка

19. shingles
черепица

20. pickax
кирка

21. shovel
лопата

22. sledgehammer
кувалда / молот

A. **paint**
красить

B. **lay** bricks
класть кирпичи

C. **measure**
мерить / измерять

D. **hammer**
забивать

Tools and Building Supplies Инструменты и стройматериалы

1. hammer
молоток

2. mallet
деревянный / резиновый молоток

3. ax
топор

4. handsaw
ручная пила

5. hacksaw
ножовка

6. C-clamp
С-образная струбцина

7. pliers
плоскогубцы

8. electric drill
электродрель

9. power sander
шлифовальный станок с электроприводом

10. circular saw
циркулярная пила

11. blade
лезвие

12. router
фасонно-фрезерный станок

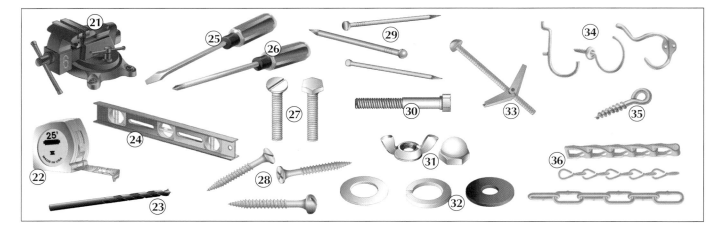

21. vise
тиски

22. tape measure
рулетка

23. drill bit
сверло

24. level
ватерпас

25. screwdriver
отвёртка

26. Phillips screwdriver
крестовая отвёртка

27. machine screw
мелкий крепёжный винт

28. wood screw
шуруп

29. nail
гвоздь

30. bolt
болт

31. nut
гайка

32. washer
шайба

33. toggle bolt
шарнирный болт

34. hook
крюк

35. eye hook
крюк с проушиной

36. chain
цепь

Use the new language.

1. Which tools are used for plumbing?

2. Which tools are used for painting?

3. Which tools are used for electrical work?

4. Which tools are used for working with wood?

13. wire
провод

14. extension cord
удлинитель

15. yardstick
деревянный метр

16. pipe
труба

17. fittings
арматура

18. wood
дерево

19. spray gun
краскопульт

20. paint
краска

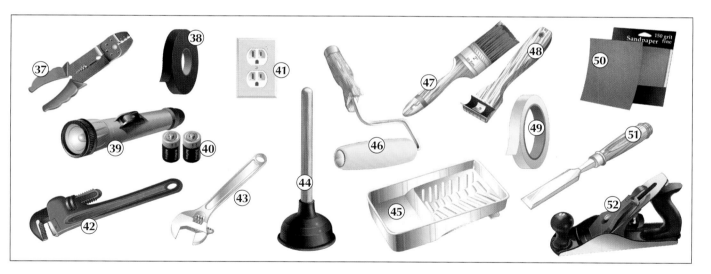

37. wire stripper
клещи для удаления
изоляции

38. electrical tape
изоляционная лента

39. flashlight
фонарик

40. battery
батарея / батарейка

41. outlet
розетка

42. pipe wrench
разводной ключ

43. wrench
гаечный ключ

44. plunger
вантуз

45. paint pan
лоток для краски

46. paint roller
валик для краски

47. paintbrush
кисть для краски

48. scraper
скребок

49. masking tape
маскировочная липкая
лента

50. sandpaper
наждачная бумага

51. chisel
долото

52. plane
рубанок

Use the new language.

Look at **Household Problems and Repairs,**
pages **48–49.**

Name the tools you use to fix the problems you see.

Share your answers.

1. Which tools do you have in your home?

2. Which tools can be dangerous to use?

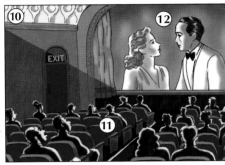

1. zoo
зоопарк

2. animals
животные

3. zookeeper
служитель зоопарка

4. botanical gardens
ботанический сад

5. greenhouse
оранжерея

6. gardener
садовник

7. art museum
художественный музей

8. painting
картина

9. sculpture
скульптура

10. the movies
кино

11. seat
место

12. screen
экран

13. amusement park
парк с аттракционами

14. puppet show
кукольный театр

15. roller coaster
американские горки

16. carnival
карнавал

17. rides
катание

18. game
игра

19. county fair
окружная ярмарка

20. first place/first prize
первое место/первый приз

21. exhibition
выставка

22. swap meet/flea market
толкучка/барахолка

23. booth
будка

24. merchandise
товар

25. baseball game
бейсбольный матч

26. stadium
стадион

27. announcer
диктор

Talk about the places you like to go.

I like <u>animals</u>, so I go to <u>the zoo</u>.

I like <u>rides</u>, so I go to <u>carnivals</u>.

Share your answers.

1. Which of these places is interesting to you?

2. Which rides do you like at an amusement park?

3. What are some famous places to go to in your country?

1. ball field
площадка для игры в мяч

2. bike path
велосипедная дорожка

3. cyclist
велосипедист

4. bicycle/bike
велосипед

5. jump rope
скакалка/прыгалки

6. duck pond
пруд с утками

7. tennis court
теннисный корт

8. picnic table
стол для пикника

9. tricycle
трёхколёсный велосипед

10. bench
скамейка

11. water fountain
фонтан

12. swings
качели

13. slide
горка

14. climbing apparatus
лестница для лазания

15. sandbox
песочница

16. seesaw
качалка

A. **pull** the wagon
тянуть тележку

B. **push** the swing
качать

C. **climb** on the bars
лазать по лестнице

D. **picnic/have** a picnic
устраивать пикник

153

1. camping
поход с ночёвкой

2. boating
катание на лодке

3. canoeing
гребля

4. rafting
катание на плоту / лодке

5. fishing
рыбная ловля

6. hiking
прогулка пешком

7. backpacking
поход

8. mountain biking
езда на велосипеде по горам

9. horseback riding
катание на лошадях

10. tent
палатка

11. campfire
костёр

12. sleeping bag
спальный мешок

13. foam pad
пенопластовая подстилка

14. life vest
спасательный жилет

15. backpack
рюкзак

16. camping stove
походная плита

17. fishing net
рыболовная сеть

18. fishing pole
удочка

19. rope
верёвка

20. multi-use knife
универсальный складной нож

21. matches
спички

22. lantern
фонарь

23. insect repellent
средство от насекомых

24. canteen
фляга

1. ocean/water
   океан/вода

2. fins
   ласты

3. diving mask
   водолазная маска

4. sailboat
   парусная лодка

5. surfboard
   доска для серфинга

6. wave
   волна

7. wet suit
   гидрокостюм

8. scuba tank
   акваланг

9. beach umbrella
   пляжный зонт

10. sand castle
    замок из песка

11. cooler
    переносной холодильник

12. shade
    тень

13. sunscreen/sunblock
    защитный крем от солнца

14. beach chair
    пляжное кресло

15. beach towel
    пляжное полотенце

16. pier
    пирс

17. sunbather
    загорающий/загорающая

18. lifeguard
    спасатель

19. lifesaving device
    спасательные принадлежности

20. lifeguard station
    спасательная станция

21. seashell
    морская раковина

22. pail/bucket
    ведро

23. sand
    песок

24. rock
    камень

More vocabulary

seaweed: a plant that grows in the ocean

tide: the level of the ocean. The tide goes in and out every twelve hours.

Share your answers.

1. Are there any beaches near your home?

2. Do you prefer to spend more time on the sand or in the water?

3. Where are some of the world's best beaches?

155

A. walk
ходить

B. jog
бегать трусцой

C. run
бегать / бежать

D. throw
бросать

E. catch
ловить

F. pitch
подавать

G. hit
ударять

H. pass
пасовать / передавать

I. shoot
посылать

J. jump
прыгать

K. dribble / bounce
вести / бить мячом о землю

L. kick
ударять ногой

M. tackle
перехватывать / останавливать

Practice talking about what you can do.

I can <u>swim</u>, but I can't <u>dive</u>.

I can <u>pass the ball</u> well, but I can't <u>shoot</u> too well.

Use the new language.

Look at **Individual Sports,** page **159.**

Name the actions you see people doing.

The man in number 18 is riding a horse.

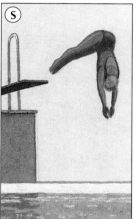
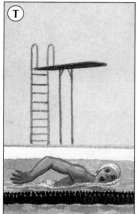

N. serve
подавать

O. swing
размахиваться

P. exercise/work out
тренироваться

Q. stretch
растягиваться

R. bend
нагибаться

S. dive
нырять

T. swim
плавать

U. ski
кататься на лыжах

V. skate
кататься на коньках

W. ride
ехать/ездить

X. start
стартовать

Y. race
участвовать в гонках

Z. finish
финишировать

Share your answers.

1. What do you like to do?
2. What do you have difficulty doing?
3. How often do you exercise? Once a week? Two or three times a week? More? Never?
4. Which is more difficult, throwing a ball or catching it?

1. score
счёт

2. coach
тренер

3. team
команда

4. fan
болельщик

5. player
игрок

6. official/referee
судья/рефери

7. basketball court
баскетбольная площадка

8. basketball
баскетбол

9. baseball
бейсбол

10. softball
софтбол

11. football
американский футбол

12. soccer
футбол

13. ice hockey
хоккей на льду

14. volleyball
волейбол

15. water polo
водное поло

More vocabulary

captain: the team leader

umpire: in baseball, the name for the referee

Little League: a baseball league for children

win: to have the best score

lose: the opposite of win

tie: to have the same score as the other team

1. archery
   стрельба из лука

2. billiards/pool
   бильярд

3. bowling
   кегли/боулинг

4. cycling/biking
   велосипедные гонки

5. fencing
   фехтование

6. flying disc*
   фрисби

7. golf
   гольф

8. gymnastics
   гимнастика

9. inline skating
   катание на роликовых
   коньках

10. martial arts
    спортивная борьба

11. racquetball
    рэкетбол

12. skateboarding
    катание на скейтборде

13. table tennis/
    Ping-Pong™
    настольный теннис/
    пинг-понг

14. tennis
    теннис

15. weightlifting
    тяжёлая атлетика

16. wrestling
    борьба

17. track and field
    лёгкая атлетика

18. horse racing
    скачки/бега

*Note: One brand is Frisbee®
(Mattel, Inc.)

Talk about sports.

Which sports do you like?

   I like <u>tennis</u> but I don't like <u>golf</u>.

Share your answers.

1. Which sports are good for children to learn? Why?

2. Which sport is the most difficult to learn? Why?

3. Which sport is the most dangerous? Why?

159

1. downhill skiing
скоростной спуск на лыжах

2. snowboarding
катание на сноуборде

3. cross-country skiing
лыжные гонки

4. ice skating
катание на коньках

5. figure skating
фигурное катание

6. sledding
катание на санках

7. waterskiing
воднолыжный спорт

8. sailing
парусный спорт

9. surfing
серфинг

10. sailboarding
катание на парусной доске

11. snorkeling
подводное плавание с
дыхательной трубкой

12. scuba diving
подводное плавание с
аквалангом

Use the new language.

Look at **The Beach,** page **155.**

Name the sports you see.

Share your answers.

1. Which sports are in the Winter Olympics?

2. Which sports do you think are the most exciting
to watch?

1. golf club
клюшка/бита для гольфа

2. tennis racket
теннисная ракетка

3. volleyball
волейбол

4. basketball
баскетбол

5. bowling ball
шар для игры в кегли

6. bow
лук

7. arrow
стрела

8. target
мишень

9. ice skates
коньки

10. inline skates
роликовые коньки

11. hockey stick
хоккейная клюшка

12. soccer ball
футбольный мяч

13. shin guards
щиток для защиты голени

14. baseball bat
бейсбольная бита

15. catcher's mask
маска кетчера

16. uniform
форма

17. glove
перчатка

18. baseball
бейсбол

19. weights
гири

20. football helmet
шлем для игры в американский футбол

21. shoulder pads
наплечники

22. football
мяч для игры в американский футбол

23. snowboard
сноуборд

24. skis
лыжи

25. ski poles
лыжные палки

26. ski boots
лыжные ботинки

27. flying disc*
фрисби

*Note: One brand is Frisbee®
(Mattel, Inc.)

Share your answers.

1. Which sports equipment is used for safety reasons?

2. Which sports equipment is heavy?

3. What sports equipment do you have at home?

Use the new language.

Look at **Individual Sports,** page **159.**

Name the sports equipment you see.

A.   collect things
коллекционировать

B.   play games
играть в игры

C.   build models
собирать модели

D.   do crafts
делать поделки

1. video game system
система для видеоигр

2. cartridge
кассета

3. board game
настольные игры

4. dice
игральные кости

5. checkers
шашки

6. chess
шахматы

7. model kit
сборная модель

8. glue
клей

9. acrylic paint
акриловая краска

10. figurine
статуэтка

11. baseball card
бейсбольная карточка

12. stamp collection
коллекция марок

13. coin collection
коллекция монет

14. clay
пластилин

15. doll making kit
кукольный набор

16. woodworking kit
столярный набор

Talk about how much time you spend on your hobbies.

I _do crafts_ all the time.

I _play chess_ sometimes.

I never _build models_.

Share your answers.

1. How often do you play video games? Often?
   Sometimes? Never?

2. What board games do you know?

3. Do you collect anything? What?

E. paint
красить

F. knit
вязать

G. pretend
притворяться/
придумывать

H. play cards
играть в карты

17. yarn
пряжа

18. knitting needles
вязальные спицы

19. embroidery
вышивка

20. crochet
вязальный крючок

21. easel
мольберт

22. canvas
холст

23. paintbrush
кисть

24. oil paint
масляная краска

25. watercolor
акварель

26. clubs
трефи

27. diamonds
бубны

28. spades
пики

29. hearts
черви

30. paper doll
бумажные куклы

31. action figure
фигурка персонажа

32. model trains
модели поездов

Share your answers.

1. Do you like to play cards? Which games?

2. Did you pretend a lot when you were a child? What did you pretend to be?

3. Is it important to have hobbies? Why or why not?

4. What's your favorite game?

5. What's your hobby?

1. clock radio
радио с часами

2. portable radio-cassette player
портативное радио / магнитофон

3. cassette recorder
магнитофон

4. microphone
микрофон

5. shortwave radio
коротковолновое радио

6. TV (television)
телевизор

7. portable TV
переносной телевизор

8. VCR (videocassette recorder)
видеомагнитофон

9. remote control
дистанционное управление

10. videocassette
видеокассета

11. speakers
колонки

12. turntable
проигрыватель

13. tuner
тюнер

14. CD player
проигрыватель компактных дисков

15. personal radio-cassette player
переносной радио-магнитофон

16. headphones
наушники

17. adapter
адаптер

18. plug
вилка

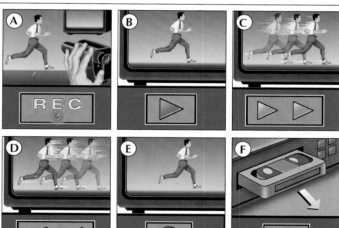

19. video camera
видеокамера

20. tripod
тренога

21. camcorder
видеокамера

22. battery pack
батарейка

23. battery charger
зарядное устройство для
батареек

24. 35 mm camera
35-миллиметровый фотоаппарат

25. zoom lens
объектив с переменным
фокусным расстоянием

26. film
плёнка

27. camera case
футляр для фотоаппарата

28. screen
экран

29. carousel slide projector
диапроектор с вращающимся
магазином

30. slide tray
диамагазин

31. slides
слайды

32. photo album
фотоальбом

33. out of focus
не в фокусе

34. overexposed
передержанный

35. underexposed
недодержанный

A. **record**
запись

B. **play**
пуск

C. **fast forward**
быстрая перемотка вперёд

D. **rewind**
перемотка назад

E. **pause**
пауза

F. **stop** and **eject**
стоп и выброс

Types of entertainment Виды развлечений

1. film/movie
фильм/кино

2. play
пьеса

3. television program
телевизионная
программа

4. radio program
радиопрограмма

5. stand-up comedy
театр одного актёра

6. concert
концерт

7. ballet
балет

8. opera
опера

Types of stories Виды рассказа

9. western
вестерн

10. comedy
комедия

11. tragedy
трагедия

12. science fiction story
научно-фантастический
рассказ

13. action story/
adventure story
приключенческий
рассказ

14. horror story
рассказ ужасов

15. mystery
детектив

16. romance
роман

Types of TV programs   Виды телевизионных программ

17. news
новости

18. sitcom (situation comedy)
ситуационная комедия

19. cartoon
мультфильм

20. talk show
ток-шоу

21. soap opera
мыльная опера

22. nature program
передача о природе

23. game show/quiz show
игровое представление/
телевикторина

24. children's program
детская программа

25. shopping program
программа «покупки по
телевизору»

26. serious book
серьёзная книга

27. funny book
смешная книга

28. sad book
грустная книга

29. boring book
скучная книга

30. interesting book
интересная книга

1. New Year's Day
Новый год

2. parade
парад

3. confetti
конфетти

4. Valentine's Day
день св. Валентина

5. card
открытка

6. heart
сердце

7. Independence Day/4th of July
День независимости / 4-е июля

8. fireworks
салют

9. flag
флаг

10. Halloween
канун Дня всех святых

11. jack-o'-lantern
фонарь из тыквы

12. mask
маска

13. costume
костюм

14. candy
конфета

15. Thanksgiving
День благодарения

16. feast
пир / застолье

17. turkey
индейка

18. Christmas
Рождество

19. ornament
украшение

20. Christmas tree
Рождественская ёлка

A. plan a party
планировать вечеринку

B. invite the guests
приглашать гостей

C. decorate the house
украшать дом

D. wrap a gift
заворачивать подарок

E. hide
прятать

F. answer the door
открывать дверь

G. shout "surprise!"
кричать «сюрприз!»

H. light the candles
зажигать свечи

I. sing "Happy Birthday"
петь «С днём рождения»

J. make a wish
загадывать желание

K. blow out the candles
задувать свечи

L. open the presents
разворачивать подарки

Practice inviting friends to a party.

I'd love for you to come to my party <u>next week</u>.

Could <u>you and your friend</u> come to my party?

Would <u>your friend</u> like to come to a party I'm giving?

Share your answers.

1. Do you celebrate birthdays? What do you do?

2. Are there birthdays you celebrate in a special way?

3. Is there a special birthday song in your country?

Verb Guide

Verbs in English are either regular or irregular in the past tense and past participle forms.

Regular Verbs

The regular verbs below are marked 1, 2, 3, or 4 according to four different spelling patterns.
(See page 172 for the **irregular verbs** which do not follow any of these patterns.)

Spelling Patterns for the Past and the Past Participle	*Example*		
1. Add **-ed** to the end of the verb.	**ASK**	→	**ASKED**
2. Add **-d** to the end of the verb.	**LIVE**	→	**LIVED**
3. Double the final consonant and add **-ed** to the end of the verb.	**DROP**	→	**DROPPED**
4. Drop the final y and add **-ied** to the end of the verb.	**CRY**	→	**CRIED**

The Oxford Picture Dictionary List of Regular Verbs

act (1)
add (1)
address (1)
answer (1)
apologize (2)
appear (1)
applaud (1)
arrange (2)
arrest (1)
arrive (2)
ask (1)
assemble (2)
assist (1)
bake (2)
barbecue (2)
bathe (2)
board (1)
boil (1)
borrow (1)
bounce (2)
brainstorm (1)
breathe (2)
broil (1)
brush (1)
burn (1)
call (1)
carry (4)
change (2)
check (1)
choke (2)
chop (3)
circle (2)
claim (1)
clap (3)
clean (1)
clear (1)
climb (1)
close (2)
collate (2)

collect (1)
color (1)
comb (1)
commit (3)
compliment (1)
conserve (2)
convert (1)
cook (1)
copy (4)
correct (1)
cough (1)
count (1)
cross (1)
cry (4)
dance (2)
design (1)
deposit (1)
deliver (1)
dial (1)
dictate (2)
die (2)
discuss (1)
dive (2)
dress (1)
dribble (2)
drill (1)
drop (3)
drown (1)
dry (4)
dust (1)
dye (2)
edit (1)
eject (1)
empty (4)
end (1)
enter (1)
erase (2)
examine (2)
exchange (2)

exercise (2)
experience (2)
exterminate (2)
fasten (1)
fax (1)
file (2)
fill (1)
finish (1)
fix (1)
floss (1)
fold (1)
fry (4)
gargle (2)
graduate (2)
grate (2)
grease (2)
greet (1)
grill (1)
hail (1)
hammer (1)
harvest (1)
help (1)
hire (2)
hug (3)
immigrate (2)
inquire (2)
insert (1)
introduce (2)
invite (2)
iron (1)
jog (3)
join (1)
jump (1)
kick (1)
kiss (1)
knit (3)
land (1)
laugh (1)
learn (1)

lengthen (1)
listen (1)
live (2)
load (1)
lock (1)
look (1)
mail (1)
manufacture (2)
mark (1)
match (1)
measure (2)
milk (1)
miss (1)
mix (1)
mop (3)
move (2)
mow (1)
need (1)
nurse (2)
obey (1)
observe (2)
open (1)
operate (2)
order (1)
overdose (2)
paint (1)
park (1)
pass (1)
pause (2)
peel (1)
perm (1)
pick (1)
pitch (1)
plan (3)
plant (1)
play (1)
point (1)
polish (1)
pour (1)
pretend (1)
print (1)
protect (1)

pull (1)
push (1)
race (2)
raise (2)
rake (2)
receive (2)
record (1)
recycle (2)
register (1)
relax (1)
remove (2)
rent (1)
repair (1)
repeat (1)
report (1)
request (1)
return (1)
rinse (2)
roast (1)
rock (1)
sauté (2)
save (2)
scrub (3)
seat (1)
sentence (2)
serve (2)
share (2)
shave (2)
ship (3)
shop (3)
shorten (1)
shout (1)
sign (1)
simmer (1)
skate (2)
ski (1)
slice (2)
smell (1)
sneeze (2)
sort (1)
spell (1)
staple (2)

start (1)
stay (1)
steam (1)
stir (3)
stir-fry (4)
stop (3)
stow (1)
stretch (1)
supervise (2)
swallow (1)
tackle (2)
talk (1)
taste (2)
thank (1)
tie (2)
touch (1)
transcribe (2)
transfer (3)
travel (1)
trim (3)
turn (1)
type (2)
underline (2)
unload (1)
unpack (1)
use (2)
vacuum (1)
vomit (1)
vote (2)
wait (1)
walk (1)
wash (1)
watch (1)
water (1)
weed (1)
weigh (1)
wipe (2)
work (1)
wrap (3)
yield (1)

Irregular Verbs

These verbs have irregular endings in the past and/or the past participle.

The Oxford Picture Dictionary List of Irregular Verbs

simple	past	past participle	simple	past	past participle
be	was	been	leave	left	left
beat	beat	beaten	lend	lent	lent
become	became	become	let	let	let
begin	began	begun	light	lit	lit
bend	bent	bent	make	made	made
bleed	bled	bled	pay	paid	paid
blow	blew	blown	picnic	picnicked	picnicked
break	broke	broken	put	put	put
build	built	built	read	read	read
buy	bought	bought	rewind	rewound	rewound
catch	caught	caught	rewrite	rewrote	rewritten
come	came	come	ride	rode	ridden
cut	cut	cut	run	ran	run
do	did	done	say	said	said
draw	drew	drawn	see	saw	seen
drink	drank	drunk	sell	sold	sold
drive	drove	driven	send	sent	sent
eat	ate	eaten	set	set	set
fall	fell	fallen	sew	sewed	sewn
feed	fed	fed	shoot	shot	shot
feel	felt	felt	sing	sang	sung
find	found	found	sit	sat	sat
fly	flew	flown	speak	spoke	spoken
get	got	gotten	stand	stood	stood
give	gave	given	sweep	swept	swept
go	went	gone	swim	swam	swum
hang	hung	hung	swing	swung	swung
have	had	had	take	took	taken
hear	heard	heard	teach	taught	taught
hide	hid	hidden	throw	threw	thrown
hit	hit	hit	wake	woke	woken
hold	held	held	wear	wore	worn
keep	kept	kept	withdraw	withdrew	withdrawn
lay	laid	laid	write	wrote	written

Index

Two numbers are shown after words in the index: the first refers to the page where the word is illustrated and the second refers to the item number of the word on that page. For example, cool [ko͞ol] **10**-3 means that the word *cool* is item number 3 on page 10. If only the bold page number appears, then that word is part of the unit title or subtitle, or is found somewhere else on the page. A bold number followed by ◆ means the word can be found in the exercise space at the bottom of that page.

Words or combinations of words that appear in **bold** type are used as verbs or verb phrases. Words used as other parts of speech are shown in ordinary type. So, for example, **file** (in bold type) is the verb *file*, while file (in ordinary type) is the noun *file*. Words or phrases in small capital letters (for example, HOLIDAYS) form unit titles.

Phrases and other words that form combinations with an individual word entry are often listed underneath it. Rather than repeating the word each time it occurs in combination with what is listed under it, the word is replaced by three dots (...), called an ellipsis. For example, under the word *bus*, you will find ...driver and ...stop meaning *bus driver* and *bus stop*. Under the word *store* you will find shoe... and toy..., meaning *shoe store* and *toy store*.

Pronunciation Guide

The index includes a pronunciation guide for all the words and phrases illustrated in the book. This guide uses symbols commonly found in dictionaries for native speakers. These symbols, unlike those used in pronunciation systems such as the International Phonetic Alphabet, tend to use English spelling patterns and so should help you to become more aware of the connections between written English and spoken English.

Consonants

[b] as in back [băk]	[k] as in key [kē]	[sh] as in shoe [sho͞o]
[ch] as in cheek [chēk]	[l] as in leaf [lēf]	[t] as in tape [tāp]
[d] as in date [dāt]	[m] as in match [măch]	[th] as in three [thrē]
[dh] as in this [dhĭs]	[n] as in neck [nĕk]	[v] as in vine [vīn]
[f] as in face [fās]	[ng] as in ring [rĭng]	[w] as in wait [wāt]
[g] as in gas [găs]	[p] as in park [pärk]	[y] as in yams [yămz]
[h] as in half [hăf]	[r] as in rice [rīs]	[z] as in zoo [zo͞o]
[j] as in jam [jăm]	[s] as in sand [sănd]	[zh] as in measure [mĕzhʹər]

Vowels

[ā] as in bake [bāk]	[ĭ] as in lip [lĭp]	[ow] as in cow [kow]
[ă] as in back [băk]	[ï] as in near [nïr]	[oy] as in boy [boy]
[ä] as in car [kär] or box [bäks]	[ō] as in cold [kōld]	[ŭ] as in cut [kŭt]
[ē] as in beat [bēt]	[ö] as in short [shört]	[ü] as in curb [kürb]
[ĕ] as in bed [bĕd]	or claw [klö]	[ə] as in above [ə bŭvʹ]
[ë] as in bear [bër]	[o͞o] as in cool [ko͞ol]	
[ī] as in line [līn]	[o͝o] as in cook [ko͝ok]	

All the pronunciation symbols used are alphabetical except for the schwa [ə]. The schwa is the most frequent vowel sound in English. If you use the schwa appropriately in unstressed syllables, your pronunciation will sound more natural.

Vowels before [r] are shown with the symbol [¨] to call attention to the special quality that vowels have before [r]. (Note that the symbols [ä] and [ö] are also used for vowels not followed by [r], as in *box* or *claw*.) You should listen carefully to native speakers to discover how these vowels actually sound.

Stress

This index follows the system for marking stress used in many dictionaries for native speakers.

1. Stress is not marked if a word consisting of a single syllable occurs by itself.
2. Where stress is marked, two levels are distinguished:

   a bold accent [ʹ] is placed after each syllable with primary (or strong) stress, a light accent [ʹ] is placed after each syllable with secondary (or weaker) stress.

In phrases and other combinations of words, stress is indicated for each word as it would be pronounced within the whole phrase or other unit. If a word consisting of a single syllable is stressed in the combinations listed below it, the accent mark indicating the degree of stress it has in the phrases (primary or secondary) is shown in parentheses. A hyphen replaces any part of a word or phrase that is omitted. For example, bus [bŭs(ʹ–)] shows that the word *bus* is said with primary stress in the combinations shown below it. The word ...driver [–drīʹvər], listed under *bus*, shows that *driver* has secondary stress in the combination *bus driver*: [bŭsʹ drīʹvər]

Syllable Boundaries

Syllable boundaries are indicated by a single space or by a stress mark.

Note: The pronunciations shown in this index are based on patterns of American English. There has been no attempt to represent all of the varieties of American English. Students should listen to native speakers to hear how the language actually sounds in a particular region.

Index

abdomen [ăb/də mən] **74**–3
above [ə bŭv/] **13**–6
accelerator [ĭk sĕl/ə rā/tər] **109**–47
ACCESSORIES [ĭk sĕs/ə rēz] **68**–**69**
accident [ăk/sə dənt] **102**–2
accordion [ə kör/dē ən] **120**–21
accountant [ə kown/tnt] **136**–1
acid rain [ăs/əd rān/] **126**–11
across [ə krös/] **105**–3
acrylic paint [ə krĭl/ĭk pănt/] **162**–9
act [ăkt] **140** ✦
action [ăk/shən]
  …figure [–fĭg/yər] **163**–31
  …story [–stör/ē] **166**–13
actor [ăk/tər] **136**–2
acupuncture [ăk/yə pŭngk/chər] **81**–G
adapter [ə dăp/tər] **164**–17
add [ăd] **58**–Q, **72**–B
addition [ə dĭsh/ən] **118**–1
address [ə drĕs/] **96**–A
address [ə drĕs/, ă/drĕs] **4**–5, **96**–7,8
adhesive bandage [əd hē/sĭv băn/dĭj] **83**–3
administrative assistant [əd mĭn/ə strā/tĭv ə sĭs/tənt] **136**–3
administrator [əd mĭn/ə strā/tər] **5** ✦
adults [ə dŭlts/, ăd/ŭlts] **22**–9
adult school [ə dŭlt/ skōol/, ăd/ŭlt–] **112**–8
adventure story [əd vĕn/chər stör/ē] **166**–13
aerogramme [ĕr/ə grăm/] **96**–13
afternoon [ăf/tər nōon/] **17**–18
aftershave [ăf/tər shāv/] **77**–28
AGE AND PHYSICAL DESCRIPTION [āj/ ən fĭz/ĭ kəl
  dĭ skrĭp/shən] **22**
AIDS (acquired immunodeficiency syndrome) [ādz] **79** ✦
air [ĕr(/–)] **109**–59
  …bag [–băg/] **108**–16
  …conditioner [–kən dĭsh/ə nər] **37**–19
  …conditioning [–kən dĭsh/ə nĭng] **108**–28
  …letter [–lĕt/ər] **96**–13
  …pollution [–pə lōo/shən] **126**–10
  …purifier [–pyōor/ə fī ər] **80**–4
airline [ĕr/līn/]
  …representative [–rĕp rĭ zĕn/tə tĭv] **110**–2
  …terminal [–tür/mə nəl] **110**–1
airplane [ĕr/plān/] **110**–9
  …crash [–krăsh/] **102**–3
AIRPORT [ĕr/pört/] **110**
airsickness bag [ĕr/sĭk/nəs băg/] **110**–15
aisle [īl] **54**–5
Alaska time [ə lăs/kə tīm/] **17**–25
alfalfa [ăl făl/fə] **148**–5
algebra [ăl/jə brə] **118**–25
allergies [ăl/ər jēz] **79**–8
alley [ăl/ē] **37**–21
alligator [ăl/ə gā/tər] **131**–36
alphabet [ăl/fə bĕt/] **3**–30
ALTERATIONS [öl/tə rā/shənz] **73**
aluminum foil [ə lōo/mə nəm foyl/] **55**–55
a.m. [ā/ĕm/] **16** ✦
American cheese [ə mĕr/ə kən chēz/] **53**–9
AMPHIBIANS [ăm fĭb/ē ənz] **130**–**131**
amusement park [ə myōoz/mənt pärk/] **152**–13
anesthesiologist [ăn/əs thē/zē ăl/ə jĭst] **87**–35
angle [ăng/gəl] **118**–24
angry [ăng/grē] **31**–29
animals [ăn/ə məlz] **152**–2
ANIMALS, DOMESTIC [də mĕs/tĭk ăn/ə məlz] **133**

ankle [ăng/kəl] **75**–61, **78**–18
anniversary [ăn/ə vür/sə rē] **19**–42
announcer [ə nown/sər] **152**–27
answer [ăn/sər]
  …a question [–ə kwĕs/chən] **6**–H
  …the door [–dhə dör/] **169**–F
answering machine [ăn/sə rĭng mə shēn/] **9**–14
answer sheet [ăn/sər shēt/] **7**–T
antacid [ănt ăs/əd] **81**–18
anteater [ănt/ē/tər] **135**–24
antelope [ăn/tə lōp/] **135**–35
antibacterial ointment [ăn/tē băk tĭr/ē əl oynt/mənt] **83**–9
antihistamine cream [ăn/tī hĭs/tə mēn krēm/] **83**–10
antler [ănt/lər] **134**–16
ants [ănts] **49**–24
apartment [ə pärt/mənt]
  …building [–bĭl/dĭng] **34**–5
  …number [–nŭm/bər] **4**–6
APARTMENTS [ə pärt/mənts] **36**–**37**
apologize [ə päl/ə jīz/] **8**–I
apostrophe [ə päs/trə fē] **113**–11
appear in court [ə pĭr/ ĭn kört/] **99**–C
applaud [ə plöd/] **32**–B
apple juice [ăp/əl jōos/] **55**–50, **57**–5
apples [ăp/əlz] **50**–4
application [ăp/lə kā/shən] **144**–21
appointment [ə poynt/mənt] **19**–45, **85**
  …book [–bōok/] **143**–27
apricots [ăp/rə kăts/] **50**–7
April [ā/prəl] **19**–28
archery [är/chə rē] **159**–1
architect [är/kə tĕkt/] **136**–4
area [ĕr/ē ə] **34**–(1, 4)
area code [ĕr/ē ə kōd/] **4**–10
arm [ärm] **74**–9
armadillo [är/mə dĭl/ō] **134**–8
armchair [ärm/chĕr/] **42**–24
around [ə rownd/] **105**–10
arrange [ə rānj/] **35**–K
arrest [ə rĕst/] **99**–A
arrival and departure monitors
  [ə rī/vəl ən dĭ pär/chər män/ə tərz] **110**–4
arrival time [ə rī/vəl tīm/] **111** ✦
arrive [ə rīv/] **111**–O
arrow [ăr/ō] **161**–7
art [ärt] **121**–1
artery [är/tə rē] **75**–43
artichokes [är/tə chōks/] **51**–20
artist [är/tĭst] **136**–2
art museum [ärt/ myōo zē/əm] **152**–7
ask [ăsk(/–)]
  …about benefits [–ə bowt/ bĕn/ə fĭts] **141**–J
  …about the hours [–ə bowt/ dhē ow/ərz] **141**–F
  …a question [–ə kwĕs/chən] **6**–G
asparagus [ə spăr/ə gəs] **51**–24
assault [ə sölt/] **100**–7
assemble [ə sĕm/bəl] **140**–A
assembler [ə sĕm/blər] **136**–6
assembly line [ə sĕm/blē līn/] **146**–8
assist [ə sĭst/] **140**–B
Associate of Arts (AA) [ə sō/shē ĭt əv ärts/, –sē ĭt–] /
  [ā/ā/] **112** ✦
asteroid belt [ăs/tə royd bĕlt/] **127**–12
asthma [ăz/mə] **79**–11
astronaut [ăs/trə nöt/] **127**–17
astronomer [ə strän/ə mər] **127**–20

athletic [ăth lĕt/ĭk]
...shoes [–shōoz/] **68**–23
...supporter [–sə pör/tər] **67**–14
Atlantic time [ət lăn/tĭk tīm/] **17**–30
atlas [ăt/ləs] **98**–3
ATM (automated teller machine) [ā/tē/ĕm/] **97**–3
ATM card [ā/tē/ĕm/ kärd/] **97**–9
atom [ăt/əm] **119**–17
attorney [ə tür/nē] **99**–4
attractive [ə trăk/tĭv] **22**–23
audience [ö/dē əns] **32**–10
audiocassette [ö/dē ō kə sĕt/] **98**–12
audiologist [ö/dē äl/ə jĭst] **81**–32
auditorium [ö/də tör/ē əm] **5**–3
August [ö/gəst] **19**–32
aunt [ănt] **24**–10
author [ö/thər] **98**–22, **139**–64
automatic transmission
  [ö/tə măt/ĭk trănz mĭsh/ən, –trăns–] **109**
auto mechanic [ö/tō mə kăn/ĭk] **136**–7
average [ăv/rĭj]
...height [–hīt/] **22**–17
...weight [–wāt/] **22**–21
avocadoes [ä/və kä/dōz, ăv/ə–] **50**–14
ax [ăks] **150**–3
baboon [bă boon/] **135**–32
baby [bā/bē] **22**–2
...backpack [–băk/păk/] **95**–15
...carrier [–kăr/ē ər] **95**–14
...food [–food/] **95**–28
...monitor [–män/ə tər] **45**–9
...powder [–pow/dər] **95**–18
baby-sitter [bā/bē sĭt/ər] **136**–12
Bachelor's degree [băch/lərz də grē/] **112** ✦
back [băk(/–)] **74**–11
...support [–sə pört/] **147**–16
backache [băk/āk/] **78**–5
backhoe [băk/hō/] **149**–8
backpack [băk/păk/] **69**–28, **95**–15, **154**–15
backpacking [băk/păk/ĭng] **154**–7
backseat [băk/sēt/] **109**–38
backyard [băk/yärd/] **38**–2
bacon [bā/kən] **52**–11, **61**–7
bad [băd] **11**–18
bag [băg] (market) **55**–22, 23, **56**–7, 19 (purse) **69**–27, 28, 29
baggage claim area [băg/ĭj klām/ ĕr/ē ə] **110**–17
bagger [băg/ər] **55**–21
baggy [băg/ē] **71**–42
bag of flour [băg/ əv flow/ər] **56**–19
bags (luggage) [băgz] **111**–B
bailiff [bā/ləf] **99**–13
bake [bāk] **58**–L
baked [bākt(/–)]
...goods [–goodz/] **54**–6
...potato [–pə tā/tō] **61**–14
baker [bā/kər] **136**–8
bakery [bā/kə rē] **89**–16
baking products [bā/kĭng präd/ŭkts] **55**–13
balance [băl/əns] (bank) **97**–11, (science) **119**–11
balcony [băl/kə nē] **37**–17
bald [böld] **23**–12
ball [böl] **45**–16, **161**–3, 4, 5, 12, 18, 22
ballet [bă lā/] **166**–7
ball field [böl/ fēld/] **153**–1
ballroom [böl/room/] **145**–20

bananas [bə năn/əz] **50**–3
bandage [băn/dĭj] **83**–3, 12
bangs [băngz] **23**–8
BANK [băngk] **97**
bank [băngk] **88**–3
banner [băn/ər] **33**–15
barbecue [bär/bĭ kyoo/] **58**–T
barbecue grill [bär/bĭ kyoo grĭl/] **39**–7
barber shop [bär/bər shäp/] **88**–15
bar code [bär/ kōd/] **21**–4
barn [bärn] **148**–11
barrette [bə rĕt/] **76**–18
baseball [bās/böl/] **158**–9, **161**–18
...bat [–băt/] **161**–14
...cap [–kăp/] **66**–27
...card [–kärd/] **162**–11
...game [–gām/] **152**–25
basement [bās/mənt] **36** ✦
basket [băs/kət] **42**–2
basketball [băs/kət böl/] **158**–8, **161**–4
...court [–kört/] **158**–7
bass (fish) [băs] **130**–11
bass (instrument) [bās] **120**–10
bassoon [bə soon/] **120**–6
bat [băt] (animal) **134**–7, (baseball) **161**–14
bath [băth(/–)]
...mat [–măt/] **43**–27
...powder [–pow/dər] **76**–3
...towel [–tow/əl] **43**–12
bathe [bādh] **76**–B
bathing suit [bā/dhĭng soot/] **66**–26
bathrobe [băth/rōb/] **67**–8
BATHROOM [băth/room/] **43**
bathtub [băth/tŭb/] **43**–2
battery [băt/ə rē] (car) **109**–43, (flashlight) **151**–40
...charger [–chär/jər] **165**–23
...pack [–păk/] **165**–22
bay [bā] **117**–9
be [bē]
...18 years old [–ā/tēn/ yïrz/ ōld/] **116**–A
...**born** [–börn/] **28**–A
...**hurt** [–hürt/] **82**–A
...**injured** [–ĭn/jərd] **82**–A
...in school [–ĭn skool/] **26**–J
...in shock [–ĭn shäk/] **82**–C
...**released** [–rĭ lēst/] **99**–H
...**unconscious** [–ŭn kän/shəs] **82**–B
BEACH [bēch] **155**
beach [bēch(/–)] **117**–10
...chair [–chër/] **155**–14
...towel [–tow/əl] **155**–15
...umbrella [–ŭm brĕl/ə] **155**–9
beads [bēdz] **69**–32
beak [bēk] **132**–1
beaker [bē/kər] **119**–13
beam [bēm] **149**–3
beans [bēnz] **51**–25, **54**–26
bear [bër] **134**–11
beard [bïrd] **23**–6
beat [bēt] **58**–B
beautiful [byoo/tə fəl] **11**–21
beauty shop [byoo/tē shäp/] **92** ✦
beaver [bē/vər] **134**–9
become a citizen [bĭ kŭm/ ə sĭt/ə zən] **28**–H
bed [bĕd(/–)] **44**–8

Index

...control [–kən trōl/] **86**–12
...frame [–frām/] **44**–27
...table [–tā/bəl] **86**–9
bedpan [bĕd/păn/] **86**–13
BEDROOM [bĕd/rōōm/] **44**
bedspread [bĕd/sprĕd/] **44**–11
Beef [bēf] **52**
beef ribs [bēf/ rĭbz/] **52**–5
beetle [bēt/l] **132**–19
beets [bēts] **51**–6
begin [bĭ gĭn/] **8**–B
behind [bĭ hīnd/] **13**–3
beige [bāzh] **12**–9
bell captain [bĕl/ kăp/tən] **145**–4
bellhop [bĕl/häp/] **145**–5
below [bĭ lō/] **13**–7
belt buckle [bĕlt/ bŭk/əl] **69**–41
belts [bĕlts] **69**–11
bench [bĕnch] **153**–10
bend [bĕnd] **157**–R
berries [bĕr/ēz] **128**–20
between [bĭ twēn/] **13**–10
beverages [bĕv/rə jəz] **55**–15, **61**
bib [bĭb] **95**–8
bicycle [bī/sĭ kəl] **153**–4
big [bĭg] **11**–2
bike [bīk(/–)] **153**–4
...path [–păth/] **153**–2
...shorts [–shörts/] **67**–3
biking [bī/kĭng] **159**–4
bikini panties [bə kē/nē păn/tēz] **67**–16
bill (bird) [bĭl] **132**–1
bill (invoice) [bĭl] **21** ✦
billiards [bĭl/yərdz] **159**–2
billion [bĭl/yən] **14**
bills (paper money) [bĭlz] **20, 20** ✦
bin [bĭn] **37**–20
binder [bīn/dər] **3**–24
biohazard [bī/ō hăz/ərd] **147**–5
biology [bī äl/ə jē] **119**–1
birch [bürch] **128**–8
BIRDS, INSECTS, AND ARACHNIDS
  [bürdz/ ĭn/sĕkts ən ə răk/nĭdz] **132**
birth certificate [bürth/ sər tĭf/ə kət] **29**–1
birthday [bürth/dā/] **19**–41, **169**–I
bison [bī/sən] **134**–6
black [blăk(/–)] **12**–15
...hair [–hër/] **23**–15
bladder [blăd/ər] **75**–47
blade [blād] **150**–11
blanket [blăng/kət] **44**–12
...sleeper [–slē/pər] **67**–7
bleach [blēch] **72**–8
bleachers [blē/chərz] **5**–10
bleed [blēd] **82**–M
blender [blĕn/dər] **40**–12
blind [blīnd] **22**–26
blinds [blīndz] **43**–11
blister [blĭs/tər] **78**–15
blizzard [blĭz/ərd] **103**–11
block [bläk] **107**–2
blocks [bläks] **45**–15
blond [bländ] **23**–16
blood [blŭd(/–)] **79**–15
...pressure gauge [–prĕsh/ər gāj/] **84**–12

...test [–tĕst/] **86**–17
...work [–würk/] **86**–17
bloody nose [blŭd/ē nōz/] **78**–17
blouse [blows] **64**–9
blow dryer [blō/ drī/ər] **23**–20, **76**–16
blow out [blō/ owt/] **169**–K
blue [blōō] **12**–1
blueberries [blōō/bĕr/ēz] **50**–19
blue jay [blōō/ jā/] **132**–7
blush [blŭsh] **77**–36
board game [börd/ gām/] **162**–3
boarding area [bör/dĭng ër/ē ə] **110**–6
board the plane [börd/ dhə plān/] **111**–F
boating [bō/tĭng] **154**–2
bobby pins [bäb/ē pĭnz/] **76**–19
BODY [bäd/ē] **74**–**75**
body lotion [bäd/ē lō/shən] **76**–7
body of water [bäd/ē əv wö/tər] **117** ✦
boil [boyl] **58**–P
bolt [bōlt] **37**–29, **150**–30, 33
bone [bōn] (body) **75**–49, (broken) **82**–P
boneless [bōn/ləs] **52** ✦
bookbag [bŏŏk/băg/] **69**–28
bookcase [bŏŏk/kās/] **3**–8, **42**–1
bookstore [bŏŏk/stör/] **92**–4
booth [bōōth] **60**–19, **152**–23
boots [bōōts] **68**–18
bored [börd] **31**–26
boring [bör/ĭng] **167**–29
borrow [bär/ō, bör/ō] **20** ✦
botanical gardens [bə tăn/ĭ kəl gär/dnz] **152**–4
bottle [bät/l] **56**–1, **95**–26
...of soda [–əv sō/də] **56**–13
bottled water [bät/ld wö/tər] **55**–53
bottle return [bät/l rĭ türn/] **54**–1
bounce [bowns] **156**–K
bouquet [bō kā/, bōō–] **129**–27
bow [bō] **161**–6
bowl [bōl] **41**–25
bowling [bō/lĭng] **159**–3
...ball [–böl/] **161**–5
bow tie [bō/ tī/] **69**–40
box [bäks(/–)] **56**–6
...of cereal [–əv sïr/ē əl] **56**–18
...spring [–sprĭng/] **44**–26
boxer shorts [bäk/sər shörts/] **67**–12
boy [boy] **22**–4, 7
bra [brä] **67**–20
brace [brās] **81**–31
bracelet [brās/lət] **69**–35, **83**–14
braces [brā/səz] **84**–24
brain [brān(/–)] **75**–35
...cancer [–kăn/sər] **79**–12
brainstorm [brān/störm/] **6**–K
brake [brāk(/–)]
...light [–līt/] **108**–13
...pedal [–pĕd/l] **109**–46
branch [brănch] **128**–2
Branches of government [brăn/chəz əv gŭv/ər mənt] **116**
Brass [brăs] **120**
bread [brĕd(/–)] **53**–1, 2, 3, **54**–29
...basket [–băs/kət] **63**–8
bread-and-butter plate [brĕd/ n bŭt/ər plāt/] **63**–16
break [brāk(/–)]
...a bone [–ə bōn/] **82**–P

...three eggs [–thrē′ ĕgz′] **58**–A
Breakfast [brĕk′fəst] **61**
breast (body) [brĕst] **74**–14
breasts (chicken) [brĕsts] **52**–19
bricklayer [brĭk′lā′ər] **136**–9
bricks [brĭks] **149**–11
bridge [brĭj] **105**–2
briefs [brēfs] **67**–13, 17
broccoli [bräk′ə lē] **51**–15, **58**–I
broil [broyl] **58**–V
broiler [broy′lər] **40**–21
broken [brō′kən] **48**–5, 6, 7, **49**–15, **70**–24
broom [broōm] **47**–10
brother [brŭdh′ər] / [–brŭdh′ər] **24**–9
   half... [hăf′–] **25**–29
brother-in-law [brŭdh′ər ĭn lö′] **24**–16
brown [brown(′–)] **12**–11
   ...hair [–hër′] **23**–17
bruise [broōz] **78**–12
brush [brŭsh(′–)]
   ...hair [–hër′] **76**–I
   ...teeth [–tēth′] **77**–J
brush [(–)brŭsh(′)] **23**–18, **76**–14
   paint... [pānt′–] **151**–47, **163**–23
   scrub... [skrŭb′–] **47**–19
   toilet... [toy′lət–] **43**–16
bucket [bŭk′ət] **47**–20, **155**–22
buckle [bŭk′əl] **69**–41
bud [bŭd] **129**–6
buffalo [bŭf′ə lō] **134**–6
buffet [bə fā′] **33**–13
building [bĭl′dĭng] **34**–5
BUILDING SUPPLIES [bĭl′dĭng sə plīz′] **150–151**
build models [bĭld′ mäd′lz] **162**–C
bulb [bŭlb] **129**–9
bulldozer [boōl′dō′zər] **149**–6
bulletin board [boōl′ə tn börd′] **3**–14
bumper [bŭm′pər] **108**–7
bumper pad [bŭm′pər păd′] **45**–7
bunk [bŭngk] **45**–1
Bunsen burner [bŭn′sən bür′nər] **119**–9
bureau [byoōr′ō] **44**–2
burglary [bür′glə rē] **100**–6
burner [bür′nər] **40**–19
burn (your)self [bürn′ (yər)sĕlf′] **82**–H
bus [bŭs(′–)] **90**–15, **104**–4
   ...driver [–drī′vər] **104**–8
   ...stop [–stäp′] **91**–16, **104**–1
bush [boōsh] **39**–20
business education [bĭz′nəs ĕj ə kā′shən] **121**–2
businessman [bĭz′nəs măn′] **136**–10
businesswoman [bĭz′nəs woōm′ən] **136**–10
busperson [bŭs′pür′sən] **63**–9
butcher [boōch′ər] **136**–11
butter [bŭt′ər] **54**–36
butterfly [bŭt′ər flī′] **132**–20
buttocks [bŭt′əks] **74**–12
button [bŭt′n] **73**–21
buttonhole [bŭt′n hōl′] **73**–12
buy [bī(′–)] **21**–C
   ...a house [–ə hows′] **29**–O
   ...your ticket [–yər tĭk′ət] **111**–A
Buying a house [bī′ĭng ə hows′] **35**
cab [kăb] **104**–18, **106**–16
cabbage [kăb′ĭj] **51**–2

cabinet [kăb′ə nət] **40**–1
cable [kā′bəl] **144**–16
cactus [kăk′təs] **128**–21
cafeteria [kăf′ə tïr′ē ə] **5**–4
cake [kāk(′–)] **54**–32, **61**–19
   ...mix [–mĭks′] **55**–47
   ...pan [–păn′] **59**–26
calculator [kăl′kyə lā′tər] **142**–8
calculus [kăl′kyə ləs] **118**–28
CALENDAR [kăl′ən dər] **18–19**
calf [kăf] **74**–18
call [köl] **141**–E
call button [köl′ bŭt′n] **86**–10
calm [käm] **30**–10
camcorder [kăm′kör′dər] **165**–21
camel [kăm′əl] **135**–38
camera [kăm′rə] **165**–19, 24, 27
   ...case [–kās′] **165**–27
camisole [kăm′ə sōl′] **67**–21
camper [kăm′pər] **106**–11
campfire [kămp′fīr′] **154**–11
camping [kăm′pĭng] **154**–1
   ...stove [–stōv′] **154**–16
can [kăn(′–)] **56**–3
   ...of soup [–əv soōp′] **56**–15
   ...opener [–ō′pə nər] **40**–14, **59**–1
cancer [kăn′sər] **79**–12
candle [kăn′dl] **41**–7
candles [kăn′dlz] **169**–H, K
candlestick [kăn′dl stĭk′] **41**–8
candy [kăn′dē] **55**–41, **168**–14
   ...bar [–bär′] **55**–41
   ...store [–stör′] **92**–3
cane [kān] **80**–7
canned goods [kănd′ goōdz′] **54**–4
canoeing [kə noō′ĭng] **154**–3
cantaloupes [kăn′tə lōps′] **50**–15
can't breathe [kănt′ brēdh′] **82**–N
canteen [kăn tēn′] **154**–24
canvas [kăn′vəs] **163**–22
canyon [kăn′yən] **117**–17
cap [kăp] (graduation) **32**–3, (clothing) **66**–6
capsule [kăp′səl] **81**–27
captain [kăp′tən] **158** ✦
car [kär(′–)]
   ...accident [–ăk′sə dənt] **102**–2
   ...dealership [–dē′lər shĭp′] **88**–4
   ...safety seat [–sāf′tē sēt′] **95**–13
card [kärd(′–)] **96**–4, **168**–5
   ...catalog [–kăt′l ög, –äg] **98**–10
   ...store [–stör′] **92**–7
cardigan sweater [kär′də gən swĕt′ər] **65**–27
Cardinals [kärd′nəlz] **14**
cardiologist [kär′dē äl′ə jĭst] **86**–3
cards [kärdz] **163**–H
careful [kër′fəl] **147**–24
caregiver [kër′gĭv′ər] **136**–12
careless [kër′ləs] **147**–23
CAR MAINTENANCE [kär′ mān′tn əns] **108–109**
carnation [kär nā′shən] **129**–18
carnival [kär′nə vəl] **152**–16
carousel [kăr′ə sĕl′] **110**–18
carousel slide projector [kăr′ə sĕl′ slīd′ prə jĕk′tər] **165**–29
carpenter [kär′pən tər] **48**–12, **136**–13
carpet [kär′pət] **42**–27

Index

carriage [kăr/ĭj] **95**–16
carrots [kăr/əts] **51**–3
carry [kăr/ē] **62**–H
carry-on bag [kăr/ē än băg/, –ön–] **111**–H
CARS AND TRUCKS [kärz/ ən trŭks/] **106**
cart [kärt] **54**–3, **91**–31
carton [kär/tn] **56**–4
  …of eggs [–əv ĕgz/] **56**–16
cartoon [kär tōōn/] **167**–19
cartridge [kär/trĭj] / [–kär/trĭj] **162**–2
  typewriter… [tīp/rī/tər–] **143**–31
carving knife [kär/vĭng nīf/] **59**–12
cash [kăsh(/–)] **20**–13, **97**–D
  …register [–rĕj/ə stər] **55**–18, **140**–N
cashier [kă shïr/] **136**–14
casserole dish [kăs/ə rōl dĭsh/] **59**–11
cassette [kə sĕt/]
  …player [–plā/ər] **3**–11, **164**–2, 15
  …recorder [–rī kör/dər] **164**–3
cast [kăst] **81**–29
casual [kăzh/ōō əl] **71**–37
cat [kăt] **133**–9
catch [kăch] **156**–E
catcher's mask [kăch/ərz măsk/] **161**–15
caterer [kā/tər ər] **33**–12
caterpillar [kăt/ə pĭl/ər, kăt/ər–] **132**–21
catfish [kăt/fĭsh/] **53**–17
cattle [kăt/l] **148**–21
cauliflower [kö/lĭ flow/ər, kä/–] **51**–16
cavity [kăv/ə tē] **84**–20
C-clamp [sē/klămp/] **150**–6
CD (compact disc) [sē/dē/] **98**–14
  …player [–plā/ər] **164**–14
  …ROM disc [–räm/ dĭsk/] **144**–2
ceiling [sē/lĭng] **42**–5
  …fan [–făn/] **41**–4
celery [sĕl/ə rē] **51**–9
cello [chĕl/ō] **120**–9
cellular phone [sĕl/yə lər fōn/] **9**–13
Celsius [sĕl/sē əs] **10**
cent [sĕnt] **20**–1
centimeter (cm) [sĕn/tə mē/tər] **15**–12
CENTRAL AMERICA [sĕn/trəl ə mĕr/ə kə] **122**–123
central time [sĕn/trəl tīm/] **17**–28
cents [sĕnts] **20**–2, 3, 4
cereal [sïr/ē əl] **56**–18
Ceremony [sĕr/ə mō/nē] **32**
Certificate of Naturalization
  [sər tĭf/ə kət əv năch/rə lə zā/shən] **29**–6
certified mail [sür/tə fīd/ māl/] **96**–11
chain [chān] (hardware) **37**–28, **150**–36, (jewelry) **69**–31
chair [(–)chër(/–)] **2**–7
  dining room… [dī/nĭng rōōm/–] **41**–16
  easy… [ē/zē–] **42**–24
  high… [hī/–] **95**–7
  rocking… [räk/ĭng–] **94**–6
  swivel… [swĭv/əl–] **143**–22
chalk [chök] **3**–16
chalkboard [chök/börd/] **2**–1
  …eraser [–ī rā/sər] **3**–17
change [chānj(/–)] **21**–9
  …purse [–pürs/] **69**–25
change [chānj(/–)]
  …diapers [–dī/pərz] **94**–E
  …the sheets [–dhə shēts/] **46**–P

…your diet [–yər dī/ət] **80**–C
changing table [chān/jĭng tā/bəl] **45**–12, **95**–9
cheap [chēp] **11**–20
check [chĕk(/–)]
  …blood pressure [–blŭd/ prĕsh/ər] **85**–B
  …your bags [–yər băgz/] **111**–B
  …your work [–yər würk/] **7**–Y
checkbook [chĕk/bŏŏk/] **97**–7
checked [chĕkt] **70**–11
checker [chĕk/ər] **55**–19
checkers [chĕk/ərz] **162**–5
check in [chĕk/ ĭn/] **111**–D
check-in counter [chĕk/ĭn kown/tər] **110**–3
checking account number [chĕk/ĭng ə kownt/ nŭm/bər] **97**–8
check out [chĕk/ owt/] **98** ✦
checkout desk [chĕk/owt dĕsk/] **98**–16
checkstand [chĕk/stănd/] **55**–17
cheddar cheese [chĕd/ər chēz/] **53**–10
cheek [chēk] **74**–29
cheese [chēz] **53**–9, 10, 11, 12, **54**–38
cheeseburger [chēz/bür/gər] **60**–3
chef [shĕf] **63**–11
chef's salad [shĕfs/ săl/əd] **61**–9
chemistry [kĕm/ə strē] **119**–2
cherries [chĕr/ēz] **50**–16
cherry picker [chĕr/ē pĭk/ər] **149**–5
chess [chĕs] **162**–6
chest (body) [chĕst] **74**–13
chest of drawers [chĕst/ əv drörz/] **45**–8
chicken [chĭk/ən] **52**–16, **61**–12
  …soup [–sōōp/] **58**
chicken pox [chĭk/ən päks/] **79**–6
Chief Justice [chēf/ jŭs/təs] **116**–9
CHILDCARE CENTER [chīld/kër sĕn/tər] **94**–95
childcare worker [chīld/kër wür/kər] **94**–3
Childhood diseases [chīld/hŏŏd dĭ zē/zəz] **79**
children [chĭl/drən] **11**–11, 12, **22**–1
CHILDREN'S BEDROOM [chĭl/drənz bĕd/rōōm/] **45**
children's program [chĭl/drənz prō/grăm] **167**–24
child safety seat [chīld/ săf/tē sēt/] **109**–39
chili peppers [chĭl/ē pĕp/ərz] **51**–8
chills [chĭlz] **78**–9
chimney [chĭm/nē] **38**–21
chimpanzee [chĭm/păn zē/] **135**–28
chin [chĭn] **74**–31
china cabinet [chī/nə kăb/ə nət] **41**–1
chipmunk [chĭp/mŭngk/] **133**–20
chiropractor [kī/rə prăk/tər] **81**–H
chisel [chĭz/əl] **151**–51
choke [chōk] **82**–L
chop [chäp] **58**–G
chorus [kör/əs] **121**–3
Christmas [krĭs/məs] **168**–18
  …tree [–trē/] **168**–20
chrysanthemum [krĭ săn/thə məm] **129**–19
church [chürch] **88**–6
cigarette lighter [sĭg/ə rĕt/ lī/tər, sĭg/ə rĕt–] **108**–32
circle [sür/kəl] **7**–5
circle [sür/kəl] **118**–5
circular saw [sür/kyə lər sö/] **150**–10
circumference [sər kŭm/frəns] **118**–15
Citizen application requirements
  [sĭt/ə zən ăp/lə kā/shən rĭ kwīr/mənts] **116**
CITIZENSHIP [sĭt/ə zən shĭp/] **116**
city [sĭt/ē] **4**–7, **34**–1

...center [–sĕn/tər] **88** ✦
...hall [–höl/] **89**–17
CITY STREETS [sĭt/ē strēts/] **88–89**
claim your baggage [klām/ yər băg/ĭj] **111**–P
clams [klămz] **53**–28
clap [klăp] **32**–B
clarinet [klăr/ə nĕt/] **120**–4
CLASSROOM [klăs/rōom/] **2–3**
classroom [klăs/rōom/] **5**–1
Class work [klăs/ würk/] **7**
claw [klö] **132**–4
clay [klā] **162**–14
clean [klēn] (household) **27**–N, **46**–C, **72**–D, (teeth) **85**–I
clean [klēn] **72**–16
CLEANING SUPPLIES [klē/nĭng sə plīz/] **47**
cleanser [klĕn/zər] **47**–23
clear [klïr(/–)] **10**–6
...tape [–tāp/] **143**–39
clear [klïr] **62**–G
clear [klïr] **10**–6
clerk [(–)klürk(/)] **5**–18
desk... [dĕsk/–] **145**–8
file... [fīl/–] **142**–12
library... [lī/brĕr ē–] **98**–17
shipping... [shĭp/ĭng–] **146**–15
stock... [stäk/–] **139**–55
climb [klīm] **153**–C
climbing apparatus [klī/mĭng ăp ə răt/əs] **153**–14
CLINICS [klĭn/ĭks] **84**
clipboard [klĭp/börd/] **143**–26
clip-on earrings [klĭp/än ïr/ĭngz, –ön–] **69**–38
clock [kläk(/–)] **3**–10
...radio [–rā/dē ō] **44**–16, **164**–1
close [klōz] **2**–J
closet [kläz/ət] **11**–15, 16, **43** ✦, **44**–4
cloth diapers [klöth/ dī/pərz] **95**–21
clothesline [klōz/līn/] **72**–9
clothespin [klōz/pĭn/] **72**–10
CLOTHING I, II, III [klō/dhĭng] **64–67**
cloudy [klow/dē] **10**–7
clubs [klŭbz] **163**–26
clutch [klŭch] **109**–45
coach [kōch] **5** ✦, **158**–2
coal [kōl] **126**–4
coat [kōt] (clothing) **66**, (animal) **134**–19
cobra [kō/brə] **131**–40
cockpit [käk/pĭt/] **110**–11
cockroaches [käk/rō/chəz] **49**–25
coconuts [kō/kə nŭts/] **50**–22
cod [käd] **130**–8
coffee [kö/fē] **55**–51, **61**–22
...cup [–kŭp/] **41**–27
...shop [–shäp/] **88**–2
...table [–tā/bəl] **42**–23
instant... [ĭn/stənt–] **55**–51
coffeemaker [kö/fē mā/kər] **40**–11
COFFEE SHOP MENU [kö/fē shäp/ mĕn/yōo] **61**
coin collection [koyn/ kə lĕk/shən] **162**–13
Coins [koynz] **20**
colander [käl/ən dər] **59**–17
cold [kōld] (weather) **10**–4, (feeling) **30**–4
cold (illness) [kōld(/–)] **79**–1
...tablets [–tăb/ləts] **81**–17
cold water [kōld/ wö/tər] **43**–7
coleslaw [kōl/slö/] **53**–14

collar [käl/ər] **73**–7
collate [kō/lāt/, kə lāt/] **142**–F
collect [kə lĕkt/]
...the papers [–dhə pā/pərz] **7**–Q
...things [–thĭngz/] **162**–A
collection [kə lĕk/shən] **162**–12, 13
college [käl/ĭj] **112**–10
...degree [–də grē/] **29**–7
...dormitory [–dör/mə tör/ē] **34**–9
community... [kə myōo/nə tē–] **112** ✦
cologne [kə lōn/] **76**–5
colon [kō/lən] **113**–12
color hair [kŭl/ər hër/] **23**–D
coloring book [kŭl/ə rĭng bōok/] **45**–20
COLORS [kŭl/ərz] **12**
comb...hair [kōm/ hër/] **76**–G
comb [kōm] **23**–22, **76**–13
comedy [käm/ə dē] **166**–10
come home [kŭm/ hōm/] **27**–Q
comet [käm/ət] **127**–25
comfortable [kŭmf/tə bəl, –tər–] **30**–7
comforter [kŭm/fər tər] **45**–2
comma [käm/ə] **113**–10
commercial fisher [kə mür/shəl fĭsh/ər] **136**–15
commit a crime [kə mĭt/ ə krīm/] **100** ✦
Common illnesses and childhood diseases
[käm/ən ĭl/nə səz ən chīld/hōod dĭ zē/zəz] **79**
community college [kə myōo/nə tē käl/ĭj] **112** ✦
compact [käm/păkt] **106**–2
compact disc (CD) [käm/păkt dĭsk/] **98**–14
compliment [käm/plə mĕnt/] **8**–G
components [kəm pō/nənts] **140**–A
composition [käm/pə zĭsh/ən] **113**–2
compost pile [käm/pōst pīl/] **39**–10
computer [kəm pyōo/tər] **3**–15
...programmer [–prō/grăm ər] **136**–16
...science [–sī/əns] **121**–4
...workstation [–würk/stā/shən] **143**–21
COMPUTERS [kəm pyōo/tərz] **144**
concert [kän/sərt] **166**–6
concierge [kän/sē ërzh/, kōn/–] **145** ✦
concrete [käng/krēt, kän krēt/] **149**–10
condiments [kän/də mənts] **60** ✦
conditioner [kən dĭsh/ə nər] **76**–10
condominium [kän/də mĭn/ē əm] **34** ✦
conductor [kən dŭk/tər] **104**–16
cone [kōn] **118**–11
confetti [kən fĕt/ē] **168**–3
confused [kən fyōozd/] **31**–27
congestion [kən jĕs/chən] **78**–7
Congressman [käng/grəs mən] **116**–2
Congresswoman [käng/grəs wŏom/ən] **116**–2
Conservation [kän/sər vā/shən] **126**
conserve [kən sürv/] **126**–B, C
constellation [kän/stə lā/shən] **127**–24
CONSTRUCTION [kən strŭk/shən] **149**
construction worker [kən strŭk/shən wür/kər] **149**–1
contact lenses [kän/tăkt lĕn/zəz] **81**–36
container [kən tā/nər] **56**–5, **59**–3
...of cottage cheese [–əv kät/ĭj chēz/] **56**–17
CONTAINERS AND PACKAGED FOODS
[kən tā/nərz ən păk/ĭjd fōodz/] **56**
Continents [kän/tə nənts] **124**
control tower [kən trōl/ tow/ər] **110**–7
convenience store [kən vēn/yəns stör/] **90**–3

Index

CONVERSATION, EVERYDAY [ĕv/rē dā/ kän/vər sā/shən] **8**
convertible [kən vür/tə bəl] **106**–5
convert the measurements
   [kən vürt/ dhə mĕzh/ər mənts] **57**–C
conveyor belt [kən vā/ər bĕlt/] **146**–12
convict [kən vĭkt/] **99**–14
cook [kŏŏk] **27**–P, **58**–F, **140**–C
cook [kŏŏk] **137**–17
cooked chicken [kŏŏkt/ chĭk/ən] **52**–25
cookies [kŏŏk/ēz] **54**–31, **56**–20
cookie sheet [kŏŏk/ē shēt/] **59**–27
cool [kŏŏl] **10**–3
coolant [kŏŏ/lənt] **109**–56
cooler [kŏŏ/lər] **155**–11
co-op [kō/äp/] **34** ✦
copy [käp/ē] **6**–F
copy center [käp/ē sĕn/tər] **91**–22
cord [körd] **9**–3, **151**–14
cordless phone [körd/ləs fōn/] **9**–12
core course [kör/ körs/] **121** ✦
corn [körn] **51**–27, **148**–4
corned beef [körnd/ bēf/] **53**–8
corner [kör/nər] **91**–17, **105**–10, **107**–1
corral [kə räl/] **148**–17
correct [kə rĕkt/] **7**–Z
correction fluid [kə rĕk/shən flŏŏ/əd] **143**–33
corrosive [kə rō/sĭv] **147**–4
cost [köst] **21**–6
costume [käs/tŏŏm] **168**–13
cottage cheese [kät/ĭj chēz/] **56**–17
cotton [kät/n] **70**–16, **148**–6
couch [kowch] **42**–19
cough [köf] **78**–A
cough syrup [köf/ sĭr/əp, –sür/–] **81**–20
counselor [kown/slər] **5**–16
counselor's office [kown/slərz ö/fəs] **5**–15
count [kownt] **15** ✦
counter [kown/tər] **40**–22, **46**–O, **60**–13, **80**–12, **110**–3
country [kŭn/trē] **34**–4
county fair [kown/tē fër/] **152**–19
courier [kür/ē ər, kŏŏr/–] **138**–38
court [kört(/–)] **99**–C
   ...reporter [–rĭ pör/tər] **99**–12
courthouse [kört/hows/] **89**–18
courtroom [kört/rŏŏm/] **99**–7
courtyard [kört/yärd/] **37**–18
cousin [kŭz/ən] **24**–12
cover-up [kŭv/ər ŭp/] **66**–25
cow [kow] **133**–3
coyote [kī ō/tē, kī/ōt/] **134**–3
CPR (cardiopulmonary resuscitation) [sē/pē/är/] **83**–17
CPU (central processing unit) [sē/pē/yŏŏ/] **144**–1
crab [krăb] **53**–22, **130**–16
cracked [krăkt] **48**–4
cradle [krād/l] **45**–19
crane [krān] **149**–7
crash [krăsh] **102**–3
crayons [krā/änz] **45**–21
creamer [krē/mər] **41**–13
credit card [krĕd/ət kärd/] **20**–15
creek [krēk, krĭk] **117** ✦
crescent moon [krĕs/ənt mŏŏn/] **127**–14
crewneck sweater [krŏŏ/nĕk/ swĕt/ər] **71**–26
crib [krĭb] **45**–6
cricket [krĭk/ət] **132**–24

CRIME [krīm] **100**
criminal [krĭm/ə nəl] **100** ✦
crochet [krō shā/] **163**–20
crocodile [kräk/ə dīl/] **131**–37
crocus [krō/kəs] **129**–25
Crops [kräps] **148**
cross-country skiing [krös/kŭn/trē skē/ĭng] **160**–3
cross out [krös/ owt/] **7**–U
cross the street [krös/ dhə strēt/] **90**–A
crosswalk [krös/wök/] **90**–8
crucible tongs [krŏŏ/sə bəl tängz/, –töngz/] **119**–15
crutches [krŭch/əz] **80**–1
cry [krī] **32**–C
cubby [kŭb/ē] **94**–4
cube [kyŏŏb] **118**–10
cucumbers [kyŏŏ/kŭm bərz] **51**–12
cuff [kŭf] **73**–5
cup [kŭp(/–)] **63**–21
   ...of flour [–əv flow/ər] **57**–10
   ...of oil [–əv oyl/] **57**–2
curb [kürb] **90**–10
curling iron [kür/lĭng ī/ərn] **76**–15
curly [kür/lē] **23**–11
curtains [kür/tnz] **44**–5
curved [kürvd] **118**–19
custodian [kŭ stō/dē ən] **138**–35
customs [kŭs/təmz] **110**–20
   ...officer [–ö/fə sər] **110**–21
cut [kŭt] **23**–A, **77**–N
cut [kŭt] **78**–13
cute [kyŏŏt] **22**–24
cutting board [kŭt/ĭng börd/] **40**–27
cut up [kŭt/ ŭp/] **58**–M
cycling [sī/klĭng] **159**–4
cyclist [sī/klĭst] **153**–3
cylinder [sĭl/ən dər] **118**–12
daffodil [dăf/ə dĭl/] **129**–26
DAILY ROUTINES [dā/lē rŏŏ tēnz/] **26**–27
dairy section [dër/ē sĕk/shən] **54**–9
daisy [dā/zē] **129**–14
dance [dăns] **33**–J
dance floor [dăns/ flör/] **33**–16
dangerous situation [dān/jər əs sĭch/ŏŏ ā/shən] **147**–8
dark blue [därk/ blŏŏ/] **12**–2
dashboard [dăsh/börd/] **108**–17
data [dā/tə, dăt/ə] **144** ✦
date [dāt(/–)] **18**–14
   ...of birth [–əv bürth/] **4**–16
dates (fruit) [dāts] **50**–25
daughter [dö/tər] **24**–21
daughter-in-law [dö/tər ĭn lö/] **24** ✦
day [dā] **18**–10
daylight saving time [dā/līt/ sā/vĭng tīm/] **17**–33
Days of the week [dāz/ əv dhə wēk/] **18**
dead-bolt lock [dĕd/bōlt/ läk/] **37**–29
dead end [dĕd/ĕnd/] **107**–8
deaf [dĕf] **22**–27
decaf coffee [dē/kăf/ kö/fē] **61**–23
December [dĭ sĕm/bər] **19**–36
deck [dĕk] **38**–16
declaration form [dĕk/lə rā/shən förm/] **110**–22
decorate [dĕk/ə rāt/] **169**–C
deer [dïr] **134**–14
defendant [dĭ fĕn/dənt] **99**–5
defense attorney [dĭ fĕns/ ə tür/nē] **99**–4

degree [də grē/] **29**–7, **112** ✦
degrees [də grēz/]
...Celsius [–sĕl/sē əs] **10**
...Fahrenheit [–făr/ən hīt/] **10**
DELI AND SEAFOOD [dĕl/ē ən sē/food/] **53**
deliver [də lĭv/ər] **96**–C
delivery person [də lĭv/ə rē pür/sən] **137**–18
dental [dĕn/təl]
...assistant [–ə sĭs/tənt] **84**–19, **137**–19
...floss [–flös/, –fläs/] **77**–22
...hygienist [–hī jē/nĭst, –jĕn/ĭst] **84**–16
Dental clinic [dĕn/təl klĭn/ĭk] **84**
DENTAL EXAMS [dĕn/təl ĭg zămz/] **85**
dentist [dĕn/tĭst] **84**–18, **137**–20
deodorant [dē ō/dər ənt] **76**–4
department store [dĭ pärt/mənt stör/] **93**–13
departure time [dĭ pär/chər tīm/] **111** ✦
deposit [dĭ päz/ət] **9**–C
deposit [dĭ päz/ət] **97**–C
...slip [–slĭp/] **97**–12
depth [dĕpth] **15**–15
DESCRIBING CLOTHES [dĭ skrī/bĭng klōz/] **70**–**71**
DESCRIBING HAIR [dĭ skrī/bĭng hër/] **23**
DESCRIBING THINGS [dĭ skrī/bĭng thĭngz/] **11**
desert [dĕz/ərt] **117**–4
design [dĭ zīn/] **146**–A
designated drivers [dĕz/ĭg nā/təd drī/vərz] **101** ✦
designer [dĭ zī/nər] **146**–3
desk [dĕsk/–)] **2**–6, **142**–1
...calendar [–kăl/ən dər] **142**–6
...clerk [–klürk/] **145**–9
...pad [–păd/] **142**–7
dessert tray [dĭ zürt/ trā/] **63**–7
destination [dĕs/tə nā/shən] **111** ✦
diabetes [dī/ə bē/tēz, –təs] **79**–9
diagonal [dī ăg/ə nəl, –ăg/nəl] **118**–23
dial [dī/əl] **9**–D
dial tone [dī/əl tōn/] **9**–B
diameter [dī ăm/ə tər] **118**–17
diamonds [dī/məndz] **163**–27
diaper [dī/pər]
...pail [–pāl/] **45**–13, **95**–23
...pins [–pĭnz/] **95**–22
dice [dīs] **162**–4
dictate [dĭk/tāt] **6**–N
dictionary [dĭk/shə nër/ē] **3**–28
Dictionary work [dĭk/shə nër ē würk/] **6**
die [dī] **29**–R
dietician [dī/ə tĭsh/ən] **87**–25
difference [dĭf/rəns] **118** ✦
difficult [dĭf/ĭ kŭlt/] **11**–24
dime [dīm] **20**–3
Dimensions [də mĕn/shənz] **15**
diner [dī/nər] **62**–5
DINING AREA [dī/nĭng ër/ē ə] **41**
dining room [dī/nĭng room/] **62**–2
...chair [–chër/] **41**–16
...table [–tā/bəl] **41**–17
dinner [dĭn/ər]
...fork [–förk/] **63**–25
...plate [–plāt/] **63**–15
diploma [də plō/mə] **29**–2, **32**–7
direct flight [də rĕkt/ flīt/, dī–] **111** ✦
Directions [də rĕk/shənz, dī–] **107**

DIRECTIONS AND TRAFFIC SIGNS
[də rĕk/shənz ən trăf/ĭk sīnz/, dī–] **107**
directory [də rĕk/tə rē, dī–] **9**–8, **93**–19
directory assistance (411) [də rĕk/tə rē ə sĭs/təns, dī–] **9**–8
dirty [dür/tē] **72**–15
discuss [dĭ skŭs/] **6**–L
disgusted [dĭ skŭs/təd] **30**–9
dish [dĭsh(/–)]
...drainer [–drā/nər] **40**–3
...towel [–tow/əl] **47**–22
dishroom [dĭsh/room/] **63**–12
dishwasher [dĭsh/wä/shər, –wö/–] (machine) **40**–4,
(person) **63**–13
dishwashing liquid [dĭsh/wä/shĭng lĭk/wəd, –wö/–] **47**–21
disinfectant [dĭs/ən fĕk/tənt] **95**–19
disk [dĭsk(/–)] **144**–5
...drive [–drīv/] **144**–3
display case [dĭ splā/ kās/] **69**–7
disposable diapers [dĭ spō/zə bəl dī/pərz] **95**–20
dissection kit [dĭ sĕk/shən kĭt/, dī–] **119**–7
dive [dīv] **157**–5
diving mask [dī/vĭng măsk/] **155**–3
division [də vĭzh/ən] **118**–4
divorced [də vörst/] **25**–24
DJ (disc jockey) [dē/jā/] / [dĭsk/ jäk/ē] **33**–17
do [doo(/–)]
...an experiment [–ən ĭk spĕr/ə mənt] **119**–A
...crafts [–krăfts/] **162**–A
...errands [–ĕr/əndz] **90** ✦
...homework [–hōm/würk/] **27**–T
...manual labor [–măn/yoo əl lā/bər] **140**–D
dockworker [däk/wür/kər] **137**–21
doctor [däk/tər] **84**–6, **137**–22
Doctorate [däk/tər ət] **112** ✦
dog [dög] **11**–17, 18, **133**–11
dogwood [dög/wood/] **128**–16
DOING THE LAUNDRY [doo/ĭng dhə lön/drē] **72**–2
doll [däl] **45**–18
dollar [däl/ər] **20**–7
dollhouse [däl/hows/] **45**–14
doll making kit [däl/ mā/kĭng kĭt/] **162**–15
dolphin [däl/fən, döl/–] **131**–30
DOMESTIC ANIMALS AND RODENTS
[də mĕs/tĭk ăn/ə məlz ən rōd/nts] **133**
domesticated animals [də mĕs/tə kā/təd ăn/ə məlz] **133** ✦
donkey [däng/kē, dŭng/–, döng/–] **133**–2
do not enter [doo/ nät/ ĕn/tər] **107**–4
do not wash [doo/ nät/ wäsh/, –wösh/] **72** ✦
don't [dōnt(/–)]
...**drink** and **drive** [–drĭngk/ ən drīv/] **101**–G
...**open** [–ō/pən] **101**–F
donut shop [dō/nŭt shäp/] **91**–20
doorbell [dör/bĕl/] **38**–10
door chain [dör/ chān/] **37**–28
doorknob [dör/näb/] **37**–30
doorman [dör/măn/] **36**–10, **145**–2
dosage [dō/sĭj] **80** ✦
double boiler [dŭb/əl boy/lər] **59**–8
doughnut [dō/nŭt] **60**–15, **60** ✦
down (feathers) [down(/–)]
...jacket [–jăk/ət] **66**–15
...vest [–vĕst/] **66**–13
down (preposition) [down] **105**–8
downhill skiing [down/hĭl/ skē/ĭng] **160**–1
downstairs [down/stërz/] **38** ✦

Index

downtown [down/town/] **88** ✦
drain [drān] **43**–4
drapes [drāps] **42**–16
draw a picture [drö/ ə pĭk/chər] **6**–M
draw blood [drö/ blŭd/] **85**–G
drawer [drör] **40**–23, **44**–3
dress [(–)drĕs(/)] **64**–3
   maternity… [mə tür/nə tē–] **65**–19
dress [drĕs] **94**–J
dresser [drĕs/ər] **44**–2
dressmaker [drĕs/mā/kər] **73**–2
dress shop [drĕs/ shäp/] **92** ✦
dribble [drĭb/əl] **156**–K
drill [drĭl(/–)] **84**–21, **150**–8, 23
   …bit [–bĭt/] **150**–23
drill a tooth [drĭl/ ə tooth/] **85**–K
drink [drĭngk(/–)] / [–drĭngk/] **60**–B
   …fluids [–floo/ədz] **80**–B
   don't… [dōnt–] **101**–G
dripping [drĭp/ĭng] **49**–16
drive [drīv] **26**–I, **90**–C, **140**–E
drive (computer) [drīv] **144**–3, 20
driver's [drī/vərz]
   …education [–ĕj/ə kā/shən] **121**–5
   …license [–lī/səns] **29**–4
drive-thru window [drīv/throo/ wĭn/dō] **90**–13
driveway [drīv/wā/] **38**–5
drop off [dräp/ öf/] **94**–A
dropper [dräp/ər] **119**–14
drought [drowt] **103**–10
drown [drown] **82**–I
drugs [drŭgz] **100**–4
drugstore [drŭg/stör/] **90**–2
drums [drŭmz] **120**–18
drumsticks [drŭm/stĭks/] **52**–22
drunk driving [drŭngk/ drī/vĭng] **100**–3
dry [drī(/–)]
   …hair [–hër/] **76**–H
   …the dishes [–dhə dĭsh/əz] **46**–N
dry [drī] **72**–18
dry-clean [drī/klēn/] **72** ✦
dry cleaners [drī/ klē/nərz] **72** ✦, **91**–24
dryer [drī/ər] **72**–4
   …sheets [–shēts/] **72**–5
Dry measures [drī/ mĕzh/ərz] **57**
drywall [drī/wöl/] **149**–18
duck [dŭk(/–)] **52**–18, **132**–13
   …pond [–pänd/] **153**–6
dump truck [dŭmp/ trŭk/] **106**–12
duplex house [doo/plĕks hows/] **34** ✦
dust [dŭst] **46**–A
dust [dŭst(/–)]
   …mop [–mäp/] **47**–17
   …ruffle [–rŭf/əl] **44**–22
   …storm [–störm/] **10**–21
dustpan [dŭst/pän/] **47**–11
dye hair [dī/ hër/] **23**–D
eagle [ē/gəl] **132**–10
ear [ïr(/–)] **74**–28
   …infection [–ĭn fĕk/shən] **79**–3
earache [ïr/āk/] **78**–3
early [ür/lē] **17**–22
earmuffs [ïr/mŭfs/] (outdoor) **66**–12, (safety) **147**–14
earplugs [ïr/plŭgz/] **147**–13
earrings [ïr/ĭngz] **69**–37

Earth [ürth] **127**–7
earthquake [ürth/kwāk/] **102**–5
easel [ē/zəl] **163**–21
east [ēst] **107, 123, 124**
eastern time [ē/stərn tīm/] **17**–29
easy [ē/zē] **11**–23
   …chair [–chër/] **42**–24
eat [ēt(/–)] **60**–B
   …breakfast [–brĕk/fəst] **26**–E
eat out [ēt/ owt/] **62** ✦
eclipse [ĭ klĭps/]
   lunar… [loo/nər–] **127** ✦
   solar… [sō/lər–] **127** ✦
economics [ĕk/ə näm/ĭks, ē/kə–] **121**–6
edit [ĕd/ət] **113**–B
eel [ēl] **130**–5
eggbeater [ĕg/bē/tər] **59**–20
eggplants [ĕg/plänts/] **51**–18
eggs [(–)ĕgz(/)] **54**–34
   scrambled… [skrăm/bəld–] **61**–1
eight [āt] **14**
eighteen [ā/tēn/] **14**
eighteenth [ā/tēnth/] **14**
eighth [ātth, āth] **14, 15**–1
eighty [ā/tē] **14, 15**–10
eject [ĭ jĕkt/] **165**–F
elastic bandage [ĭ lăs/tĭk băn/dĭj] **83**–12
elbow [ĕl/bō] **74**–15
elderly [ĕl/dər lē] **22**–15
Election [ĭ lĕk/shən] **115**
elective [ĭ lĕk/tĭv] **121** ✦
electric [ĭ lĕk/trĭk]
   …can opener [–kăn/ ō/pə nər] **40**–14
   …drill [–drĭl/] **150**–8
   …keyboard [–kē/börd/] **120**–20
   …mixer [–mĭk/sər] **40**–25
   …pencil sharpener [–pĕn/səl shär/pə nər] **142**–9
   …shaver [–shā/vər] **77**–24
electrical [ĭ lĕk/trĭ kəl] **151**–38
   …hazard [–hăz/ərd] **147**–1
   …tape [–tāp/] **151**–38
electrician [ĭ lĕk trĭsh/ən] **48**–9
ELECTRONICS AND PHOTOGRAPHY
   [ĭ lĕk trän/ĭks ən fə täg/rə fē] **164**–**165**
electronics store [ĭ lĕk trän/ĭks stör/] **93**–18
elementary school [ĕl/ə mĕn/trē skool/] **112**–5
elephant [ĕl/ə fənt] **135**–42
elevator [ĕl/ə vā/tər] **37**–34, **145** ✦
eleven [ĭ lĕv/ən] **14**
eleventh [ĭ lĕv/ənth] **14**
ellipse [ĭ lĭps/] **118**–9
elm [ĕlm] **128**–17
embarrassed [ĭm băr/əst] **31**–25
embroidery [ĭm broy/də rē] **163**–19
EMERGENCIES AND NATURAL DISASTERS [ĭ mür/jən sēz ən
   năch/rəl dĭ zăs/tərz, –năch/ər əl–] **102**–**103**
emergency [ĭ mür/jən sē]
   …brake [–brāk/] **109**–44
   …card [–kärd/] **111**–K
   …exit [–ĕg/zət, –ĕk/sət] **111**–J
   …medical technician (EMT)
      [–mĕd/ĭ kəl tĕk nĭsh/ən] / [ē/ĕm/tē/] **87**–26
   …service (911) [–sür/vəs] **9**–9
Emergency room [ĭ mür/jən sē room/] **87**
emery board [ĕm/ə rē börd/, ĕm/rē–] **77**–30

empty [ĕmp/tē] **46**–F
empty [ĕmp/tē] **11**–10
encyclopedia [ĭn sī/klə pē/dē ə] **98**–18
end table [ĕnd/ tā/bəl] **42**–21
end the conversation [ĕnd/ dhə kän/vər sā/shən] **8**–C
ENERGY AND THE ENVIRONMENT
  [ĕn/ər jē ən dhē ĭn vī/rən mənt, –vī/ərn–] **126**
Energy resources [ĕn/ər jē rē/sör səz, –rī sör/səz] **126**
engine [ĕn/jən] **109**–41
engineer [ĕn/jə nïr/] **137**–23
English as a second language
  [ĭng/glĭsh əz ə sĕk/ənd lăng/gwĭj] **121**–7
ENGLISH COMPOSITION [ĭng/glĭsh käm/pə zĭsh/ən] **113**
ENTERTAINMENT [ĕn/tər tān/mənt] **166**–**167**
enter your PIN number [ĕn/tər yər pĭn/ nŭm/bər] **97**–B
entrance [ĕn/trəns] **36** ✦
Entryway [ĕn/trē wā/] **37**
envelope [ĕn/və lōp/] **96**–1, **143**–20
ENVIRONMENT [ĭn vī/rən mənt, –vī/ərn–] **126**
Equivalents [ĭ kwĭv/ə lənts] **15**
erase [ĭ rās/] **2**–H
eraser [ĭ rā/sər] **3**–21
escalator [ĕs/kə lā/tər] **93**–21
evening [ēv/nĭng] **17**–19
  ...gown [–gown/] **65**–29
every day [ĕv/rē dā/] **18**–21
EVERYDAY CONVERSATION [ĕv/rē dā/ kän/vər sā/shən] **8**
evidence [ĕv/ə dəns] **99**–9
examination table [ĭg zăm/ə nā/shən tā/bəl] **84**–13
examine [ĭg zăm/ən] **85**–F
examining room [ĭg zăm/ə nĭng rōōm/] **84**–9
exchange [ĭks chānj/] **21**–G
excited [ĭk sī/təd] **31**–23
exclamation mark [ĕk/sklə mā/shən märk/] **113**–8
Excuse me. [ĭk skyōōz/ mē] **8**
Executive [ĭg zĕk/yə tĭv] **116**
exercise [ĕk/sər sīz/] **27**–W, **80**–D, **157**–P
exhausted [ĭg zö/stəd] **30** ✦
exhibition [ĕk/sə bĭsh/ən] **152**–21
expensive [ĭk spĕn/sĭv] **11**–19
experience turbulence [ĭk spïr/ē əns tür/byə ləns] **111**–N
expiration date [ĕk/spə rā/shən dāt/] **80** ✦
Exploration [ĕk/splə rā/shən] **114**
explosion [ĭk splō/zhən] **102**–4
Express Mail [ĭk sprĕs/ māl/] **96**–15
extension cord [ĭk stĕn/shən körd/] **151**–14
exterminate [ĭk stür/mə nāt/] **49** ✦
exterminator [ĭk stür/mə nā/tər] **49**–21
extra [ĕk/strə]
  ...large [–lärj/] **70**–5
  ...small [–smöl/] **70**–1
extract a tooth [ĭk străkt/ ə tōōth/] **85** ✦
eye [ī(/–)] / [–ī/] **73**–23, **74**–27
  ...chart [–chärt/] **84**–11
  ...glasses [–glăs/əz] **81**–35
  ...hook [–hook/] **150**–35
  ...shadow [–shăd/ō] **77**–34
  hook and... [hook/ ən–] **73**–23
eyebrow [ī/brow/] **74**–32
  ...pencil [–pĕn/səl] **77**–33
eyedrops [ī/dräps/] **81**–22
eyelashes [ī/lăsh/əz] **74**–34
eyelid [ī/lĭd/] **74**–33
eyeliner [ī/lī/nər] **77**–35
fabric softener [făb/rĭk sö/fə nər] **72**–6

Face [fās] **74, 77**
face powder [fās/ pow/dər] **77**–39
FACTORY [făk/tə rē, –trē] **146**
factory [făk/tə rē, –trē]
  ...owner [–ō/nər] **146**–2
  ...worker [–wür/kər] **146**–6
fall [föl] **82**–O
fall [föl] **19**–39
fall in love [föl/ ĭn lŭv/] **28**–K
FAMILY [făm/lē, făm/ə lē] **24**–**25**
fan [făn] (appliance) **41**–4, (person) **158**–4
fancy [făn/sē] **71**–39
fare [fër(/–)] **104**–5
  ...card [–kärd/] **104**–12
far from [fär/ frŭm/, –frəm] **13** ✦
farm [färm(/–)] **34**–13
  ...equipment [–ĭ kwĭp/mənt] **148**–10
Farm animals [färm/ ăn/ə məlz] **133**
farmer [fär/mər] **148**–15
FARMING AND RANCHING [fär/mĭng ən răn/chĭng] **148**
farmworker [färm/wür/kər] **148**–8
fashion designer [făsh/ən dĭ zī/nər] **73** ✦
fast [făst] **11**–3
fasten your seat belt [făs/ən yər sēt/ bĕlt/] **111**–I
FAST FOOD [făst/ fōōd/] **60**
fast food restaurant [făst/ fōōd/ rĕs/tə rənt, –ränt] **90**–14
fast forward [făst/ för/wərd] **165**–C
fat [făt] **11**–7
father [fä/dhər] **24**–6, **25**–26
father-in-law [fä/dhər ĭn lö/] **24**–14
faucet [fö/sət] **43**–6, **49**–16
fax [făks] **142**–B
fax machine [făks/ mə shēn/] **143**–23
feast [fēst] **168**–16
feather [fĕdh/ər] **132**–5
  ...duster [–dŭs/tər] **47**–1
February [fĕb/yōō ër/ē, fĕb/rōō–] **19**–26
feed [fēd] **94**–D, **148**–D
feel [fēl(/–)]
  ...dizzy [–dĭz/ē] **78**–C
  ...nauseous [–nö/shəs, –zē əs] **78**–D
FEELINGS [fē/lĭngz] **30**–**31**
feet [fēt] **15** ✦
female [fē/māl/] **4**–14
fence [fĕns] **38**–3, **148**–19
fencing [fĕn/sĭng] **159**–5
ferry [fĕr/ē] **104**–23
fever [fē/vər] **78**–8
fiction [fĭk/shən] **98, 166**
field [fēld] (school) **5**–12, (farm) **148**–7, (sports) **159**–17
fifteen [fĭf/tēn/] **14**
fifteenth [fĭf/tēnth/] **14**
fifth [fĭfth] **14**
fifty [fĭf/tē] **14**
  ...dollars [–däl/ərz] **20**–11
  ...percent [–pər sĕnt/] **15**–9
figure skating [fĭg/yər skā/tĭng] **160**–5
figurine [fĭg/yə rēn/] **162**–10
file [fīl] **142**–H
file [fīl(/–)]
  ...cabinet [–kăb/ə nət] **142**–10
  ...clerk [–klürk/] **142**–12
  ...folder [–fōl/dər] **142**–11
filet of sole [fĭ lā/ əv sōl/] **53**–21
fill a cavity [fĭl/ ə kăv/ə tē] **85**–L

fill in the blank [fĭl/ ĭn dhə blăngk/] **7**–R
fill out [fĭl/ owt/] / [fĭl/ owt/–]
...a form [–ə förm/] **4**–B
...an application [–ən ăp/lə kā/shən] **141**–G
filling [fĭl/ĭng] **84**–22
film [fĭlm] (camera) **165**–26, (movie) **166**–1
fin [fĭn] **130**–1
find your seat [fīnd/ yər sēt/] **111**–G
FINDING A HOME [fīn/dĭng ə hōm/] **35**
fingernail [fĭng/gər nāl/] **75**–58
fingers [fĭng/gərz] **75**–57
finish [fĭn/ĭsh] **157**–Z
fins [fĭnz] **155**–2
fire [fīr(/–)] **42**–10, **102**–7
...escape [–ĭ skāp/] **36**–7
...exit [–ĕg/zət, –ĕk/sət] **37**–23
...extinguisher [–ĭk stĭng/gwĭ shər] **147**–22
...hydrant [–hī/drənt] **91**–28
...screen [–skrēn/] **42**–11
...station [–stā/shən] **88**–1
...truck [–trŭk/] **102**–9
firefighter [fīr/fī/tər] **102**–8, **137**–24
fireplace [fīr/plās/] **42**–9
fireworks [fīr/würks/] **168**–8
first [fürst(/–)] **14**
...draft [–drăft/] **113**–A
...floor [–flör/] **36**–1
...name [–nām/] **4**–2
...place [–plās/] **152**–20
...prize [–prīz/] **152**–20
FIRST AID [fürst/ ād/] **83**
first aid [fürst/ ād/]
...kit [–kĭt/] **83**–1
...manual [–măn/yoo əl] **83**–7
Fish [fĭsh] **53**
fish [fĭsh] **61**–17, **130**–12, 14, 15
fishing [fĭsh/ĭng] **154**–5
...net [–nĕt/] **154**–17
...pole [–pōl/] **154**–18
fitted sheet [fĭt/əd shēt/] **44**–14
fittings [fĭt/ĭngz] **151**–17
five [fīv(/–)] **14**–5, **20**
...after one [–ăf/tər wŭn/] **16**–5
...to two [tə tōō/] **16**–15
Five ways to cook chicken [fīv/ wāz/ tə kŏŏk/ chĭk/ən] **58**
fix [fĭks] **49** ✦
flag [flăg] **168**–9
flammable [flăm/ə bəl] **147**–2
flashlight [flăsh/līt/] **151**–39
flat sheet [flăt/ shēt/] **44**–13
flea market [flē/ mär/kət] **152**–22
fleas [flēz] **49**–23
flight attendant [flīt/ ə tĕn/dənt] **110**–13
flood [flŭd] **103**–16
floor [flör(/–)] / [–flör/] **44**–24
...lamp [–lămp/] **42**–15
...plan [–plăn/] **38**–1
dance... [dăns/–] **33**–16
floppy [flăp/ē] **144**–5
floral [flör/əl] **70**–12
florist [flör/ĭst] **92**–12, **137**–25
floss [flös, fläs] **77**–K
flounder [flown/dər] **130**–13
flour [flow/ər] **55**–45, **57**–10
flower [flow/ər] **39**–19, **129**–7

...bed [–bĕd/] **39**–A
...pot [–pät/] **39**–18
Parts of a... [pärts/ əv ə–] **129**
FLOWERS [flow/ərz] **129**
flu [flōō] **79**–2
fluid ounce [flōō/əd owns/] **57**–1
flute [flōōt] **120**–3
fly [flī] **140** ✦
fly [flī] **132**–29
flying disc [flī/ĭng dĭsk/] **159**–6, **161**–27
foam pad [fōm/ păd/] **154**–13
foggy [fö/gē, fäg/ē–] **10**–11
fold [fōld] **72**–F
Follow directions [fäl/ō də rek/shənz, –dī–] **7**
food [fōōd(/–)]
...court [–kört/] **93**–14
...processor [–prä/sē sər] **40**–26
FOOD PREPARATION [fōōd/ prĕp ə rā/shən] **58**
Foot [fŏŏt] **75**
foot [fŏŏt] (measurement) **15** ✦, (body) **74**–7
football [fŏŏt/böl/] **158**–11, **161**–22
...helmet [–hĕl/mət] **161**–20
forceps [för/səps, –sĕps] **119**–8
forehead [för/əd, –hĕd/, fär/–] **74**–20
foreign language [för/ən lăng/gwĭj, fär/–] **121**–8
forest [för/əst, fär/–] **117**–11
fork [förk] **41**–21, **63**–24, 25, ✦
forklift [förk/lĭft/] **146**–14
form [(–)förm(/)]
declaration... [dĕk/lə rā/shən–] **110**–22
registration... [rĕj/ə strā/shən–] **4**
formal [för/məl] **71**–36
former husband [för/mər hŭz/bənd] **25** ✦
former wife [för/mər wīf/] **25** ✦
formula [för/myə lə] **95**–25, **119**–19
forty [för/tē] **14**, **16**–12
foundation [fown dā/shən] **77**–40
fountain [fown/tn] / [–fown/tn] **92**–11
water... [wö/tər–] **153**–11
four [för] **14**
fourteen [för/tēn/] **14**
fourteenth [för/tēnth/] **14**
fourth [förth(/–)] **14**, **15**–2
...floor [–flör/] **36**–4
fox [fäks] **134**–15
Fractions [frăk/shənz] **15**
freezer [frē/zər] **40**–10
freezing [frē/zĭng] **10**–5
french fries [frĕnch/ frīz/] **60**–2
French horn [frĕnch/ hörn/] **120**–15
fresh [frĕsh] **53**–29
Friday [frī/dā, –dē] **18**–6
fried [frīd] **61**–17
frog [frög, fräg] **130**–25
front... [frŭnt(/–)]
...desk [–dĕsk/] **145**–8
...door [–dör/] **38**–11
...office [–ö/fəs] **146**–1
...seat [–sēt/] **109**–35
...walk [–wök/] **38**–14
...yard [–yärd/] **38**–15
frozen [frō/zən]
...fish [–fĭsh/] **53**–30
...foods [–fōōdz/] **55**–12
...vegetables [–vĕj/tə bəlz] **55**–43

...yogurt [–yō/gərt] **60**–11
FRUIT [frōot] **50**
frustrated [frŭs/trā/təd] **31**–28
fry [frī] **58**–5
frying pan [frī/ĭng păn/] **59**–5
fuel injection system [fyōo/əl ĭn jĕk/shən sĭs/təm] **109**–40
full [fŏol] (not empty) **11**–9, (satisfied) **30**–6
full [fŏol(/–)]
...moon [–mōon/] **127**–16
...slip [–slĭp/] **67**–22
full-size car [fŏol/sīz/ kär/] **106**–4
funnel [fŭn/əl] **119**–12
funny [fŭn/ē] **167**–27
fur [für] **134**–19
furious [fyŏor/ē əs] **30** ✦
furniture [für/nĭ chər] / [–für/nĭ chər] **35**–K
...polish [–päl/ĭsh] **47**–18
...store [–stör/] **88**–13
patio... [păt/ē ō–] **39**–5
fuse box [fyōoz/ bäks/] **48**–13
galaxy [găl/ək sē] **127**–26
gallbladder [göl/blăd/ər] **75**–40
gallon [găl/ən] **57**–5
game [gām(/–)] **152**–18
...show [–shō/] **167**–23
GAMES [gām(/–)] **162**–**163**
gang violence [găng/ vī/ə ləns] **100**–2
garage [gə räzh/, –räj/] / [–gə räzh/, –räj/] **36, 38**–6
...door [–dör/] **38**–7
garbage [gär/bĭj] **46**–Q
...can [–kăn/] **39**–3
...disposal [–dĭ spō/zəl] **40**–5
...truck [–trŭk/] **91**–27
garden [gär/dn] (vegetable) **148**–12, (botanical) **152**–4
gardener [gärd/nər, gär/dn ər] **137**–26, **152**–6
gardenia [gär dēn/yə] **129**–16
gargle [gär/gəl] **77**–L
garlic [gär/lĭk] **51**–29
...bread [–brĕd/] **61**–16
...press [–prĕs/] **59**–10
garment worker [gär/mənt wür/kər] **73** ✦, **137**–27
garter belt [gär/tər bĕlt/] **67**–19
garter snake [gär/tər snāk/] **131**–39
gas [găs(/–)] / [–găs/] **109**–54
...gauge [–gāj/] **108**–22
...meter [–mē/tər] **48**–14
...pedal [–pĕd/l] **109**–47
...station [–stā/shən] **88**–12, **137**–28
...station attendant [–stā/shən ə tĕn/dənt] **137**–28
...tank [–tăngk/] **108**–12
natural... [năch/rəl, năch/ər əl–] **126**–3
gate [gāt] (garage) **36**, (airport) **110**–5, **111**–D
gauge [gāj] **84**–12, **108**–19, 22, 23
gauze [göz] **83**–6
gearshift [gĭr/shĭft/] **108**–27
GEOGRAPHY [jē ăg/rə fē] **117**
geometry [jē äm/ə trē] **118**–26
geothermal energy [jē/ō thür/məl ĕn/ər jē] **126**–7
get [gĕt(/–)]
...a checkup [–ə chĕk/ŭp/] **85** ✦
...acupuncture [–ăk/yə pŭngk/chər] **81**–G
...a job [–ə jäb/] **28**–G
...a loan [–ə lōn/] **35**–I
...an electric shock [–ən ĭ lĕk/trĭk shäk/] **82**–F
...an injection [–ən ĭn jĕk/shən] **80**–E
...an X ray [–ən ĕks/ rā/] **85**–H
...bed rest [–bĕd/ rĕst/] **80**–A
...feedback [–fēd/băk/] **113**–C
...frostbite [–fröst/bīt/] **82**–G
...home [–hōm/] **27**–Q
...your boarding pass [–yər bör/dĭng păs/] **111**–E
get dressed [gĕt/ drĕst/] **26**–D
get hired [gĕt/ hīrd/] **141**–L
get married [gĕt/ măr/ēd] **28**–L
get up [gĕt/ ŭp/] **26**–B
gift [gĭft(/–)] **169**–D
...shop [–shäp/] **145**–7
gifts [gĭfts] **33**–18
gills [gĭlz] **130**–2
giraffe [jə răf/] **135**–33
girder [gür/dər] **149**–3
girdle [gür/dl] **67**–18
girl [gürl] **22**–5, 8
give [gĭv(/–)] **21**–D
...a shot of anesthetic [–ə shät/ əv ăn/əs thet/ĭk] **85**–J
...a speech [–ə spēch/] **32**–E
...the verdict [–dhə vür/dĭkt] **99**–E
gizzards [gĭz/ərdz] **52**–23
glass [glăs(/–)] **11**–9, 10, **41**–26, **63**–19, 20, ✦
...cleaner [–klē/nər] **47**–8
glasses [glăs/əz] **81**–35
globe [glōb] **3**–9
glove [glŭv(/–)] **161**–17
...compartment [–kəm pärt/mənt] **108**–33
gloves [glŭvz] **66**–5
glue [glōo] **143**–37, **162**–8
go [gō(/–)]
...on an interview [–än ən ĭn/tər vyōo/, –ön–] **141**–H
...straight [–strāt/] **107**–A
...through security [–thrōo sĭ kyŏor/ə tē] **111**–C
...to a chiropractor [–tōo ə kī/rə prăk/tər] **81**–H
...to bed [–tə bĕd/] **27**–X
...to college [–tə käl/ĭj] **28**–J
...to jail [–tə jāl/] **99**–G
...to prison [–tə prĭz/ən] **99**–G
...to sleep [–tə slēp/] **27**–Y
...to the market [–tə dhə mär/kət] **26**–L
...to work [–tə würk/] **26**–I
goat [gōt] **133**–1
goggles [gäg/əlz] **147**–9
goldfish [gōld/fĭsh/] **133**–16
golf [gälf(/–), gölf(/–)] **159**–7
...club [–klŭb/] **161**–1
good [gŏod] **11**–17
good-bye [gŏod bī/, gə–] **8**
goose [gōos] **132**–14
gopher [gō/fər] **133**–19
gorilla [gə rĭl/ə] **135**–30
gown [gown] **32**–2, **65**–29
graduate [grăj/ōo āt/] **28**–D, **32**–A
graduate [grăj/ōo ət] **32**–6
...school [–skōol/] **112** ✦
graduated cylinder [grăj/ōo ā/təd sĭl/ən dər] **119**–10
graduating class [grăj/ōo ā/tĭng klăs/] **32**–1
GRADUATION [grăj/ōo ā/shən] **32**–**33**
grams [grămz] **57** ✦
grandchild [grăn/chīld/, grănd/–] **29**–Q
granddaughters [grăn/dö/tərz] **24** ✦
grandfather [grăn/fä/dhər, grănd/–] **24**–3
grandmother [grăn/mŭdh/ər, grănd/–] **24**–2

Index

grandparents [grăn′për′ənts, grănd′–] **24**−1
grandson [grăn′sŭn′, grănd′–] **24**−7
grapefruit [grāp′frōot′] **50**−9
grapes [grāps] **50**−1
graphic artist [grăf′ĭk är′tĭst] **137**−29
grasshopper [grăs′häp′ər] **132**−25
grate [grāt] **58**−J
grater [grā′tər] **59**−2
gray [grā′–] **12**−5
　...hair [–hër′] **23**−13
grease [grēs] **58**−C
green [grēn] **12**−8
greenhouse [grēn′hows′] **152**−5
green salad [grēn′ săl′əd] **60**−8
greeting card [grē′tĭng kärd′] **96**−4
greet someone [grēt′ sŭm′wŭn] **8**−A
grill [grĭl] **58**−T
grilled cheese sandwich [grĭld′ chēz′ săn′wĭch, –sănd′–] **61**−8
ground beef [grownd′ bēf′] **52**−4
ground post [grownd′ pōst′] **96**−14
grower [grō′ər] **148**−15
guard [gärd] **97**−4, **99**−3
guest [gĕst′–] **32**−9, **145**−11
　...room [–rōom′] **145**−10
　...speaker [–spē′kər] **32**−9
guests [gĕsts] **33**−14, **169**−B
guilty [gĭl′tē] **99**
guinea pig [gĭn′ē pĭg′] **133**−14
guitar [gĭ tär′] **120**−11
gum [gŭm] **55**−42
gums [gŭmz] **74**−24
gun [gŭn] **100**−9
gurney [gŭr′nē] **87**−28
gutter [gŭt′ər] **38**−19
gym [jĭm] **5**−9
gymnastics [jĭm năs′tĭks] **159**−8
gynecologist [gī′nə käl′ə jĭst] **86** ✦
hacksaw [hăk′sö′] **150**−5
hail [hāl] **10**−19
hail a taxi [hāl′ ə tăk′sē] **104** ✦
hailstorm [hāl′störm′] **10**−18
hair [hër′–] **23**, **74**−19
　...clip [–klĭp′] **76**−17
　...gel [–jĕl′] **76**−11
　...net [–nĕt′] **147**−18
　...salon [–sə län′] **23** ✦, **93**−16
　...spray [–sprā′] **76**−12
　...stylist [–stī′lĭst] **23** ✦
hairdresser [hër′drĕs′ər] **137**−30
half [hăf′–] **15**−4, **16**−10, **20**−5
　...bath [–băth′] **43** ✦
　...brother [–brŭdh′ər] **25**−29
　...cup of raisins [–kŭp′ əv rā′zənz] **57**−9
　...past one [–păst′ wŭn′] **16**
　...sister [–sĭs′tər] **25**−30
　...slip [–slĭp′] **67**−23
halibut [hăl′ə bət] **53**−20
hall [höl] **89**−17, **145**−13
Halloween [hăl′ə wēn′, häl′–] **168**−10
Hallway [höl′wā′] **37**
ham [hăm] **52**−9
hamburger [hăm′bür′gər] **60**−1
hammer [hăm′ər] **149**−D
hammer [hăm′ər] **150**−1
hammock [hăm′ək] **39**−2

hamper [hăm′pər] **43**−1
Hand [hănd] **75**
hand [hănd′–] **2, 11, 74**−8
　...towel [–tow′əl] **43**−13
　...truck [–trŭk′] **146**−11
handbags [hănd′băgz′] **69**−6
handcuffs [hănd′kŭfs′] **99**−2
handicapped parking [hăn′dē kăpt pär′kĭng] **107**−14
handkerchief [hăng′kər chĭf, –chēf′] **69**−42
handsaw [hănd′sö′] **150**−4
hanger [hăng′ər] **72**−11
hang up [hăng′ ŭp′] / [hăng′ ŭp′–]
　...the clothes [–dhə klōz′] **72**−H
　...the receiver [–dhə rĭ sē′vər] **9**−F
happy [hăp′ē] **31**−32
Happy Birthday [hăp′ē bürth′dā] **169**
hard [härd] (surface) **11**−5, (difficult) **11**−24
hard [härd′–]
　...disk drive [–dĭsk′ drīv′] **144**−20
　...hat [–hăt′] **147**−19
Hardware [härd′wër′] **144**
hardware [härd′wër′] **150**
　...store [–stör′] **88**−14
harvest [här′vəst] **148**−B
hat [hăt] **66**−1
hats [hăts] **68**−5
have [hăv′–]
　...a baby [–ə bā′bē] **29**−M
　...a grandchild [–ə grăn′chīld′, grănd′–] **29**−Q
　...a heart attack [–ə härt′ ə tăk′] **82**−D
　...an allergic reaction [–ən ə lür′jĭk rē ăk′shən] **82**−E
　...a picnic [–ə pĭk′nĭk] **153**−D
　...dinner [–dĭn′ər] **27**−R
Hawaii-Aleutian time [hə wī′ē ə lōo′shən tīm′] **17**−24
hay [hā] **148**−18
hazardous [hăz′ər dəs]
　...materials [–mə tïr′ē əlz] **147**−7
　...waste [–wāst′] **126**−9
head [hĕd] **74**−1
headache [hĕd′āk′] **78**−1
headboard [hĕd′börd′] **44**−15
headlight [hĕd′līt′] **108**−5
headphones [hĕd′fōnz′] **164**−16
HEALTH CARE [hĕlth′ kër′] **80**−81
health [hĕlth′–]
　...club [–klŭb′] **89**−21
　...insurance card [–ĭn shŏor′əns kärd′] **84**
hear [hïr] **75**−B
hearing aid [hïr′ĭng ād′] **81**−33
hearing impaired [hïr′ĭng ĭm përd′] **22**−27
heart (symbol) [härt] **168**−6
heart (body) [härt′–] **75**−38, **79**−14
　...disease [–dĭ zēz′] **79**−14
　　listen to... [lĭs′ən tə–] **85**−D
hearts [härts] **163**−29
heater [hē′tər] **48**−1, **108**−29
heating pad [hē′tĭng păd′] **80**−3
heat wave [hēt′ wāv′] **10**−15
heavy [hĕv′ē] **11**−13, **71**−41
　...machinery [–mə shē′nə rē] **140**−F
heavyset [hĕv′ē sĕt′] **22**−20
hedge [hĕj′–] **39**−1
　...clippers [–klĭp′ərz] **39**−12
heel [hēl] (shoe) **68**−13, (foot) **75**−62
height [hīt] **15**−14, **22**

Heimlich maneuver [hīm/lĭk mə noo/vər] **83**–18

helicopter [hĕl/ə käp/tər] **110**–8

hello [hə lō/, hĕ–] **8**

help [hĕlp] **6**–J

help wanted sign [hĕlp/ wän/təd sīn/, –wŏn/–] **141**–C

hemline [hĕm/līn/] **73**–1

hen [hĕn] **133**–5

Hi! [hī] **8**

hibiscus [hī bĭs/kəs, hĭ–] **129**–12

hide [hīd] **169**–E

high [hī(/–)]

   ...chair [–chër/] **95**–7

   ...heels [–hēlz/] **68**–17, **71**–47

high blood pressure [hī/ blŭd/ prĕsh/ər] **79**–15

high-rise building [hī/rīz/ bĭl/dĭng] **89**–25

high school [hī/ skool/] **112**–7

hiking [hī/kĭng] **154**–6

   ...boots [–boots/] **68**–21

hills [hĭlz] **117**–16

hip [hĭp] **74**–5

hippopotamus [hĭp/ə pät/ə məs] **135**–43

hire [hīr] **99**–B

hired hand [hīrd/ hănd/] **148**–20

hit [hĭt] **156**–G

HIV (human immunodeficiency virus) [ăch/ī/vē/]
   [hyoo/mən ĭm/yə nō dĭ fĭsh/ən sē vī/rəs] **79**–10

HOBBIES AND GAMES [häb/ēz ən gāmz/] **162–163**

hockey stick [häk/ē stĭk/] **161**–11

hold [hōld] **94**–B, **101**–C

holiday [häl/ə dā/] **19**–43, 44

HOLIDAYS [häl/ə dāz/] **168**

holly [häl/ē] **128**–19

home [hōm(/–)]

   ...attendant [–ə tĕn/dənt] **137**–31

   ...economics [–ĕk/ə näm/ĭks, –ē/kə–] **121**–9

homemaker [hōm/mā/kər] **137**–32

homesick [hōm/sĭk/] **31**–21

honeybee [hŭn/ē bē/] **132**–26

hood [hood] **108**–6

hoof [hoof] **134**–17

hook [hook(/–)] **150**–34, 35

   ...and eye [–ən ī/] **73**–23

horn [hörn] (car) **108**–24, (music) **120**–13, (animal) **134**–21

horror story [hör/ər stör/ē, här/–] **166**–14

horse [hörs(/–)] **133**–4

   ...racing [–rā/sĭng] **159**–18

horseback riding [hörs/băk rī/dĭng] **154**–9

hose [hōz] **39**–9

HOSPITAL [häs/pĭ tl] **86–87**

hospital [häs/pĭ tl] **88**–7

   ...bed [–bĕd/] **86**–11

   ...gown [–gown/] **86**–15

Hospital staff [häs/pĭ tl stăf/] **86**

hostess [hō/stəs] **62**–1

hot [hät] (weather) **10**–1, (feeling) **30**–1

hot dog [hät/ dög/] **60**–6

HOTEL [hō tĕl/] **145**

hotel [hō tĕl/] **88**–5

hot water [hät/ wö/tər] **43**–5

hour [ow/ər] **16**–3

HOUSE [hows] **38**

house [(–)hows(/)] **34**–6

   buy a... [bī/ ə–] **29**–O

   clean the... [klēn/ dhə–] **27**–N

Household Pests [hows/hōld/ pĕsts/] **49**

HOUSEHOLD PROBLEMS AND REPAIRS
   [hows/hōld/ präb/ləmz ən rī përz/] **48–49**

housekeeper [hows/kē/pər] **138**–33, **145**–15

housekeeping cart [hows/kē/pĭng kärt/] **145**–14

House of Representatives [hows/ əv rĕp/rĭ zĕn/tə tĭvz] **116**–1

houseplant [hows/plănt/] **129**–29

HOUSEWORK [hows/würk/] **46**

hubcap [hŭb/kăp/] **108**–9

hug [hŭg] **33**–G

humid [hyoo/məd] **10**–12

humidifier [hyoo mĭd/ə fī/ər] **80**–2

humiliated [hyoo mĭl/ē ā/təd] **30** ✦

hummingbird [hŭm/ĭng bürd/] **132**–11

hump [hŭmp] **135**–51

hundred [hŭn/drəd] **14**

hungry [hŭng/grē] **30**–5

hurricane [hür/ə kān/] **103**–12

hurt [hürt] (feeling) **30**–17, (medical) **82**–A

husband [hŭz/bənd] **24**–19

hydrant [hī/drənt] **91**–28

hydroelectric power [hī/drō ĭ lĕk/trĭk pow/ər] **126**–5

hydrogen peroxide [hī/drə jən pə räk/sīd] **83**–8

hyena [hī ē/nə] **135**–31

hygienist [hī jē/nĭst, –jĕn/ĭst] **84**–16

hypertension [hī/pər tĕn/shən] **79** ✦

hypoallergenic [hī/pō ăl/ər jĕn/ĭk] **77** ✦

I beam [ī/ bēm/] **149**–3

ice [īs(/–)]

   ...hockey [–häk/ē] **158**–13

   ...machine [–mə shēn/] **145**–18

   ...pack [–păk/] **83**–13

   ...skates [–skāts/] **161**–9

   ...skating [–skā/tĭng] **160**–4

ice cream [īs/ krēm/] **55**–44

ice cream stand [īs/ krēm stănd/] **93**–20

iced tea [īst/ tē/] **60**–5

icy [ī/sē] **10**–13

ignition [ĭg nĭsh/ən] **108**–25

illegal drugs [ĭ lē/gəl drŭgz/] **100**–4

ILLNESSES AND MEDICAL CONDITIONS
   [ĭl/nə səz ən mĕd/ĭ kəl kən dĭsh/ənz] **79**

immigrate [ĭm/ə grāt/] **28**–C

Immigration [ĭm/ə grā/shən] **114**

immunization [ĭm/yə nə zā/shən] **80** ✦

in [ĭn] **13**–5

   ...fashion [–făsh/ən] **64** ✦

   ...front of [–frŭnt/ əv] **13**–4

   ...love [–lŭv/] **28**–K, **30**–19

   ...pain [–pān/] **30**–12

   ...shock [–shäk/] **82**

inch (in.) [ĭnch] **15**–13

Independence Day [ĭn/də pĕn/dəns dā/] **168**–7

INDIVIDUAL SPORTS [ĭn/də vĭj/oo əl spörts/] **159**

industrial arts [ĭn dŭs/trē əl ärts/] **121**–10

infectious disease [ĭn fĕk/shəs dĭ zēz/] **79** ✦

influenza [ĭn/floo ĕn/zə] **79** ✦

information booth [ĭn/fər mā/shən booth/] **93**–22

ingredients [ĭn grē/dē ənts] **58**–K

INJURIES [ĭn/jə rēz] **78**

ink pad [ĭngk/ păd/] **143**–41

inline [ĭn/līn/]

   ...skates [–skāts/] **161**–10

   ...skating [–skā/tĭng] **159**–9

inquire about the salary [ĭn kwīr/ ə bowt/ dhə săl/ə rē] **141**–K

insect [ĭn/sĕkt]

Index

...bite [–bīt/] **78**–11
...repellent [–rĭ pĕl/ənt] **154**–23
INSECTS [ĭn/sĕkts] **132**
insert [ĭn sürt/] **97**–A
Inside the body [ĭn/sīd/ dhə bäd/ē] **75**
instant coffee [ĭn/stənt kö/fē] **55**–51
instructor [ĭn strŭk/tər] **5** ✦, **139**–58
instrument [ĭn/strə mənt] **120**–A
insulation [ĭn/sə lā/shən] **149**–13
insurance [ĭn shŏŏr/əns]
...card [–kärd/] **84**–4
...form [–förm/] **84**–5
intercom [ĭn/tər käm/] **36**–8
interesting [ĭn/trə stĭng, ĭn/tə rĕs/tĭng] **167**–30
international call [ĭn/tər näsh/ə nəl köl/] **9**–6
internist [ĭn/tür/nĭst] **86**–2
interpreter [ĭn tür/prə tər] **138**–34
INTERSECTION [ĭn/tər sĕk/shən] **90–91**
interview [ĭn/tər vyōō/] **141**–H
intestinal parasites [ĭn tĕs/tə nəl păr/ə sīts/] **79**–16
intestines [ĭn tĕs/tənz] **75**–42
into [ĭn/tōō, –tə] **105**–4
introduce [ĭn/trə dōōs/] **8**–D, F
Invention [ĭn vĕn/shən] **115**
invite [ĭn vīt/] **169**–B
iris [ī/rəs] **129**–20
iron [ī/ərn] **72**–G
iron [ī/ərn] **72**–13
ironed shirt [ī/ərnd shürt/] **72**–20
ironing board [ī/ər nĭng börd/] **72**–14
island [ī/lənd] **117**–8
IV (intravenous drip) [ī/vē/] / [ĭn/trə vē/nəs drĭp/] **87**–27
jack [jăk] **109**–51
jack cheese [jăk/ chēz/] **53**–12
jacket [jăk/ət] **66**–7
jack hammer [jăk/ hăm/ər] **149**–9
jack-o'-lantern [jăk/ə lăn/tərn] **168**–11
jam [jăm] **56**–14
janitor [jăn/ə tər] **138**–35
January [jăn/yōō ër/ē] **19**–25
jar [jär(/–)] **56**–2
...of jam [–əv jăm/] **56**–14
jasmine [jăz/mən] **129**–21
jaw [jö] **74**–23
jeans [jēnz] **64**–5
jellyfish [jĕl/ē fĭsh] **130**–14
jewelry [jōō/əl rē] **69**–8
...store [–stör/] **92**–2
job [jäb(/–)] / [–jäb/]
...board [–börd/] **141**–B
get a... [gĕt/ ə–] **28**–G
JOB SAFETY [jäb/ sāf/tē] **147**
JOB SEARCH [jäb/ sürch/] **141**
JOB SKILLS [jäb/ skĭlz/] **140**
JOBS AND OCCUPATIONS A-H [jäbz/ ən äk/yə pā/shənz]
136–137
JOBS AND OCCUPATIONS H-W [jäbz/ ən äk/yə pā/shənz]
138–139
jockstrap [jäk/străp/] **67**–14
jog [jäg] **156**–B
join the army [joyn/ dhē är/mē] **28**–F
joystick [joy/stĭk/] **144**–9
judge [jŭj] **99**–6
Judicial [jōō dĭsh/əl] **116**
July [jōō lī/] **19**–31, **168**–7
jump [jŭmp] **156**–J

jumper [jŭm/pər] **65**–18
jumper cables [jŭm/pər kā/bəlz] **109**–52
jump rope [jŭmp/ rōp/] **153**–5
jumpsuit [jŭmp/sōōt/] **65**–16
June [jōōn] **19**–30
junior high school [jōōn/yər hī/ skōōl] **112**–6
Jupiter [jōō/pə tər] **127**–5
jury [jŏŏr/ē] **99**–8, **116**
Justices [jŭs/tə səz] **116**–10
kangaroo [kăng/gə rōō/] **135**–44
keep [kēp] **21**–E
ketchup [kĕch/əp, kăch/–] **60**–23
key [kē(/–)] **37**–31
...chain [–chān/] **69**–43
keyboard [kē/börd/] **120**–20, **144**–7
kick [kĭk] **156**–L
kidney [kĭd/nē] **75**–45
kilometers [kĭ läm/ə tərz, kĭl/ə mē/tərz] **15** ✦
kiss [kĭs] **33**–F
KITCHEN [kĭch/ən] **40**
kitchen [kĭch/ən] **63**–10
...timer [–tī/mər] **59**–18
KITCHEN UTENSILS [kĭch/ən yōō tĕn/səlz] **59**
kitten [kĭt/n] **133**–10
knee [nē(/–)] **74**–17
...socks [–säks/] **67**–25
knee-highs [nē/hīz/] **67**–24
knife [(–)nīf(/)] **41**–22, **63**–27
carving... [kär/vĭng–] **59**–12
multi-use... [mŭl/tē yōōs/–, mŭl/tī–] **154**–20
paring... [për/ĭng–] **59**–16
knit [nĭt] **163**–F
knit shirt [nĭt/ shürt/] **65**–20
knitting needles [nĭt/ĭng nēd/lz] **163**–18
koala [kō ä/lə] **135**–45
label [lā/bəl] / [–lā/bəl] **143**–35
prescription... [prĭ skrĭp/shən–] **80**–14
lab technician [lăb/ tĕk nĭsh/ən] **86**–16
ladder [lăd/ər] **149**–2
ladle [lād/l] **59**–7
ladybug [lā/dē bŭg/] **132**–27
lake [lāk] **117**–13
lamb [lăm(/–)] **52**–13, 14, 15
...chops [–chäps/] **52**–15
...shanks [–shăngks/] **52**–13
lamp [lămp] **42**–15, **44**–17
lampshade [lămp/shād/] **44**–18
land [lănd] **111**–O
landlord [lănd/lörd/] **37**–32
language [lăng/gwĭj]
English as a second... [ĭng/glĭsh əz ə sĕk/ənd–] **141**–7
foreign... [för/ən–, fär/–] **141**–8
speak another... [spēk/ ə nä/thər] **140**–J
use the new... [yōōz/ thə nū/–] **143** ✦
lantern [lăn/tərn] **154**–22
laptop [lăp/täp/] **144**–14
large [lärj] **70**–4
last [lăst(/–)]
...name [–nām/] **4**–4
...week [–wēk/] **18**–18
late [lāt] **17**–23
latex gloves [lā/tĕks glŭvz/] **87**–33, **147**–17
laugh [lăf] **33**–H
Laundromat [lön/drə mät/] **90**–1
laundry [lön/drē] **72**–1

...basket [–băs/kət] **72**–2
...detergent [–dĭ tür/jənt] **72**–7
...room [–rōōm/] **36**
lawn [lön(/–)] **39**–21
...mower [–mō/ər] **39**–22
lawyer [lö/yər] **99**–B, **138**–36
lay bricks [lā/ brĭks/] **149**–B
leaf [lēf(/–)] **128**–6, **129**–5
...blower [–blō/ər] **39**–4
leaking [lē/kĭng] **48**–3
learn to drive [lürn/ tə drīv/] **28**–E
lease [lēs] **35** ✦
leather [lĕdh/ər]
...boots [–bōōts/] **70**–18
...jacket [–jăk/ət] **66**–3
leave [lēv(/–)] **111**–L
...a message [–ə mĕs/ĭj] **9**–E
...a tip [–ə tĭp/] **62**–J
...work [–würk/] **26**–M
left [lĕft] **13**–1
leg [lĕg(/–)] **74**–6
...of lamb [–əv lăm/] **52**–14
legal [lē/gəl]
...holiday [–häl/ə dā/] **19**–43
...pad [–păd/] **143**–18
LEGAL SYSTEM [lē/gəl sĭs/təm] **99**
leggings [lĕg/ĭngz] **65**–23
Legislative [lĕj/əs lā/tĭv] **116**
lemons [lĕm/ənz] **50**–11
lend [lĕnd] **20** ✦
length [lĕngkth] **15**–16
lengthen [lĕngk/thən] **73**–C
leopard [lĕp/ərd] **135**–25
leotard [lē/ə tärd/] **67**–1
let out [lĕt/ owt/] **73**–F
letter [lĕt/ər] / [–lĕt/ər] **96**–2, **142**–B, D
...carrier [–kăr/ē ər] **96**–6
air... [ër/–] **96**–13
letterhead paper [lĕt/ər hĕd pā/pər] **143**–19
lettuce [lĕt/əs] **51**–1, **60**–17
level [lĕv/əl] **150**–24
librarian [lī brër/ē ən] **98**–1
LIBRARY [lī/brër ē] **98**
library [lī/brër ē] **5**–6, **89**–28, **98**–17, 19, 20
...book [–bōōk/] **98**–20
...card [–kärd/] **98**–19
...clerk [–klürk/] **98**–17
license plate [lī/səns plāt/] **108**–15
lid [lĭd] **59**–24
LIFE EVENTS [līf/ ĭ vĕnts/] **28**–29
lifeguard [līf/gärd/] **155**–18
...station [–stā/shən] **155**–20
lifesaving device [līf/sā/vĭng dĭ vīs/] **155**–19
life vest [līf/ vĕst/] **154**–14
light [līt] **169**–H
light [līt] (weight) **11**–14, **71**–40, (color) **12**–3
light (appliance) [līt(/–)] / [–līt/]
...fixture [–fĭks/chər] **41**–5
...switch [–swĭch/] **44**–19
porch... [pörch/–] **38**–9
lightbulb [līt/bŭlb/] **42**–4
lightning [līt/nĭng] **10**–17
lily [lĭl/ē] **129**–24
limb [lĭm] **128**–3
limes [līmz] **50**–12

line [līn(/–)] / [–līn/] **55**–20
...supervisor [–sōō/pər vī zər] **146**–5
assembly... [ə sĕm/blē–] **146**–8
line dry [līn/ drī/] **72** ✦
linen [lĭn/ən] **70**–17
linen closet [lĭn/ən kläz/ət] **43** ✦
Lines [līnz] **118**
lingerie [län/zhə rā/, –jə–] **67** ✦
lion [lī/ən] **135**–36
lip [lĭp] **74**–30
lipstick [lĭp/stĭk/] **77**–37
Liquid measures [lĭk/wəd mĕzh/ərz] **57**
list [lĭst] **6**–L
listen [lĭs/ən] **2**–C, **85**–D
listen for the dial tone [lĭs/ən fər dhə dī/əl tōn/] **9**–B
liters [lē/tərz] **57** ✦
little [lĭt/l] **11**–1
Little League [lĭt/l lēg/] **158** ✦
live [lĭv] **116**–B
liver [lĭv/ər] (food) **52**–7, (body) **75**–39
livestock [līv/stäk/] **148**–13
LIVING ROOM [lĭv/ĭng rōōm/] **42**
lizard [lĭz/ərd] **131**–41
llama [lä/mə] **135**–26
loading dock [lō/dĭng däk/] **146**–16
load the washer [lōd/ dhə wä/shər, –wö/–] **72**–C
loaf [lōf(/–)] **56**–10
...of bread [–əv brĕd/] **56**–22
loafers [lō/fərz] **68**–19
loan [lōn] **35**–I
Lobby [läb/ē] **37**
lobby [läb/ē] **145**–3
lobster [läb/stər] **53**–23
local call [lō/kəl köl/] **9**–4
lock [läk] **101**–E
lock [läk] (house) **37**–29, **48**–6, (car) **109**–34
lockers [läk/ərz] **5**–7
locket [läk/ət] **69**–33
locksmith [läk/smĭth/] **48**–11
logs [lögz, lägz] **42**–12
lonely [lōn/lē] **30**–18
long [löng(/–)] **23**–3, **71**–34
...underwear [–ŭn/dər wër/] **67**–11
long-distance call [löng/dĭs/təns köl/] **9**–5
long-sleeved shirt [löng/slēvd/ shürt/] **71**–31
look at [lōōk/ ăt/, –ət] **111**–K, **141**–B
look for [lōōk/ för/] / [lōōk/ fər]
...a help wanted sign [–ə hĕlp/ wän/təd sīn/, –wön/–] **141**–C
...a new apartment [–ə nōō/ ə pärt/mənt] **35**–A
...the emergency exit
[–dhē ĭ mür/jən sē ĕg/zət, –ĕk/sət] **111**–J
look in [lōōk/ ĭn]
...the classifieds [–dhə kläs/ə fīdz/] **141**–D
...throat [–thrōt/] **85**–E
look up a word [lōōk/ ŭp ə würd/] **6**–A
loose [lōōs] **71**–42
lose [lōōz] **158** ✦
lost child [löst/ chīld/] **102**–1
loud [lowd] **11**–11
loungewear [lownj/wër/] **67** ✦
love [lŭv(/–)] **30**–19
...seat [–sēt/] **42**–25
low [lō] **71**–46
LPN (licensed practical nurse)
[ĕl/pē/ĕn/] / [lī/sənst prăk/tĭ kəl nürs/] **87**–24

luggage [lŭg/ĭj]
   ...carrier [–kăr/ē ər] **110**–19
   ...cart [–kärt/] **145**–6
lug wrench [lŭg/ rĕnch/] **109**–50
lumber [lŭm/bər] **149**–17, **151**
lunar eclipse [lōō/nər ī klĭps/] **127** ✦
lunch [lŭnch(/–)] **61**
   ...benches [–bĕn/chəz] **5**–5
lung [lŭng] **75**–37
LVN (licensed vocational nurse)
   [ĕl/vē/ĕn] / [lī/sənst vō kā/shə nəl nürs/] **87**–24
machine [mə shēn/]
   ...operator [–äp/ə rā tər] **138**–37
   ...screw [–skrōō/] **150**–27
magazine [măg/ə zēn/, măg/ə zēn/] **98**–7
   ...holder [–hōl/dər] **42**–22
magnet [măg/nət] **119**–21
magnolia [măg nōl/yə] **128**–9
mailbox [māl/bäks/] **38**–4, **90**–12
mailboxes [māl/bäk/səz] **37**–36
mailer [mā/lər] **143**–32
mailing address [mā/lĭng ə drĕs/, –ă/drĕs] **96**–8
mail [māl/ ĭt] **96**–B
main office [mān/ ö/fəs] **5**–17
make [māk] **106** ✦
make [māk(/–)]
   ...a deposit [–ə dĭ päz/ət] **97**–C
   ...an appointment [–ən ə poynt/mənt] **85**–A
   ...an offer [–ən ö/fər] **35**–H
   ...a toast [–ə tōst/] **33**–I
   ...a wish [–ə wĭsh/] **169**–J
   ...copies [–käp/ēz] **142**–E
   ...lunch [–lŭnch/] **26**–F
   ...the bed [–dhə bĕd/] **46**–G
make sure you **understand**
   [māk/ shōōr/ yōō ŭn/dər stănd/] **8**–E
male [māl] **4**–13
MALL [möl] **92**–93
mallet [măl/ət] **150**–2
MAMMALS [măm/əlz] **134**–135
Mammals, Sea [sē/ măm/əlz] **131**
man [măn] **22**–11
manager [măn/ī jər] **35**–B, **36**–12, **54**–8, **143**–25
mane [mān] **135**–49
mangoes [măng/gōz] **50**–21
mantel [măn/təl] **42**–8
manual [măn/yōō əl] **144**–22
manual labor [măn/yōō əl lā/bər] **140**–D
manufacture [măn/yə făk/chər] **146**–B
map [măp] **3**–12
maple [mā/pəl] **128**–13
March [märch] **19**–27
margarine [mär/jər ən] **54**–39
marigold [măr/ə gōld/] **129**–13
MARINE LIFE, AMPHIBIANS, AND REPTILES
   [mə rēn/ līf/ ăm fĭb/ē ənz ən rĕp/tīlz] **130**–131
mark [märk] **7**–T
marker [mär/kər] **3**–19
MARKET [mär/kət] **54**–55
market [mär/kət] **89**–20
marriage license [măr/ĭj lī/səns] **29**–8
married [măr/ēd] **25**–23, **28**–L
Mars [märz] **127**–6
martial arts [mär/shəl ärts/] **159**–10
mascara [mă skär/ə] **77**–38

mashed potatoes [măsht/ pə tā/tōz] **61**–11
mask [măsk] **168**–12
masking tape [măs/kĭng tāp/] **151**–49
Master's degree [măs/tərz də grē/] **112** ✦
match [măch] **7**–X
matches [măch/əz] **154**–21
maternity dress [mə tür/nə tē drĕs/] **65**–19
maternity shop [mə tür/nə tē shäp/] **93**–17
MATHEMATICS [măth/ə măt/ĭks] **118**
mattress [mă/trəs] **44**–25
May [mā] **19**–29
mayonnaise [mā/ə nāz/, mā/ə nāz/] **60**–25
meadow [mĕd/ō] **117**–20
measles [mē/zəlz] **79**–5
measure [mĕzh/ər] **15** ✦, **149**–C
Measurement [mĕzh/ər mənt] **15**
MEASUREMENTS [mĕzh/ər mənts] **14**–15
MEASURES [mĕzh/ərz] **57**
measure the ingredients [mĕzh/ər dhē ĭn grē/dē ənts] **57**–A
MEAT AND POULTRY [mĕt/ n pōl/trē] **52**
meat and poultry section [mĕt/ n pōl/trē sĕk/shən] **54**–2
media section [mē/dē ə sĕk/shən] **98**–11
medical [mĕd/ī kəl]
   ...charts [–chärts/] **87**–20
   ...emergency bracelet [–ī mür/jən sē brās/lət] **83**–14
   ...waste disposal [–wāst/ dĭ spō/zəl] **86**–14
MEDICAL AND DENTAL EXAMS
   [mĕd/ī kəl ən dĕn/təl ĭg zămz/] **85**
Medical clinic [mĕd/ī kəl klĭn/ĭk] **84**
MEDICAL CONDITIONS [mĕd/ī kəl kən dĭsh/ənz] **79**
Medical conditions and serious diseases
   [mĕd/ī kəl kən dĭsh/ənz ən sĭr/ē əs dĭ zē/zəz] **79**
MEDICAL EMERGENCIES [mĕd/ī kəl ī mür/jən sēz] **82**
medication [mĕd/ə kā/shən] **80**–11, 12
   ...tray [–trā/] **87**–23
medicine cabinet [mĕd/ə sən kăb/ə nət] **43**–19
medium [mē/dē əm] **70**–3
meeting room [mē/tĭng rōōm/] **145**–19
memory [mĕm/ə rē] **144** ✦
men's store [mĕnz/ stör/] **90** ✦
menu [mĕn/yōō] **62**–3
MENU, COFFEE SHOP [kö/fē shäp/ mĕn/yōō] **61**
merchandise [mür/chən dīz/, –dīs/] **152**–24
Mercury [mür/kyə rē] **127**–9
messenger [mĕs/ən jər] **138**–38
messy [mĕs/ē] **11**–16
meter [mē/tər] (measurement) **15**, (taxi) **104**–21
meter [mē/tər] / [–mē/tər]
   gas... [găs/–] **48**–14
   parking... [pär/kĭng–] **91**–18
mice [mīs] **49**–26
microcassette transcriber [mī/krō kə sĕt/ trăn skrī/bər] **142**–4
microfilm [mī/krə fĭlm/] **98**–5
microfilm reader [mī/krə fĭlm rē/dər] **98**–4
microphone [mī/krə fōn/] **164**–4
microscope [mī/krə skōp/] **119**–4
microwave oven [mī/krə wāv/ ŭv/ən] **40**–13
middle-aged [mĭd/l ājd/] **22**–14
middle initial [mĭd/l ī nĭsh/əl] **4**–3
middle school [mĭd/l skōōl/] **112**–6
midnight [mĭd/nīt/] **17**–21
midsize car [mĭd/sīz/ kär/] **106**–3
mile [mīl] **15** ✦
milk [mĭlk] **148**–C
milk [mĭlk(/–)] **54**–35

...shake [–shāk/] **60**–12
milliliters [mĭl/ə lē/tərz] **57** ✦
million [mĭl/yən] **14**
miniblinds [mĭn/ē blīndz/] **43**–11
minivan [mĭn/ē văn/] **106**–10
minute [mĭn/ət] **16**–2
mirror [mïr/ər] **43**–18, **44**–1
   rearview... [rïr/vyoo/–] **108**–1
   sideview... [sīd/vyoo/–] **108**–8
missing [mĭs/ĭng] **70**–25
miss the bus [mĭs/ dhə bŭs/] **104** ✦
mistake [mĭ stāk/] **7**–2
mittens [mĭt/nz] **66**–9
mix [mĭks] **58**–K
mixing bowl [mĭk/sĭng bōl/] **59**–31
mobile [mō/bēl] **45**–4
mobile home [mō/bəl hōm/] **34**–8
model (occupation) [mäd/l] **138**–39
model (hobby) [mäd/l] **106** ✦
   ...kit [–kĭt/] **162**–7
   ...trains [–trānz/] **163**–32
models [mäd/lz] **162**–C
modem [mō/dəm, –dĕm] **144**–11
moisturizer [moys/chə rī/zər] **76**–8
molecule [mäl/ĭ kyool/] **119**–18
Monday [mŭn/dā, –dē] **18**–2
MONEY [mŭn/ē] **20**
money order [mŭn/ē ör/dər] **20**–16
monitor [män/ə tər] **144**–6
monitors [män/ə tərs] **110**–4
monkey [mŭng/kē] **135**–27
month [mŭnth] **4**–16, **18**–9
monthly statement [mŭnth/lē stāt/mənt] **97**–10
Months of the year [mŭnths/ əv dhə yïr/] **19**
moon [moon] **127**–13, 14, 15, 16
moose [moos] **134**–1
mop [mäp] **46**–J
mop [(–)mäp(/)]
   dust... [dŭst/–] **47**–17
   wet... [wĕt/–] **47**–16
MORE SCHOOL SUBJECTS [mör/ skool/ sŭb/jĭkts] **121**
morning [mör/nĭng] **17**–16
mosque [mäsk] **89**–23
mosquito [mə skē/tō] **132**–23
motel [mō tĕl/] **89**–22
moth [möth] **132**–22
mother [mŭdh/ər] **24**–5, **25**–25
motherboard [mŭdh/ər börd/] **144**–18
mother-in-law [mŭdh/ər ĭn lö/] **24**–13
motorcycle [mō/tər sī/kəl] **91**–19
mountain [mown/tn]
   ...biking [–bī/kĭng] **154**–8
   ...lion [lī/ən] **134**–2
   ...peak [–pēk/] **117**–14
   ...range [–rānj/] **117**–15
   ...time [–tīm/] **17**–27
mouse [mows] (animal) **133**–17, (computer) **144**–8
mouth [mowth] **74**–22
mouthwash [mowth/wäsh/, –wösh/] **77**–23
move [moov] **29**–P
move in [moov/ ĭn/] **35**–D
Movement [moov/mənt] **115**
mover [moo/vər] **138**–40
movie [moo/vē] **166**–1
movies [moo/vēz] **152**–10

movie theater [moo/vē thē/ə tər] **88**–11
moving van [moo/vĭng văn/] **106**–14
mow [mō] **39**–C
mudslide [mŭd/slīd/] **102**–6
muffin [mŭf/ən] **60**–14
muffler [mŭf/lər] (clothing) **66**–4, (car part) **108**–11
mug [mŭg] **41**–28
mugging [mŭg/ĭng] **100**–5
multiplication [mŭl/tə plə kā/shən] **118**–3
multi-use knife [mŭl/tē yoos/ nīf/, mŭl/tī–] **154**–20
mumps [mŭmps] **79**–7
murder [mür/dər] **100**–8
muscle [mŭs/əl] **75**–48
mushrooms [mŭsh/roomz/] **51**–26
MUSIC [myoo/zĭk] **120**
musician [myoo zĭsh/ən] **138**–41
music store [myoo/zĭk stör/] **92**–1
mussel [mŭs/əl] **130**–17
mussels [mŭs/əlz] **53**–26
mustache [mŭs/tăsh] **23**–5
mustard [mŭs/tərd] **60**–24
mystery [mĭs/tə rē] **166**–15
nachos [nä/chōz] **60**–10
nail (hardware) [nāl] **150**–29
nail (body) [nāl(/–)]
   ...clipper [–klĭp/ər] **77**–29
   ...polish [–päl/ĭsh] **77**–31
   ...polish remover [–päl/ĭsh rĭ moo/vər] **77**–32
   ...salon [–sə län/] **91**–25
name [nām] **4**–1, 2, 3, 4, A, C, D
napkin [năp/kĭn] **41**–19, **63**–23
narrow [năr/ō] **71**–45
nasal congestion [nā/zəl kən jĕs/chən] **78**–7
nasal spray [nā/zəl sprā/] **81**–23
NATURAL DISASTERS
   [năch/rəl dĭ zăs/tərz, năch/ər əl–] **102**–103
natural gas [năch/rəl găs/, năch/ər əl–] **126**–3
nature program [nā/chər prō/grăm] **167**–22
near [nïr] **13** ✦
neat [nēt] **11**–15
neck [nĕk] **74**–2
necklaces [nĕk/lə səz] **69**–9
need [nēd] **109**–(54–59)
needle [nēd/l] (sewing) **73**–22, (pine) **128**–12
neighbor [nā/bər] **37**–22
neighborhood [nā/bər hood/] **90** ✦
Neighborhood Watch
   [nā/bər hood/ wäch/, –wöch/] **101** ✦
nephew [nĕf/yoo] **24**–18
Neptune [nĕp/toon] **127**–2
nerve [nürv] **75**–50
nervous [nür/vəs] **30**–11
nest [nĕst] **132**–5
new [noo(/–)] **71**–32
   ...moon [–moon/] **127**–13
Newfoundland time [noo/fən lənd tīm/, –fənd–] **17**–31
news [nooz] **167**–17
newspaper [nooz/pā/pər] **98**–8
newsstand [nooz/stănd/] **90**–11
newt [noot] **130**–26
New Year's Day [noo/ yïrz/ dā/] **168**–1
next to [nĕkst/ too, –tə] **13**–1, 2
next week [nĕkst/ wēk/] **18**–20
nickel [nĭk/əl] **20**–2
niece [nēs] **24**–17

night [nīt] **17**–20
nightgown [nīt/gown/] **67**–5
night-light [nīt/līt/] **45**–3
nightshirt [nīt/shürt/] **67**–9
night table [nīt/ tā/bəl] **44**–21
nine [nīn] **14**
nineteen [nīn/tēn/] **14**
nineteenth [nīn/tēnth/] **14**
nineteen-year-old [nīn/tēn/yïr ōld/] **22**–8
ninety [nīn/tē] **14**
ninth [nīnth] **14**
nipple [nĭp/əl] **95**–27
noisy children [noy/zē chĭl/drən] **11**–11
nonfiction [nän/fĭk/shən] **98** ✦
noon [noon] **17**–17
no outlet [nō/ owt/lĕt, –lət] **107**–8
no parking [nō/ pär/kĭng] **107**–12
north [nörth] **107, 123, 124**
NORTH AMERICA AND CENTRAL AMERICA
   [nörth/ ə mĕr/ə kə ən sĕn/trəl ə mĕr/ə kə] **122**–**123**
nose [nōz] **74**–21
not [nät(/–)]
   ...guilty [–gĭl/tē] **99**
   ...ripe [–rīp] **50**–28
notebook [nōt/book/] **3**–24
   ...paper [–pā/pər] **3**–25
note pad [nōt/ păd/] **143**–36
November [nō vĕm/bər] **19**–35
nuclear energy [noo/klē ər ĕn/ər jē] **126**–8
numbers [nŭm/bərz] **3**–31
NUMBERS AND MEASUREMENTS
   [nŭm/bərz ən mĕzh/ər mənts] **14**–**15**
nurse [nürs] **94**–C
nurse [nürs(/–)] **84**–10, **87**–22, 24, 29, ✦, **138**–42, ✦
   ...midwife [–mĭd/wīf/] **86** ✦
   ...practitioner [–prăk tĭsh/ə nər] **86** ✦
Nurse's station [nür/səz stā/shən] **87**
nursing home [nür/sĭng hōm/] **34**–11
nut (hardware) [nŭt] **150**–31
nuts (food) [nŭts] **50**–23
nylon [nī/län] **70**–19
oak [ōk] **128**–18
obey the law [ō bā/ dhə lö/] **116**–H
oboe [ō/bō] **120**–5
observatory [əb zür/və tör/ē] **127**–19
observe [əb zürv/] **119**–B
obstetrician [äb/stə trĭsh/ən] **86**–1
OCCUPATIONS (A-H) [äk/yə pā/shənz] **136**–**137**
OCCUPATIONS (H-W) [äk/yə pā/shənz] **138**–**139**
ocean [ō/shən] **117**–6, **155**–1
o'clock [ə kläk/] **16**–4
October [äk tō/bər] **19**–34
octopus [äk/tə pəs] **130**–4
odometer [ō däm/ə tər] **108**–21
off [öf] **105**–7
OFFICE [ö/fəs] **142**–**143**
Office [ö/fəs] **37**
office [ö/fəs] **5**–13, 15, 17, **146**–1
   ...building [–bĭl/dĭng] **89**–24
   ...manager [–măn/ĭ jər] **143**–25
official [ə fĭsh/əl] **158**–6
oil (cooking) [oyl] **55**–49, **57**–2
oil (petroleum) [oyl(/–)] **109**–55, **126**–6
   ...gauge [–gāj/] **108**–19
   ...paint [–pānt/] **163**–24

...spill [–spĭl/] **126**–15
ointment [oynt/mənt] **81**–24, **83**–9
old [ōld] **71**–33
on [än, ön] **13**–8
   ...the left [–dhə lĕft/] **13**–1
   ...the right [–dhə rīt/] **13**–2
once a week [wŭns/ə wēk/] **18**–22
one [wŭn(/–)] **14, 15**–1, 2, 3, 4, 5, 11, **16**–4, 15, **20**–1, 12
   ...o'clock [–ə kläk/] **16**–4
   ...way [–wā/] **107**–6
one billion [wŭn/ bĭl/yən] **14**
one-eighth [wŭn/ātth/, –āth/] **15**–1
one-fifteen [wŭn/fĭf/tēn/] **16**–7
one-fifty [wŭn/fĭf/tē] **16**–14
one-forty [wŭn/för/tē] **16**–12
one-fourth [wŭn/förth/] **15**–2
one-half [wŭn/hăf/] **15**–4
one-hundred percent [wŭn/ hŭn/drəd pər sĕnt/] **15**–11
one-oh-five [wŭn/ ō fīv/] **16**–5
one-ten [wŭn/tĕn/] **16**–6
one-third [wŭn/thürd/] **15**–3
one-thirty [wŭn/thür/tē] **16**–10
one-twenty [wŭn/twĕn/tē] **16**–8
onions [ŭn/yənz] **51**–28, **58**–G, H
online catalog [än/līn/ kăt/l ög/, –äg/, ön/–] **98**–9
on time [än/ tīm/, ön/–] **17** ✦
onto [än/too, –tə, ön/–] **105**–6
open [ō/pən] **2**–I
   ...the presents [–dhə prĕz/ənts] **169**–L
   don't... [dōnt/–] **101**–F
opera [äp/rə] **166**–8
operate heavy machinery
   [äp/ə rāt/ hĕv/ē mə shē/nə rē] **140**–F
Operating room [äp/ə rā/tĭng room/] **87**
operating table [äp/ə rā/tĭng tā/bəl] **87**–34
Operations (math) [äp/ə rā/shənz] **118**
operator [äp/ə rā/tər] **9**–7
ophthalmologist [äf/thəl mäl/ə jĭst, –thə mäl/–, äp/–] **86**–7
opossum [ə päs/əm, päs/əm] **134**–4
optician [äp tĭsh/ən] **92**–8
optometrist [äp täm/ə trĭst] **81**–34
orange [ör/ənj, är/–] **12**–6
oranges [ör/ən jəz, är/–] **50**–10
orangutan [ö răng/ə tăng/, –tăn/] **135**–40
orbit [ör/bət] **127**–11
orchard [ör/chərd] **148**–16
orchestra [ör/kə strə] **120**–1
orchid [ör/kĭd] **129**–17
order [ör/dər] **62**–D
orderly [ör/dər lē] **87**–18
order puller [ör/dər pool/ər] **146**–10
Ordinals [ör/dn əlz, örd/nəlz] **14**
organ [ör/gən] **120**–22
organizer [ör/gə nī/zər] **143**–30
ornament [ör/nə mənt] **168**–19
orthodontist [ör/thə dän/tĭst] **84**–23
orthopedist [ör/thə pē/dĭst] **81**–28
Other instruments [ŭdh/ər ĭn/strə mənts] **120**
otter [ät/ər] **131**–35
ounce [owns] **57**–11
out [owt(/–)] **48**–2
   ...of focus [–əv fō/kəs] **165**–33
   ...of the taxi [–əv dhə tăk/sē] **105**–5
OUTDOOR RECREATION [owt/dör rĕk/rē ā/shən] **154**
outfit [owt/fĭt] **64** ✦

outlet [owt/lĕt, –lət] **44**–20, **107**–8, **151**–41
oval [ō/vəl] **118**–9
oven [ŭv/ən] **40**–20, **46**–C, **47**–3
  ...cleaner [–klē/nər] **47**–3
  microwave...[mī/krə wāv/–] **40**–13
over [ō/vər] **105**–2
overalls [ō/vər ölz/] **65**–21
overcoat [ō/vər kōt/] **66**–2
overdose [ō/vər dōs, ō/vər dōs/] **82**–K
overdrawn account [ō/vər drön/ ə kownt/] **97** ✦
overexposed [ō/vər ĭk spōzd/] **165**–34
overflowing [ō/vər flō/ĭng] **49**–17
overhead [ō/vər hĕd/]
  ...compartment [–kəm pärt/mənt] **110**–10
  ...projector [–prə jĕk/tər] **2**–4
overjoyed [ō/vər joyd/] **30** ✦
overnight mail [ō/vər nīt/ māl/] **96**–15
over-the-counter medication
  [ō/vər dhə kown/tər mĕd/ə kā/shən] **80**–12
owl [owl] **132**–6
owner [ō/nər] **139**–56
oxfords [äks/fərdz] **68**–20
oxygen mask [äk/sĭ jən mäsk/] **110**–14
oysters [oy/stərz] **53**–27
Pacific time [pə sĭf/ĭk tīm/] **17**–26
pacifier [päs/ə fī/ər] **95**–29
package [päk/ĭj] **56**–8, **96**–5
  ...of cookies [–əv kook/ēz] **56**–20
PACKAGED FOODS [päk/ĭjd foodz/] **56**
packer [päk/ər] **146**–13
packing tape [päk/ĭng tāp/] **143**–42
pager [pā/jər] **9**–16
pail [pāl] **45**–13, **47**–20, **155**–22
pain [pān(/–)]
  ...reliever [–rĭ lē/vər] **81**–16
paint [pānt] **149**–A, **163**–E
paint [pānt(/–) / [–pānt/] **151**–20
  ...pan [–pän/] **151**–45
  ...roller [–rō/lər] **151**–46
  acrylic... [ə krĭl/ĭk–] **162**–47
paintbrush [pānt/brŭsh/] **151**–9, **163**–23
painter [pān/tər] **138**–43
painting [pān/tĭng] **42**–7, **152**–8
pair of scissors [për/ əv sĭz/ərz] **73**–18
paisley [pāz/lē] **70**–13
pajamas [pə jä/məz, –jä/–] **67**–4
palm [päm] (hand) **75**–59, (tree) **128**–15
pan [pän] **40**–24, **59**–5, 13, 26, 28
pancakes [pän/kāks/] **61**–6
pancreas [päng/krē əs] **75**–46
panda [pän/də] **135**–41
panther [pän/thər] **135**–39
panties [pän/tēz] **67**–16
pants [pänts] **64**–8
pantyhose [pän/tē hōz/] **67**–27
papayas [pə pī/əz] **50**–20
paper [pā/pər] (composition) **113**–2
paper [pā/pər] / [–pā/pər]
  ...bag [–băg/] **55**–22
  ...clip [–klĭp/] **143**–44
  ...cutter [–kŭt/ər] **143**–15
  ...doll [–däl/] **163**–30
  ...products [–präd/ŭkts] **55**–14
  ...shredder [–shrĕd/ər] **143**–24
  ...towels [–tow/əlz] **40**–2, **56**–23

notebook... [nōt/book/–] **3**–24, 25, 26
parade [pə rād/] **168**–2
paragraph [păr/ə grăf/] **113**–5
parakeet [păr/ə kēt/] **133**–15
parallel [păr/ə lĕl/] **118**–21
parcel post [pär/səl pōst/] **96**–14
parent [për/ənt] **94**–1
parents [për/ənts] **24**–4
paring knife [për/ĭng nīf/] **59**–16
park [pärk] **91**–D
park [pärk] **88**–8
parka [pär/kə] **66**–8
PARK AND PLAYGROUND [pärk/ ən plā/grownd/] **153**
parking [pär/kĭng]
  ...garage [–gə räzh/, –räj/] **89**–26
  ...meter [–mē/tər] **91**–18
  ...space [–spās/] **36**–15, **90**–5
parochial school [pə rō/kē əl skool/] **112**–3
parsley [pär/slē] **51**–10
part [pärt] **23**–4
partner [pärt/nər] **6**–J
parts [pärts] **146**–7
Parts of a bird [pärts/ əv ə bürd/] **132**
PARTS OF A CAR AND CAR MAINTENANCE
  [pärts/ əv ə kär/ ən kär/ mān/tn əns] **108–109**
Parts of a circle [pärts/ əv ə sür/kəl] **118**
Parts of a fish [pärts/ əv ə fĭsh/] **130**
Parts of a flower [pärts/ əv ə flow/ər] **129**
Parts of a square [pärts/ əv ə skwër/] **118**
Parts of a tree [pärts/ əv ə trē/] **128**
PARTY [pär/tē] **169**
Party [pär/tē] **33**
pass [päs] **156**–H
passbook [päs/book/] **97**–5
passenger [päs/ən jər] **104**–7, **110**–23
pass out [päs/ owt/] **7**–O
passport [päs/pört/] **29**–9
pasta [päs/tə] **61**–15
  ...salad [–säl/əd] **53**–15
pastrami [pə strä/mē] **53**–6
patient [pā/shənt] **84**–3
Patient's room [pā/shənts room/] **86**
patio [păt/ē ō] **39**–6
  ...furniture [–für/nĭ chər] **39**–5
patron [pā/trən] **62**–5
pattern (clothes) [păt/ərn] **73**–8
pattern maker [păt/ərn mā/kər] **73** ✦
Patterns (fabric) [păt/ərnz] **70**
pause [pöz] **165**–E
paw [pö] **134**–42
pay [pā(/–)]
  ...taxes [–tăk/səz] **116**–E
  ...the check [–dhə chĕk/] **62**–I
  ...the mortgage [–dhə mör/gĭj] **35**–L
  ...the rent [–dhə rĕnt/] **35**–F
pay phone [pā/ fōn] **9**–11
pay back [pā/ băk/] **20** ✦
pay for [pā/ för/, –fər] **21**–C
PE (physical education) [pē/ē/] / [fĭz/ĭ kəl ĕj/ə kā/shən]
  121–11
peaches [pē/chəz] **50**–5
peacock [pē/käk/] **132**–15
peak [pēk] **117**–14
pearls [pürlz] **69**–30
pears [përz] **50**–6

peas [pēz] **51**–19
pedestrian [pə dĕs/trē ən] **90**–7
   …crossing [–krö/sĭng] **107**–10
pediatrician [pē/dē ə trĭsh/ən] **86**–4
peel [pēl] **58**–N
peephole [pēp/hōl/] **37**–27
pelvis [pĕl/vəs] **75**–55
pen [pĕn] **3**–18
pencil [pĕn/səl] **3**–20
   …eraser [–ĭ rā/sər] **3**–21
   …sharpener [–shär/pə nər] **3**–13, **142**–9
penguin [pĕng/wĭn] **132**–12
peninsula [pə nĭn/sə lə] **117**–7
penny [pĕn/ē] **20**–1
peppers [pĕp/ərz] **51**–7
pepper shaker [pĕp/ər shā/kər] **41**–15
Percents [pər sĕnts/] **15**
Percussion [pər kŭsh/ən] **120**
perfume [pür/fyoom/, pər fyoom/] **76**–5
period [pïr/ē əd] **113**–6
periodical section [pïr/ē äd/ĭ kəl sĕk/shən] **98**–6
perm hair [pürm/ hër/] **23**–B
perpendicular [pür/pən dĭk/yə lər] **118**–20
personal check [pür/sə nəl chĕk/] **20**–14
PERSONAL HYGIENE [pür/sə nəl hī/jēn] **76**–**77**
personal identification number (PIN)
   [pür/sə nəl ī dĕn/tə fə kā/shən nŭm/bər] **97**–B
PERSONAL INFORMATION [pür/sə nəl ĭn/fər mā/shən] **4**
personal radio-cassette player
   [pür/sə nəl rā/dē ō kə sĕt/ plā/ər] **164**–15
pesticide [pĕs/tə sīd/] **49** ✦
   …poisoning [–poy/zə nĭng] **126**–14
pet [pĕt(/–)]
   …food [–food/] **54**–10
   …store [–stör/] **92**–6
petal [pĕt/l] **129**–8
petri dish [pē/trē dĭsh/] **119**–6
petroleum [pə trō/lē əm] **126**–6
Pets [pĕts] **133**
pharmacist [fär/mə sĭst] **80**–10
pharmacy [fär/mə sē] **80**–9, **90**–2
Phillips screwdriver [fĭl/ĭps skroo/drī/vər] **150**–26
phone [fōn(/–)] **9**–1
   …card [–kärd/] **9**–10
photo [fō/tō]
   …album [–ăl/bəm] **165**–32
   …shop [–shäp/] **90**–4
photocopier [fō/tə käp/ē ər] **142**–14
photograph [fō/tə grăf/] **44**–7
photographer [fə täg/rə fər] **32**–11
PHOTOGRAPHY [fə täg/rə fē] **164**-**165**
PHYSICAL DESCRIPTION [fĭz/ĭ kəl dĭ skrĭp/shən] **22**
physically challenged [fĭz/ĭ klē chăl/ənjd] **22**–25
physical therapist [fĭz/ĭ kəl thër/ə pĭst] **81**–30
physics [fĭz/ĭks] **119**–3
pi (π) [pī] **118** ✦
piano [pē ăn/ō] **120**–16
pickax [pĭk/ăks/] **149**–20
pick up [pĭk/ ŭp/] / [pĭk/ ŭp/–] **94**–G
   …the children [–dhə chĭl/drən] **27**–O
   …the receiver [–dhə rĭ sē/vər] **9**–A
pickup truck [pĭk/ŭp trŭk/] **106**–7
picnic [pĭk/nĭk] **153**–D
picnic table [pĭk/nĭk tā/bəl] **153**–8
picture [pĭk/chər]

…book [–book/] **45**–17
   …dictionary [–dĭk/shə nër ē] **3**–29
pie [pī(/–)] **61**–21
   …pan [–păn/] **59**–28
pier [pïr] **155**–16
pierced earrings [pïrst/ ïr/ĭng] **69**–37
pig [pĭg] **133**–8
pigeon [pĭj/ən] **132**–16
pill [pĭl] **81**–26
pillow [pĭl/ō] **42**–20, **44**–9
pillowcase [pĭl/ō kās/] **44**–10
pilot [pī/lət] **110**–12
PIN (personal identification number) [pĭn] **97**–B
pin [pĭn] (jewelry) **69**–36, (sewing) **73**–14
pin [pĭn(/–)] / [–pĭn/]
   …cushion [–koosh/ən] **73**–15
   push… [poosh/–] **143**–43
pine [pīn] **128**–10
pinecone [pīn/kōn/] **128**–11
pineapples [pī/năp/əlz] **50**–2
Ping-Pong [pĭng/päng/, –pöng/] **159**–13
pink [pĭngk] **12**–10
pint [pīnt] **57**–3
pipe [pīp(/–)] **151**–16
   …wrench [–rĕnch/] **151**–43
pipes [pīps] **49**–19
pitch [pĭch] **156**–F
pizza [pēt/sə] **60**–7
place [plās(/–)]
   …mat [–măt/] **41**–20
   …setting [–sĕt/ĭng] **63**–14
place of birth [plās/ əv bürth/] **4**–17
PLACES TO GO [plā/səz tə gō/] **152**
PLACES TO LIVE [plā/səz tə lĭv/] **34**
plaid [plăd] **70**–9
plain [plān] **71**–38
plains [plānz] **117**–19
plan [plăn] **169**–A
plane (tool) [plān] **151**–52
PLANE TRIP [plān/ trĭp/] **111**
Planets [plăn/əts] **127**
plant [plănt] **39**–D, **148**–A
plant [plănt] **39**–B, **42**–18
PLANTS [plănts] **128**
plastic [plăs/tĭk] **70**
   …bag [–băg/] **55**–23
   …storage container [–stör/ĭj kən tā/nər] **59**–3
   …wrap [–răp/] **55**–54
plate [plāt] **41**–24, **63**–15, 16, 17
platform [plăt/förm/] **104**–15
platter [plăt/ər] **41**–3
platypus [plăt/ĭ pəs, –poos/] **135**–46
play [plā(/–)] **94**–K, **165**–B
   …an instrument [–ən ĭn/strə mənt] **120**–A
   …cards [–kärdz/] **163**–H
   …games [–gāmz/] **162**–C
play [plā] **166**–2
player [plā/ər] **158**–5, **164**–2, 14, 15
PLAYGROUND [plā/grownd/] **153**
playground [plā/grownd/] **36**–6
playpen [plā/pĕn/] **95**–11
pliers [plī/ərz] **150**–7
plug [plŭg] **164**–18
plumber [plŭm/ər] **49**–20
plums [plŭmz] **50**–8

plunger [plŭn/jər] **151**–44
Pluto [plōō/tō] **127**–1
plywood [plī/wŏŏd/] **149**–16
p.m. [pē/ĕm/] **16**
pneumatic drill [nŏŏ măt/ĭk drĭl/] **149**–9
pocket [päk/ət] **73**–4
podium [pō/dē əm] **32**–5
poinsettia [poyn sĕt/ē ə, –sĕt/ə] **129**–23
point [poynt] **2**–F
poison [poy/zən] **82**–J, **147**–3
...ivy [–ī/vē] **128**–25
...oak [–ōk/] **128**–23
...sumac [–sōō/măk, –shōō/–] **128**–24
police [pə lēs/]
...officer [–ö/fə sər] **99**–1, **138**–44
...station [–stā/shən] **89**–19
polish [päl/ĭsh]
...nails [–nālz/] **77**–O
...the furniture [–dhə für/nĭ chər] **46**–K
polka-dotted [pō/kə dät/əd] **70**–8
Pollution [pə lōō/shən] **126**
polyester [päl/ē ĕs/tər, päl/ē ĕs/tər] **70**
poncho [pän/chō] **66**–18
pond [pänd] **117**–21, **153**–6
pool (game) [pōōl] **159**–2
pool (swimming) [pōōl(/–)] **37**–16, **145**–16
...service [–sür/vəs] **145**–17
porch light [pörch/ līt/] **38**–9
porcupine [pör/kyə pīn/] **134**–10
Pork [pörk] **52**
pork chops [pörk/ chäps/] **52**–10
porpoise [pör/pəs] **131**–31
port [pört] **144**–17
portable [pör/tə bəl]
...radio-cassette player [–rā/dē ō kə sĕt/ plā/ər] **164**–2
...TV [–tē/vē/] **164**–7
postage [pō/stĭj] **96**–10
postal [pō/stəl]
...scale [–skāl/] **143**–16
...worker [–wür/kər] **138**–45
postcard [pōst/kärd/] **96**–3
Post-it notes [pōst/ĭt nōts/] **143**–34
postmark [pōst/märk/] **96**–9
post office [pōst/ ö/fəs] **89**–29
pot [pät(/–)] **40**–16, **59**–6
...holders [–hōl/dərz] **59**–29
potato [pə tā/tō]
...chips [–chĭps/] **55**–40
...salad [–săl/əd] **53**–13
potatoes [pə tā/tōz] **51**–21, **61**–11
potty seat [pät/ē sēt/] **95**–10
pouch [powch] **135**–50
POULTRY [pōl/trē] **52**
poultry section [pōl/trē sĕk/shən] **54**–2
pound [pownd] **57**–12
pour [pör(/–)]
...the eggs into the pan [–dhē ĕgz/ ĭn/tə dhə pän/] **58**–D
...the water [–dhə wö/tər] **62**–C
power [pow/ər] **48**–2
...sander [–săn/dər] **150**–9
...switch [–swĭch/] **144**–4
prairie dog [prër/ē dög/] **133**–22
pregnant [prĕg/nənt] **22**–19
PREPOSITIONS [prĕp/ə zĭsh/ənz] **13**
PREPOSITIONS OF MOTION [prĕp/ə zĭsh/ənz əv mō/shən] **105**

preschool [prē/skōōl/] **112**–4
prescription [prĭ skrĭp/shən] **80**–13
...label [–lā/bəl] **80**–14
...medication [–mĕd/ə kā/shən] **80**–11
President [prĕz/ə dənt] **116**–6
pretend [prĭ tĕnd/] **163**–G
price [prīs(/–)] **21**–6
...tag [–tăg/] **21**–1
principal [prĭn/sə pəl] **5**–14
principal's office [prĭn/sə pəlz ö/fəs] **5**–13
print [prĭnt] **4**–C
print [prĭnt] **70**–10
printer [prĭn/tər] (occupation) **138**–46, (computer) **144**–12
print shop [prĭnt/ shäp/] **91**–22
priority mail [prī ör/ə tē māl/, –är/–] **96**–12
prism [prĭz/əm] **119**–20
prison [prĭz/ən] **99**–G
private school [prī/vət skōōl/] **112**–2
Problems (clothing) [präb/ləmz] **70**
PROBLEMS, HOUSEHOLD [hows/hōld/ präb/ləmz] **48**–49
produce section [prō/dōōs sĕk/shən] **54**–11
product [präd/ŭkt] **118**✦
program (computer) [prō/grăm] **144**–21
Programs (TV) [prō/grămz] **167**
projector [prə jĕk/tər] / [–prə jĕk/tər]
carousel slide... [kăr/ə sĕl/ sīld/–] **165**–29
overhead... [ō/vər hĕd/–] **2**–4
prosecuting attorney [präs/ĭ kyōō/tĭng ə tür/nē] **99**–10
protect your wallet [prə tĕkt/ yər wä/lət, –wö/–] **101**–D
proud [prowd] **31**–22
prunes [prōōnz] **50**–26
pruning shears [prōō/nĭng shïrz/] **39**–15
psychiatrist [sī kī/ə trĭst, sə–] **86**–6
PUBLIC SAFETY [pŭb/lĭk sāf/tē] **101**
public school [pŭb/lĭk skōōl/] **112**–1
public telephone [pŭb/lĭk tĕl/ə fōn/] **91**–21
PUBLIC TRANSPORTATION
[pŭb/lĭk trăns/pər tā/shən] **104**
pudding [pŏŏd/ĭng] **61**–20
pull [pŏŏl(/–)]
...a tooth [–ə tōōth/] **85**–M
...the wagon [–dhə wăg/ən] **153**–A
pullover sweater [pŏŏl/ō vər swĕt/ər] **64**–11
pumps [pŭmps] **68**–16
Punctuation [pŭngk/chōō ā/shən] **113**
puppet show [pŭp/ət shō/] **152**–14
puppy [pŭp/ē] **133**–12
purple [pür/pəl] **12**–7
purses [pür/səz] **69**–6
push [pŏŏsh] **153**–B
pushpin [pŏŏsh/pĭn/] **143**–43
put away [pŏŏt/ə wā/] / [pŏŏt/ə wā/–]
...the toys [–dhə toyz/] **46**–H
...your pencil [–yər pĕn/səl] **2**–L
put in order [pŏŏt/ ĭn ör/dər] **7**–W
put on [pŏŏt/ än/, –ön/] / [pŏŏt/ än–, –ön–]
...makeup [–māk/ŭp/] **77**–P
...sunscreen [–sŭn/skrēn/] **76**–D
puzzle [pŭz/əl] **45**–22
pyramid [pïr/ə mĭd] **118**–13
quart [kwört] **57**–4
quarter [kwör/tər] (time) **16**, (money) **20**–4
quarter cup [kwör/tər kŭp/] **57**–8
quarter moon [kwör/tər mōōn/] **127**–15
question mark [kwĕs/chən märk/] **113**–7

Index

quiet [kwī/ət] 11–12
quill [kwĭl] 134–23
quiz show [kwĭz/ shō/] 167–23
quotation marks [kwō tā/shən märks/] 113–9
quotient [kwō/shənt] 118 ✦
rabbit [răb/ət] 133–13
raccoon [ră kōōn/] 134–13
race [rās] 157–Y
racquetball [răk/ət böl/] 159–11
radiation [rā/dē ā/shən] 126–13
radiator [rā/dē ā/tər] 109–42, 56
radio [rā/dē ō] 44–16, 108–31
   …program [-prō/grăm] 166–4
radioactive [rā/dē ō ăk/tĭv] 147–6
radiologist [rā/dē äl/ə jĭst] 86–5
radishes [răd/ĭ shəz] 51–5
radius [rā/dē əs] 118–16
rafting [răf/tĭng] 154–4
rags [răgz] 47–6
railroad crossing [rāl/rōd krö/sĭng] 107–11
rain boots [rān/ bōōts/] 66–19
raincoat [rān/kōt/] 66–17
rain forest [rān/ för/əst, fär/–] 117–1
raining [rā/nĭng] 10–8
raise [rāz] 2–A
raisins [rā/zənz] 50–27
rake [rāk] 39–F
rake [rāk] 39–11
ranch [rănch] 34–12
rancher [răn/chər] 148–22
RANCHING [răn/chĭng] 148
rash [răsh] 78–10
raspberries [răz/bĕr/ēz] 50–18
rat [răt] 133–18
rats [răts] 49–27
rattle [răt/l] 95–31
rattlesnake [răt/l snāk/] 131–38
raw [rö] 52–24
ray [rā] 130–6
rayon [rā/än] 70
razor [rā/zər] 77–25
   …blade [–blād/] 77–26
read [rēd] 6–B, 27–V, 94–F
Realtor [rē/əl tər] 35
rearview mirror [rĭr/vyōō/ mĭr/ər] 108–1
receipt [rĭ sēt/] 21–5
receive [rĭ sēv/] 96–D
receiver [rĭ sē/vər] 9–2
receptionist [rĭ sĕp/shə nĭst] 84–2, 138–47
recharging [rē chär/jĭng] 109–58
record [rĕk/ərd] 98–15
record [rĭ körd/] (science) 119–C, (cassette player) 165–A
Recreation room [rĕk/rē ā/shən rōōm/] 36
rec room [rĕk/ rōōm/] 36 ✦
rectangle [rĕk/tăng/gəl] 118–8
recycle [rē sī/kəl] 46–B, 126–A
recycling bin [rē sī/klĭng bĭn/] 47–2
red [rĕd(/–)] 12–13
   …hair [–hër/] 23–14
redwood [rĕd/wōōd/] 128–1
referee [rĕf/ə rē/] 158–6
reference [rĕf/rəns]
   …desk [–dĕsk/] 98–2
   …librarian [lī brër/ē ən] 98–1
refrigerator [rĭ frĭj/ə rā/tər] 40–9

register [rĕj/ə stər] 116–F
registered [rĕj/ə stərd]
   …nurse (RN) [–nürs/] 87–22
regular price [rĕg/yə lər prĭs/] 21–2
relax [rĭ lăks/] 27–U
relieved [rĭ lēvd/] 30–16
religious holiday [rĭ lĭj/əs häl/ə dā/] 19–44
relish [rĕl/ĭsh] 60–26
remarried [rē mär/ēd] 25–27
remote control [rĭ mōt/ kən trōl/] 164–9
remove [rĭ mōōv/] 97–F
rent [rĕnt] 28–I
Renting an apartment [rĕn/tĭng ən ə pärt/mənt] 35
repair [rĭ për/] 140–G
repair person [rĭ për/ pür/sən] 48–10, 138–48
REPAIRS [rĭ përz/] 48–49
repeat [rĭ pēt/] 6–D
report crimes [rĭ pört/ krīmz/] 101–H
reporter [rĭ pör/tər] 99–12, 139–49
Reptiles [rĕp/tīlz] 131
request [rĭ kwĕst/] 111–M
rescue breathing [rĕs/kyōō brē/dhĭng] 83–16
Resident Alien card [rĕz/ə dənt ā/lē ən kärd/] 29–3
respirator [rĕs/pə rā/tər] 147–12
Responsibilities (of citizenship)
   [rĭ spän/sə bĭl/ə tēz əv sĭt/ə zən shĭp/] 116
RESTAURANT [rĕs/tə rənt, –ränt/] 62–63
restaurant [rĕs/tə rənt, –ränt/] 90–14
rest rooms [rĕst/ rōōmz/] 5–8
retire [rĭ tīr/] 29 ✦
return [rĭ türn/] 21–F
return address [rĭ türn/ ə drĕs/, –ā/drĕs/] 96–7
rewind [rē wīnd/] 165–D
rewrite [rē rīt/] 113–D
rhinoceros [rī näs/ər əs] 135–29
rib cage [rĭb/ kāj/] 75–53
rice [rīs(/–)] 54–28, 148–1
   …pilaf [–pē/läf, –pī läf/] 61–18
ride [rīd] 91–E, 157–W
rides [rīdz] 152–17
right [rīt(/–)] / [–rīt/]
   …turn only [–türn/ ōn/lē] 107–9
   on the… [än dhə–, ön–] 13–2
right-of-way [rīt/əv wā/] 107 ✦
Rights and responsibilities [rīts/ ən rĭ spän/sə bĭl/ə tēz] 116
ring [rĭng] 69–39
rinse [rĭns] 76–F
rip [rĭp] 70–23
ripe [rīp] 50–29
river [rĭv/ər] 117–3
RN (registered nurse) [är/ĕn/] 87–22
roast [rōst] 58–U
roast [rōst(/–)]
   …beef [–bēf/] 52–1, 53–7, 57–12
   …chicken [–chĭk/ən] 61–12
roasting [rō/stĭng]
   …pan [–păn/] 59–13
   …rack [–răk/] 59–14
robin [räb/ən] 132–17
rock [räk] 94–H
rock [räк(/–)] 155–24
rock band [räk/ bănd/] 120–2
rocking chair [räk/ĭng chër/] 94–6
RODENTS [rōd/nts] 133
roll [rōl(/–)] 56–11

...of paper towels [–əv pā/pər tow/əlz] **56**–23
roller coaster [rō/lər kō/stər] **152**–15
rollers [rō/lərz] **23**–21
rolling pin [rō/lĭng pĭn/] **59**–30
rolls [rōlz] **54**–30
romance [rō măns/, rō/măns] **166**–16
Roman numerals [rō/mən nōō/mər əlz] **14**
roof [rōōf] **38**–20, **48**–3
roofer [rōō/fər] **48**–8
roof garden [rōōf/ gär/dn] **36**–5
room service [rōōm/ sür/vəs] **145**–12
rooster [rōō/stər] **133**–6
root [rōōt] **128**–5, **129**–3
rope [rōp] **154**–19
rose [rōz] **129**–15
rotary card file [rō/tə rē kärd/ fīl/] **143**–17
rotten [rät/n] **50**–30
rouge [rōōzh] **77**–36
route [rōōt, rowt] **104**–2
router [row/tər] **150**–12
rubber [rŭb/ər]
　...band [–bănd/] **143**–45
　...cement [–sə mĕnt/] **143**–38
　...gloves [–glŭvz/] **47**–4
　...mat [–măt/] **43**–3
　...stamp [–stămp/] **143**–40
rug [rŭg] **44**–23
ruler [rōō/lər] **3**–27
run [rŭn] **156**–C
rural area [rōōr/əl ĕr/ē ə] **34**–4
rye bread [rī/ brĕd/] **53**–3
sad [săd] **31**–20, **167**–28
safe-deposit box [sāf/dĭ päz/ət bäks/] **97**–13
safety [sāf/tē]
　...boot [–bōōt/] **147**–20
　...earmuffs [–ïr/mŭfs/] **147**–14
　...glasses [–glăs/əz] **147**–10
　...goggles [–gäg/əlz] **147**–9
　...pin [–pĭn/] **73**–24
　...seat [–sēt/] **109**–39
　...vest [–vĕst/] **147**–15
　...visor [–vī/zər] **147**–11
SAFETY, PUBLIC [pŭb/lĭk sāf/tē] **101**
sailboarding [sāl/bör/dĭng] **160**–10
sailboat [sāl/bōt/] **155**–4
sailing [sā/lĭng] **160**–8
salad [săl/əd]
　...bar [–bär/] **60**–16
　...dressing [–drĕs/ĭng] **60**–18
　...fork [–förk/] **63**–24
　...plate [–plāt/] **63**–17
salamander [săl/ə măn/dər] **130**–27
salami [sə lä/mē] **53**–5
sale price [sāl/ prīs/] **21**–3
salesclerk [sālz/klürk/] **68**–1, **139**–50
salesperson [sālz/pür/sən] **139**–50
sales tax [sālz/ tăks/] **21**–7
salmon steak [săm/ən stāk/] **53**–19
saltshaker [sölt/shā/kər] **41**–14
sand [sănd(/–)] **155**–23
　...castle [–kăs/əl] **155**–10
　...dune [–dōōn/] **117**–5
sandals [săn/dlz] **68**–24
sandbox [sănd/bäks/] **153**–15
sandpaper [sănd/pā/pər] **151**–50

sanitation worker [săn/ə tā/shən wür/kər] **139**–51
Saturday [săt/ər dā/, –dē] **18**–7
Saturn [săt/ərn] **127**–4
saucepan [sös/păn/] **59**–25
saucer [sö/sər] **63**–22
sausage [sö/sĭj] **52**–12, **61**–2
sauté [sö tā/, sō–] **58**–H
save [sāv] **126**–B, C
savings account number [sā/vĭngz ə kownt/ nŭm/bər] **97**–6
saxophone [săk/sə fōn/] **120**–7
say [sā] **6**–C
scaffolding [skăf/əl dĭng] **149**–4
scale (weight) [skāl] **43**–26, **84**–7
scales (fish) [skālz] **130**–3
scallions [skăl/yənz] **51**–17
scallop [skăl/əp, skäl/–] **130**–18
scallops [skăl/əps, skäl/–] **53**–25
scanner [skăn/ər] **144**–13
scared [skërd] **31**–24
scarf [skärf] **66**–4, **70**–15
schedule [skĕj/ōōl, –ōō əl] **104**–3
SCHOOL [skōōl] **5**
school **89**–27
　...crossing [–krö/sĭng] **107**–13
　adult... [ə dŭlt/–, ăd/ŭlt–] **112**–8
　elementary... [ĕl/ə mĕn/trē–] **112**–5
　high... [hī/–] **112**–7
　junior high... [jōōn/yər hī/–] **112**–6
　middle... [mĭd/l–] **112**–6
　parochial... [pə rō/kē əl–] **112**–3
　private... [prī/vət–] **112**–2
　trade... [trād/–] **112**–9
　vocational... [vō kā/shə nəl–] **112**–9
School Registration Form [skōōl/ rĕj/ə strā/shən förm/] **4**
SCHOOLS, TYPES OF [tīps/ əv skōōlz/] **112**
SCHOOL SUBJECTS, MORE [mör/ skōōl/ sŭb/jĭkts] **121**
SCIENCE [sī/əns] **119**
science fiction story [sī/əns fĭk/shən stör/ē] **166**–12
scissors [sĭz/ərz] **23**–19, **73**–18
score [skör] **158**–1
scorpion [skör/pē ən] **132**–31
scrambled eggs [skrăm/bəld ĕgz/] **58**, **61**–1
scraper [skrā/pər] **151**–48
screen [skrēn] **2**–2, **144**–6, **152**–12, **165**–28
screen door [skrēn/ dör/] **38**–8
screwdriver [skrōō/drī/vər] **150**–25
　Phillips... [fĭl/ĭps–] **150**–26
scrub [skrŭb] **46**–L
scrub brush [skrŭb/ brŭsh/] **47**–19
scuba [skōō/bə]
　...diving [–dī/vĭng] **160**–12
　...tank [–tăngk/] **155**–8
sculpture [skŭlp/chər] **152**–9
sea [sē(/–)]
　...anemone [–ə nĕm/ə nē] **130**–21
　...horse [–hörs/] **130**–23
　...lion [–lī/ən] **131**–34
　...urchin [–ür/chən] **130**–20
Sea animals [sē/ ăn/ə məlz] **130**
SEAFOOD [sē/fōōd/] **53**
seal [sēl] **131**–33
seam [sēm(/–)] **73**–11
　...ripper [–rĭp/ər] **73**–19
Sea mammals [sē/ măm/əlz] **131**
search and rescue team [sürch/ ən rĕs/kyōō tēm/] **103**–17

Index

seashell [sē/shĕl/] **155**–21
Seasons [sē/zənz] **19**
seat [sēt(/–)] **2**–E, **152**–11
...belt [–bĕlt/] **109**–36
seat [sēt] **62**–B
seaweed [sē/wēd/] **155** ✦
second [sĕk/ənd] **14**, **16**–1
...floor [–flör/] **36**–2
secretary [sĕk/rə tër/ē] **139**–52, **142**–3
section [sĕk/shən] / [–sĕk/shən]
    dairy... [dër/ē–] **54**–9
    produce... [prō/dōōs–] **54**–11
security [sĭ kyōōr/ə tē] **111**–C
    ...gate [–gāt/] **36**–13
    ...guard [–gärd/] **97**–4
    ...system [–sĭs/təm] **36**–9
see [sē] **75**–A
seed [sēd] **129**–1
seedling [sēd/lĭng] **129**–2
seesaw [sē/sö/] **153**–16
See you [sē/ yə] **8**
Selective Service [sə lĕk/tĭv sür/vəs] **116**–F
sell [sĕl] **21**–B, **140**–H
semi [sĕm/ī] **106**–15
semicolon [sĕm/ē kō/lən] **113**–13
Senate [sĕn/ət] **116**–3
Senator [sĕn/ə tər] **116**–4
send [sĕnd] **96**–B
senior citizen [sēn/yər sĭt/ə zən] **22**–12
Senses [sĕn/səz] **75**
sentence [sĕn/tns] **113**–4
sentence the defendant [sĕn/tns dhə dĭ fĕn/dənt] **99**–F
September [sĕp tĕm/bər] **19**–33
serious [sïr/ē əs] **167**–26
Serious Diseases [sïr/ē əs dĭ zē/zəz] **79**
serve (sports) [sürv] **157**–N
serve on a jury [sürv/ än ə jōōr/ē, –ön–] **116**–G
server [sür/vər] **62**–4, **63**–6, **139**–53
serve the meal [sürv/ dhə mēl/] **62**–F
service elevator [sür/vəs ĕl/ə vā tər] **145** ✦
serviceman [sür/vəs măn/, –mən] **139**–54
servicewoman [sür/vəs wōōm/ən] **139**–54
serving dish [sür/vĭng dĭsh/] **41**–6
set [sĕt(/–)]
    ...hair [–hër/] **23**–C
    ...the table [–dhə tā/bəl] **62**–A
set of dishes [sĕt/ əv dĭsh/əz] **41**–2
seven [sĕv/ən] **14**
seventeen [sĕv/ən tēn/] **14**
seventeenth [sĕv/ən tēnth/] **14**
seventh [sĕv/ənth] **14**
seventy [sĕv/ən tē] **14**
sew [sō(/–)]
    ...by hand [–bī hănd/] **73**–A
    ...by machine [–bī mə shēn/] **73**–B
    ...clothes [–klōz/] **140**–L
SEWING AND ALTERATIONS [sō/ĭng ən öl/tə rā/shənz] **73**
sewing machine [sō/ĭng mə shēn/] **73**–10
sex [sĕks] **4**–12
shade [shād] **155**–11
shampoo [shăm pōō/] **76**–9
Shapes [shāps] **118**
share [shër] **6**–I
shark [shärk] **130**–7
shave [shāv] **77**–M

shaving cream [shā/vĭng krēm/] **77**–27
shears [shïrz] **39**–15
sheep [shēp] **133**–7
sheet [shēt] **44**–13, 14
shelf [shĕlf] **40**–8
Shellfish [shĕl/fĭsh/] **53**
shelter [shĕl/tər] **34**–10
shingles [shĭng/gəlz] **149**–19
shin guards [shĭn/ gärdz/] **161**–13
ship [shĭp] **146**–C
shipping clerk [shĭp/ĭng klürk/] **146**–15
shirt [shürt] **64**–4, **65**–20
shock [shäk] **82**–C
shoe [shōō(/–)]
    ...department [–dĭ pärt/mənt] **68**–3
    ...store [–stör/] **92**–10
shoelace [shōō/lās/] **68**–14
SHOES AND ACCESSORIES [shōōz/ ən ĭk sĕs/ə rēz] **68**–69
shoot [shōōt] **156**–I
shop [shäp] **21**–A
shop [shäp] **121**–10
SHOPPING [shäp/ĭng] **21**
shopping [shäp/ĭng]
    ...basket [–băs/kət] **54**–7
    ...cart [–kärt/] **54**–3
    ...program [–prō/grăm] **167**–25
shore [shör] **117**–12
short [shört] **22**–18, **23**–1, **71**–35
shorten [shör/tn] **73**–D
short-sleeved [shört/slēvd/] **71**–30
shorts [shörts] **64**–13, **67**–3, 12
shortwave radio [shört/wāv/ rā/dē ō] **164**–5
shoulder [shōl/dər] **74**–10
    ...bag [–băg/] **69**–27
    ...harness [–här/nəs] **109**–37
    ...pads [–pădz/] **161**–21
shoulder-length [shōl/dər lĕngkth/] **23**–2
shout [showt] **169**–G
shovel [shŭv/əl] **39**–13, **149**–21
show (puppet) [shō] **152**–14
shower cap [show/ər kăp/] **76**–1
showerhead [show/ər hĕd/] **43**–10
shrimp [shrĭmp] **53**–24, **130**–19
shutter [shŭt/ər] **38**–18
sick [sĭk] **30**–14
side [sīd] **118**–22
sideburns [sīd/bürnz/] **23**–7
sideview mirror [sīd/vyōō/ mïr/ər] **108**–8
sidewalk [sīd/wök/] **91**–26
sight impaired [sīt/ ĭm përd/] **22**–26
sign [sīn(/–)]
    ...a rental agreement [–ə rĕn/təl ə grē/mənt] **35**–C
    ...your name [–yər nām/] **4**–D
sign [sīn] **91**–29
signature [sĭg/nə chər] **4**–18
Signs [sīnz] **107**
silk [sĭlk] **70**–15
silk scarves [sĭlk/ skärvz/] **68**–4
silver dollar [sĭl/vər däl/ər] **20**–6
simmer [sĭm/ər] **58**–R
sing [sĭng] **120**–B, **169**–I
single [sĭng/gəl]
    ...father [–fä/dhər] **25**–25
    ...mother [–mŭdh/ər] **25**–26
sink [sĭngk] **40**–6, **43**–22, **49**–17

sister [sĭs/tər] **24**–8, **25**–30, 32
sister-in-law [sĭs/tər ĭn lö/] **24**–15
sitcom [sĭt/käm/] **167**–18
sit down [sĭt/ down/] **2**–E
situation comedy [sĭch/ōō ā/shən käm/ə dē] **167**–18
six [sĭks] **14**
six-pack [sĭks/păk/] **56**–9
six-pack of soda [sĭks/păk/ əv sō/də] **56**–21
sixteen [sĭks/tēn/] **14**
sixteenth [sĭks/tēnth/] **14**
sixth [sĭksth] **14**
sixty [sĭks/tē] **14**
six-year-old [sĭks/yïr ōld/] **22**–4
Sizes [sī/zəz] **70**
skate [skāt] **157**–V
skateboarding [skāt/bör/dĭng] **159**–12
skating [skā/tĭng] **160**–4, 5
Skeleton [skĕl/ə tn] **75**
ski [skē] **157**–V
ski [skē(/–)]
...boots [–bōōts/] **161**–26
...cap [–kăp/] **66**–10
...mask [–măsk/] **66**–14
...poles [–pōlz/] **161**–25
skiing [skē/ĭng] **160**–1, 3, 7
skin [skĭn] **75**–51
skinless [skĭn/ləs] **52** ✦
skirt [skürt] **64**–10, **65**–25
skis [skēz] **161**–24
skull [skŭl] **75**–52
skunk [skŭngk] **134**–12
skyscraper [skī/skrā/pər] **88** ✦
slacks [slăks] **64**–8
sledding [slĕd/ĭng] **160**–6
sledgehammer [slĕj/hăm/ər] **149**–22
sleeping bag [slē/pĭng băg/] **154**–12
sleepy [slē/pē] **30**–3
sleeve [slēv] **73**–6
sleeveless [slēv/ləs] **71**–29
slice [slīs] **58**–O
slide [slīd] (science) **119**–5, (park) **153**–13
slides [slīdz] **165**–31
slide tray [slīd/ trā/] **165**–30
slim [slĭm] **22**–22
sling [slĭng] **80**–8
slippers [slĭp/ərz] **67**–6
slot [slät] **144**–19
slow [slō] **11**–4
small [smöl(/–)] **70**–2
...town [–town/] **34**–3
smell [smĕl] **75**–C
smog [smäg(/–), smög(/–)] **126**–10
...check [–chĕk/] **109**–57
smoggy [smä/gē, smö/–] **10**–14
smoke detector [smōk/ dĭ tĕk/tər] **37**–25, **45**–11
smoked turkey [smōkt/ tür/kē] **53**–4
snack foods [snăk/ fōōdz/] **55**–16
snail [snāl] **130**–24
snake [snāk] **131**–38, 39
sneeze [snēz] **78**–B
snorkeling [snör/kə lĭng] **160**–11
snowboard [snō/börd/] **161**–23
snowboarding [snō/bör/dĭng] **160**–2
snowing [snō/ĭng] **10**–9
snowstorm [snō/störm/] **10**–20

soap [sōp(/–)] **43**–23, **76**–2
...dish [–dĭsh/] **43**–24
...pads [–pădz/] **47**–5
soap opera [sōp/ äp/rə] **167**–21
soccer [säk/ər] **158**–12
...ball [–böl/] **161**–12
Social Security card [sō/shəl sĭ kyŏŏr/ə tē kärd/] **29**–5
Social Security number [sō/shəl sĭ kyŏŏr/ə tē nŭm/bər] **4**–15
socks [säks] **67**–15
soda [sō/də] **55**–52, **60**–4
sofa [sō/fə] **42**–19
soft [söft] **11**–6
softball [söft/böl/] **158**–10
Software [söft/wër/] **144**
solar [sō/lər]
...eclipse [–ī klĭps/] **127** ✦
...energy [–ĕn/ər jē] **126**–1
...system [–sĭs/təm] **127**
sole [sōl] (fish) **53**–21, (shoe) **68**–12
solid [säl/əd] **70**–6
Solids [säl/ədz] **118**
son [sŭn] **24**–22
son-in-law [sŭn/ĭn lö/] **24** ✦
sore throat [sör/ thrōt/] **78**–6
Sorry. [sär/ē, sör/ē] **8**
sort [sört] **72**–A
soup [sōōp(/–)] **54**–24
...bowl [–bōl/] **63**–18
...of the day [–əv dhə dā/] **61**–10
soupspoon [sōōp/spōōn/] **63**–29
sour cream [sow/ər krēm/] **54**–37
south [sowth] **107, 123, 124**
soybeans [soy/bēnz/] **148**–3
space [spās(/–)] **127**–22
...station [–stā/shən] **127**–18
spades [spādz] **163**–28
spaghetti [spə gĕt/ē] **54**–27
spare tire [spër/ tīr/] **109**–53
sparrow [spär/ō] **132**–8
spatula [spăch/ə lə] **59**–19
speak [spēk] **140**–J
speaker [spē/kər] **36**–8
speakers [spē/kərz] **164**–11
specialist [spĕsh/ə lĭst] **86** ✦
speed [spēd(/–)] **144** ✦
...limit [–lĭm/ət] **107**–5
speedometer [spĭ däm/ə tər] **108**–20
spell [spĕl] **4**–A, **6**–E
sphere [sfïr] **118**–14
spices [spī/səz] **55**–46
spider [spī/dər] **132**–30
spinach [spĭn/ĭch] **51**–11
spinal column [spī/nəl käl/əm] **75**–54
spiral notebook [spī/rəl nōt/bōōk/] **3**–26
splint [splĭnt] **83**–11
split skirt [splĭt/ skürt/] **65**–25
sponge [spŭnj] **47**–24
spool of thread [spōōl/ əv thrĕd/] **73**–17
spoon [spōōn] **41**–23, **59**–9
SPORTS [spörts] **158**–**160**
sports [spörts(/–)]
...car [–kär/] **106**–6
...coat [–kōt/] **64**–6
...shirt [–shürt/] **65**–26
SPORTS EQUIPMENT [spörts/ ĭ kwĭp/mənt] **161**

Index

SPORTS VERBS [spörts/ vürbz/] **156–157**
sprained ankle [sprānd/ ăng/kəl] **78**–18
spray [sprā(/–)]
...gun [–gŭn/] **151**–19
...starch [–stärch/] **72**–12
spring [sprĭng] **19**–37
sprinkler [sprĭng/klər] **39**–8
square [skwër] **118**–6
squash [skwäsh, skwösh] **51**–13
squeegee [skwē/jē] **47**–9
squid [skwĭd] **130**–10
squirrel [skwür/əl] **133**–21
stacking tray [stăk/ĭng trā/] **142**–5
stadium [stā/dē əm] **152**–26
stage [stāj] **32**–4
stain [stān] **70**–22
stairs [stërz] **37**–35, **105**–8, 9
stairway [stër/wā/] **37**–26
stall shower [stöl/ show/ər] **43** ✦
stamp [stămp(/–)] **96**–10
...collection [–kə lĕk/shən] **162**–12
standard [stăn/dərd]
...time [–tīm/] **17**–32
...transmission [–trănz mĭsh/ən, –trăns–] **109**
stand trial [stănd/ trī/əl, –trīl/] **99**–D
stand up [stănd/ ŭp/] **2**–D
stand-up comedy [stănd/ŭp/ kăm/ə dē] **166**–5
staple [stā/pəl] **142**–G
staple [stā/pəl] **143**–29
stapler [stā/plər] **143**–28
star [stär] **127**–23
starfish [stär/fĭsh/] **130**–15
start [stärt(/–)] **157**–X
...school [–skōōl/] **28**–B
starving [stär/vĭng] **30** ✦
state [stāt] **4**–8
station wagon [stā/shən wăg/ən] **106**–8
stay [stā] **101**–B
steak [stāk(/–)] **52**–2, **61**–13
...knife [–nīf/] **63**–26
steam [stēm] **58**–I
steamer [stē/mər] **59**–4
steel-wool soap pads [stēl/wōōl/ sōp/ pădz/] **47**–5
steering wheel [stïr/ĭng wēl/] **108**–26
steers [stïrz] **148**–21
stem [stēm] **129**–4
stepbrother [stĕp/brŭdh/ər] **25**–33
stepdaughter [stĕp/dö/tər] **25** ✦
stepfather [stĕp/fä/dhər] **25**–28
stepladder [stĕp/lăd/ər] **47**–7
stepmother [stĕp/mŭdh/ər] **25**–31
steps [stĕps] **38**–13, **48**–7
stepsister [stĕp/sĭs/tər] **25**–32
stereo system [stĕr/ē ō sĭs/təm] **42**–14
sterile pad [stĕr/əl păd/] **83**–4
stethoscope [stĕth/ə skōp/] **84**–8
stewing beef [stōō/ĭng bēf/] **52**–3
stick shift [stĭk/ shĭft/] **109**–48
stir [stür] **58**–E
stir-fry [stür/frī/] **58**–W
stitches [stĭch/əz] **83**–15
stock clerk [stäk/ klürk/] **139**–55
stockings [stäk/ĭngz] **67**–26
stomach [stŭm/ək] **75**–41
stomachache [stŭm/ək āk/] **78**–4

stop [stäp] **165**–F
stop [stäp] **107**–3
stopover [stäp/ō/vər] **111** ✦
stopped up [stäpt/ ŭp/] **49**–18
storage locker [stör/ĭj läk/ər] **36**–14
store [stör(/–)] / [–stör/]
...owner [–ō/nər] **139**–56
candy... [kăn/dē–] **92**–3
card... [kärd/–] **92**–7
convenience... [kən vēn/yəns–] **90**–3
department... [dĭ pärt/mənt–] **93**–13
electronics... [ĭ lĕk trän/ĭks–] **93**–18
jewelry... [jōō/əl rē–] **92**–2
music... [myōō/zĭk–] **92**–1
pet... [pĕt/–] **92**–6
shoe... [shōō/–] **92**–10
toy... [toy/–] **92**–5
video... [vĭd/ē ō–] **93**–15
storm [störm] **10**–16, 18, 20, 21
storm door [störm/ dör/] **38**–12
stove [stōv] **40**–18, **154**–16
stow [stō] **111**–H
straight [strāt(/–)]
...hair [–hër/] **23**–9
...line [–līn/] **118**–18
strainer [strā/nər] **59**–22
stranger [strān/jər] **101**–F
straw [strö] **60**–20
strawberries [strö/bĕr/ēz] **50**–17
straw hat [strö/ hăt/] **66**–23
stream [strēm] **117** ✦
street [strēt(/–)] **90**–9
...vendor [–vĕn/dər] **91**–30
streetlight [strēt/līt/] **91**–23
strep throat [strĕp/ thrōt/] **79**–4
stretch [strĕch] **157**–Q
stretcher [strĕch/ər] **87**–28
string beans [strĭng/ bēnz/] **51**–25
string of pearls [strĭng/ əv pürlz/] **69**–30
Strings [strĭngz] **120**
striped [strīpt] **70**–7
stroller [strö/lər] **94**–2
stucco [stŭk/ō] **149**–14
student [stōōd/nt] **2**–3, **139**–57
STUDYING [stŭd/ē ĭng] **6**–7
stuffed animals [stŭft/ ăn/ə məlz] **45**–23
subcompact [sŭb/käm/păkt] **106**–1
subtraction [səb trăk/shən] **118**–2
suburbs [sŭb/ürbz] **34**–2
subway [sŭb/wā/] **104**–9
sugar [shōōg/ər] **55**–48, **60**–21
...bowl [–bōl/] **41**–12
...substitute [–sŭb/stə tōōt/] **60**–22
suit [sōōt] (clothing) **64**–2, (diving) **155**–7
summer [sŭm/ər] **19**–38
sun [sŭn] **127**–10
sunbather [sŭn/bā/dhər] **155**–17
sunblock [sŭn/bläk/] **155**–13
sunburn [sŭn/bürn/] **78**–14
Sunday [sŭn/dā, –dē] **18**–1
sunflower [sŭn/flow/ər] **129**–10
sunglasses [sŭn/glăs/əz] **66**–21
sunny [sŭn/ē] **10**–6
sunscreen [sŭn/skrēn/] **76**–6, **155**–13
superintendent [sōō/prĭn tĕn/dənt, sōō/pər ĭn–] **36**–12

supervise people [sōō/pər vīz pē/pəl] **140**–K
supply cabinet [sə plī/ kăb/ə nət] **142**–13
Supreme Court [sə prēm/ kört/] **116**–8
surfboard [sürf/börd/] **155**–5
surfing [sür/fĭng] **160**–9
surgeon [sür/jən] **87**–30
surge protector [sürj/ prə tĕk/tər] **144**–10
surgical [sür/jĭ kəl]
   ...cap [–kăp/] **87**–31
   ...gown [–gown/] **87**–32
   ...nurse [–nürs/] **87**–29
surprised [sər prīzd/, sə–] **31**–31
suspect [sŭs/pĕkt] **99**–A
suspenders [sə spĕn/dərz] **68**–2
SUV (sports utility vehicle)
   [ĕs/yōō/vē/] / [spörts/ yōō tĭl/ə tē vē/ĭ kəl] **106**–9
swallow [swäl/ō] **82**–J
swap meet [swäp/ mēt/] **152**–22
sweater [swĕt/ər]
   cardigan... [kär/də gən–] **65**–27
   crewneck... [krōō/nĕk/–] **71**–26
   pullover... [pōōl/ō/vər–] **64**–11
   turtleneck... [tür/tl nĕk/–] **71**–28
   V-neck... [vē/nĕk/–] **71**–27
sweatpants [swĕt/pănts/] **64**–15
sweatshirt [swĕt/shürt/] **64**–14
sweep [swēp] **46**–E
sweet peppers [swĕt/ pĕp/ərz] **51**–7
swim [swĭm] **157**–T
swimming [swĭm/ĭng]
   ...pool [–pōōl/] **37**–16
   ...trunks [–trŭngks/] **66**–22
swimsuit [swĭm/sōōt/] **66**–26
swing [swĭng] **157**–O
swings [swĭngz] **153**–12
Swiss cheese [swĭs/ chēz/] **53**–11
swivel chair [swĭv/əl chĕr/] **143**–22
swollen [swō/lən] **78**–16
swordfish [sörd/fĭsh/] **130**–12
SYMPTOMS AND INJURIES [sĭmp/təmz ən ĭn/jə rēz] **78**
synagogue [sĭn/ə gäg/] **88**–9
synthetic materials [sĭn thĕt/ĭk mə tïr/ē əlz] **70**
syringe [sə rĭnj/] **84**–14
syrup [sïr/əp, sür/–] **61**–5
table [tā/bəl] / [–tā/bəl]
   dining room... [dī/nĭng rōōm/–] **41**–17
   night... [nīt/–] **44**–21
   picnic... [pĭk/nĭk–] **153**–8
tablecloth [tā/bəl klöth/] **41**–18
tablespoon [tā/bəl spōōn/] **57**–7
tablet [tăb/lət] **81**–25
table tennis [tā/bəl tĕn/əs] **159**–13
tackle [tăk/əl] **156**–M
taco [tä/kō] **60**–9
tail [tāl] **134**–22
taillight [tāl/līt/] **108**–14
tailor [tā/lər] **73**–9
take [tāk(/–)]
   ...a bath [–ə băth/] **76**–B
   ...a citizenship test [–ə sĭt/ə zən shĭp tĕst/] **116**–C
   ...a message [–ə mĕs/ĭj] **142**–A
   ...a nap [–ə năp/] **94**–L
   ...a picture [–ə pĭk/chər] **32**–D
   ...a seat [–ə sēt/] **2**–E
   ...a shower [–ə show/ər] **26**–C, **76**–A

   ...medicine [–mĕd/ə sən] **80**–F
   ...ownership [–ō/nər shĭp/] **35**–J
   ...the bus [–dhə bŭs/] **26**–H, **104** ✦
   ...the children to school [–dhə chĭl/drən tə skōōl/] **26**–G
   ...the order [–dhē ör/dər] **62**–E
   ...(your) temperature [–yər tĕm/prə chər] **85**–C
take care of [tāk/ kër/ əv] **140**–L
take in [tāk/ ĭn/] **73**–E
take off [tāk/ öf/] **111**–L
take out [tāk/ owt/] **2**–K, **46**–Q
take out (food) [tāk/ owt/] **62** ✦
talcum powder [tăl/kəm pow/dər] **76**–3
talk [tök] **2**–B, **7**–P, **35**–B, G, **141**–A, I
talk show [tök/ shō/] **167**–20
tall [töl] **22**–16
tambourine [tăm/bə rēn/] **120**–19
tangerines [tăn/jə rēnz/] **50**–13
tank top [tăngk/ täp/] **67**–2
tape [tāp(/–)] **83**–5, **143**–39, 42
   ...deck [–dĕk/] **108**–30
   ...measure [–mĕzh/ər] **73**–13, **150**–22
target [tär/gət] **161**–8
tartar [tär/tər] **84**–17
taste [tāst] **75**–D
taxi [tăk/sē] **104**–18
   ...driver [–drī/vər] **104**–20
   ...license [–lī/səns] **104**–22
   ...stand [–stănd/] **104**–19
TB (tuberculosis) [tē/bē/] / [tōō bür/kyə lō/səs] **79**–13
tea [tē] **60**–5, **61**–24
teach [tēch] **140** ✦
teacher [tē/chər] **2**–5, **5**–2, **139**–58
teakettle [tē/kĕt/l] **40**–17
team [tēm] **103**–17, **158**–3
TEAM SPORTS [tēm/ spörts/] **158**
teapot [tē/pät/] **41**–11
tear [tër] **70**–23
teaspoon [tē/spōōn/] **57**–6, **63**–28
technician [tĕk nĭsh/ən] **86**–8, 16
teddy bear [tĕd/ē bër/] **45**–10
teenagers [tē/nā/jərz] **22**–6
teeth [tēth] **74**–25, **77**–J, K, **85**–I
teething ring [tē/dhĭng rĭng/] **95**–30
telemarketer [tĕl/ə mär/kə tər] **139**–59
TELEPHONE [tĕl/ə fōn/] **9**
telephone [tĕl/ə fōn/] **9**–1, 15
   ...book [–bŏŏk/] **9**–15
   ...card [–kärd/] **9**–10
   ...number [–nŭm/bər] **4**–11
telescope [tĕl/ə skōp/] **127**–21
television (TV) [tĕl/ə vĭzh/ən] **42**–26, **164**–6
   ...program [–prō/grăm] **166**–3
teller [tĕl/ər] **97**–1
Temperature (weather) [tĕm/prə chər] **10**
temperature (fever) [tĕm/prə chər] **78**–8
temperature gauge [tĕm/prə chər gāj/] **108**–23
ten [tĕn] **14**, **15**–7, **16**–6, **20**–9
tenant [tĕn/ənt] **37**–33
tennis [tĕn/əs] **159**–14
   ...court [–kört] **153**–7
   ...racket [–răk/ət] **161**–2
   ...shoes [–shōōz/] **68**–22
tent [tĕnt] **154**–10
tenth [tĕnth] **14**
ten-year-old [tĕn/yïr ōld/] **22**–5

termites [tür/mīts] **49**–22

terrified [tĕr/ə fīd/] **30** ✦

test tube [tĕst/ tōōb/] **119**–16

textbook [tĕkst/bŏŏk/, tĕks/–] **3**–22

thank [thăngk] **8**–H

Thanksgiving [thăngks gĭv/ĭng] **168**–15

Thank you [thăngk/ yōō] **8**

theater [thē/ə tər] / [thē/ə tər] **88**–10

...arts [–ärts/] **121**–12

movie... [–mōō/vē–] **88**–11

thermometer [thər măm/ə tər] **84**–15

thick book [thĭk/ bŏŏk/] **11**–7

thigh [thī] **74**–16

thighs [thīz] **52**–21

thimble [thĭm/bəl] **73**–20

thin [thĭn] **11**–8, **22**–22

third [thürd(/–)] **14**

...floor [–flör/] **36**–3

thirsty [thür/stē] **30**–2

thirteen [thür/tēn/] **14**

thirteenth [thür/tēnth/] **14**

thirteen-year-old [thür/tēn/yïr ōld/] **22**–7

thirty [thür/tē] **14**

this week [dhĭs/ wēk/] **18**–19

thorn [thörn] **129**–28

thousand [thow/zənd] **14**

thread [thrĕd] **73**–17

three [thrē(/–)] **14**

...times a week [–tīmz/ ə wēk/] **18**–24

three-fourths [thrē/förths/] **15**–5

three-piece suit [thrē/pēs/ sōōt/] **64**–1

throat [thrōt(/–)] **75**–36

...lozenges [–lăz/ən jəz] **81**–21

through [thrōō] **105**–11

throw [thrō] **156**–D

throw pillow [thrō/ pĭl/ō] **42**–20

throw up [thrō/ ŭp/] **78**–E

thumb [thŭm] **75**–56

thunderstorm [thŭn/dər störm/] **10**–16

Thursday [thürz/dā, –dē] **18**–5

tick [tĭk] **132**–28

ticket [tĭk/ət] **104**–14

tidal wave [tīd/l wāv/] **103**–15

tide [tīd] **155** ✦

tie [tī] **94**–I

tie [tī] (clothing) **69**–40, (sports) **158** ✦

ties [tīz] (clothing) **69**–10

tiger [tī/gər] **135**–37

tight [tīt] **71**–43

tights [tīts] **66**–11

tile [tīl] **43**–9

TIME [tīm] **16**–**17**

time clock [tīm/ klăk/] **146**–4

Time zones [tīm/ zōnz/] **17**

tire [tīr] **108**–10, **109**–53

tired [tīrd] **31**–33

tires [tīrz] **109**–59

title [tīt/l] **98**–21, **113**–3

toad [tōd] **130**–28

toast [tōst] **33, 61**–3

toaster [tō/stər] **40**–7

...oven [–ŭv/ən] **40**–15

today [tə dā/] **18**–15

toddler [täd/lər] **22**–3

toe [tō(/–)] **68**–15, **75**–63

...guard [–gärd/] **147**–21

toenail [tō/nāl/] **75**–64

toggle bolt [täg/əl bōlt/] **150**–33

toilet [toy/lət] **43**–17, **49**–18

...brush [–brŭsh/] **43**–16

...paper [–pā/pər] **43**–15

token [tō/kən] **104**–11

tomatoes [tə mā/tōz] **51**–23

tomorrow [tə măr/ō, –mör/ō] **18**–16

tongs [tängz, töngz] **59**–23, **119**–15

tongue [tŭng] **74**–26

too big [tōō/ bĭg/] **70**–21

TOOLS AND BUILDING SUPPLIES

[tōōlz/ ən bĭl/dĭng sə plīz/] **150**–**151**

too small [tōō/ smöl/] **70**–20

toothache [tōōth/āk/] **78**–2

toothbrush [tōōth/brŭsh/] **43**–20, **77**–20

...holder [–hōl/dər] **43**–21

toothpaste [tōōth/pāst/] **77**–21

tornado [tör nā/dō] **103**–13

total [tōt/l] **21**–8, **118** ✦

tote bag [tōt/ băg/] **69**–29

touch [tŭch] **75**–E

towel [tow/əl] **43**–8, 12, 13

...rack [–răk/] **43**–8

townhouse [town/hows/] **34**–7

tow truck [tō/ trŭk/] **106**–13

toy [toy(/–)]

...chest [–chĕst/] **45**–24

...store [–stör/] **92**–5

toys [toyz] **46**–H, **94**–5

track [trăk] (athletic) **5**–11, (train) **104**–10

track and field [trăk/ ən fēld/] **159**–17

trackball [trăk/böl/] **144**–15

track lighting [trăk/ lī/tĭng] **42**–3

tractor [trăk/tər] **148**–9

...trailer [–trā/lər] **106**–15

trade school [trād/ skōōl/] **112**–9

traffic light [trăf/ĭk līt/] **90**–6

TRAFFIC SIGNS [trăf/ĭk sīnz/] **107**

tragedy [trăj/ə dē] **166**–11

trailer [trā/lər] **106**–17

train [trān(/–)] **104**–17

...station [–stā/shən] **104**–13

training pants [trā/nĭng pănts/] **95**–24

transcribe [trăn skrīb/] **142**–C

transcriber (medical) [trăn skrī/bər] **142**–4

transfer [trăns für/, trăns/fər] **97**–E

transfer [trăns/fər] **104**–6

translator [trănz/lā/tər, trăns/–] **138**–34

transmission [trănz mĭsh/ən, trăns–]

automatic... [ö/tə măt/ĭk–] **109**

standard... [stăn/dərd–] **109**

TRANSPORTATION, PUBLIC [pŭb/lĭk trăns/pər tā/shən] **104**

trash [trăsh(/–)]

...bags [–băgz/] **47**–12

...bin [–bĭn/] **37**–20

...chute [–shōōt/] **37**–24

travel [trăv/əl] **29**–N

travel [trăv/əl]

...agency [–ā/jən sē] **92**–9

...agent [–ā/jənt] **139**–60

traveler's check [trăv/lərz chĕk/] **20**–17

tray [trā(/–)] **41**–10, **62**–H, **63**–7

...table [–tā/bəl] **110**–16

treatment [trēt/mənt] **80** ✦
TREES AND PLANTS [trēz/ ən plănts/] **128**
trench coat [trĕnch/ kōt/] **66**–20
triangle [trī/ăng/gəl] **118**–7
tricycle [trī/sĭ kəl] **153**–9
trigonometry [trĭg/ə näm/ə trē] **118**–27
trim [trĭm] **39**–E
tripe [trīp] **52**–8
tripod [trī/päd] **165**–20
trombone [träm bōn/] **120**–12
trout [trowt] **53**–16
trowel [trow/əl] **39**–14, **149**–12
truck driver [trŭk/ drī/vər] **139**–61
TRUCKS [trŭks] **106**
trumpet [trŭm/pət] **120**–13
trunk [trŭngk] (car) **109**–49, (tree) **128**–4, (animal) **135**–47
T-shirt [tē/shürt/] **64**–12, **70**–16, **72**–15, 16, 17, 18
tuba [too/bə] **120**–14
tube [toob(/–)] **56**–12
    …of toothpaste [–əv tooth/pāst/] **56**–24
Tuesday [tooz/dā, –dē] **18**–3
tulip [too/ləp] **129**–11
tuna [too/nə] **54**–25, **130**–9
tuner [too/nər] **164**–13
tunic [too/nĭk] **65**–22
tunnel [tŭn/əl] **105**–11
turbulence [tür/byə ləns] **111**–N
turkey [tür/kē] **52**–17, **53**–4, **168**–17
turn [türn(/–)]
    …left [–lĕft/] **107**–C
    …right [–rīt/] **107**–B
turn in [türn/ ĭn/] **113**–E
turnips [tür/nəps] **51**–14
turn signal [türn/ sĭg/nəl] **108**–4
turntable [türn/tā/bəl] **164**–12
turquoise [tür/koyz, –kwoyz] **12**–4
turtle [tür/tl] **131**–42
turtleneck [tür/tl nĕk/] **64**–7
    …sweater [–swĕt/ər] **71**–28
tusk [tŭsk] **135**–48
tuxedo [tŭk sē/dō] **65**–28
TV (television) [tē/vē/] **42**–26, **164**–6
    …antenna [–ăn tĕn/ə] **38**–22
tweezers [twē/zərz] **83**–2
twelfth [twĕlfth] **14**
twelve [twĕlv] **14**
twentieth [twĕn/tē əth] **14**
twenty [twĕn/tē] **14, 16**–8, 9, **20**–10
twenty-five after one [twĕn/tē fīv/ ăf/tər wŭn/] **16**–9
twenty-five to two [twĕn/tē fīv/ tə too/] **16**–11
twenty percent [twĕn/tē pər sĕnt/] **15**–8
twenty to two [twĕn/tē tə too/] **16**–12
twice a week [twīs/ ə wēk/] **18**–23
twig [twĭg] **128**–1
two [too] **14**
two-story house [too/stör/ē hows/] **38** ✦
type [tīp] **140**–M, **142**–D
Types of entertainment [tīps/ əv ĕn/tər tān/mənt] **166**
Types of material [tīps/ əv mə tïr/ē əl] **70**
Types of math [tīps/ əv măth/] **118**
TYPES OF SCHOOLS [tīps/ əv skoolz/] **112**
Types of stories [tīps/ əv stör/ēz] **166**
Types of TV programs [tīps/ əv tē/vē/ prō/grămz] **167**
typewriter [tīp/rī/tər] **142**–2
    …cartridge [–kär/trĭj] **143**–31

ugly [ŭg/lē] **11**–22
umbrella [ŭm brĕl/ə] **66**–16, **155**–9
umpire [ŭm/pīr] **158** ✦
uncle [ŭng/kəl] **24**–11
uncomfortable [ŭn kŭmf/tə bəl, –tər–] **30**–8
under [ŭn/dər] **13**–9, **105**–1
underexposed [ŭn/dər ĭk spōzd/] **165**–35
underline [ŭn/dər līn/] **7**–V
underpants [ŭn/dər pănts/] **67**–17
undershirt [ŭn/dər shürt/] **67**–10
uniform [yoo/nə förm/] **65**–17, **161**–16
UNIVERSE [yoo/nə vürs/] **127**
university [yoo/nə vür/sə tē] **112**–10
unload [ŭn lōd/] **72**–E
unpack [ŭn păk/] **35**–E
unscented [ŭn sĕn/təd] **77** ✦
up [ŭp] **105**–9
upset [ŭp sĕt/] **31**–30
upstairs [ŭp/stërz/] **38** ✦
Uranus [yoor/ə nəs, yoo rā/nəs] **127**–3
urban area [ür/bən ër/ē ə] **34**–1
use [yooz(/–)] **140**–N
    …deodorant [–dē ō/dər ənt] **76**–C
user's manual [yoo/zərz măn/yoo əl] **144**–22
U.S. GOVERNMENT AND CITIZENSHIP
    [yoo/ĕs/ gŭv/ər mənt ən sĭt/ə zən shĭp/] **116**
U.S. HISTORY [yoo/ĕs/ hĭs/tə rē] **114**–**115**
Using a pay phone [yoo/zĭng ə pā/ fōn/] **9**
Using the ATM machine [yoo/zĭng dhē ā/tē/ĕm/ mə shēn/] **97**
U.S. MAIL [yoo/ĕs/ māl/] **96**
utilities [yoo tĭl/ə tēz] **35** ✦
U-turn OK (sign) [yoo/türn/ ō kā/] **107**–7
vacancy sign [vā/kən sē sīn/] **36**–11
vacation [vā kā/shən] **19**–46
vaccination [văk/sə nā/shən] **80** ✦
vacuum [văk/yoom] **46**–I
vacuum cleaner [văk/yoom klē/nər] **47**–13
    …attachments [–ə tăch/mənts] **47**–14
    …bag [–băg/] **47**–15
valedictorian [văl/ə dĭk tör/ē ən] **32**–8
Valentine's Day [văl/ən tīnz dā/] **168**–4
valet parking [văl/ā pär/kĭng] **145**–1
valley [văl/ē] **117**–18
van [văn] **106**–10, 14
vandalism [văn/də lĭz/əm] **100**–1
vase [vās, vāz, väz] **41**–9
vault [völt] **97**–2
VCR (videocassette recorder)
    [vē/sē/är/] / [vĭd/ē ō kə sĕt/ rĭ kör/dər] **164**–8
veal cutlets [vēl/ kŭt/ləts] **52**–6
vegetable [vĕj/tə bəl]
    …casserole [–kăs/ə rōl/] **58**
    …garden [–gär/dn] **148**–12
    …peeler [–pē/lər] **59**–15
VEGETABLES [vĕj/tə bəlz] **51**
vegetables [vĕj/tə bəlz] **55**–43
vegetarian [vĕj/ə tër/ē ən] **52** ✦
vein [vān] **75**–44
vendor [vĕn/dər] **91**–30
Venus [vē/nəs] **127**–8
vest [vĕst] **65**–24, **66**–13
veterinarian [vĕt/ər ə nër/ē ən] **139**–62
Vice President [vīs/ prĕz/ə dənt] **116**–7
victim [vĭk/təm] **100** ✦
video [vĭd/ē ō]

Index

...camera [–kăm/rə] **165**–19
...game system [–gām/ sĭs/təm] **162**–1
...store [–stör/] **93**–15
videocassette [vĭd/ē ō kə sĕt/] **98**–13, **164**–8, 10
view [vyoo] **11**–21, 22
vine [vīn] **128**–22
vineyard [vĭn/yərd] **148**–14
violet [vī/ə lət, vī/lət] **129**–22
violin [vī/ə lĭn/] **120**–8
vise [vīs] **150**–21
visor [vī/zər] **147**–11
vital signs monitor [vīt/l sīnz/ män/ə tər] **87**–21
vitamins [vī/tə mənz] **81**–19
V-neck sweater [vē/nĕk/ swĕt/ər] **71**–27
vocational school [vō kā/shə nəl skool/] **112**–9
volcanic eruption [väl kăn/ĭk ĭ rŭp/shən] **103**–14
volleyball [väl/ē böl/] (sport) **158**–14, (equipment) **161**–3
Volume [väl/yəm, –yoom] **57**
volunteer [väl/ən tĭr/] **87**–19
vomit [väm/ət] **78**–E
vote [vōt] **116**–D
waffles [wä/fəlz, wö/–] **61**–4
waist [wāst] **74**–4
waistband [wāst/bănd/] **73**–3
wait [wāt] **90**–B
waiter [wā/tər] **62**–4
waiting room [wā/tĭng room/] **84**–1
wait on customers [wāt/ än kŭs/tə mərz, –ön–] **140**–O
waitress [wā/trəs] **63**–6
wake up [wāk/ ŭp/] **26**–A
walk [wök] **101**–A, **156**–A
walker [wö/kər] **80**–5, **95**–12
wall [wöl(/–)] **42**–6, **48**–4
...unit [–yoo/nət] **42**–13
wallet [wä/lət, wö/–] **69**–26
wallpaper [wöl/pā/pər] **45**–5
walrus [wöl/rəs] **131**–32
War [wör] **114**
warehouse [wër/hows/] **146**–9
warm [wörm] **10**–2
warning label [wör/nĭng lā/bəl] **80**–15
wash [wäsh(/–), wösh(/–)]
...hair [–hër/] **76**–E
...the dishes [–dhə dĭsh/əz] **46**–M
...the windows [–dhə wĭn/dōz] **46**–D
washcloth [wäsh/klöth/, wösh/–] **43**–14
washer [wä/shər, wö/–] **72**–3, **150**–32
wasp [wäsp, wösp] **132**–18
wastebasket [wāst/băs/kət] **43**–25, **46**–F
watch [wäch, wöch] **69**–34
watch TV [wäch/ tē/vē/, wöch/–] **27**–5
water [wö/tər] **39**–B
water [wö/tər] **117**, **155**–1
...fountain [–fown/tn] **153**–11
...glass [–glăs/] **63**–19
...pollution [–pə loo/shən] **126**–12
...polo [–pō/lō] **158**–15
watercolor [wö/tər kŭl/ər] **163**–25
waterfall [wä/tər föl/] **117**–2
watering can [wö/tər ĭng kăn/] **39**–17
watermelons [wö/tər mĕl/ənz] **50**–24
waterskiing [wö/tər skē/ĭng] **160**–7
WATER SPORTS [wö/tər spörts/] **160**
wave [wāv] **155**–6
wavy [wā/vē] **23**–10

Ways to pay [wāz/ tə pā/] **20**
WEATHER [wĕdh/ər] **10**
Wednesday [wĕnz/dā, –dē] **18**–4
weed [wēd] **39**–A
week [wēk] **18**–11
weekdays [wēk/dāz/] **18**–12
weekend [wēk/ĕnd/] **18**–13
weigh [wā] **57**–B
weight [wāt] **22**–21, **57**
weightlifting [wāt/lĭf/tĭng] **159**–15
weights [wāts] **161**–19
WEIGHTS AND MEASURES [wāts/ ən mĕzh/ərz] **57**
welder [wĕl/dər] **139**–63
well [wĕl] **30**–15
west [wĕst] **107**, **123**, **124**
western [wĕs/tərn] **166**–9
wet [wĕt(/–)] **72**–17
...mop [–mäp/] **47**–16
...suit [–soot/] **155**–7
whale [wāl] **131**–29
wheat [wēt(/–)] **148**–2
...bread [–brĕd/] **53**–2
wheelbarrow [wēl/băr/ō] **39**–16
wheelchair [wēl/chër/] **80**–6
whisk [wĭsk] **59**–21
whiskers [wĭs/kərz] **134**–18
white [wīt(/–)] **12**–14
...bread [–brĕd/] **53**–1
White House [wīt/ hows/] **116**–5
whole [hōl(/–)] **15**–6
...salmon [–săm/ən] **53**–18
wide [wīd] **71**–44
widow [wĭd/ō] **29** ✦
widower [wĭd/ō ər] **29** ✦
width [wĭdth, wĭtth] **15**–17
wife [wīf] **24**–20, **25** ✦
wild animals [wīld/ ăn/ə məlz] **133** ✦
willow [wĭl/ō] **128**–14
win [wĭn] **158** ✦
wind [wĭnd] **126**–2
windbreaker [wĭnd/brā/kər] **66**–24
window [wĭn/dō] **38**–17, **42**–17
...pane [–pān/] **149**–15
...shade [–shād/] **44**–6
windshield [wĭnd/shēld/] **108**–2
...wipers [–wī/pərz] **108**–3
windy [wĭn/dē] **10**–10
wine glass [wīn/ glăs/] **63**–20
wing [wĭng] **132**–2
wings [wĭngz] **52**–20
winter [wĭn/tər] **19**–40
WINTER SPORTS AND WATER SPORTS [wĭn/tər spörts/ ən wö/tər spörts/] **160**
wipes [wīps] **95**–17
wipe the counter [wīp/ dhə kown/tər] **46**–O
wire [wīr(/–)] **151**–13
...stripper [–strĭp/ər] **151**–37
wish [wĭsh] **169**–J
withdraw cash [wĭdh drö/ kăsh/, wĭth–] **97**–D
witness [wĭt/nəs] **99**–11
wolf [woolf] **134**–5
woman [woom/ən] **22**–10
wood [wood(/–)] **149**–17, **151**–18
...screw [–skroo/] **150**–28
wooden spoon [wood/n spoon/] **59**–9

woodpecker [wŏŏd/pĕk/ər] **132**–9
Woodwinds [wŏŏd/wĭndz/] **120**
woodworking kit [wŏŏd/wŭr/kĭng kĭt/] **162**–16
wool [wŏŏl(/–)] **70**–14
   ...scarf [–skärf/] **66**–4
work [wŭrk/] **26**–K, **140**–P
workbook [wŭrk/bŏŏk/] **3**–23
Work in a group [wŭrk/ ĭn ə grŏŏp/] **6**
working [wŭr/kĭng] **48**–1
work out [wŭrk/ owt/] **157**–P
Work with a partner [wŭrk/wĭdh/ ə pärt/nər, –wĭth/–] **6**
WORLD [wŭrld] **124–125**
worm [wŭrm] **130**–22
worried [wŭr/ēd] **30**–13
wrap [răp] **169**–D
wrench [rĕnch] **109**–50, **151**–42, 43
wrestling [rĕs/lĭng] **159**–16
wrinkled [rĭng/kəld] **72**–19
wrist [rĭst] **69**–34, **75**–60
wristwatch [rĭst/wäch/, –wöch/] **69**–34
write [rīt] **2**–G, **113**–A
writer [rī/tər] **139**–64
writing assignment [rī/tĭng ə sīn/mənt] **113**–1
wrong [röng(/–)]
   ...number [–nŭm/bər] **9** ✦
   ...way [–wā/] **107**–4
X-ray [ĕks/rā/]
   ...technician [–tĕk nĭsh/ən] **86**–8
xylophone [zī/lə fōn/] **120**–17
yams [yămz] **51**–22
YARD [yärd] **39**
yard [(–)yärd(/)]
   front... [frŭnt/–] **38**–15
yard (measurement) [yärd] **15** ✦
yardstick [yärd/stĭk/] **151**–15
yarn [yärn] **163**–17
year [yïr] **4**–16, **18**–8
yellow [yĕl/ō] **12**–12
yesterday [yĕs/tər dā/, –dē] **18**–17
yield [yēld] **107** ✦
yogurt [yō/gərt] **54**–33, **60**–11
young [yŭng] **22**–13
zebra [zē/brə] **135**–34
zero [zïr/ō] **14**
ZIP code [zĭp/ kōd/] **4**–9
zipper [zĭp/ər] **73**–16
zoo [zŏŏ] **152**–1
zookeeper [zŏŏ/kē/pər] **152**–3
zoom lens [zŏŏm/ lĕnz/] **165**–25
zucchini [zŏŏ kē/nē] **51**–4

Geographical Index

Continents

Africa [ăf**/**rĭ kə] **125**–5
Antarctica [ănt ärk**/**tĭ kə, –är**/**tĭ–] **125**–7
Asia [ā**/**zhə] **125**–4
Australia [ö strāl**/**yə] **125**–6
Europe [yŏŏr**/**əp] **125**–3
North America [nörth**/** ə mĕr**/**ə kə] **124**–1
South America [sowth**/** ə mĕr**/**ə kə] **124**–2

Countries and other locations

Afghanistan [ăf găn**/**ə stăn**/**] **124–125**
Albania [ăl bā**/**nē ə] **124–125**
Algeria [ăl jǐr**/**ē ə] **124–125125**
American Samoa [ə mĕr**/**ə kən sə mō**/**ə] **124–125**
Andorra [ăn dör**/**ə] **124–125**
Angola [ăng gō**/**lə] **124–125**
Argentina [är**/**jən tē**/**nə] **124–125**
Armenia [är mē**/**nē ə] **124–125**
Australia [ö strāl**/**yə] **124–125**
Austria [ö**/**strē ə] **124–125**
Azerbaijan [ăz**/**ər bī jän**/**] **124–125**
Bahamas [bə hä**/**məz] **122–125**
Bahrain [bä rän**/**] **124–125**
Bangladesh [băng**/**glə dĕsh**/**, băng**/**–] **124–125**
Barbados [bär bā**/**dōs] **124–125**
Belarus [bē**/**lə rŏŏs**/**, byĕl**/**ə–] **124–125**
Belgium [bĕl**/**jəm] **124–125**
Belize [bə lēz**/**] **124–125**
Benin [bə nĭn**/**, –nēn**/**] **124–125**
Bermuda [bər myŏŏ**/**də] **122–125**
Bhutan [bŏŏ tän**/**] **124–125**
Bolivia [bə lĭv**/**ē ə] **124–125**
Borneo [bör**/**nē ō] **124–125**
Bosnia-Herzegovina [băz**/**nē ə hĕr**/**tsə gō vē**/**nə] **124–125**
Botswana [băt swä**/**nə] **124–125**
Brazil [brə zĭl**/**] **124–125**
Brunei [brŏŏ nī**/**] **124–125**
Bulgaria [bŭl gër**/**ē ə] **124–125**
Burkina Faso [bər kē**/**nə fä**/**sō] **124–125**
Burundi [bŏŏ rŏŏn**/**dē] **124–125**
Cambodia [kăm bō**/**dē ə] **124–125**
Cameroon [kăm**/**ə rŏŏn**/**] **124–125**
Canada [kăn**/**ə də] **122–125**
Cape Verde [kāp**/** vürd**/**] **124–125**
Central African Republic [sĕn**/**trəl ăf**/**rĭ kən rĭ pŭb**/**lĭk] **124–125**
Chad [chăd] **124–125**
Chile [chĭl**/**ē] **124–125**
China [chī**/**nə] **124–125**
Colombia [kə lŭm**/**bē ə] **124–125**
Comoros [kăm**/**ə rōz] **124–125**
Congo [kăng**/**gō] **124–125**
Costa Rica [kōs**/**tə rē**/**kə, käs**/**–] **122–125**
Croatia [krō ā**/**shə] **124–125**
Cuba [kyŏŏ**/**bə] **122–125**
Cyprus [sī**/**prəs] **124–125**
Czech Republic [chĕk**/** rĭ pŭb**/**lĭk] **124–125**
Democratic Republic of the Congo [dĕm**/**ə krăt**/**ĭk rĭ pŭb**/**lĭk əv dhə käng**/**gō] **124–125**
Denmark [dĕn**/**märk] **124–125**
Djibouti [jĭ bŏŏ**/**tē] **124–125**
Dominica [däm**/**ə nē**/**kə] **124–125**
Dominican Republic [də mĭn**/**ĭ kən rĭ pŭb**/**lĭk] **122–125**
Ecuador [ĕk**/**wə dör**/**] **124–125**
Egypt [ē**/**jĭpt] **124–125**
El Salvador [ĕl săl**/**və dör**/**] **122–125**

Equatorial Guinea [ē**/**kwə tör**/**ē əl gĭn**/**ē, ĕk**/**wə–] **124–125**
Eritrea [ĕr**/**ə trē**/**ə] **124–125**
Estonia [ē stō**/**nē ə] **124–125**
Ethiopia [ē**/**thē ō**/**pē ə] **124–125**
Fiji [fē**/**jē] **124–125**
Finland [fĭn**/**lənd] **124–125**
France [frăns] **124–125**
French Guiana [frĕnch**/** gē ăn**/**ə, –ä**/**nə] **124–125**
French Polynesia [frĕnch**/** päl**/**ə nē**/**zhə] **124–125**
Gabon [gă bōn**/**] **124–125**
Georgia [jör**/**jə] **124–125**
Germany [jür**/**mə nē] **124–125**
Ghana [gä**/**nə] **124–125**
Greece [grēs] **124–125**
Greenland [grēn**/**lənd, –lănd**/**] **122–125**
Grenada [grə nā**/**də] **124–125**
Guatemala [gwä**/**tə mä**/**lə] **122–125**
Guinea [gĭn**/**ē] **124–125**
Guinea-Bissau [gĭn**/**ē bĭ sow**/**] **124–125**
Guyana [gī ăn**/**ə] **124–125**
Haiti [hā**/**tē] **122–125**
Honduras [hän dŏŏr**/**əs] **122–125**
Hong Kong [häng**/** käng**/**] **124–125**
Hungary [hŭng**/**gə rē] **124–125**
Iceland [īs**/**lənd] **124–125**
India [ĭn**/**dē ə] **124–125**
Indonesia [ĭn**/**də nē**/**zhə] **124–125**
Iran [ĭ răn**/**, ī răn**/**] **124–125**
Iraq [ĭ räk**/**, ī räk**/**] **124–125**
Ireland [īr**/**lənd] **124–125**
Israel [ĭz**/**rē əl, –rā–] **124–125**
Italy [ĭt**/**l ē] **124–125**
Ivory Coast [īv**/**rē kōst**/**] **124–125**
Jamaica [jə mā**/**kə] **122–125**
Japan [jə păn**/**] **124–125**
Java [jä**/**və] **124–125**
Jordan [jör**/**dn] **124–125**
Kazakhstan [kä**/**zäk stän**/**] **124–125**
Kenya [kĕn**/**yə, kēn**/**–] **124–125**
Kiribati [kĭr**/**ə băs**/**] **124–125**
Kuwait [kŏŏ wāt**/**] **124–125**
Kyrgyzstan [kĭr**/**gĭ stän**/**, –stän**/**] **124–125**
Laos [lows, lä**/**ōs] **124–125**
Latvia [lăt**/**vē ə] **124–125**
Lebanon [lĕb**/**ə nən, –nän**/**] **124–125**
Lesotho [lə sō**/**tō, –sŏŏ**/**tŏŏ] **124–125**
Liberia [lī bĭr**/**ē ə] **124–125**
Libya [lĭb**/**ē ə] **124–125**
Liechtenstein [lĭk**/**tən stīn**/**] **124–125**
Lithuania [lĭth**/**ŏŏ ā**/**nē ə] **124–125**
Luxembourg [lŭk**/**səm bürg**/**] **124–125**
Macedonia [măs**/**ə dō**/**nē ə] **124–125**
Madagascar [măd**/**ə găs**/**kər] **124–125**
Malawi [mə lä**/**wē] **124–125**
Malaysia [mə lā**/**zhə] **124–125**
Maldives [möl**/**dēvz, –dīvz] **124–125**
Mali [mä**/**lē] **124–125**
Malta [möl**/**tə] **124–125**
Marshall Islands [mär**/**shəl ī**/**ləndz] **124–125**
Mauritania [mör**/**ə tā**/**nē ə] **124–125**
Mauritius [mö rĭsh**/**əs] **124–125**
Mexico [mĕk**/**sĭ kō**/**] **122–125**
Micronesia [mī**/**krə nē**/**zhə] **124–125**
Moldova [mäl dō**/**və, möl–] **124–125**
Monaco [män**/**ə kō**/**] **124–125**

Mongolia [mäng gō/lē ə] **124–125**
Montenegro [män/tə nē/grō, –nē/–] **124–125**
Morocco [mə räk/ō] **124–125**
Mozambique [mō/zəm bēk/] **124–125**
Myanmar [myän/mär] **124–125**
Namibia [nə mīb/ē ə] **124–125**
Nauru [nä o͞o/ro͞o] **124–125**
Nepal [nə pöl/, –päl/] **124–125**
Netherlands [nĕdh/ər ləndz] **124–125**
New Guinea [no͞o/ gĭn/ē] **124–125**
New Zealand [no͞o/ zē/lənd] **124–125**
Nicaragua [nĭk/ə rä/gwə] **122–125**
Niger [nī/jər, nē zhër/] **124–125**
Nigeria [nī jïr/ē ə] **124–125**
North Korea [nörth/ kə rē/ə] **124–125**
Norway [nör/wā] **124–125**
Oman [ō män/] **124–125**
Pakistan [păk/ə stän/] **124–125**
Palau [pə low/] **124–125**
Panama [păn/ə mä/] **122–125**
Papua New Guinea [păp/yo͞o ə no͞o/ gĭn/ē] **124–125**
Paraguay [păr/ə gwī/, –gwā/] **124–125**
Peru [pə ro͞o/] **124–125**
Philippines [fĭl/ə pēnz/, fĭl/ə pēnz/] **124–125**
Poland [pō/lənd] **124–125**
Portugal [pör/chə gəl] **124–125**
Puerto Rico [pwër/tə rē/kō, pör/tə–] **122–125**
Qatar [kä/tär, kə tär/] **124–125**
Romania [rō mā/nē ə, ro͞o–] **124–125**
Russia [rŭsh/ə] **124–125**
Rwanda [ro͞o än/də] **124–125**
Saudi Arabia [sow/dē ə rā/bē ə, sö/dē–] **124–125**
Senegal [sĕn/ə göl/, –gäl/] **124–125**
Serbia [sür/bē ə] **124–125**
Seychelles [sā shĕlz/, –shĕl/] **124–125**
Sierra Leone [sē ĕr/ə lē ōn/, –lē ō/nē] **124–125**
Singapore [sĭng/ə pör/] **124–125**
Slovakia [slō vä/kē ə] **124–125**
Slovenia [slō vē/nē ə] **124–125**
Solomon Islands [säl/ə mən ī/ləndz] **124–125**
Somalia [sə mä/lē ə] **124–125**
South Africa [sowth/ ăf/rĭ kə] **124–125**
South Korea [sowth/ kə rē/ə] **124–125**
Spain [spān] **124–125**
Sri Lanka [srē/ läng/kə, shrē–] **124–125**
Sudan [so͞o dän/] **124–125**
Sumatra [so͞o mä/trə] **124–125**
Suriname [so͞or/ə nä/mə] **124–125**
Swaziland [swä/zē länd/] **124–125**
Sweden [swēd/n] **124–125**
Switzerland [swĭt/sər lənd] **124–125**
Syria [sïr/ē ə] **124–125**
Tahiti [tə hē/tē] **124–125**
Taiwan [tī/wän/] **124–125**
Tajikistan [tä jĭk/ə stän/, –stän/] **124–125**
Tanzania [tăn/zə nē/ə] **124–125**
Tasmania [tăz mā/nē ə] **124–125**
Thailand [tī/länd/, –lənd] **124–125**
The Gambia [dhə găm/bē ə] **124–125**
Togo [tō/gō] **124–125**
Tonga [täng/gə] **124–125**
Tunisia [to͞o nē/zhə] **124–125**
Turkey [tür/kē] **124–125**
Turkmenistan [türk mĕn/ə stän/, –stän/] **124–125**
Uganda [yo͞o găn/də] **124–125**

Ukraine [yo͞o/krān, yo͞o krān/] **124–125**
United Arab Emirates [yo͞o nī/təd är/əb ĕm/ər əts] **124–125**
United Kingdom [yo͞o nī/təd kĭng/dəm] **124–125**
United States of America [yo͞o nī/təd stäts/ əv ə mĕr/ə kə] **122–125**
Uruguay [yo͞or/ə gwī/, –gwā/] **124–125**
Uzbekistan [o͞oz bĕk/ə stän/, –stän/] **124–125**
Venezuela [vĕn/ə zwā/lə] **124–125**
Vietnam [vē/ĕt näm/, –näm/] **124–125**
Western Sahara [wĕs/tərn sə här/ə] **124–125**
Western Samoa [wĕs/tərn sə mō/ə] **124–125**
Yemen [yĕm/ən] **124–125**
Zambia [zăm/bē ə] **124–125**
Zimbabwe [zĭm bäb/wā] **124–125**

Bodies of water

Arabian Sea [ə rā/bē ən sē/] **124–125**
Arctic Ocean [ärk/tĭk ō/shən] **122–125**
Baffin Bay [băf/ən bā/] **122–125**
Baltic Sea [böl/tĭk sē/] **124–125**
Barents Sea [băr/ənts sē/] **124–125**
Beaufort Sea [bō/fərt sē/] **122–125**
Bering Sea [bër/ĭng sē/, bïr/–] **122–125**
Black Sea [blăk/ sē/] **124–125**
Caribbean Sea [kăr/ə bē/ən sē/, kə rĭb/ē ən–] **122–125**
Caspian Sea [kăs/pē ən sē/] **124–125**
Coral Sea [kör/əl sē/] **124–125**
East China Sea [ēst/ chī/nə sē/] **124–125**
Greenland Sea [grēn/lənd sē/, –länd/–] **124–125**
Gulf of Alaska [gŭlf/ əv ə lăs/kə] **122–125**
Gulf of California [gŭlf/ əv kăl/ə förn/yə] **122–125**
Gulf of Honduras [gŭlf/ əv hän do͞or/əs] **122–125**
Gulf of Mexico [gŭlf/ əv mĕk/sĭ kō/] **122–125**
Gulf of St. Lawrence [gŭlf/ əv sänt/ lör/əns, –lär/–] **122–125**
Hudson Bay [hŭd/sən bā/] **122–125**
Indian Ocean [ĭn/dē ən ō/shən] **124–125**
Labrador Sea [lăb/rə dör/ sē/] **122–125**
Mediterranean Sea [mĕd/ə tə rā/nē ən sē/] **124–125**
North Atlantic Ocean [nörth/ ət lăn/tĭk ō/shən] **122–125**
North Pacific Ocean [nörth/ pə sĭf/ĭk ō/shən] **122–125**
North Sea [nörth/ sē/] **124–125**
Norwegian Sea [nör wē/jən sē/] **124–125**
Persian Gulf [pür/zhən gŭlf/] **124–125**
Philippine Sea [fĭl/ə pēn/ sē/] **124–125**
Red Sea [rĕd/ sē/] **124–125**
Sea of Japan [sē/ əv jə păn/] **124–125**
Sea of Okhotsk [sē/ əv ō kätsk/] **124–125**
South Atlantic Ocean [sowth/ ət lăn/tĭk ō/shən] **124–125**
South China Sea [sowth/ chī/nə sē/] **124–125**
Southern Ocean [sŭdh/ərn ō/shən] **124–125**
South Pacific Ocean [sowth/ pə sĭf/ĭk ō/shən] **124–125**

The United States of America

Capital: Washington, D.C. (District Of Columbia)
  [wä/shĭng tən dē/sē/, wö/–]

Regions of the United States

Mid-Atlantic States [mĭd/ət lăn/tĭk stāts/] **123**–10
Midwest [mĭd/wĕst/] **123**–9
New England [no͞o/ ĭng/glənd] **123**–11
Pacific States [pə sĭf/ĭk stāts/] **123**–7
Rocky Mountain States [räk/ē mown/tn stāts/] **123**–8
South [sowth] **123**–13
Southeast [sowth/ēst/] **123**–13
Southwest [sowth/wĕst/] **123**–12
West Coast [wĕst/ kōst/] **123**–7

Geographical Index

States of the United States

Alabama [ăl/ə băm/ə] **122–123**
Alaska [ə lăs/kə] **122–125**
Arizona [ăr/ə zō/nə] **122–123**
Arkansas [är/kən sö/] **122–123**
California [kăl/ə förn/yə] **122–123**
Colorado [kăl/ə răd/ō, –ra/dō] **122–123**
Connecticut [kə nĕt/ĭ kət] **122–123**
Delaware [dĕl/ə wër/] **122–123**
Florida [flör/ə də, flär/–] **122–123**
Georgia [jör/jə] **122–123**
Hawaii [hə wī/ē] **122–123**
Idaho [ī/də hō/] **122–123**
Illinois [ĭl/ə noy/] **122–123**
Indiana [ĭn/dē ăn/ə] **122–123**
Iowa [ī/ə wə] **122–123**
Kansas [kăn/zəs] **122–123**
Kentucky [kən tŭk/ē] **122–123**
Louisiana [lōō ē/zē ăn/ə] **122–123**
Maine [mān] **122–123**
Maryland [mër/ə lənd] **122–123**
Massachusetts [măs/ə chōō/səts] **122–123**
Michigan [mĭsh/ĭ gən] **122–123**
Minnesota [mĭn/ə sō/tə] **122–123**
Mississippi [mĭs/ə sĭp/ē] **122–123**
Missouri [mə zŏŏr/ē, –zŏŏr/ə] **122–123**
Montana [măn tăn/ə] **122–123**
Nebraska [nə brăs/kə] **122–123**
Nevada [nə văd/ə, –vä/də] **122–123**
New Hampshire [nōō/ hămp/shər] **122–123**
New Jersey [nōō/ jür/zē] **122–123**
New Mexico [nōō/ mĕk/sĭ kō/] **122–123**
New York [nōō/ yörk/] **122–123**
North Carolina [nörth/ kăr/ə lī/nə] **122–123**
North Dakota [nörth/ də kō/tə] **122–123**
Ohio [ō hī/ō] **122–123**
Oklahoma [ō/klə hō/mə] **122–123**
Oregon [ör/ĭ gən, –găn/, är/–] **122–123**
Pennsylvania [pĕn/səl vān/yə] **122–123**
Rhode Island [rōd/ ī/lənd] **122–123**
South Carolina [sowth/ kăr/ə lī/nə] **122–123**
South Dakota [sowth/ də kō/tə] **122–123**
Tennessee [tĕn/ə sē/] **122–123**
Texas [tĕk/səs] **122–123**
Utah [yōō/tö, –tä] **122–123**
Vermont [vər mänt/] **122–123**
Virginia [vər jĭn/yə] **122–123**
Washington [wä/shĭng tən, wö/–] **122–123**
West Virginia [wĕst/ vər jĭn/yə] **122–123**
Wisconsin [wĭs kän/sən] **122–123**
Wyoming [wī ō/mĭng] **122–123**

Canada
Capital: Ottawa [ät/ə wə]

Regions of Canada
Atlantic Provinces [ət lăn/tĭk präv/ən səz] **123 – 6**
British Columbia [brĭt/ĭsh kə lŭm/bē ə] **123 – 2**
Northern Canada [nör/dhərn kăn/ə də] **123 – 1**
Ontario [än tër/ē ō/] **123 – 4**
Prairie Provinces [prë/ē präv/ən səz] **123 – 3**
Quebec [kwĭ bĕk/] **123 – 5**

Provinces of Canada
Alberta [ăl bür/tə] **122–123**
British Columbia [brĭt/ĭsh kə lŭm/bē ə] **122–123**
Manitoba [măn/ə tō/bə] **122–123**
New Brunswick [nōō/ brŭnz/wĭk] **122–123**
Newfoundland [nōō/fən lənd] **122–123**
Northwest Territories [nörth/wĕst/ tĕr/ə tör/ēz] **122–123**
Nova Scotia [nō/və skō/shə] **122–123**
Ontario [än tër/ē ō/] **122–123**
Prince Edward Island [prĭns/ ĕd/wərd ī/lənd] **122–123**
Quebec [kwĭ bĕk/] **122–123**
Saskatchewan [să skăch/ə wən, –wän/] **122–123**
Yukon Territory [yōō/kän tĕr/ə tör/ē] **122–123**

Mexico
Capital: Mexico (City) [mĕk/sĭ kō/ (sĭt/ē)]

Regions of Mexico
Chiapas Highlands [chē ä/pəs hī/ləndz] **123 – 18**
Gulf Coastal Plain [gŭlf/ kō/stəl plän/] **123 – 16**
Pacific Northwest [pə sĭf/ĭk nörth/wĕst] **123 – 14**
Plateau of Mexico [plă tō/ əv mĕk/sĭ kō/] **123 – 15**
Southern Uplands [sŭdh/ərn ŭp/ləndz] **123 – 17**
Yucatan Peninsula [yōō/kə tän/ pə nĭn/sə lə, yōō/kə tän/–] **123 – 19**

States of Mexico
Aguascalientes [ä/gwəs käl yĕn/tās] **122–123**
Baja California Norte [bä/hä kăl/ə förn/yə nör/tä] **122–123**
Baja California Sur [bä/hä kăl/ə förn/yə sŏŏr/] **122–123**
Campeche [käm pā/chä, käm pē/chē] **122–123**
Chiapas [chē ä/pəs] **122–123**
Chihuahua [chĭ wä/wä, –wə] **122–123**
Coahuila [kō/ə wē/lə] **122–123**
Colima [kə lē/mə] **122–123**
Distrito Federal [dī strē/tō fĕd/ə räl/] **122–123**
Durango [dŏŏ răng/gō, –räng/–] **122–123**
Guanajuato [gwä/nə hwä/tō] **122–123**
Guerrero [gə rër/ō] **122–123**
Hidalgo [hĭ dăl/gō, ē dhäl/gō] **122–123**
Jalisco [hə lĭs/kō, –lēs/–] **122–123**
México [mĕk/sĭ kō/, mĕ/hē kō] **122–123**
Michoacán [mē/chō ä kän/] **122–123**
Morelos [mö rĕl/ōs] **122–123**
Nayarit [nä/yə rēt/] **122–123**
Nuevo León [nwä/vō lā ōn/] **122–123**
Oaxaca [wə hä/kə, wä–] **122–123**
Puebla [pwĕb/lä] **122–123**
Querétaro [kə rēt/ə rō/] **122–123**
Quintana Roo [kēn tä/nə rō/] **122–123**
San Luis Potosí [sän/ lōō ēs/ pō/tə sē/] **122–123**
Sinaloa [sē/nə lō/ə] **122–123**
Sonora [sə nör/ə] **122–123**
Tabasco [tə bäs/kō] **122–123**
Tamaulipas [tä/mow lē/pəs] **122–123**
Tlaxcala [tlä skä/lə] **122–123**
Veracruz [vĕr/ə krōōz/, –krōōs/] **122–123**
Yucatán [yōō/kə tän/, –tän/] **122–123**
Zacatecas [zä/kə tä/kəs, sä/–] **122–123**

абажур **44**–18
абзац **113**–5
абрикосы **50**–7
аварийный тормоз **109**–44
август **19**–32
авиакатастрофа **102**–3
авокадо **50**–14
авоська **69**–29
Австралия **125**–6
автобус **90**–15, **104**–4
автобусная остановка **104**–1
автомат со льдом **145**–18
автомеханик **136**–7
автомобильная авария **102**–2
автоответчик **9**–14
автор **98**–22, **139**–64
автосалон и автосервис **88**–4
агент бюро путешествий **139**–60
адаптер **164**–17
административное здание **89**–24
адрес **4**–5
Азия **125**–4
акваланг **155**–8
акварель **163**–25
аккордеон **120**–21
акриловая краска **162**–9
акт о выселении индейцев **114**
актёр **136**–2
актиния **130**–21
актовый зал **5**–3
акула **130**–7
акушер-гинеколог **86**–1
алгебра **118**–25
аллергия **79**–8
аллигатор **131**–36
алфавит **3**–30
амбар **148**–11
американские горки **152**–15
американский салат из свежей
    капусты **53**–14
американский сыр **53**–9
американский футбол **158**–11
амфибии **130**–**131**
анализ крови **86**–17
ананасы **50**–2
ангина **78**–6
английская булавка **73**–24
английские исследователи **114**
английский как второй язык **121**–7
анестезиолог **87**–35
Антарктида **125**–7
антацидное средство **81**–18
антигистаминный крем **83**–10
антилопа **135**–35
апельсины **50**–10
аплодировать **32**–B
апостроф **113**–11
аппарат для измерения кровяного
    давления **84**–12
апрель **19**–28
аптека (американского образца) **90**–2
аптека **80**–9
аптекарь **80**–10
аптечка **43**–19
аптечка первой медицинской
    помощи **83**–1
арбузы **50**–24

арестовать подозреваемого **99**–A
арматура **151**–17
Армстронг на луне **115**
армяне **115**
ароматизирующие салфетки для
    сушки **72**–5
артерия **75**–43
артишоки **51**–20
архитектор **136**–4
ассистент дантиста **84**–19, **137**–19
ассистент зубного врача **137**–19
астма **79**–11
астронавт **127**–17
астроном **127**–20
атлас **98**–3
атом **119**–17
атомная энергия **126**–8
аттестат зрелости **32**–7
аудиокассета **98**–12
аудиолог **81**–32
аудитория **32**–10
Африка **125**–5
аэровокзал авиакомпании в
    аэропорту **110**–1
аэрозоль от насморка **81**–23
Аэропорт **110**
бабочка **132**–20
бабуин **135**–32
бабушка **24**–2
бабушка и дедушка **24**–1
багажная тележка **110**–19, **145**–6
багажник **109**–40
бакенбарды **23**–7
баклажаны **51**–18
бактерицидная мазь **83**–9
баланс **97**–11
балет **166**–7
балка **149**–3
балкон **37**–17
бальный зал **145**–20
бампер **108**–7
бананы **50**–3
банк **88**–3, **97**
банка варенья **56**–14
банка джема **56**–14
банка повидла **56**–14
банка супа **56**–15
банка творога **56**–17
банкомат **97**–3
банкоматная карточка **97**–9
банное полотенце **43**–12
Баранина **52**
бараньи отбивные **52**–15
баранья нога **52**–14
барахолка **152**–22
бардачок **108**–33
баскетбол **158**–8, **161**–4
баскетбольная площадка **158**–7
бассейн **37**–16, **145**–16
батарейка **151**–40, **165**–22
батарея **109**–43, **151**–40
батат **51**–22
батончик **55**–41
бега **159**–18
бегать **156**–C
бегать трусцой **156**–B
бегемот **135**–43

беговая дорожка **5**–11
бедро **74**–5, **74**–16
бежать **156**–C
бежевый **12**–9
Безопасность труда **147**
бейсбол **158**–9, **161**–18
бейсбольная бита **161**–14
бейсбольная карточка **162**–11
бейсбольная кепка **66**–27
бейсбольный матч **152**–25
бекон **52**–11, **61**–7
белка **133**–21
бельевая верёвка **72**–9
белый **12**–14
Белый дом **116**–5
белый хлеб **53**–1
бензиномер **108**–22
бензобак **108**–12
бензозаправочная станция **88**–12
берег **117**–12
беременная **22**–19
берёза **128**–8
бетон **149**–10
без десяти два **16**–14
без двадцати два **16**–12
без двадцати пяти два **16**–11
без пяти два **16**–15
без четверти два **16**–13
безобразный вид **11**–22
безрукавка **65**–24
библиотека **5**–6, **89**–28, **98**
библиотекарь **98**–17
библиотекарь справочного
    стола **98**–1
библиотечная карточка **98**–19
библиотечная книга **98**–20
бивень **135**–48
бигуди **23**–21
бизнес **121**–2
бизнесмен **136**–10
бизон **134**–6
бикини **67**–16
билет **104**–14
Билль о правах **115**
бильярд **159**–2
биологически опасно **147**–5
биология **119**–1
бирка **83**–21
бирюзовый **12**–4
бисер **69**–32
бита для гольфа **161**–1
битва при Вундид-Ни **115**
бить мячом о землю **156**–K
бифштекс **52**–2, **61**–13
Бланк о зачислении в школу **4**
бланк страховки **84**–5
блендер **40**–12
блины **61**–6
блок предохранителей **48**–13
блокнот **3**–26, **143**–36
блондин **23**–16
блондинка **23**–16
блоха **49**–23
блохи **49**–23
блузка **64**–9
Блюда быстрого приготовления **60**
блюдо **41**–3, **41**–6

блюдце **63**–22
бобр **134**–9
бобы **54**–26
божья коровка **132**–27
бокал **63**–20
боксёрские трусы **67**–12
Болезни **79**
болезнь сердца **79**–14
болельщик **158**–4
болеутоляющее **81**–16
болт **150**–30
боль в желудке **78**–4
боль в спине **78**–5
боль в ухе **78**–3
больная **30**–14
больница **86–87, 88**–7
больничная койка **86**–11
больничная пижама **86**–15
больничный халат **86**–15
больной **30**–14
большая рука **11**–2
большой **70**–4
большой палец **75**–56
бордюр из подушек **45**–7
борода **23**–6
борьба **159**–16
босоножки **68**–24
ботанический сад **152**–4
боулинг **159**–3
браслет **69**–35
брат **24**–9
брать...кровь **85**–G
брелок для ключей **69**–43
Британская Колумбия **123**–2
бритва (станок) **77**–25
бриться **77**–M
бровь **74**–32
бройлер **40**–21
брокколи **51**–15
броненосец **134**–8
бросать **156**–D
брошь **69**–36
брус **149**–3
брюква **51**–14
брюки **64**–8
брюнет **23**–15
брюнетка **23**–15
бубны **163**–27
будка **152**–23
будни **18**–12
буйвол **134**–6
букет **129**–27
булавка **73**–14
булавки для пелёнок **95**–22
булочка **56**–11
булочка с горячей сосиской **60**–6
булочки **54**–30
бульдозер **149**–6
бумага формата 35 на 42 см **143**–18
бумагорежущая машина **143**–24
бумагорезатель **143**–15
бумажник **69**–26
бумажные изделия **55**–14
бумажные куклы **163**–30
бумажные мешки для пылесоса **47**–15
бумажные полотенца **40**–2

бумажный пакет **55**–22
буран **103**–11
бурундук **133**–20
бусы **69**–9
бутылка **56**–1, **95**–26
бутылка газированной воды **56**–13
буфет **33**–13, **41**–1
буханка **56**–10
буханка хлеба **56**–22
бухгалтер **136**–1
быстрая перемотка вперёд **165**–C
быть без сознания **82**–B
быть в школе **26**–J, **82**–C
быть раненным **82**–A
бюро путешествий **92**–9
бюстгальтер **67**–20
в **13**–5
в горошек **70**–8
в Калифорнии найдено золото **115**
в клетку **70**–11
в крапинку **70**–8
в полоску **70**–7
в такси **105**–4
в цветочек **70**–12
ваза **41**–9
валик для краски **151**–46
валторна **120**–15
вандализм **100**–1
ванна **43**–2
Ванная **43**
вантуз **151**–44
варежки **66**–9
Варите 1 час на медленном огне **58**–R
ватерпас **150**–24
вафли **61**–4
Вашингтон 1-ый президент **115**
вверх по лестнице **105**–9
ведро **47**–20, **155**–22
ведро для грязных подгузников **95**–23
ведро для использованных подгузников **45**–13
ведро для сбора вторсырья **47**–2
веко **74**–33
велик/а/о **70**–21
Великая депрессия **114**
велосипед **153**–4
велосипедист **153**–3
велосипедная дорожка **153**–2
велосипедные гонки **159**–4
велосипедные шорты **67**–3
вена **75**–44
венгры **115**
Венера **127**–8
веник **47**–10
веничек **59**–21
верёвка **154**–19
веранда с деревянным настилом **38**–16
верблюд **135**–38
вернуть **21**–F
вертолёт **110**–8
Верховный суд **116**–8
вершина горы **117**–14
Вес **57**
весна **19**–37

вестерн **166**–9
вести **156**–K
вестибюль **145**–3
весы **43**–26, **84**–7
ветвь **128**–2, **128**–3
ветер **126**–2
ветеринар **139**–62
ветка **128**–2
ветренно **10**–10
ветровка **66**–24
ветровое стекло **108**–2
ветрянка **79**–6
ветчина **52**–9
вечер **17**–19
Вечеринка **169**
вечернее платье **65**–29
вешалка **72**–11
вешалка для полотенец **43**–8
Взвешивать продукты **57**–B
взволнованная **31**–23
взволнованный **31**–23
взлететь **111**–L
взрослые **22**–9
взрыв **102**–4
вид на жительство **29**–3
видеокамера **165**–19, **165**–21
видеокассета **98**–13, **164**–10
видеомагнитофон **164**–8
видеть **75**–A
Виды развлечений **166**
Виды рассказа **166**
Виды телевизионных программ **167**
вилка **41**–21, **164**–18
вилка для салата **63**–24
вилопогрузчик **146**–14
виноград **50**–1
виноградник **148**–14
виолончель **120**–9
витамины **81**–19
витрина **69**–7
вице-президент **116**–7
вишни **50**–16
владелец завода **146**–2
владелец магазина **139**–56
влажно **10**–12
влюбиться **28**–K
влюблённая **30**–19
влюблённый **30**–19
внешняя дверь **38**–12
вниз по лестнице **105**–8
внук **24**–7
Внутренние органы **75**
внутренний дворик **37**–18
внутривенное капельное введение **87**–27
вода **155**–1
вода в бутылке **55**–54
водитель автобуса **104**–8
водитель грузовика **139**–61
водитель такси **104**–20
водительские права **29**–4
водить машину **90**–C, **140**–E
водное поло **158**–15
воднолыжный спорт **160**–7
водные виды спорта **160**
водным транспортом **105**–3

водолазка 64–7, 71–28
водолазная маска 155–3
водопад 117–2
водопроводчик 49–20
водосточный жёлоб 38–19
военнослужащая 139–54
военнослужащий 139–54
вождение автомобиля 121–5
вождение машины в нетрезвом
    состоянии 100–3
воздуходувка для уборки листьев 39–4
воздушная подушка 108–16
Возраст 22
война 1812 года 114
война США с Мексикой 114
война в Корее 115
Война в Персидском заливе 115
война во Вьетнаме 115
Война за независимость 115
волдырь 78–15
волейбол 158–14, 161–3
волк 134–5
волна 155–6
волнистая 118–19
волнистые волосы 23–10
волосы 74–19
волосы до плеч 23–2
волы 148–21
вопросительный знак 113–7
воробей 132–8
воронка 119–12
воротник 73–7
восемнадцатый 14
восемнадцать 14
восемь 14
восемьдесят 14
восемьдесят процентов 15–10
восклицательный знак 113–8
воскресенье 18–1
воспаление уха 79–3
воспитатель сада 94–3
воспитатель яслей 94–3
Восстановите правильный порядок
    слов 7–W
восьмой 14
врач 84–6, 137–22
врач-терапевт 86–2
вращающийся стул 143–22
вредители 49
Времена года 19
Время 16–17
время в Центральной части
    США 17–28
время в восточной части США 17–29
время в районе
    Ньюфаундленда 17–31
время в районе Скалистых гор 17–27
время на Аляске 17–25
время на Атлантическом
    побережье 17–30
время на Гаваях 17–24
время на Тихоокеанском
    побережье 17–26
Вселенная 127
вставать 26–B
Вставьте карточку в банкомат 97–C
Вставьте пропущенное слово 7–R

Встаньте 2–C
встречное движение 107–4
встроенный кассетный
    магнитофон 108–30
вступить во владение
    собственностью 35–J
Вторая мировая война 114
вторично женатый 25–27
вторник 18–3
второй 14
второй инициал 4–3
второй этаж 36–2
входная дверь 38–11
вчера 18–17
въехать в (квартиру) 35–D
выбрасывать мусор из корзины 46–F
вывеска 91–29
вывеска о сдаче квартиры в
    аренду 36–11
Выгладить одежду 72–G
выдвижной ящик 40–23, 44–3
выдра 131–35
выйти замуж 28–L
выйти из заключения 99–H
выключатель 44–19, 144–4
выкройка 73–8
Вылейте яйца в сковородку 58–D
вынести приговор 99–E
выносить мусор 46–Q
Вынуть бельё из сушилки 72–E
Выньте карточку из банкомата 97–F
Выпишите слово 6–F
выплачивать ссуду 35–L
выпускать 73–F
выпускник 32–6
выпускник, отличившийся в
    учёбе 32–8
выпускной класс 32–1
выпускной курс 32–1
Выслушайте мнение о своей
    работе 113–C
высокие каблуки 68–17, 71–47
высокая 22–16
высокий 22–16
высокое кровяное давление 79–15
высота 15–14
высотное здание 89–25
выставка 152–21
выступать с речью 32–E
вытирать кухонный стол 46–O
вытирать посуду 46–N
вытирать пыль с мебели 46–A
Вытрите доску 2–H
выход на посадку 110–5
выходное платье 71–36
выходные (дни) 18–13
Вычеркните слово 7–U
Вычистить фильтр в сушилке 72–D
вычитание 118–2
ВИЧ вирус иммунодефицита
    человека (возбудитель
    СПИДа) 79–10
вышедшая замуж 25–27
вышивка 163–19
вьющиеся волосы 23–11
вьющиеся растения 128–22
вяз 128–17

вязальные спицы 163–18
вязальный крючок 163–20
вязать 163–F
гаечный ключ 151–43
газета 98–8
газетный киоск 90–11
газированная вода 55–52, 60–4
газовый счётчик 48–14
газон 39–21
газонокосилка 39–22
Гаитянцы 115
гайка 150–31
галактика 127–26
галлон яблочного сока 57–5
галстук «бабочка» 69–40
галстуки 69–10
гамак 39–2
гамбургер 60–1
гамбургер с сыром 60–3
гараж 38–6, 89–26
гаражная дверь 38–7
гардения 129–16
гвоздика 129–18
гвоздь 150–29
гель для волос 76–11
География 117
Геометрические тела 118
Геометрические фигуры 118
геометрия 118–26
геотермическая энергия 126–7
гибискус 129–12
гибкий диск 144–5
гигиенист 84–16
гидрокостюм 155–7
гидроэлектроэнергия 126–5
гиена 135–31
гимнастика 159–8
гиппопотам 135–43
гипс 81–29
гири 161–19
гитара 120–11
главный судья 116–9
Глаголы, относящиеся к
    спорту 156–157
гладильная доска 72–14
глаженная рубашка 72–20
глаз 74–27
глазные капли 81–22
глазок 37–27
глобус 3–9
глубина 15–15
глубокая миска 59–31
глубокая тарелка 41–25
глухая 22–27
глухой 22–27
глушитель 108–11
гнездо 132–3
гнилой/ая/ое 50–30
гобой 120–5
Говорите с учителем 2–B
говорить на другом языке 140–J
говорить с агентом по продаже
    недвижимости 35–G
говорить с друзьями 141–A
говорить с менеджером 35–B
Говядина 52
говяжий фарш 52–4

говяжьи рёбрышки 52–5
год 4, 18–8
годовщина 19–42
голеностопный сустав 75–61
голова 74–1
головная боль 78–1
головной убор 32–3
головоломка 45–22
голоден 30–5
голодна 30–5
гололёд 10–13
голосовать 116–D
голубая сойка 132–7
голубой 12–1
голубь 132–16
гольф 159–7
гольфы 67–24
горб 135–51
горбуша целиком 53–18
гордая 31–22
гордый 31–22
горелка 40–19
горелка Бунзена 119–9
горилла 135–30
горка 153–13
горло 75–36
горничная 137–31, 145–15
горный хребет 117–15
город 4–7, 34–1
городской район 34–1
горох 51–19
горчица 60–24
горячая вода 43–5
горячий компресс 80–3
горячий хлеб с чесноком и
    маслом 61–16
гости 33–14
Гостиная 42
гостиница 88–5, 145
государственная школа 112–1
государственный праздник 19–43
готовить 140–C
готовить на гриле 58–T
готовить (мясо) на медленном
    огне 58–U
готовить обед 26–F
готовить ужин 27–P
Готовьте в духовке 45 минут
    при температуре 350° по
    Фаренгейту 58–L
грабли 39–11
град 10–19
граждане и свободные негры 114
Гражданская Война 115
гражданство США 116
грация 67–21
гребешки 53–25
гребля 154–3
грейпфрут 50–9
гремучая змея 131–38
грибы 51–26
грива 135–49
гриль 39–7
грипп 79–2
гроза 10–16
гроза с градом 10–18
груди 74–14

грудки 52–19
грудная клетка 75–53
грудь 74–13
грузо-пассажирский автофургон (на
    шасси легкового автомобиля) 106–8
грузовой автомобиль на легковом
    шасси 106–7
грузовой автомобиль-тягач 106–13
грузовые автомобили 106
групповое насилие 100–2
грустная 31–20
грустная книга 167–28
грустный 31–20
груши 50–6
грызуны 133
грязная футболка 72–15
грязное бельё 72–1
губа 74–30
губка 3–17, 47–24
гусеница 132–21
гусь 132–14
дамские сумки 69–6
дантист 84–18, 137–20
дары моря 53
дата рождения 4–16
датчики давления 87–21
датчики дыхания 87–21
датчики пульса 87–21
дать (сдачу) 21–D
два 14
два раза в неделю 18–23
двадцатый 14
двадцать 14
двадцать два 14
двадцать долларов 20–10
двадцать минут второго 16–8
двадцать один 14
двадцать процентов 15–8
двадцать пять минут второго 16–9
двадцать пять центов 20–4
двенадцатый 14
двенадцать 14
дверная ручка 37–30
дверная цепочка 37–28
дверь с сеткой 38–8, 38–12
двигатель 109–41
движение за гражданские права 115
двоеточие 113–12
двойная пароварка 59–8
Двор 39
дворник 138–35
дворники 108–2
двоюродная сестра 24–12
двухэтажная кровать 45–1
деверь 24–16
девяносто 14
девятнадцатилетняя девушка 22–8
девятнадцатый 14
девятнадцать 14
девятый 14
девять 14
дедушка 24–3
дежурный суп 61–10
дезинсектор 49–21
дезинфицирующее
    средство 47–23, 95–19
дезодорант 76–4

декабрь 19–36
декларация 110–22
Декларация независимости 115
декоративные подушки 42–20
Делайте упражнения 80–D
делать гимнастику 27–W
делать домашнюю работу 27–T
делать копии 142–E
делать поделки 162–D
делать снимок 32–D
делать стрижку 23–A
делать укладку 23–C
делать химическую завивку 23–B
деление 118–4
Деликатесы 53
деловая женщина 136–10
дельфин 131–30
денежный перевод 20–16
день 17–18, 18–10
День благодарения 168–15
День независимости 168–7
день рождения 19–41
день св. Валентина 168–4
Деньги 20
депозитная квитанция 97–12
деревня 34–4
дерево 149–17, 151–18
Деревья 128
деревянная ложка 59–9
деревянный 150–2
деревянный метр 151–15
деревянный молоток 150–2
держать 94–B
десятилетняя девочка 22–5
десятый 14
десять 14
десять долларов 20–9
десять минут второго 16–6
десять процентов 15–7
десять тысяч 14
десять центов 20–3
детали 146–7
Детали автомобиля 108–109
детектив 166–15
дети 22–1
Детская 45
детская коляска 95–16
детская кроватка 45–6
детская площадка 36–6
детская присыпка 95–18
детская программа 167–24
детские болезни 79
детский сад 94–95
детский стул с высоким
    сиденьем 95–7
детское питание 95–28
детское сиденье безопасности 109–39
детское сиденье для
    автомобиля 95–13
детское сухое молоко 95–25
дешёвое кольцо 11–20
дёсны 74–24
джемпер 65–18
джинсы 64–5
джойстик 144–9
диабет 79–9
диагональ 118–23

диамагазин 165–30
диаметр 118–17
диапроектор с вращающимся
    магазином 165–29
диван 42–19
диван на двоих 42–25
диетолог 87–25
дикобраз 134–10
диктор 152–27
диплом 29–2
диплом колледжа 29–7
дипломированная медсестра 87–22
дипломированная практикующая
    медсестра 87–24
директор 5–14
диск CD ROM 144–2
диск-жокей 33–17
дискета 144–5
дисковод 144–3
дисковод жёсткого диска 144–20
диспетчерская башня 110–7
дистанционное управление 164–9
длина 15–16
длинная юбка 71–34
длинные волосы 23–3
длинные носки 67–25
Дни недели 18
Добавить стиральный порошок 72–B
Добавьте овощи 58–Q
доброволец 87–19
дождевой лес 117–1
Дождитесь гудка 9–B
доить 148–C
доктор 84–6, 137–22
Должности 136–139
долина 117–18
доллар 20–7
долото 151–51
дом 34–6, 38
дом для престарелых 34–11
дом ленточной застройки 34–7
дом на колёсах 106–11
Домашние животные 133
Домашние животные 133
домашние паразиты 49
домик для игр 94–4
домкрат 109–51
домовладелец 37–32
домоводство 121–9
домохозяйка 137–32
дорогое кольцо 11–19
дорожка перед домом 38–14
дорожные знаки 107
дорожный чек 20–17
доска 2–1, 40–27
доска для серфинга 155–5
доска объявлений 3–14
доставить 96–C
доставщик 137–18
Достаньте карандаш 2–K
достичь 18-летнего возраста 116–A
дочь 24–21
дошкольное учебное заведение 112–4
драгоценности 69–8
Дроби 15
дрозд 132–17

дуб 128–18
дупло (в зубе) 84–20
дупло в зубе 85–L
дуршлаг 59–17
духи 76–5
духовка 40–20
духовка-тостер 40–15
душ 43–10
дымоуловитель 37–25, 45–11
дюйм 15–13
дядя 24–11
дятел 132–9
Европа 125–3
ежемесячный банковский отчёт 97–10
езда на велосипеде по горам 154–8
ездить 157–W
енот 134–13
его обслуживание 108–109
есть 60–A
ехать 157–W
ехать в школу на автобусе 26–H
ехать на велосипеде 91–E
ехать на работу на машине 26–I
ёмкость 56–5
жаба 130–28
жабры 130–2
жалюзи 43–11
жар 78–8
жара 10–15
жареная рыба 61–17
жареный картофель 60–2
жарить на сковородке 58–S
жарить на углях 58–T
жарить переворачивая 58–W
жарко 10–1, 30–1
жаровня 59–13
Жарьте до готовности 58–F
жасмин 129–1
жвачка 55–42
ждать сигнала светофора 90–B
железнодорожная станция 104–13
железнодорожные пути 104–10
железнодорожный переезд 107–11
желудки 52–23
желудок 75–41
жёлтый 12–12
жёлчный пузырь 75–40
жёсткая щётка 47–19
жёсткий стул 11–5
жена 24–20
женатый 25–23
жениться 28–L
женские трусики 67–16
женский 4–14
женщина 22–10
женщина-конгрессмен 116–2
женщины получают право
    голосовать 114
жетон 104–11
живая изгородь 39–1
живот 74–3
животные 152–2
жидкая унция воды 57–1
жидкий крахмал в распылителе 72–12
жидкость для исправления
    опечаток 143–33

жидкость для мытья окон 47–8
жидкость для мытья посуды 47–21
жидкость для полоскания рта 77–23
жидкость для снятия лака 77–32
жилет 65–24
Жильё 34
жираф 135–33
жить в США в течение пяти
    лет 116–B
жук 132–19
журнал 98–7
журнал регистрации
    посетителей 143–27
журнальный столик 42–23
за 13–3
за угол 105–10
забивать 149–D
забор 38–3, 148–19
забрать детей 27–O
заведующий отделом 54–8
заведующий отправкой 146–15
Завод 146
заворачивать подарок 169–D
завтра 18–16
завтракать 26–E
завуч 5–16
завязывать ботинки 94–I
загадывать желание 169–J
загон 148–17
загорающая 155–17
загорающий 155–17
Загрузить стиральную машину 72–C
загрязнение воды 126–12
загрязнение воздуха 126–10
Загрязнение окружающей среды 126
Задайте вопрос 6–G
заднее сиденье 109–38
задний двор 38–2
задняя фара 108–14
задувать свечи 169–K
задыхаться 82–N
зажигалка 108–32
зажигание 108–25
зажигать свечи 169–H
зажим 119–8
зажим для волос 76–17
Займите своё место 2–E
заказать блюдо из меню 62–D
заказная почта 96–11
заколка 76–18
закончить вуз 28–D
закончить разговор 8–C
закончить школу 28–D
Закройте книгу 2–J
закуски 55–16
зал суда 99–7
залив 117–9
заменитель сахара 60–22
замок 109–34
замок из песка 155–10
замок с засовом 37–29
Замок сломан 48–6
замужняя 25–23
занавески 44–6
заниматься ручным трудом 140–D
Занятия 6–7

занять своё место 111–G
Западное побережье 123–7
запасное колесо 109–53
Запирайте двери 101–E
запирающиеся ворота 36–13
запирающиеся шкафчики 5–7
записаться...на приём к врачу 85–A
записная книжка 143–30
записывать результаты 119–C
запись 165–A
запломбировать дупло в зубе 85–L
запломбировать зуб 85–L
Заполните бланк 4–B
заполнять заявление 141–G
заправка для салата 60–18
запрещённые наркотики 100–4
запястье 75–60
запятая 113–10
зарядное устройство для
    батареек 165–23
заслонка 42–11
засов 37–29
застилать постель 46–G
застолье 168–16
засуха 103–10
защитная вставка для пальцев
    ног 147–21
защитная раковина спортсмена 67–14
защитник 99–4
защитные наушники 147–14
защитные очки 147–9, 147–10
защитный ботинок 147–20
защитный жилет 147–15
защитный козырёк 147–11
защитный крем от солнца 155–13
звезда 127–23
звонок 38–10
звуковой сигнал 108–24
здание муниципалитета 89–17
здание суда 89–18
Здравоохранение 80–81
зебра 135–34
зелёный 12–8
зелёный лук 51–17
зелёный/ая/ое 50–28
Земледелие 148
землетрясение 102–5
Земля 127–7
зеркало 43–18, 44–1
зеркало бокового вида 108–8
зеркало заднего вида 108–1
зима 19–40
Зимние виды спорта 160
знак 91–29
знамя 33–15
золовка 24–15
золотая рыбка 133–16
зонтик 66–16
зоомагазин 92–6
зоопарк 152–1
зубная боль 78–2
зубная паста 77–21
Зубная поликлиника 84
зубная щётка 43–20, 77–20
зубной врач 84–18, 137–20
зубной камень 84–17

зубоврачебный осмотр 85
зубы 74–25
зять 24–16
ива 128–14
игла 73–22, 134–23
иголка 128–12
игра 152–18
игральные кости 162–4
играть 94–K
играть в игры 162–B
играть в карты 163–H
играть на музыкальном
    инструменте 120–A
игровая площадка 153
игровое представление 167–23
игрок 158–5
игрушечный дом 45–14
игрушки 94–5
игры 162–163
идёт дождь 10–8
идёт снег 10–9
идите прямо 107–A
идти на работу 26–I
идти на рынок 26–L
идти на собеседование 141–H
идти спать 27–Y
из такси 105–5
из Центральной Америки 115
извержение вулкана 103–14
извиниться 8–I
изготавливать 146–B
Измените режим питания 80–C
измеритель уровня масла 108–19
измерить...температуру 85–C
измерять 149–C
Измерять ингредиенты 57–A
изоляционная лента 151–38
изоляция 149–13
изюм 50–27
икра 74–18
иметь внука 29–Q
иметь внучку 29–Q
иммигранты из Юго-восточной
    Азии 115
иммигранты из Южной и Восточной
    Европы 115
Иммиграция 114
иммиграция беженцев Второй
    мировой войны 114
иммигрировать 28–C
имя 4–1, 4–2
инвалидное кресло 80–6
индейка 52–17, 168–17
индекс 4–9
Индивидуальные виды спорта 159
индикатор температуры 108–23
инженер 137–23
иностранный язык 121–8
Инструменты 150–151
интересная книга 167–30
интерком 36–8
интернирование японцев 114
информационная схема 93–19
ирис 129–20
ирландцы 114
искать новую квартиру 35–A

искать объявления о предложении
    работы 141–C
искусственное дыхание 83–16
искусственный массаж сердца и
    искусственное дыхание 83–17
искусство 121–1
Испано-американская война 115
испанские исследователи 114
испанцы в Санта-Фе 114
использовать дезодорант 76–C
Исправьте ошибку 7–Z
испуганная 31–24
испуганный 31–24
испытывать болтанку 111–N
испытывать головокружение 78–C
испытывать тошноту 78–D
испытывающая боль 30–12
испытывающая неловкость 31–25
испытывающая отвращение 30–9
испытывающий боль 30–12
испытывающий неловкость 31–25
испытывающий отвращение 30–9
истории болезней 87–20
Исторические и политические
    события 114
История США 114–115
исчисление 118–28
итого 21–8
июль 19–30, 19–31
йогурт 54–33
кабачок 51–13
кабели аварийного пуска
    двигателя 109–52
кабель 144–16
кабина 106–16
кабина пилота 110–11
кабинет директора 5–13
кабинет завуча 5–15
каблук 68–13
кавычки 113–9
каждый день 18–21
кактус 128–21
Календарь 18–19
календула 129–13
калькулятор 142–8
кальмар 130–10
кальсоны 67–11
камбала 130–13
каменщик 136–9
камень 155–24
камин 42–9
каминная полка 42–8
канталупа 50–15
канун Дня всех святых 168–10
каньон 117–17
капельница 87–27
капот 108–6
капсула 81–27
капуста 51–2
карандаш 3–20, 77–35
карандаш для бровей 77–33
кардиган 65–27
кардиолог 86–3
карман 73–4
карнавал 152–16
карта 3–12

картина 42–7, 152–8
картотека 98–10
картофель 51–21
картофельное пюре 61–11
картофельные чипсы 55–40
картофельный салат 53–13
карточка с номером социального обеспечения 29–5
карточка страховой компании 84–4
каска 147–19
касса 55–18
кассета 162–2
кассета для пишущей машинки 143–31
кассир 55–19, 97–1, 136–14
кассовая стойка 55–17
кастрюля 40–16, 40–24, 59–6, 59–25
кастрюля для тушения 59–11
каталка 87–28
катание 152–17
катание на коньках 160–4
катание на лодке 154–2, 154–4
катание на лошадях 154–9
катание на парусной доске 160–10
катание на плоту 154–4
катание на роликовых коньках 159–9
катание на санках 160–6
катание на скейтборде 159–12
катание на сноуборде 160–2
кататься на коньках 157–V
кататься на лыжах 157–U
катушка ниток 73–17
кафе 88–2
кафедра 32–5
кафель 43–9
кафетерий 5–4
качалка 153–16
качать 94–H, 153–B
качели 153–12
кашлять 78–A
кашне 66–4
квадрат 118–6
кварта молока 57–4
квартал 107–2
квартиросъёмщик 37–33
Квартиры 36–37
Квебек 123–5
кегли 159–3
кекс 54–32, 61–19
кенгуру 135–44
кепка 66–6
кетчуп 60–23
кизил 128–16
кино 152–10, 166–1
кинотеатр 88–11
киоск 60–19
киоск «мороженое» 93–20
кирка 149–20
кирпичи 149–11
кислородная маска 110–14
кислотный дождь 126–11
кисточка для век 77–35
кисть 163–23
кисть для краски 151–47
кисть руки 74–8
кит 131–29
китайцы 115

кишечник 75–42
кишечные паразиты 79–16
клавиатура 144–7
кладовка 36–14
кларнет 120–4
Класс 2–3, 5–1
класть кирпичи 149–B
клей 143–37, 162–8
клейкая лента 83–5
клерк 5–18
клерк по обслуживанию картотеки 142–12
клещ 132–28
клещи для удаления изоляции 151–37
клён 128–13
Клиники 84
клипсы 69–38
клуб здоровья 89–21
клубника 50–17
клык 135–48
клюв 132–1
ключ 37–31
клюшка 161–1
книжка с картинками 45–17
книжка для раскрашивания 45–20
книжный магазин 92–4
книжный шкаф 3–8, 42–1
кнопка 143–43
кнопка для вызова медперсонала 86–10
кнопка регулирования положения высоты койки 86–12
коала 135–45
кобра 131–40
ковёр 42–27, 44–23
коврик для ванной 43–27
коготь 132–4
код города 4–10
кожа 75–51
кожаная куртка 66–3
кожаные сапоги 70–18
коза 133–1
койот 134–3
кокосовые орехи 50–22
колбаса 52–12, 61–2
колготки 67–27
колено 74–17
колибри 132–11
Количественные числительные 14
колледж 32–A, 112–10
коллекционировать 162–A
коллекция марок 162–12
коллекция монет 162–13
колонии на атлантическом побережье, основанные северо-европейцами 114
колонисты 114
колонисты и свободные негры 115
колонки 164–11
колпак ступицы колеса 108–9
колыбель 45–19
кольцо 69–39
кольцо для прорезывания зубов 95–30
команда 158–3
Командные виды спорта 158
комар 132–23

комбинация 67–22
комбинезон 65–16, 65–21
комедия 166–10
комендант 36–12
комета 127–25
комнатный цветок 129–29
комод 44–2, 45–8
компакт-диск 98–14
комплектовать листы 142–F
компьютер 3–15
компьютерная рабочая станция 143–21
компьютерные науки 121–4
компьютерный каталог 98–9
Компьютеры 144
конвейер 146–12
конвейерная лента 146–12
конверт 96–1, 143–20
конверт для младенца 67–7
конгрессмен 116–2
кондитерская смесь 55–47
кондитерский магазин 92–3
кондиционер 37–19, 108–28
кондиционер для волос 76–10
кондуктор 104–16
консервная банка 56–3
консервы 54–4
Конституция США 115
конструктор 146–3
контактные линзы 81–36
контейнер для медицинских отходов 86–14
Континенты 124
контрабас 120–10
конус 118–11
конференц-зал 145–19
конфета 55–41, 168–14
конфетти 168–3
концерт 166–6
коньки 161–9
копировальная машина 142–14
копировальный 91–22
копчёная грудинка 52–11
копчёная индейка 53–4
копыто 134–17
корейцы 115
Коренные американцы 114, 115
корень 128–5, 129–3
корзина 42–2
корзина для грязного белья 43–1, 72–2
корзина для мусора 43–25
корзина для покупок 54–7
корзинка с хлебом 63–8
коридор 145–13
коридорный 145–5
коричневый 12–11
кормить 94–D, 148–D
кормить грудью 94–C
коробка 56–4, 56–6
коробка печенья 56–20
коробка яиц 56–16
корова 133–3
короткая юбка 71–35
короткие волосы 23–1
коротковолновое радио 164–5
корродирующее вещество 147–4

корсаж **73**–3
корсет **67**–18
корь **79**–5
косить траву **39**–C
космическая станция **127**–18
космос **127**–22
костёр **154**–11
костыли **80**–1
кость **75**–49
костюм **64**–2, **168**–13
костюм-тройка **64**–1
кот **133**–9
котёнок **133**–10
кофе **61**–22
кофе без кофеина **61**–23
кофеварка **40**–11
кофейная чашка **41**–27
кошелёк **69**–25
кошка **133**–9
краб **53**–22, **130**–16
край тротуара **90**–10
кран **43**–6, **149**–7
кран-балка **149**–5
Кран течёт **49**–16
красивый вид **11**–21
красить **149**–A, **163**–E
красить волосы **23**–D
красить...ногти **77**–O
краситься **77**–P
краска **151**–20
краскопульт **151**–19
красный **12**–13
крах фондовой биржи **114**
креветка **53**–24, **130**–19
кредитная карточка **20**–15
крем для бритья **77**–27
крем от загара **76**–6
кресло **42**–24
кресло-качалка **94**–6
крестовая отвёртка **150**–26
кричать «сюрприз!» **169**–G
кровать **44**–8
кровельщик **48**–8
кровотечение из носа **78**–17
кровоточить **82**–M
крокодил **131**–37
крокус **129**–25
кролик **133**–13
кроссовки **68**–23
круг **118**–5
кружка **41**–28
крупногабаритный автомобиль **106**–4
крупные куски баранины **52**–13
крыло **132**–2
крылышки **52**–20
крыса **49**–27, **133**–18
крысы **49**–27
крытый грузовик-фургон для
    перевозки мебели **106**–14
крыша **38**–20
Крыша течёт **48**–3
крышка **59**–24
крюк **150**–34
крюк с проушиной **150**–35
крючок и петелька **73**–23
ксилофон **120**–17

куб **118**–10
кубики **45**–15
кубинцы **115**
кувалда **149**–22
кудрявые волосы **23**–11
кузнечик **132**–25
кукла **45**–18
кукольный набор **162**–15
кукольный театр **152**–14
кукуруза **51**–27, **148**–4
купальная шапочка **76**–1
купальник **66**–26
купальный костюм **66**–26
купальный халат **66**–25
купаться **76**–B
купить **21**–C
купить билет **111**–A
купить дом **29**–O
куриные ножки **52**–22
куриные окорочка **52**–21
Куриный суп **58**
курица **52**–16, **133**–5
курица, зажаренная в духовке **61**–12
куртка **66**–7
курьер **138**–38
кусок горбуши **53**–19
кусок лосося **53**–19
куст **39**–20
Кухня **40, 63**–10
Кухонная утварь **59**
кухонное полотенце **47**–22
кухонный комбайн **40**–26
кухонный стол **40**–22
кухонный таймер **59**–18
кухонный шкаф **40**–1
куча удобрений **39**–10
кушетка для осмотра **84**–13
лаборант **86**–16
ладонь **75**–59
лазать по лестнице **153**–C
лаймы **50**–12
лак для волос **76**–12
лак для ногтей **77**–31
лама **135**–26
лампа **44**–17
лампочка **42**–4
лапа **134**–20
ласты **155**–2
лев **135**–36
леггинсы **65**–23
лёгкая атлетика **159**–17
лёгкая задача **11**–23
лёгкая куртка **71**–40
лёгкий ящик **11**–14
лёгкое **75**–37
Легковые **106**
легче **30**–16
леденцы от боли в горле **81**–21
лезвие **77**–26, **150**–11
лейка **39**–17
лейкопластырь **83**–3
лекарства по рецепту **80**–11
лекарства, отпускаемые без
    рецепта **80**–12
леопард **135**–25
лепесток **129**–8

лес **117**–11
лестница **37**–35
лестница для лазания **153**–14
лестничная клетка **37**–26
летнее время **17**–33
лето **19**–38
летучая мышь **134**–7
лилия **129**–24
лиловый **12**–7
лимоны **50**–11
линейка **3**–27
Линии **118**
линия подшива **73**–1
линованная бумага **3**–25
лиса **134**–15
лист **128**–6, **129**–5
лифт **37**–34
лифчик **67**–20
лихой водитель **11**–3
лицензия водителя такси **104**–22
Лицо **74**
Личная гигиена **76**–77
Личные данные **4**
личный банковский сейф **97**–13
личный чек **20**–14
лоб **74**–20
ловить **156**–E
лодочки **68**–16
лодыжка **75**–61
ложиться спать **27**–X
ложка **41**–23
локоть **74**–15
лопата **39**–13, **149**–21
лопатка **59**–19
лосось **53**–18
лось **134**–1
лосьон для бритья **77**–28
лосьон для тела **76**–7
лоток для краски **151**–45
лошадь **133**–4
луг **117**–20
луговая собачка **133**–22
лук **51**–28, **161**–6
луковица **129**–9
лыжи **161**–24
лыжная маска **66**–41
лыжная шапочка **66**–10
лыжные ботинки **161**–26
лыжные гонки **160**–3
лыжные палки **161**–25
лысина **23**–12
льняная куртка **70**–17
люцерна **148**–5
лягушка **130**–25
магазин видеотоваров **93**–15
магазин для будущих матерей **93**–17
магазин игрушек **92**–5
магазин открыток **92**–7
магазин скобяных изделий **88**–14
магазин удобства **90**–3
магазин фототоваров **90**–4
магазин электронных товаров **93**–18
магнит **119**–21
магнитофон **164**–2, **164**–3
магнолия **128**–9
мазь **81**–24

май **19**–29
майка **67**–2, **67**–10
майонез **60**–25
макароны **54**–27, **61**–15
мал/а/о **70**–20
маленькая рука **11**–1
маленький **70**–2
малина **50**–18
малогабаритный автомобиль **106**–2
малыш **22**–2
манго **50**–21
мандарины **50**–13
манеж **95**–11
манжета **73**–5
маникюрный салон **91**–25
мантия **32**–2
маргарин **54**–39
маргаритка **129**–14
марка **96**–10
марля **83**–6
Марс **127**–6
март **19**–27
маршрут **104**–2
маска **168**–12
маска кетчера **161**–15
маскировочная липкая лента **151**–49
масло **54**–36
масляная краска **163**–24
масляный манометр **108**–19
мастер **48**–10
мастерок **39**–14, **149**–12
мастерская **121**–10
Математика **118**
математические действия **118**
материнская плата **144**–18
матерчатые пелёнки **95**–21
матрас **44**–25
мать **24**–5
мать-одиночка **25**–25
мачеха **25**–31
машина с откидным верхом **106**–5
мебельный магазин **88**–13
медальон **69**–33
медведь **134**–11
медицинский браслет **83**–14
Медицинский осмотр **85**
медицинский техник по оказанию
  первой помощи **87**–26
медоносная пчела **132**–26
Медперсонал больницы **86**
медсестра **84**–10, **138**–42
медсестра помощи на дому **87**–24
медуза **130**–14
между **13**–10
междугородний звонок **9**–5
международный звонок **9**–6
Мексиканское плоскогорье **123**–15
мексиканцы **114**
мел **3**–16
мелкая тарелка **63**–15
мелкий крепёжный винт **150**–27
менеджер **36**–12
менеджер офиса **143**–25
мензурка **119**–13
меню **62**–3
Меню кафе **61**

менять пеленки **94**–E
менять постельное бельё **46**–P
мерить **149**–C
Меркурий **127**–9
Меры жидкостей **57**
Меры сыпучих тел **57**
Места проведения досуга **152**
местный звонок **9**–4
место **2**–7, **152**–11
место рождения **4**–17
место сбора пассажиров для выхода
  на посадку **110**–6
месяц **4**, **18**–9, **127**–14
Месяцы года **19**
металлические-войлочные
  губки, пропитанные моющим
  средством **47**–5
метёлка из перьев для смахивания
  пыли **47**–1
метель **10**–20, **103**–11
метла **47**–10
метрдотель **62**–1
метро **104**–9
мех **134**–19
механизм переключения
  передач **108**–28
меховые наушники **66**–12
мечеть **89**–23
мешковатые брюки **71**–42
мешок **56**–7
мидии **53**–26
мидия **130**–17
микроавтобус **106**–10
микроволновая печь **40**–13
микрокассетный аппарат для
  транскрибирования **142**–4
микроскоп **119**–4
микрофильм **98**–5
микрофон **164**–4
микстура от кашля **81**–20
милиция **9**–9
миллиард **14**
миллион **14**
милая **22**–24
милый **22**–24
мини-автомобиль **106**–1
минута **16**–2
Мир **124**–**125**
миска **41**–25
Миссурийский компромисс **114**
мишень **161**–8
мишка **45**–10
младшие классы средней школы **112**–6
Млекопитающие **134**–**135**
многоквартирный дом **34**–5
модели поездов **163**–32
модель **138**–39
модем **144**–11
мозг **75**–35
мойка **40**–6
мокасины **68**–19
мокрая футболка **72**–17
молекула **119**–18
моллюски **53**–28
молния **10**–17, **73**–16
молния сломана **70**–24

молодая **22**–13
молодой **22**–13
молоко **54**–35
молот **149**–22
молоток **150**–1
молочай красивейший **129**–23
молочник **41**–13
молочный коктейль **60**–12
молочный отдел **54**–9
моль **132**–22
мольберт **163**–21
Монеты **20**
монитор **144**–6
монитор «электронная няня» **45**–9
мониторы прилёта и отлёта **110**–4
морж **131**–32
морковь **51**–3
мороженая рыба **53**–30
мороженое **55**–44
мороженое из йогурта **60**–11
мороженые овощи **55**–43
мороженые продукты **55**–12
морозилка **40**–10
морозно **10**–5
морская звезда **130**–15
морская раковина **155**–21
морская свинка **133**–14
морская свинья **131**–31
Морская фауна **130**–**131**
Морские животные **130**
Морские млекопитающие **131**
морской ёж **130**–20
морской гребешок **130**–18
морской конёк **130**–23
морской лев **131**–34
мотель **89**–22
мотор **109**–41
мотоцикл **91**–19
мочалка из махровой ткани **43**–14
мочевой пузырь **75**–47
моющее средство **47**–23
Моющие средства **47**
муж **24**–19
мужские трусы **67**–13, **67**–17
мужской **4**–13
мужчина **22**–11
Музыка **120**
музыкальный магазин **92**–1
музыкант **138**–41
мука **55**–45
мультфильм **167**–19
муравей **49**–24
муравьед **135**–24
муравьи **49**–24
мускусная дыня **50**–15
мусорное ведро **37**–20
мусорный бак **39**–3
мусоровоз **91**–27
мусоропровод **37**–24
муха **132**–29
мыло **43**–23, **76**–2
мыльная опера **167**–21
мыльница **43**–24
мыть духовку **46**–C
мыть окна **46**–D
мыть пол **46**–J

мыть пол щёткой **46**–L
мыть посуду **46**–M
мыть...голову **76**–E
мыши **49**–26
мышца **75**–48
мышь **49**–26, **133**–17, **144**–8
мякие игрушки **45**–23
мягкий стул **11**–6
мясник **136**–11
Мясо **52**
мятая рубашка **72**–19
мяч **45**–16
мяч для игры в американский
    футбол **161**–22
на **13**–8
на шоссе **105**–6
Наберите личный код **97**–B
Наберите номер **9**–D
набивная ткань **70**–10
наблюдать **119**–B
набор для вскрытия **119**–7
наводнение **103**–16
наволочка **44**–10
нагибаться **157**–R
Нагорье Чьяпас **123**–18
Нагреватель воды не работает **48**–1
над **13**–6
надставлять **73**–F
наёмный работник **148**–20
наждачная бумага **151**–50
название **98**–21, **113**–3
Найдите пары **7**–X
Найдите слово в словаре **6**–A
найти работу **28**–G
накладывать...макияж **77**–P
наклейка с адресом **143**–35
накрыть на стол **62**–A
налить воды **62**–C
наличные (деньги) **20**–13
налог на продажу **21**–7
намазаться кремом от загара **76**–D
нанять адвоката **99**–B
нанять юриста **99**–B
нападение **100**–7
напёрсток **73**–20
написать адрес на почтовой
    открытке **96**–A
напитки **55**–15
Напишите на черновике **113**–A
Напишите своё имя печатными
    буквами **4**–C
наплечники **161**–21
направленное освещение **42**–3
Нарежьте лук **58**–G
Нарежьте морковь **58**–O
Нарисуйте картинку **6**–M
наручники **99**–2
наручные часы **69**–34
нарцисс **129**–26
нарядная блузка **71**–39
нарядное платье **71**–36
насадки для пылесоса **47**–14
насекомые **132**
Население **114**
насильственное переселение
    индейцев Чироки **114**
насморк **78**–7

настольные игры **162**–3
настольный календарь **142**–6
настольный теннис **159**–13
Натрите сыр на тёрке **58**–J
Наука **119**
научно-фантастический
    рассказ **166**–12
наушники **164**–16
начальная школа **112**–5
начать разговор **8**–B
начос **60**–10
не в фокусе **165**–33
Не открывайте дверь незнакомым
    людям **101**–F
Не пейте за рулём **101**–G
не хватает пуговицы **70**–25
небольшого роста **22**–18
небольшой город **34**–3
небоскрёб **89**–25
невестка **24**–15
невидимки **76**–19
неделя **18**–11
недодержанный **165**–35
нейлоновые чулки **70**–19
неопрятный шкаф **11**–16
неосторожно **147**–23
Неполадки **48–49**
Нептун **127**–2
нерв **75**–50
нервная **30**–11
нервный **30**–11
неспелый/ая/ое **50**–28
нести поднос **62**–H
несчастные случаи **82**
Несчастные случаи **102–103**
неудобно **30**–8
нефть **126**–6
нижнее бельё **67**–11
нижняя юбка **67**–23
низкие каблуки **71**–46
нитка для зубов **77**–22
нитка жемчуга **69**–30
Новая Англия **123**–11
новолуние **127**–13
новости **167**–17
новые туфли **71**–32
Новый год **168**–1
нога **74**–6
ноготь **75**–58
ноготь на пальце ноги **75**–64
нож **41**–22, **63**–27
нож для мяса **63**–26
нож для порки швов **73**–19
нож для чистки овощей **59**–15
нож для чистки фруктов и
    овощей **59**–16
ножницы **23**–19, **73**–18
ножовка **150**–5
ноль **14**
номер **145**–10
№ квартиры **4**–6
номер сберегательного счёта **97**–6
номер социального обеспечения **4**–15
номер телефона **4**–11
номер чекового счёта **97**–8
номера **3**–31
номерной знак **108**–15

нос **74**–21
носилки **87**–28
носки **67**–15
носовой платок **69**–42
носок **68**–15
носорог **135**–29
ночная рубашка **67**–5
ночная сорочка **67**–9
ночник **45**–3
ночной столик **44**–21
ночь **17**–20
ноябрь **19**–35
Нужно залить антифриз в
    радиатор **109**–56
Нужно залить масло в машину **109**–55
Нужно заправить машину **109**–54
Нужно подзарядить батарею **109**–58
Нужно подкачать шины **109**–59
Нужно проверить выхлопные газы
    на содержание загрязняющих
    веществ **109**–57
нырять **157**–S
нюхать **75**–C
няня **136**–12
Обведите правильный ответ **7**–S
обвиняемый **99**–5
Обжарьте лук **58**–H
обедающий **62**–5
обеденный зал **62**–2
обеденный стол **41**–17
обезьяна **135**–27
Оберегайте кошелёк **101**–D
обеспокоенная **30**–13
обеспокоенный **30**–13
обжечься **82**–H
обиженная **30**–17
обиженный **30**–17
облачно **10**–7
обменять **21**–G
обморозиться **82**–G
обнимать **33**–G
обниматься **33**–G
обои **45**–5
обочина **90**–10
Образцы тканей **70**
Обратитесь к хиропрактику **81**–H
обратный адрес **96**–7
обращаться за справкой по
    телефону **141**–E
обсерватория **127**–19
обслуживание бассейна **145**–17
обслуживание в номере **145**–12
обслуживать посетителей **140**–O
Обсудите список **6**–L
обувной магазин **92**–10
обувной отдел **68**–3
Обувь **68–69**
общая сумма **21**–8
Общественная безопасность **101**
Общественный транспорт **104**
объектив с переменным фокусным
    расстоянием **165**–25
обычная блузка **71**–38
обычная цена **21**–2
обязанности **116**
овал **118**–9
Овощи **51**

овца **133**–7
огнеопасно **147**–2
огнетушитель **147**–22
огонь **42**–10
огород **148**–12
огорчённая **31**–30
огорчённый **31**–30
ограбление на улице **100**–5
ограбление со взломом **100**–6
ограда **148**–19
ограничение скорости **107**–5
огурцы **51**–12
одевать **94**–J
одеваться **26**–D
Одежда I **64**–65
Одежда II **66**
Одежда III **67**
одеколон **76**–5
одеяло **44**–12, **45**–2
один **14**
один цент **20**–1
одиннадцатый **14**
одиннадцать **14**
одинокая **30**–18
одинокий **30**–18
одна восьмая **15**–1
одна вторая **15**–4
одна третья **15**–3
одна четвёртая **15**–2
одноразовые подгузники **95**–20
одностороннее движение **107**–6
однотонная зелёная ткань **70**–6
одометр **108**–21
озеро **117**–13
ознакомиться с планом выхода при
    аварии **111**–K
ознакомиться с расположением
    аварийного выхода **111**–J
озноб **78**–9
океан **117**–6, **155**–1
окно **38**–17, **42**–17
окно выдачи на вынос для водителей
    за рулём **90**–13
Окно разбито **48**–5
оконное стекло **149**–15
Окончание школы **32**–33
окончить школу **32**–A
окружающая среда **126**
окружная ярмарка **152**–19
окружность **118**–15
октябрь **19**–34
окулист **86**–7
окунь **130**–11
оладьи **61**–6
олений рог **134**–16
олень **134**–14
омар **53**–23
Онтарио **123**–4
опасная ситуация **147**–8
опасные материалы **147**–7
опасные отходы **126**–9
опера **166**–8
оператор **9**–7
Операционная **87**
операционная сестра **87**–29
операционный стол **87**–34
описание внешности **22**

Описание одежды **70**–71
Описание предметов **11**
Описание причёски **23**
оплатить счёт **62**–I
ополаскивать...волосы **76**–F
оползень **102**–6
опоссум **134**–4
опрятный шкаф **11**–15
оптик **81**–34
оптика **92**–8
Опустите монеты **9**–C
опухший палец **78**–16
орангутан **135**–40
оранжевый **12**–6
оранжерея **152**–5
орбита **127**–11
орган **120**–22
организатор банкета **33**–12
орехи **50**–23
орёл **132**–10
оркестр **120**–1
ортодонтические скобы **84**–24
ортопед **81**–28
орхидея **129**–17
оса **132**–18
освободиться **99**–H
осень **19**–39
осёл **133**–2
осмотреть...горло **85**–E
Оставайтесь на хорошо освещённых
    улицах **101**–B
оставить **21**–E
оставить чаевые **62**–J
Оставьте сообщение **9**–E
останавливать **156**–M
остановка автобуса **91**–16
осторожно **147**–24
осторожно, дети **107**–13
осторожно, ток **147**–1
осторожный водитель **11**–4
остров **117**–8
остролист **128**–19
острый перец **51**–8
осуждённый **99**–14
осьминог **130**–4
отбеливатель **72**–8
Ответьте на вопрос **6**–H
отвёртка **150**–25
отвозить детей в школу **26**–G
отворот **73**–5
отдел «Мясо-птица» **54**–2
отдел выдачи **98**–16
отдел периодических изданий **98**–6
отдел средств массовой
    информации **98**–11
отделение для ручной
    клади, расположенное над
    сиденьями **110**–10
отделение получения багажа **110**–17
отдыхать **27**–U
отец **24**–6
отец-одиночка **25**–26
откидной столик **110**–16
Откройте книгу **2**–I
открывалка для консервов **59**–1
открывать дверь **169**–F
открытка **168**–5

отмена рабства **115**
Отметьте правильный ответ в
    экзаменационном листе **7**–T
отправить **96**–B
отправить письмо по факсу **142**–B
отправиться **111**–L
отправлять **146**–C
отпуск **19**–46
отравление пестицидами **126**–14
отчётная банковская книжка **97**–5
отчим **25**–28
Офис **142**–143
официант **62**–4
официантка **63**–6
офтальмолог **86**–7
охранник **97**–4, **99**–3
очень большой **70**–5
очень маленький **70**–1
очередь **55**–20
очиститель воздуха **80**–44
очки **81**–35
павлин **132**–15
падуб **128**–19
пакет **56**–4, **56**–7
пакет муки **56**–19
пакет со льдом **83**–13
пакеты для мусора **47**–12
Палата пациента **86**
Палата представителей **116**–1
палатка **60**–19, **154**–10
палец ноги **75**–63
палтус **53**–20
пальма **128**–15
пальто **66**–2
пальцы **75**–57
панда **135**–41
пантера **135**–39
папайя **50**–20
папка **142**–11
парад **168**–2
параллельная **118**–21
парикмахер **137**–30
парикмахерская **88**–15
парк **88**–8, **153**
парк с аттракционами **152**–13
парка **66**–8
парковать машину **91**–D
парковка для инвалидов **107**–14
парковка запрещена **107**–12
пароварка **59**–4
паром **104**–23
парта **2**–4
парусная лодка **155**–4
парусный спорт **160**–8
пасовать **156**–H
паспорт **29**–9
пассажир **104**–7, **110**–23
пастрами **53**–6
патио **39**–6
пауза **165**–E
паук **132**–30
паукообразные **132**
пациент **84**–3
пачка овсянки **56**–18
пачка хлопьев **56**–18
педаль акселератора газа **109**–47
педаль тормоза **109**–46

педиатр **86**–4
пейджер **9**–16
Пейте много жидкости **80**–В
пекарня **89**–16
пекарь **136**–8
пеленальный стол **45**–12
пенопластовая подстилка **154**–13
первая атомная бомба **114**
первая индейская резервация в
  Виргинии **114**
первая модель машины «Форд» **114**
Первая медицинская помощь **83**
Первая мировая война **114**
первое место **152**–20
первые англичане в Виргинии **114**
первые звуковые фильмы **114**
первый **14** ·
первый африканский раб продан в
  Виргинии **114**
первый полёт на самолёте **114**
первый приз **152**–20
первый этаж **36**–1
Переведите деньги **97**–Е
Перевести из одной системы мер в
  другую **57**–С
переводчик **138**–34
перевозчик **138**–40
перевязь **80**–8
переговорное устройство **36**–8
перед **13**–4
передавать **156**–Н
передача о природе **167**–22
передвижной дом **34**–8
переделка одежды **73**
передержанный **165**–34
переднее сиденье **109**–35
передний двор **38**–15
передняя фара **108**–4
переехать **29**–Р
перекись водорода **83**–8
Перекрёсток **90–91**
Перемешайте **58**–Е
Перемешайте ингредиенты **58**–К
перемотка назад **165**–D
переносная люлька **95**–14
переносной радио-
  магнитофон **164**–15
переносной телевизор **164**–7
переносной телефон **9**–12
переносной холодильник **155**–11
Перепишите работу **113**–D
пересадка **104**–6
переулок **37**–21
перехватывать **156**–М
переход **90**–8
переходить дорогу **90**–А
перечница **41**–15
перо **132**–5
перпендикулярная **118**–20
персики **50**–5
перчатка **161**–17
перчатки **66**–5
песок **155**–23
песочница **153**–15
песчаная дюна **117**–5
петлица **73**–12

петля **73**–12
петрушка **51**–10
петух **133**–6
петь песню **120**–В
петь «С днём рождения» **169**–I
печатать **140**–М
печатать письмо **142**–D
печатник **138**–46
печатный фирменный бланк **143**–19
печатный центр **91**–22
печень **75**–39
печенье **54**–31
печёнка **52**–7
печёный картофель **61**–14
печка **108**–29
Печка сломана **49**–15
печь в духовке при высокой
  температуре **58**–V
пешеход **90**–7
пешеходный переход **107**–10
пёстрая ткань **70**–13
пианино **120**–16
пижама **67**–4
пикап **106**–7
пики **163**–28
пиломатериал **149**–17
пилот **110**–12
пилочка для ногтей **77**–30
пилюля **81**–26
пинг-понг **159**–13
пингвин **132**–12
пинта йогурта **57**–3
пинцет **83**–2, **119**–8
пир **168**–16
пирамида **118**–13
пирог **61**–21
пирс **155**–16
писатель **139**–64
пистолет **100**–9
письменное задание **113**–1
письменный стол **142**–1
письмо **96**–2
письмо, доставляемое
  авиапочтой **96**–13
пить **60**–В
пицца **60**–7
Пишите на доске **2**–G
пишущая машинка **142**–2
плавать **157**–Т
плавки **66**–22
плавник **130**–1
плакать **32**–С
план этажа **38**–1
Планеты **127**
планировать вечеринку **169**–А
пластилин **162**–14
пластинка **98**–15
пластмассовый контейнер для
  хранения **59**–3
пластырь **83**–5
плата за проезд **104**–5
платить **21**–С
платить за квартиру **35**–F
платить налоги **116**–Е
платформа **104**–15
платье **64**–3

платье для беременной **65**–19
плащ **66**–17
плейер **3**–11
племянник **24**–18
племянница **24**–17
плечевые предохранительные
  ремни **109**–37
плечо **74**–10
плёнка **165**–26
плита **40**–18
плов **61**–18
пломба **84**–22
плоскогубцы **150**–7
плотник **48**–12, **136**–13
плохая собака **11**–18
площадка для игры в мяч **153**–1
Плутон **127**–1
пляж **117**–10, **155**
пляжное кресло **155**–14
пляжное полотенце **155**–15
пляжный зонт **155**–9
пневматическая дрель **149**–9
пневматический бурильный
  молоток **149**–9
по воде **105**–3
побег **128**–1
поблагодарить друга **8**–Н
повар **137**–17
поверните налево **107**–С
поверните направо **107**–В
Повесьте трубку **9**–F
повседневное платье **71**–37
Повторите слово **6**–D
Поговорите друг с другом **7**–Р
Погода **10**
погремушка **95**–31
погрузочная платформа **146**–16
под **13**–7, **13**–9
под мост **105**–1
под мостом **105**–1
подавальщик **62**–4, **139**–53
подавальщица **63**–6
подавать **156**–F, **157**–N
подавиться **82**–L
подарки **33**–18
подать на стол **62**–F
подбородок **74**–31
подвесная игрушка над кроватью
  ребёнка **45**–4
подвижная лента выдачи
  багажа **110**–18
подводное плавание с
  аквалангом **160**–12
подводное плавание с дыхательной
  трубкой **160**–11
Поделитесь книгой **6**–I
поджелудочная железа **75**–46
подкладное судно **86**–13
подметать пол **46**–Е
поднимать **94**–G
Поднимите руку **2**–А
поднос **41**–10
поднос для бумаг **142**–5
поднос с десертом **63**–7
поднос с ячейками для
  лекарств **87**–23

подошва **68**–12
подписать договор об аренде **35**–C
подпись **4**–18
подрезать кусты **39**–E
подростки **22**–6
подсвечник **41**–8
подсолнух **129**–10
подставка для журналов и
    газет **42**–22
подставка для зубных щёток **43**–21
подставка для письма с
    зажимом **143**–26
подстилка на стол **142**–7
подтяжки **68**–2
подушечка для булавок **73**–15
подушечка для иголок **73**–15
подушка **44**–9
Подчеркните слово **7**–V
подшивать документы **142**–H
подъездная дорога **38**–5
поезд **104**–17
пожар **102**–7
пожарная **9**–9
пожарная машина **102**–9
пожарная станция **88**–1
пожарник **102**–8, **137**–24
пожарный выход **36**–7, **37**–23
пожарный кран **91**–28
пожилая **22**–15
пожилой **22**–15
пожилой человек **22**–12
позвоночник **75**–54
поздно **17**–23
поздороваться **8**–A
поздравительная открытка **96**–4
позиция **144**–19
Поиск жилья **35**
Поиск работы **141**
поисково-спасательная группа **103**–17
пойти в армию **28**–F
пойти в школу **28**–B
покрывало **44**–11
покрывать лаком **77**–O
покупать **21**–A
Покупка дома **35**
покупка Луизианы **114**
Покупки **21**
пол **4**–12, **44**–24
полдень **17**–17
поле **5**–12, **148**–7
поленья **42**–12
Полёт на самолёте **111**
поливать цветы **39**–B
Поликлиника **84**
полировать мебель **46**–K
полироль **47**–18
полицейский **99**–1, **138**–44
полицейский участок **89**–19
полиция **89**–19
полка **40**–8
полнолуние **127**–16
полночь **17**–21
полная **22**–20
полный **22**–20
полный стакан **11**–9
половик **44**–23

половина второго **16**–10
половник **59**–7
полоскать рот **77**–L
полотенце для рук **43**–13
полоть клумбу **39**–A
полуботинки **68**–20
полуостров **117**–7
Полуостров Юкатан **123**–19
полупальто **66**–20
получить **96**–B
получить аллергическую
    реакцию **82**–E
получить гражданство **28**–H
получить инфаркт **82**–D
получить передозировку
    лекарств **82**–K
получить передозировку
    наркотиков **82**–K
получить посадочный талон **111**–E
получить свой багаж **111**–P
получить ссуду (в банке) **35**–I
получить травму **82**–A
получить удар электричеством **82**–F
получить электрошок **82**–F
полчашки изюма **57**–9
Пользование банкоматом **97**
Пользование телефоном-
    автоматом **9**
помада **77**–37
помидоры **51**–23
помогать пациентам **140**–B
Помогите товарищу **6**–J
помощник официанта **63**–9
помощник менеджера **136**–3
помощница официанта **63**–9
понедельник **18**–2
пончик **60**–15
пончиковая **91**–20
пончо **66**–18
попасть домой **27**–Q
попросить одеяло **111**–M
попугай **133**–15
популярность интернета **115**
популярность компьютеров **115**
популярность телевидения **115**
порван/а/о **70**–23
порез **78**–13
порошок для приготовления
    торта **55**–47
порт **144**–17
портативное радио **164**–2
портативный компьютер **144**–14
портной **73**–2, **73**–9
портовый рабочий **137**–21
портье **36**–10, **145**–9
Порядковые числительные **14**
посетитель **62**–5
послать по почте **96**–B
пособие по оказанию первой
    медицинской помощи **83**–7
Пост медсестры **87**
постоялец **145**–11
поступить в колледж **28**–J
посудомоечная **63**–12
посудомоечная машина **40**–4, **63**–13
посылать **156**–I

посылка **96**–5
посылочный отдел **96**–14
посыльный **138**–38
потерявшийся ребёнок **102**–1
потолок **42**–5
потолочный вентилятор **41**–4
поход **154**–7
поход с ночёвкой **154**–1
походная плита **154**–16
Почистите морковь **58**–N
почка **75**–45, **89**–29, **129**–6
почта, доставляемая на следующий
    день **96**–15
почта, доставляемая наземным
    транспортом **96**–14
Почта США **96**
почтальон **96**–6, **138**–45
почтовая открытка **96**–3
почтовые весы **143**–16
почтовые ящики **37**–36
почтовый адрес **96**–8
почтовый сбор **96**–10
почтовый штемпель **96**–9
почтовый ящик **38**–4, **90**–12
пояс **67**–18, **73**–3, **74**–4, **147**–16
пояс астероидов **127**–12
пояс с резинками **67**–19
пояса **69**–11
Права **116**
Правительство **116**
Правовая система **99**
Праздники **168**
прачечная **90**–1
превысить дозу лекарств **82**–K
превысить дозу наркотиков **82**–K
Предлоги **13**
Предлоги, относящиеся к
    движению **105**
предложение **113**–4
предметное стекло **119**–5
предохранительный ремень
    безопасности **109**–36
представитель авиакомпании **110**–2
представить своего друга **8**–F
представиться **8**–D
предстать перед судом **99**–D
преподаватель **5**–2, **139**–58
Прерии **123**–3
пресмыкающиеся **130**–131
Преступление **100**
приём Хаймлиха **83**–18
приём у врача **19**–45
приёмная **5**–17, **84**–1, **146**–1
приборный щиток **108**–17
Прибрежная равнина вдоль
    Мексиканского залива **123**–16
прибыть **111**–O
привлекательная **22**–23
привлекательный **22**–23
приглашать гостей **169**–B
приглашённый оратор **32**–9
приговорить обвиняемого **99**–F
пригород **34**–2
Приготовление пищи **58**
приготовленная курица **52**–25
Приготовьте на пару брокколи **58**–I

придти домой 27–Q
придумывать 163–G
Прижимайте сумку к себе 101–C
призма 119–20
прикладная программа 144–21
приключенческий рассказ 166–13
прикроватный столик 86–9
приливная волна 103–15
Примите лекарство 80–F
принадлежности туалета 68–69
принимать ванну 76–B
принимать душ 26–C, 76–A
принтер 144–12
принять заказ 62–E
принять сообщение 142–A
приправа из маринованных овощей 60–26
природный газ 126–3
приставной столик 42–21
пристегнуть привязные ремни 111–I
присыпка 76–3
присяжные 99–8
притворяться 163–G
прихватки 59–29
приходская школа 112–3
прицеп 106–17
прицеп тягача 106–15
причёсывать...волосы щёткой 76–I
прищепка 72–10
приют 34–10
пробирка 119–16
Проблемы 70
пробовать 75–D
пробор 23–4
проверить...глаза 85–F
проверить...кровяное давление 85–B
Проверьте работу 113–B
Проверьте свою работу 7–Y
Провинции побережья Атлантического океана 123–6
провод 151–13
проводить посетителя к столу 62–B
проводить эксперимент 119–A
проглотить яд 82–J
программа 144–21
программа «покупки по телевизору» 167–25
программист 136–16
программное обеспечение 144
прогулка пешком 154–6
прогулочная коляска 94–2
продавать 21–B
продавать автомобили 140–H
продавец 68–1, 139–50
Продиктуйте предложение 6–N
продукты для животных 54–10
проезд 38–5
проезд запрещён 107–4
проезда нет 107–8
проездной билет 104–12
проектировать 146–A
проектировщик 146–3
проектор 2–4
прозрачная клейкая лента 143–39
проигрыватель 164–12

проигрыватель компактных дисков 164–14
произвести посадку 111–N
производить 146–B
Произнесите своё имя по буквам 4–A
Произнесите слово 6–C
Произнесите слово по буквам 6–E
произносить тост 33–I
пройти контроль 111–C
пройти регистрацию у выхода на посадку 111–D
прокурор 99–10
промтоварный магазин 90–2
промышленные искусства 121–10
Прослушайте кассету 2–C
прослушать...сердце 85–D
просматривать объявления о работе 141–B
просматривать раздел объявлений 141–D
простуда 79–1
простыня 44–13
простыня с подзором 44–22
простыня-наматрасник 44–14
просыпаться 26–A
противень 59–27
противовес 119–11
профессии 136–139
профессионально-техническое училище 112–9
Профессиональные навыки 140
прохладно 10–3
проход между полками в магазине 54–5
Проценты 15
Прочитайте слово 6–B
прошлая неделя 18–18
пруд 117–21
пруд с утками 153–6
пружины кровати 44–26
прыгалки 153–5
прыгать 156–J
пряжа 163–17
пряжка на ремне 69–41
прямая 118–18
прямоугольник 118–8
прямые волосы 23–9
пряности 55–46
прятать 169–E
психиатр 86–6
птица 52
Птицы 132
пуговица 73–21
пудинг 61–20
пудра 77–39
пуловер 64–11, 71–27
пума 134–2
пункт сбора стеклотары 54–1
Пунктуация 113
пуск 165–B
пустой стакан 11–10
пустыня 117–4
пустышка 95–29
путешествовать 29–N
пуховая безрукавка 66–13
пуховая куртка 66–15

пуховик 66–15
пуэрториканцы 114
пшеница 148–2
пшеничный хлеб 53–2
пылесос 47–13
пылесосить ковёр 46–I
пыльная буря 10–21
пьеса 166–2
пятка 75–62
пятнадцатый 14
пятнадцать 14
пятница 18–6
пятно 70–22
пятый 14
пять 14
пять долларов 20–8
пять минут второго 16–5
Пять способов приготовления курицы 58
пять центов 20–2
пятьдесят 14
пятьдесят долларов 20–11
пятьдесят процентов 15–9
пятьдесят центов 20–5
работа 113–2
Работа в группе 6
Работа в классе 7
Работа в паре 6
Работа по дому 46
Работа со словарём 6
работать 26–K
работать в кассе 140–N
работать на компьютере 140–P
работник заправочной станции 137–28
работник ремонтной мастерской 138–48
работник телемаркетинга 139–59
работник типографии 138–46
работник фондовой биржи 139–55
работник сада 94–3
работник яслей 94–3
рабочий завода 146–6
рабочий-станочник 138–37
рабы 114, 115
равнины 117–19
радиатор 109–42
радиация 126–13
радио 108–31
радио с часами 44–16, 164–1
радиоактивность 147–6
радиограмма 96–13
радиопрограмма 166–4
радиус 118–16
раз в неделю 18–22
Разбейте 3 яйца 58–A
разбрызгиватель воды 39–8
разведённая 25–24
разведённый 25–24
Развесить одежду 72–H
Развлечения 166–167
Развлечения на открытом воздухе 154
разводной ключ 109–50, 151–42
разворачивать подарки 169–L
разворот разрешён 107–7
Разговор на бытовые темы 8

Раздайте письменные работы 7–O
Разделайте курицу 58–M
разделочный нож 59–12
Разделы математики 118
разлив нефти 126–15
размахиваться 157–O
Размеры 15, 70
разносчик 137–18
разрядник для защиты от
    перенапряжения 144–10
рак мозга 79–12
раковина 43–22
Раковина засорилась 49–17
Ракушки 53
рама 44–27
ранец 69–28
рано 17–22
ранчо 34–12
распаковать вещи 35–E
расписание 104–3
Распишитесь 4–D
распорот/а/о 70–23
Распорядок дня 26–27
Распространённые заболевания 79
рассказ ужасов 166–14
рассказывать о своём опыте 141–I
Рассортировать бельё 72–A
расставить мебель 35–K
расстроенная 31–28
расстроенный 31–28
растворимый кофе 55–51
растения 128
растительное масло 55–49
растягиваться 157–Q
растяжение голеностопного
    сустава 78–18
растяжение лодыжки 78–18
расфасованные продукты 56
расчёска 23–22, 76–131
расчёсывать...волосы 76–G
рационально использовать
    воду 126–B
рационально использовать
    энергию 126–C
рвать 78–E
Реанимация 87
ребёнок 22–2
ребёнок, начинающий ходить 22–3
Регионы Канады 123
Регионы Мексики 123
Регионы Соединённых Штатов 123
регистратор 84–2, 138–47
регистрационная стойка 110–3
регистрироваться для прохождения
    выборочной службы 116–F
редис 51–5
резидент 116–6
резинка 143–45
резиновая швабра для мытья
    окон 47–9
резиновые перчатки 47–4, 87–33, 147–17
резиновые сапоги 66–19
резиновый клей 143–38
резиновый коврик 43–3
резиновый молоток 150–2

резиновый штемпель 143–40
рейтузы 65–23, 66–11
река 117–3
рекламная брошюра 143–32
рельсы 104–10
ремесленное училище 112–9
ремни 69–11
ремонт в доме 48–49
рентгенолог 86–5
репа 51–14
репортёр 139–49
ресницы 74–34
респиратор 147–12
Ресторан 62–63
ресторан быстрого
    обслуживания 90–14
рефери 158–6
рецепт 80–13
рециркулировать 126–A
решётка для жарки 59–14
ржаной хлеб 53–3
Римские цифры 14
рис 54–28, 148–1
рог 134–21
родители 24–4
родитель 94–1
родить ребёнка 29–M
родиться 28–A
Рождественская ёлка 168–20
Рождество 168–18
рожок 120–13
роза 129–15
розетка 44–20, 151–41
розовый 12–10
рок-группа 120–2
роликовые коньки 161–10
роман 166–16
ронять 94–A
ростбиф 52–1, 53–7
рот 74–22
роторная настольная
    картотека 143–17
рубанок 151–52
рубашка 64–4
рубашка без рукавов 71–29
рубашка с длинными рукавами 71–31
рубашка с короткими рукавами 71–30
ружьё 100–9
рука 74–8, 74–9
рукав 73–6
руководить людьми 140–K
руководство пользователя 144–22
рулетка 150–22
рулон бумажного полотенца 56–23
руль 108–26
румяна 77–36
русские 115
ручка 3–18, 11–1, 86–12
ручная пила 150–4
ручная тележка 146–11
Рыба 53
рыба-меч 130–12
рыбак 136–15
рыбная ловля 154–5
рыболовная сеть 154–17

рыжие волосы 23–14
Рынок 54–55, 89–20
рычаг ручного переключения
    передач 109–48
рэкетбол 159–11
рюкзак 69–28, 154–15
рюкзак для ношения ребёнка 95–15
рядом с 13–1, 13–2
с Ближнего–Востока 115
с магистрали 105–7
с плохим зрением 22–26
с плохим слухом 22–27
с физическими недостатками 22–25
сад на крыше 36–5
Садитесь 2–E
садовая мебель 39–5
садовник 137–26, 152–6
садовые ножницы 39–12
сажать 148–A
сажать дерево 39–D
саженец 129–2
саксофон 120–7
саламандра 130–27
салат из макарон 53–15
салат из свежих овощей 60–8
салат-латук 51–1, 60–17
салон-парикмахерская 93–16
салфетка 41–19, 63–23
салфетка под столовый прибор 41–20
салфетки с пропиткой 95–17
салют 168–8
салями 53–5
самоклеющаяся бумага для
    заметок 143–34
самолёт 110–9
самосвал 106–12
сандалии 68–24
санитар 87–18, 139–51
санитарный пакет 110–15
сантиметр 73–13
сантиметр [см] 15–12
сапоги 68–18
Сатурн 127–3
сахар 55–48, 60–21
сахарин 60–22
сахарница 41–12
сбивалка для яиц 59–20
сборная модель 162–7
сборный дом 34–8
сборочная линия 146–8
сборщик 136–6
сбрасыватель 119–14
Сварите курицу 58–P
сварщик 139–63
свежая рыба 53–29
свекровь 24–13
сверлить зуб 85–K
сверло 84–21, 150–23
сверчок 132–24
светильник 41–5
светло-голубой 12–3
светофор 90–6
свёкла 51–6
свёкр 24–14
свеча 41–7

свидетель 99–11
свидетельство о браке 29–8
свидетельство о получении
    гражданства 29–6
свидетельство о рождении 29–1
Свинина 52
свинка 79–7
свиные отбивные 52–10
свинья 133–8
свитер 64–11
свитер под горло 71–26
свободные брюки 71–42
сводная сестра 25–30, 25–32
сводный брат 25–29, 25–33
свояк 24–16
свояченница 24–15
сгребать листья 39–F
сдавать газеты в макулатуру 46–В
Сдайте работу 113–Е
сдать багаж 111–В
сдать экзамен на получение
    гражданства 116–С
сдача 21–9
Сделайте акупунктуру 81–G
Сделайте вклад 97–С
Сделайте укол 80–Е
сделать...заморозку 85–J
сделать комплимент другу 8–G
сделать предложение 35–Н
сделать рентген 85–Н
сделать...обезболивающий укол 85–J
сдобная булочка 60–14
Северная Америка 124–1
Северная Канада 123–1
Северная 122–123
сегодня 18–15
седые волосы 23–13
седьмой 14
сейф 97–2
секатор 39–15
секвойя 128–7
секретарь 139–52, 142–3
секретарь в приёмной 138–47
секунда 16–1
сельдерей 51–9
сельская местность 34–4
сельскохозяйственное
    оборудование 148–10
Сельскохозяйственные животные 133
Сельскохозяйственные культуры 148
сельскохозяйственные
    продукты 54–11
сельскохозяйственный рабочий 148–8
семнадцатый 14
семнадцать 14
семь 14
семьдесят 14
Семья 24–25
семя 129–1
Сенат 116–3
сенатор 116–4
сено 148–18
сентябрь 19–33
сервант 41–1
сервиз 41–2
сердечно–лёгочная реанимация 83–17

сердитая 31–29
сердитый 31–29
сердце 75–38, 168–6
серебряный доллар 20–6
серфинг 160–9
серый 12–5
серьёзная книга 167–26
серьги 69–37
сестра 24–8
сесть в самолёт 111–F
сесть в тюрьму 99–G
сетка 69–29
сетка для волос 147–18
сигнал поворота 108–4, 108–18
сиденье 2–7
сиденье для горшка 95–10
Симптомы заболеваний 78
синагога 88–9
синий 12–2
синяк 78–12
сироп 61–5
система безопасности 36–9
система весов 57
система для видеоигр 162–1
Система мер 15, 57
система подачи топлива 109–40
системы мер 14–15
ситечко 59–22
ситуационная комедия 167–18
скакалка 153–5
скалка 59–30
скамейка 153–10
скамейки 5–5
скандинавы 115
сканер 144–13
сканирующее устройство 144–13
скат 130–6
скатерть 41–18
скачки 159–18
Скелет 75
склад 146–9
скобка 143–29
скобкосшиватель 143–28
сковородка 59–5
скорая 9–9
скоростной спуск на лыжах 160–1
скоросшиватель 3–24
скорпион 132–31
скот 148–13, 148–21
скотоводство 148
скребок 151–48
скрепка 143–44
скреплять 142–G
скрипка 120–8
скульптура 152–9
скунс 134–12
скучающая 31–26
скучающий 31–26
скучная книга 167–29
сладкий перец 51–7
слайды 165–31
слева от 13–1
Следование инструкции 7
следующая неделя 18–20
слепая 22–26
слепой 22–26

слесарь 48–11
слив 43–4
сливы 50–8
словарь 3–28
словарь в картинках 3–29
сложение 118–1
Сложить бельё 72–F
сломать кость 82–Р
слон 135–42
служащий 5–18
служба парковки 145–1
служитель зоопарка 152–3
служить в качестве
    присяжного 116–G
слуховой аппарат 81–33
слышать 75–В
слюнявчик 95–8
Смажьте сковородку маслом 58–С
смерч 103–13
сметана 54–37
смешная книга 167–27
смеяться 33–Н
смог 10–14, 126–10
смокинг 65–28
смотреть за детьми 140–L
смотреть телевизор 27–S
смотровой кабинет 84–9
смущённая 31–27
смущённый 31–27
смягчитель тканей 72–6
снежная буря 10–20, 103–11
Снимите деньги со счёта 97–D
Снимите трубку 9–А
сноуборд 161–23
снять квартиру 28–I
снять...камень с зубов 85–I
С-образная струбцина 150–6
собака 133–11
Соберите работы 7–Q
собирать детали 140–А
собирать модели 162–С
собирать урожай 148–В
Соблюдайте постельный режим 80–А
соблюдать закон 116–Н
События жизни 28–29
сова 132–6
совок для мусора 47–11
соевые бобы 148–3
созвездие 127–24
солнечная энергия 126–1
солнечно 10–6
солнечные очки 66–21
солнечный ожог 78–14
солнце 127–10
соломенная шляпа 66–23
соломка 60–20
солонина 53–8
солонка 41–14
сом 53–17
Сообщайте о преступлениях в
    полицию 101–Н
сорок 14
сосед 37–22
соска 95–27, 128–10
сосновая шишка 128–11
Составьте список 6–К

Состояние здоровья **79**
сотовый телефон **9**–13
софа **42**–19
софтбол **158**–10
сочинение **113**–2
Сочинение на английском языке **113**
спагетти **54**–27
спальный мешок **154**–12
Спальня **44**
спаржа **51**–24
спаржевая капуста **51**–15
спасатель **155**–18
спасательная станция **155**–20
спасательные
    принадлежности **155**–19
спасательный жилет **154**–14
спать **94**–L
спелый / ая / ое **50**–29
специи **55**–46
спидометр **108**–20
спина **74**–11
спинка кровати **44**–15
спички **154**–21
спокойная **30**–10
спокойные **11**–12
спокойный **30**–10
спортзал **5**–9
спортивная борьба **159**–10
спортивная кофта с начёсом **64**–14
спортивная машина **106**–6
спортивная рубашка **65**–26
Спортивное оборудование **161**
спортивные штаны с начёсом **64**–15
спортивный автомобиль общего
    назначения **106**–9
спортивный костюм **65**–16
спортивный пиджак **64**–6
Способы оплаты **20**
справа от **13**–2
справочная **9**–8
справочник **83**–7
справочное бюро **93**–22
справочный стол **98**–2
спрашивать о зарплате **141**–K
спрашивать о льготах **141**–J
спрашивать о рабочих часах **141**–F
среда **18**–4
Среднеатлантические штаты **123**–10
среднегабаритный автомобиль **106**–3
среднего роста **22**–17
средней комплекции **22**–21
средний **70**–3
Средний Запад **123**–9
средних лет **22**–14
средство для мытья духовки **47**–3
средство от насекомых **154**–23
срочная почта **96**–12
ставень **38**–18
стадион **152**–26
стакан **41**–26
стакан для воды **63**–19
стандартное время **17**–32
стартовать **157**–X
старшие классы средней школы **112**–7
старший коридорный **145**–4
старые туфли **71**–33

статуэтка **162**–10
стать гражданином **28**–H
ствол **128**–4
стебель **129**–4
стеклянная банка **56**–2
стена **42**–6
Стена потрескалась **48**–4
стенка **42**–13
стерательная резинка **3**–21
стереосистема **42**–14
стерильная прокладка **83**–4
стерильный тампон **83**–4
стетоскоп **84**–8
стиральная машина **72**–3
стиральный порошок **72**–7
стирка **72**–1
Стирка белья **72**
стихийные бедствия **102–103**
сто **14**
сто долларов **20**–12
сто один **14**
сто процентов **15**–11
сто тысяч **14**
стоимость **21**–6
стойка **60**–13
стойка портье **145**–8
стойка с выбором салатов **60**–16
стол для пеленания **95**–9
стол для пикника **153**–8
Столовая **41**
столовая вилка **63**–25
столовая ложка **63**–29
столовая ложка сахара **57**–7
столовый прибор **63**–14
столярный набор **162**–16
стоматолог-ортодонт **84**–23
стоп **107**–3
стоп и выброс **165**–F
сторона **118**–22
стоянка **36**–15, **90**–5
стоянка такси **104**–19
стрела **161**–7
стрельба из лука **159**–1
стремянка **47**–7, **149**–2
стрептококовая ангина **79**–4
стричь...ногти **77**–N
стричься **23**–A
строитель **149**–1
строительные леса **149**–4
Строительство **149**
стройматериалы **150–151**
стройная **22**–22
стройный **22**–22
стручковая фасоль **51**–25
студент **139**–57
студенческое общежитие **34**–9
стул **2**–7
стул от обеденного гарнитура **41**–16
ступеньки **37**–35, **38**–13
Ступеньки сломаны **48**–7
ступня **74**–7
стюард **110**–13
стюардесса **110**–13
суббота **18**–7
сувенирный магазин **145**–7
судебная стенографистка **99**–12

судебный исполнитель **99**–13
судьи **116**–10
судья **99**–6, **158**–6
сук **128**–3
сумах лаковый **128**–24
сумах укореняющийся **128**–23, **128**–25
сумка **135**–50
сумка через плечо **69**–27
суп **54**–24
суповая тарелка **63**–18
суслик **133**–19
сухая футболка **72**–18
сухая штукатурка **149**–18
сушилка **72**–4
сушилка для посуды **40**–3
сушить...волосы **76**–H
сфера **118**–14
сцена **32**–4
сцепление **109**–45
счастливая **31**–32
счастливый **31**–32
Счета **20**
счёт **158**–1
счётчик **104**–21
счётчик парковки автомобилей **91**–18
счётчик пробега **108**–21
считыватель микрофильма **98**–4
США закрывают границы **114**
США покупают Аляску **115**
Съём квартиры **35**
сын **24**–22
сыпь **78**–10
сыр **54**–38
сыр жак **53**–12
сыр чедер **53**–10
сырая курица **52**–24
сыт **30**–6
сыта **30**–6
табельные часы **146**–4
таблетка **81**–25
таблетки от простуды **81**–17
таблица для проверки зрения **84**–11
Таблица перевода единиц
    измерений **15**
таз **75**–55
тако **60**–9
такси **104**–18
талия **74**–4
тальк **76**–3, **95**–18
тамбурин **120**–19
таможенник **110**–21
таможня **110**–20
танцевальный зал **145**–20
танцевать **33**–J
танцплощадка **33**–16
таракан **49**–25
тараканы **49**–25
тарелка **41**–24
тарелка для салата **63**–17
тарелка с хлебом и маслом **63**–16
тачка **39**–16
театр **88**–10
театр одного актёра **166**–5
театральное искусство **121**–12
телевизионная антена **38**–22
телевизионная программа **166**–3

телевизор 42–26, 164–6
телевикторина 167–23
тележка 91–31
тележка горничной 145–14
тележка для покупок 54–3
телескоп 127–21, 115
телефон 9, 9–1, 115
телефон-автомат 9–11, 91–21
телефонная карточка 9–10
телефонная книга 9–15
Тело 74–75
телячьи отбивные 52–6
Температура 10, 78–8
тени для век 77–34
теннис 159–14
теннисная ракетка 161–2
теннисные туфли 68–22
теннисный корт 153–7
тень 155–12
тепло 10–2
термит 49–22
термиты 49–22
термометр 84–15
тесть 24–14
тетрадь 3–23, 3–24
техник-рентгенолог 86–8
Технические средства 144
тёплая куртка 71–41
тёрка 59–2
тётя 24–10
тёща 24–13
тигр 135–37
Типы материала 70
Типы тканей 70
Типы школ 112
тиски 150–21
тихие дети 11–12
Тихоокеанские штаты 123–7
Тихоокеанский Северо-Запад 123–14
товар 152–24
ток-шоу 167–20
толкучка 152–22
толстая книга 11–7
только правый поворот 107–9
тон 77–40
тонкая книга 11–8
топор 150–3
торговец цветами 137–25
Торговый центр 92–93
тормозные фары 108–13
торнадо 103–13
торт 54–32, 61–19
торшер 42–15
тост 61–3
тост с сыром 61–8
тостер 40–7
точилка для карандашей 3–13
точка 113–6
точка с запятой 113–13
травмы 78, 82
трагедия 166–11
трактор 148–9
тракторный прицеп 106–15
трансконтинентальная железная дорога 115
транскрибировать заметки 142–C

Требования при подаче заявления на гражданство 116
требуха 52–8
тренер 158–2
тренироваться 157–P
тренировочные штаны 95–24
тренога 165–20
треска 130–8
третий 14
третий этаж 36–3
треугольник 118–7
трефи 163–26
трёхколёсный велосипед 153–9
три 14
три раза в неделю 18–24
три четвёртых 15–5
трибуны 5–10
тригонометрия 118–27
35-миллиметровый фотоаппарат 165–24
тридцать 14
трико 67–1
трикотажная рубашка 65–20
тринадцатилетний мальчик 22–7
тринадцатый 14
тринадцать 14
тритон 130–26
трогать 75–E
тромбон 120–12
«тропа слёз» 114
трость 80–7
тротуар 91–26
труба 38–21, 120–13, 151–16
трубка 9–2
Трубы замёрзли 49–19
трудная задача 11–24
тряпки 47–6
туалетная бумага 43–15
туалеты 5–8
туба 120–14
туберкулёз 79–13
туловище 135–47
туманно 10–11
тунец 54–25, 130–9
туника 65–22
тупик 107–8
туристический автомобиль 106–11
туристическое агентство 92–9
туристкие ботинки 68–21
тушёная говядина 52–3
Тушёные овощи 58
тушь 77–38
тыква 51–13
тысяча 14
тысяча один 14
тюбик 56–12
тюбик зубной пасты 56–24
тюлень 131–33
тюльпан 129–11
тюнер 164–13
тяжёлая атлетика 159–15
тяжёлые заболевания 79
тяжёлый ящик 11–13
тянуть тележку 153–A
убедиться, что вы правильно поняли 8–E

Уберите карандаш 2–L
убийство 100–8
убийство Кеннеди 115
убийство Кинга 115
убийство Линкольна 115
убирать дом 27–N
убирать игрушки 46–H
уборщик 138–35
убрать со стола 62–G
увлажнитель воздуха 80–2
увлажняющий крем 76–8
угол 91–17, 107–1, 118–24
уголь 126–4
угорь 130–5
удалить зуб 85–M
ударные инструменты 120–18
ударять 156–G
ударять ногой 156–L
удивлённая 31–31
удивлённый 31–31
удлинитель 151–14
удлинять 73–C
удобно 30–7
удостоверение 104–22
удочка 154–18
уж 131–39
ужинать 27–R
узкие брюки 71–43
узкий галстук 71–45
Укажите на рисунок 2–F
Указатели 107
Указатели 107
указатель уровня бензина 108–22
укладчик 146–10
укорачивать 73–D
украшать дом 169–C
украшение 168–19
украшения 69–8
укус насекомого 78–11
улики 99–9
улитка 130–24
улица 90–9
Улицы города 88–89
уличный торговец 91–30
уличный фонарь 91–23
уложить ручную кладь 111–H
умереть 29–R
умножение 118–3
умывальник 43–22
универмаг 93–13
универсальный складной нож 154–20
университет 112–10
унитаз 43–17
Унитаз засорился 49–18
униформа 65–17
унция сыра 57–11
упаковка 56–5, 56–8
Упаковка 56
упаковка из 6 предметов 56–9
упаковка из шести банок 56–21
упаковочная коробка 143–32
упаковочная лента 143–42
упаковочная плёнка 55–54
упаковщик 55–21, 146–13
упасть 82–O

управлять тяжёлым
  оборудованием **140**–F
управляющий линией **146**–5
ураган **103**–12
Уран **127**–3
усталая **31**–33
усталый **31**–33
устраивать пикник **153**–D
устрицы **53**–27
устроиться на работу **141**–L
усы **23**–5, **134**–18
утка **52**–18, **132**–13
утконос **135**–46
утонуть **82**–I
утро **17**–16
утюг **72**–13
ухо **74**–28
уходить с работы **26**–M
участвовать в гонках **157**–Y
участок **39**
учебник **3**–22
ученик **2**–3
ученица **2**–3
учитель **2**–5, **5**–2, **139**–58
учительница **2**–5
учиться водить машину **28**–E
ушивать **73**–E
ушные вкладыши **147**–13
фагот **120**–6
факс **143**–23
фамилия **4**–4
фанера **149**–16
фармацевт **80**–10
фасоль **54**–26
фасонно-фрезерный станок **150**–12
февраль **19**–26
фен **23**–20, **76**–16
ферма **34**–13
фермер **148**–15
фехтование **159**–5
фиалка **129**–22
фигурка персонажа **163**–31
фигурное катание **160**–5
физика **119**–3
физиотерапевт **81**–30
физкультура **121**–11
филе камбалы **53**–21
филиппинцы **115**
фильм **166**–1
финики **50**–25
финишировать **157**–Z
фирменный салат **61**–9
фломастер **3**–19
флаг **168**–9
флейта **120**–3
фляга **154**–24
фольга **55**–55
фонарик **151**–39
фонарь **154**–22
фонарь из тыквы **168**–11
фонарь на крыльце **38**–9
фонтан **92**–11, **153**–11
форель **53**–16
форма **161**–16
форма для кекса **59**–26

форма для пирога **59**–28
форма для торта **59**–26
формула **119**–19
фотоальбом **165**–32
фотограф **32**–11
фотографировать **32**–D
фотография **44**–7, **164–165**
французские исследователи **114**
Французско-индейская война **115**
фрисби **159**–6, **161**–27
фруктовый сад **148**–16
Фрукты **50**
фужер **63**–20
фунт говяжьей вырезки **57**–12
футбол **158**–12
футболка **64**–12
футбольный мяч **161**–12
футляр для фотоаппарата **165**–27
фуфайка **67**–11
халат **67**–8
хвост **134**–22
химический стакан **119**–13
химия **119**–2
химчистка **91**–24
хирург **87**–30
хирургическая шапочка **87**–31
хирургический халат **87**–32
хлеб **54**–29
хлебо-булочные изделия **54**–6, **55**–13
хлопать в ладоши **32**–B
хлопок **148**–6
хлопчатобумажная футболка **70**–16
Хобби **162–163**
Ходите в сопровождении друга **101**–A
ходить **156**–A
ходунок **95**–12
ходунок (для больных людей) **80**–5
ходунок (для пожилых людей) **80**–5
хозяин (дома) **37**–32
хозяин (квартиры) **37**–32
хозяин ранчо **148**–22
хоккей на льду **158**–13
хоккейная клюшка **161**–11
холмы **117**–16
холодильник **40**–9
холодная вода **43**–7
холодная война **114**
холодно **10**–4, **30**–4
холст **163**–22
хор **121**–3
хоровое пение **121**–3
хорошая собака **11**–17
хорошо **30**–15
Хорошо взбейте **58**–B
хотеть пить **30**–2
хотеть спать **30**–3
хризантема **129**–19
художественный музей **152**–7
художник **136**–5
художник-график **137**–29
художник-живописец **138**–43
худая **22**–22
худой **22**–22
Цвета **12**
цветная капуста **51**–16

цветные карандаши **45**–21
цветок **39**–19, **42**–18, **129**–7
цветочник **137**–25
цветочный горшок **39**–18
цветочный магазин **92**–12
Цветы **129**
целлофановый пакет **55**–23
целовать **33**–F
целоваться **33**–F
целое **15**–6
цена **21**–6
цена во время распродажи **21**–3
цена со скидкой **21**–3
ценник **21**–1
центр общественного питания в
  торговом центре **93**–14
Центральная Америка **122–123**
цепочка **69**–31
цепочка для ключей **69**–43
цепь **150**–36
церковный праздник **19**–44
церковь **88**–6
цилиндр **118**–12
цилиндрическая мензурка **119**–10
циркулярная пила **150**–10
цифры **3**–31
ЦПУ (центральный процессор) **144**–1
цуккини **51**–4
чай **61**–24
чай со льдом **60**–5
чайная ложка **63**–28
чайная ложка соли **57**–6
чайник **40**–17, **41**–11
час **16**–3
час (дня) **16**–4
час (ночи) **16**–4
час двадцать **16**–8
час двадцать пять **16**–9
час десять **16**–6
час пятнадцать **16**–7
час пять (минут) **16**–5
час пятьдесят **16**–14
час пятьдесят пять **16**–15
час сорок **16**–12
час сорок пять **16**–13
час тридцать **16**–10
час тридцать пять **16**–11
Части дерева **128**
Части квадрата **118**
Части круга **118**
Части птицы **132**
Части рыбы **130**
частная школа **112**–2
часы **3**–10
чашка **63**–21
чашка масла **57**–2
чашка муки **57**–10
чашка Петри **119**–6
чек **20**–14, **21**–5
чековая книжка **97**–7
челюсть **74**–23
черви **163**–29
червяк **130**–22
через мост **105**–2
через туннель **105**–11

череп 75–52
черепаха 131–42
черепица 149–19
черника 50–19
чернослив 50–26
чеснок 51–29
чеснокодавилка 59–10
4-е июля 168–7
четверг 18–5
четвёртый 14
четвёртый этаж 36–4
четверть второго 16–7
четверть луны 127–15
четверть чашки неочищенного сахара 57–8
четыре 14
четырнадцатый 14
четырнадцать 14
чешуя 130–3
чёлка 23–8
чёрный 12–15
чинить приборы 140–G
Числа, цифры 14–15
число 4, 18–14
чистая футболка 72–16
чистить...зубы 77–J
чистить ниткой между зубами 77–K
читать газету 27–V
читать рассказ 94–F
чихать 78–B
Чувства 30–31
чувство ностальгии 31–21
чувство тоски по дому 31–21
чувство тоски по родине 31–21
чулки 67–26
шайба 150–32
шампунь 76–9
шапка 32–3
шар для игры в кегли 161–5
шар трассировки 144–15
шарнирный болт 150–33
шатен 23–17
шатенка 23–17
шахматы 162–6
шашки 162–5
швабра для мытья 47–16
швабра для пыли 47–17
шведский стол 33–13
швейная машинка 73–10
швейцар 145–2
швейцарский сыр 53–11
швея 137–27
швы 83–15
шерсть 134–19
шерстяной свитер 70–14
шерстяной шарф 66–4
шестилетний мальчик 22–4
шестнадцатый 14
шестнадцать 14
шестой 14
шесть 14
шестьдесят 14
шеф-повар 63–11
шея 74–2
шёлковые шарфы 68–4
шёлковый шарф 70–15

шимпанзе 135–28
шина 81–31, 83–11, 108–10
шип 129–28
ширина 15–17
широкий галстук 71–44
шить на машинке 73–B
шить на руках 73–A
шить руками 73–A
шить одежду 140–I
Шитьё 73
шкаф 44–4
шкаф для канцелярских принадлежностей 142–13
шкаф-картотека 142–10
Школа 5, 89–27
школа для взрослых 112–8
Школьные предметы (продолжение) 121
шланг 39–9
шлем для игры в американский футбол 161–20
шлёпанцы 67–6
шлифовальный станок с электроприводом 150–9
шляпа 66–1
шляпы 68–5
шнур 9–3, 144–16
шнурок 68–14
шов 73–11
шорты 64–13
шотландка 70–9
шотландцы, ирландцы, немцы 115
шпильки 68–17
шпинат 51–11
шприц 84–14
штаны 64–8
штат 4–8
Штаты, расположенные на Скалистых горах 123–8
штемпельная подушечка 143–41
шторы 42–16, 44–5
штриховой код 21–4
штукатурка 149–14
шумные дети 11–11
шурин 24–16
шуруп 150–28
щека 74–29
щенок 133–12
щётка 23–18, 76–14
щётка для унитаза 43–16
щипцы 59–23, 119–15
щипцы для завивки 76–15
щипчики для ногтей 77–29
щиток для защиты голени 161–13
экономика 121–6
экономить воду 126–B
экономить энергию 126–C
Экономия энергии 126
экономка 138–33
экран 2–2, 144–6, 152–12, 165–28
экскаватор 149–8
Экспресс-почта 96–15
эластичный бинт 83–12
электрик 48–9
электрическая клавиатура 120–20
электрическая лампочка 115

электрическая открывалка 40–14
электрическая точилка для карандашей 142–9
электрический миксер 40–25
Электричества нет 48–2
электробритва 77–24
электродрель 150–8
электромусоропровод 40–5
Электроника 164–165
эллипс 118–9
Энергетические ресурсы 126
Энергия 126
энциклопедия 98–18
эскалатор 93–21
эта неделя 18–19
этикетка с названием лекарства, фамилией врача и пациента 80–14
этикетка с предупредительной надписью 80–15
юбка 64–10
юбка с разрезом 65–25
ювелирный магазин 92–2
Юг 123–13
Юго-Восток 123–13
Юго-Запад 123–12
Южная Африка 124–2
Южная возвышенность 123–17
Юпитер 127–5
юрист 138–36
яблоки 50–4
яблочный сок 55–50
явиться в суд 99–C
ягодицы 74–12
ягоды 128–20
яд 147–3
язык 74–26
Яичница-болтунья 58, 61–1
яйца 54–34
ямс 51–22
январь 19–25
японцы 115
Ясли 94–95
ясно 10–6
ящерица 131–41
ящик 56–6
ящик для игрушек 45–24